NON-STATE ACTORS' RIGHTS IN MARITIME DELIMITATION

Most of the world's maritime boundary disputes involve privately held rights – relating to such matters as fishing, petroleum exploration and scientific research – that states have unilaterally granted to non-state actors in areas of overlapping national claims. An international lawyer would typically investigate the legality of a state's decision to create such rights without notifying or consulting its neighbour, and the legal consequences this action would have for the interests of the states concerned. Departing from this approach, Dr Marianthi Pappa examines such situations from the perspective of the non-state actors: what will happen to private rights in a disputed maritime area if it changes hands from state A to state B due to a subsequent delimitation treaty or judgment? Does the legal framework of maritime delimitation protect those rights effectively against a potential reallocation? To address these questions, the book considers the place that private rights have in land boundary-making.

Marianthi Pappa is Assistant Professor in Law at the University of Nottingham. She specializes in international law, ocean governance, energy and natural resources law and space law. She also provides workshops on boundary disputes and energy issues for governmental and business organizations.

Non-State Actors' Rights in Maritime Delimitation

LESSONS FROM LAND

MARIANTHI PAPPA

University of Nottingham

CAMBRIDGE
UNIVERSITY PRESS

University Printing House, Cambridge CB2 8BS, United Kingdom

One Liberty Plaza, 20th Floor, New York, NY 10006, USA

477 Williamstown Road, Port Melbourne, VIC 3207, Australia

314–321, 3rd Floor, Plot 3, Splendor Forum, Jasola District Centre,
New Delhi – 110025, India

103 Penang Road, #05–06/07, Visioncrest Commercial, Singapore 238467

Cambridge University Press is part of the University of Cambridge.

It furthers the University's mission by disseminating knowledge in the pursuit of
education, learning, and research at the highest international levels of excellence.

www.cambridge.org
Information on this title: www.cambridge.org/9781108835220
DOI: 10.1017/9781108891936

© Marianthi Pappa 2021

This publication is in copyright. Subject to statutory exception
and to the provisions of relevant collective licensing agreements,
no reproduction of any part may take place without the written
permission of Cambridge University Press.

First published 2021

A catalogue record for this publication is available from the British Library.

Library of Congress Cataloging-in-Publication Data
NAMES: Pappa, Marianthi, author.
TITLE: Non-state actors' rights in maritime delimitation : lessons from land / Marianthi
Pappa, University of Nottingham
DESCRIPTION: Cambridge, United Kingdom ; New York, NY : Cambridge University
Press, 2021. | Based on author's thesis (doctoral – University of Aberdeen, 2018) issued
under title: The unbalanced protection of private rights in land and maritime delimi-
tation : the necessity of an equilibrium. | Includes bibliographical references and index.
IDENTIFIERS: LCCN 2020058055 (print) | LCCN 2020058056 (ebook) | ISBN
9781108835220 (hardback) | ISBN 9781108891936 (ebook)
SUBJECTS: LCSH: Continental shelf – Law and legislation. | Maritime boundaries. |
Right of property. | Conflict of laws.
CLASSIFICATION: LCC KZA1660 .P37 2021 (print) | LCC KZA1660 (ebook) |
DDC 341.4/55–dc23
LC record available at https://lccn.loc.gov/2020058055
LC ebook record available at https://lccn.loc.gov/2020058056

ISBN 978-1-108-83522-0 Hardback

Cambridge University Press has no responsibility for the persistence or accuracy of
URLs for external or third-party internet websites referred to in this publication
and does not guarantee that any content on such websites is, or will remain,
accurate or appropriate.

As though by some eternal decree
Land and Sea are destined to disagree
Over where the shoreline should be.

Isam Hussain, 'Land and Sea'

Contents

Preface and Acknowledgements		*page* xi
Table of Cases		xiv
Table of Treaties and Conventions		xix
Other International Instruments		xxviii
List of Abbreviations		xxxi
1	**Prolegomena**	1
	1.1 A New Approach to International Boundary-Making	1
	1.2 Boundaries Revisited	2
	1.3 Boundaries and States	6
	1.4 Boundaries and Non-State Actors	7
	1.5 How to Compare Land and Sea?	8
	1.6 Limits on Research	11
	1.7 Book Plan	13
2	**Private Rights in Areas of Uncertain Jurisdiction**	15
	2.1 Introduction	15
	2.2 State Powers on Land and at Sea: Sovereignty vis-à-vis Sovereign Rights	16
	2.3 Private Rights on Land and at Sea: General Features	23
	2.3.1 Types of Private Rights	23
	2.3.2 Nature of Private Rights	26
	2.4 The Creation of Private Rights in Land and Maritime Areas of Overlapping Sovereign Claims	29
	2.4.1 The Cause of Overlapping Land and Maritime Claims	33

vii

viii *Contents*

| | 2.4.2 | The Legal Competence of States to Create Private Rights in Areas of Overlapping Claims | 34 |
| 2.5 | | Conclusions | 43 |

3 The Divergent Role of Private Rights in Land and Maritime Delimitation · 45

3.1		Introduction	45
3.2		Delimitation by Treaty	45
	3.2.1	The Significant Role of Private Rights in Land Delimitation Treaties	48
		3.2.1.1 The Importance of Private Rights in Boundary Allocation	49
		3.2.1.2 The Importance of Private Rights in Boundary Delimitation	51
		3.2.1.3 The Importance of Private Rights in Boundary Demarcation	54
	3.2.2	The Restricted Role of Private Rights in Maritime Delimitation Treaties	56
		3.2.2.1 The Moderate Role of Private Rights in Boundary Negotiation	57
		3.2.2.2 The Limited Role of Private Rights in Boundary Delimitation	59
		3.2.2.3 The Absence of Private Rights in Boundary Demarcation	65
3.3		Delimitation by a Court or Tribunal	66
	3.3.1	The Significant Role of Private Rights in Land Delimitation Rulings	68
		3.3.1.1 Private Rights in Support of *Uti Possidetis*	68
		3.3.1.2 Private Rights in Support of Acquiescence	69
		3.3.1.3 Private Rights in Support of *Effectivités*	71
	3.3.2	The Restricted Role of Private Rights in Maritime Delimitation Rulings	73
		3.3.2.1 The Importance of Private Rights in Early Delimitation Cases	73
		3.3.2.2 The Judicial Shift in Modern Delimitation Cases	74
3.4		Assessment of State and Judicial Practice	83
	3.4.1	Absence of an International Custom on Land and at Sea	83

Contents

	3.4.2	Absence of Coherent Case Law on Land and at Sea	88
	3.4.3	Implications for Non-State Actors	93
3.5	Conclusions		94

4 The Uneven Preservation of Reallocated Private Rights on Land and at Sea — 96

4.1	Introduction		96
4.2	Conventional Mechanisms of Protection		96
	4.2.1	The Systematic Employment of Conventional Mechanisms on Land	97
	4.2.1.1	The Widespread Use of Grandfather Clauses in Land Delimitation Treaties	97
	4.2.1.2	The Widespread Conclusion of State Cooperation Agreements on Land	99
	4.2.2	The Restricted Employment of Conventional Mechanisms at Sea	101
	4.2.2.1	The Limited Use of Grandfather Clauses in Maritime Delimitation Treaties	101
	4.2.2.2	The Limited Conclusion of State Cooperation Agreements at Sea	106
4.3	Judicial Mechanisms of Protection		114
	4.3.1	Extensive Preservation of Reallocated Private Rights in Land Delimitation Rulings	114
	4.3.2	Limited Preservation of Reallocated Private Rights in Maritime Delimitation Rulings	117
4.4	Assessment of State and Judicial Practice		123
	4.4.1	Absence of an International Custom on Land and at Sea	123
	4.4.2	Absence of Coherent Case Law on Land and at Sea	128
	4.4.3	Implications for Non-State Actors	129
4.5	Conclusions		133

5 Reassessing the Asymmetry — 136

5.1	Introduction		136
5.2	The Restricted Scope of the Sea Conventions		137
	5.2.1	Geneva Conventions	137
	5.2.2	UNCLOS	139
5.3	Maritime Delimitation's Idiosyncratic Position vis-à-vis Land Delimitation		143

	5.3.1	Differences in Delimitation Grounds	143
	5.3.2	Differences in Delimitation Rules	145
		5.3.2.1 Delimitation of the Territorial Sea	145
		5.3.2.2 Delimitation of the Exclusive Economic Zone and the Continental Shelf	147
5.4		Reasons Related to the Private Rights Themselves	152
	5.4.1	Differences between Onshore and Offshore Private Rights	152
		5.4.1.1 Duration and Socio-Economic Value	152
		5.4.1.2 Legal Value	153
	5.4.2	Protection of Offshore Rights under Private Law	156
		5.4.2.1 Contractual Clauses	156
		5.4.2.2 Insurance	159
5.5		Conclusions	161

6 Reaching an Equilibrium — 163

6.1		Introduction	163
6.2		Setting the Standards to Counteract the Asymmetry	163
	6.2.1	Embracing Inclusiveness	164
	6.2.2	Revisiting Equity	165
6.3		Choosing the Means to Counteract the Asymmetry	170
	6.3.1	Short-Term Means	170
		6.3.1.1 Means Pertaining to Maritime Delimitation Treaties	170
		6.3.1.2 Means Pertaining to Maritime Delimitation Rulings	171
	6.3.2	Long-Term Means	177
		6.3.2.1 Future Developments in International Law of the Sea	177
		6.3.2.2 Future Developments in General International Law	184
6.4		Conclusions	188

7 Epilogue — 190

7.1	The Unbalanced Protection of Non-State Actors' Rights in Land and Maritime Delimitation	190
7.2	Towards Greater Coherence	192

Bibliography	194
Index	214

Preface and Acknowledgements

This book emerged from a mere 'what if' question. While studying the world's maritime boundary disputes, I observed that a significant number of those interstate situations involved privately held rights (relating mainly to fishing and petroleum exploration, but also to scientific research), which one or both of the states concerned had unilaterally granted to non-state actors in the area of overlapping claims.[1] An international lawyer would typically investigate the legality of a state's decision to create such rights in contested waters without notifying or consulting its neighbour and the legal consequences that this action would have for the interests of the concerned states.

Departing from this approach, I examined the above cases from the perspective of the non-state actors involved, asking myself what happens to private rights attached to a disputed maritime area if this area changes hands pursuant to a subsequent delimitation treaty or judgment, passing from one state to another. Does the legal framework of maritime delimitation protect those rights effectively against potential reallocation?

In order to answer these questions, I compared the treatment of private rights in land and maritime boundary-making, doing so for two main reasons. First, the very concept of delimitation was originally developed on land. When state control eventually expanded to the oceans and maritime disputes arose, the principles of land delimitation served as basis for maritime boundary-making. Hence, maritime delimitation rules can only be effectively assessed in relation to their land counterparts. Second, land delimitation pays considerable attention to private rights. I observed that, both in transactional and judicial delimitation, it is common for private rights to determine or otherwise

---

[1] The rights granted by states to non-state actors (whether on land or at sea) are hereinafter referred to as 'private rights' or 'non-state actors' rights'. The two expressions are used interchangeably.

affect the course of land boundaries. This largely prevents the reallocation of private rights and their potential discharge by the absorbing state. And even when the reallocation of onshore private rights is inevitable, special legal mechanisms are employed by states and international courts or tribunals in order to accommodate the affected private interests post delimitation. Do the above also apply at sea?

The common features of land and maritime delimitation would initially suggest that the protection of private rights extends to oceans, too. Both on land and at sea, the purpose of boundary-making is to set the limits of two contiguous jurisdictions in a final and peaceful manner. Also, in both settings delimitation is effected by treaties concluded between the states concerned or by rulings handed down by judicial bodies on the basis of international law.

However, the comparative analysis I conducted between land and maritime delimitation revealed a significant asymmetry: while private rights have a substantial effect on the course of land boundaries, their impact on the course of maritime boundaries is barely detectable. This means that the risk of reallocation of private rights is significantly higher at sea in the first place. Also, the treatment of reallocated private rights is considerably different between the two settings. On land, a series of legal mechanisms are systematically employed by states and judicial authorities to accommodate reallocated private rights post delimitation. At sea, similar mechanisms are also available but scarcely triggered. This means that absorbed private rights have a much greater chance of surviving on land than at sea.

Hence, what began as a simple query ended up exposing a significant legal problem: when it comes to boundary-making, international law is severely fragmented. Despite their similarities, land and maritime delimitation are dissimilar in the protection of private rights. This has serious implications for non-state actors holding interests in contested waters and for international law in general. It cultivates the misconception that offshore private rights are inferior to their counterparts on land and as such do not deserve to be protected against a potential reallocation. It further creates a tension between the processes of land and maritime delimitation, which yet are both governed by international law and should therefore follow similar rules and principles.

The significantly greater protection which international law offers to private rights in the context of land delimitation provides a number of valuable lessons for maritime delimitation, demonstrating the need for changes in the rules and practices of ocean boundary-making. The recommendations of this study seek to encourage a balanced protection of private interests in all areas of overlapping sovereign claims and in all situations of boundary-making.

Preface and Acknowledgements

The book is intended for both legal theorists and practitioners interested in maritime delimitation. The nexus between maritime boundaries and private interests remains largely underexplored in literature,[2] as does the comparison between land and maritime delimitation.[3] A critical analysis of those matters enables a better understanding of maritime delimitation and a critique of its current legal framework.

The insights of this book may also inform the discussion about the place of non-state actors in the international plane, and offer inspiration for the protection of offshore private rights in other areas of law, such as human rights and international investment. Finally, beyond its scholarly importance, the book may be of practical value to individuals and corporations holding interests in undelimited waters, as well as to states seeking to grant private rights in disputed maritime areas in order to bolster their national claims.

The monograph is based on my doctoral thesis defended in Aberdeen in June 2018. I will never forget the late Professor Barbara Kwiatkowska, who encouraged me to step outside my comfort zone when I was drafting my PhD proposal and 'dive into waters where no one else had swum before'. I am thankful to my PhD supervisor, Professor Roy Andrew Partain, for believing in me, even at the hardest of times. I would also like to express my gratitude to Professors Zeray Yihdego, Guillermo Jose Garcia Sanchez, Tina Soliman Hunter, Irini Papanicolopulu and Sandesh Sivakumaran for their kind support, and to all anonymous reviewers for their useful comments. Special thanks go to Cambridge University Press for bringing this book to life. Yet this work would not have been completed without the love of my husband, Pavlos.

---

[2] The few authors who consider individuals in boundary delimitation have examined different aspects from the present study. Marcelo Kohen is concerned with the rights of communities in freshwater resources (eg rivers) in disputed territories; see M Kohen and M Tignino, 'Do People Have Rights in Boundaries' Delimitations?' in L Boisson de Chazournes and others (eds), *International Law and Freshwater: The Multiple Challenges* (Edward Elgar 2013). Others discuss private rights in the context of human or political geography; see R Sack, *Human Territoriality: Its Theory and History* (CUP 1986); D Massey, *Space, Place, and Gender* (University of Minnesota Press 1990); J Painter, *Politics, Geography and 'Political Geography': A Critical Perspective* (Arnold 1995); D Harvey, *Justice, Nature and the Geography of Difference* (Blackwell 1996).

[3] Land and maritime delimitation are examined separately in the literature, maritime delimitation being studied mainly by legal scholars and land delimitation by geographers; see Chapter 1. By way of exception, Weil observed that 'one can better understand the peculiar nature of maritime delimitation, a newcomer to the international scene, by comparing it with the long-established and well-developed institution of delimitation on land'; see P Weil, *The Law of Maritime Delimitation: Reflections* (Grotius 1989) 91.

Table of Cases

CASES FROM INTERNATIONAL COURTS AND TRIBUNALS

Aegean Sea Continental Shelf Case (Greece v Turkey) (Interim Measures) [1976] ICJ Rep 3

Aegean Sea Continental Shelf Case (Greece v Turkey) (Jurisdiction of the Court) [1978] ICJ Rep 3

Amoco International Finance Corp v the Government of the Islamic Republic of Iran, National Iranian Oil Company, National Petrochemical Company and KHARG Chemical Company Ltd (14 July 1987) 15 Iran-USCTR 189

Arbitral Award in the Matter of Delimitation of a Certain Part of the Maritime Boundary between Norway and Sweden (Grisbådarna Case) (Norway v Sweden) (1909) 11 RIAA 147

Arbitration between Barbados and Trinidad and Tobago (Barbados v Trinidad and Tobago) (2006) 45 ILM 798

Arbitration between Guyana and Suriname (Guyana v Suriname) (2007)

Arbitration between India and Pakistan for the Indo-Pakistan Western Boundary (Rann of Kutch) (India v Pakistan) (1968)

Arbitration between Newfoundland and Labrador and Nova Scotia (Newfoundland and Labrador v Nova Scotia) (2002)

Arbitration between the Republic of Croatia and the Republic of Slovenia (Croatia v Slovenia) (2017)

Arbitration Concerning the Definite Fixing of the Italian-Swiss Frontier at the Place Called Alpe de Cravairola (Italy/Switzerland) (1874)

Arbitration in the Bay of Bengal (Bangladesh v India) (2014)

Arbitration Regarding the Delimitation of the Abyei Area between the Government of Sudan and the Sudan People's Liberation Movement/Army (2009)

Asylum Case (Columbia v Peru) [1950] ICJ Rep 266

Table of Cases

Barcelona Traction, Light and Power Company Limited (Belgium v Spain) [1970] ICJ Rep 4

Case Concerning Ahmadou Sadio Diallo (Republic of Guinea v Democratic Republic of Congo) (Preliminary Objections) [2007] ICJ Rep 582

Case Concerning Avena and Other Mexican Nationals (Mexico v United States) [2004] ICJ Rep 12

Case Concerning Elettronica Sicula SpA (ELSI) (United States of America v Italy) [1989] ICJ Rep 15

Case Concerning Kasikili/Sedudu Island (Botswana/Namibia) [1999] ICJ Rep 1045

Case Concerning Maritime Delimitation in the Area between Greenland and Jan Mayen (Denmark v Norway) [1993] ICJ Rep 38

Case Concerning Military and Paramilitary Activities in and against Nicaragua (Nicaragua v United States of America) [1986] ICJ Rep 14

Case Concerning Sovereignty over Certain Frontier Land (Belgium/Netherlands) [1959] ICJ Rep 209

Case Concerning Sovereignty over Pulau Ligitan and Pulau Sipadan (Indonesia/Malaysia) [2002] ICJ Rep 625

Case Concerning Territorial and Maritime Dispute between Nicaragua and Honduras in the Caribbean Sea (Nicaragua v Honduras) [2007] ICJ Rep 659

Case Concerning the Continental Shelf (Libyan Arab Jamahiriya/Malta) [1985] ICJ Rep 13

Case Concerning the Continental Shelf (Tunisia/Libyan Arab Jamahiriya) [1982] ICJ Rep 18

Case Concerning the Delimitation of Maritime Boundary between Guinea-Bissau and Senegal (Guinea-Bissau v Senegal) (Award) (1989)

Case Concerning the Frontier Dispute (Benin/Niger) [2005] ICJ Rep 90

Case Concerning the Frontier Dispute (Burkina Faso/Republic of Mali) [1986] ICJ Rep 554

Case Concerning the Temple of Preah Vihear (Cambodia v Thailand) [1962] ICJ Rep 6

Case Concerning the Territorial Dispute (Libyan Arab Jamahiriya/Chad) [1994] ICJ Rep 6

Case Concerning the Land and Maritime Boundary between Cameroon and Nigeria (Cameroon v Nigeria; Equatorial Guinea Intervening) [2002] ICJ Rep 303

Certain Activities Carried out by Nicaragua in the Border Area (Nicaragua v Costa Rica) [2015] ICJ Rep 665

Certain German Interests in Polish Upper Silesia (Germany v Poland) PCIJ Rep Series A No 7 (1926)

xvi   *Table of Cases*

Certain Questions Relating to Settles of German Origin in the Territory
    Ceded by Germany to Poland (German Settlers) (Advisory Opinion)
    PCIJ Rep Series B No 6 (1923)
Channel Continental Shelf Arbitration (UK v France) (1978)
Decision Regarding Delimitation of the Border between Eritrea and Ethiopia
    (2002) 25 RIAA 83
Delimitation of Maritime Areas between Canada and the French Republic
    (St Pierre et Miquelon) (Arbitral Award) (1992)
Delimitation of the Continental Shelf between the United Kingdom of Great
    Britain and Northern Ireland and the French Republic (UK v France)
    (Arbitral Award) (1977)
Delimitation of the Maritime Boundary in the Gulf of Maine Area (Canada/
    United States) [1984] ICJ Rep 292
Deutsche Continental Shelf Gas-Gesellschaft v Polish State (1929) PCIJ AD
    No 5
Dispute Concerning Delimitation of the Maritime Boundary between Ghana
    and Côte d'Ivoire in the Atlantic Ocean (Ghana/Côte d'Ivoire) (Provisional
    Measures) (2015) ITLOS
Dispute Concerning Delimitation of the Maritime Boundary between Ghana
    and Côte d'Ivoire in the Atlantic Ocean (Ghana/Côte d'Ivoire) (Judgment)
    (2017) ITLOS
Dispute Concerning Delimitation of the Maritime Boundary between
    Guinea and Guinea-Bissau (Guinea v Guinea-Bissau) (1985) 24 ILM 252
Dispute Concerning Delimitation of the Maritime Boundary in the Bay of
    Bengal (Bangladesh/Myanmar) (2012) 51 ILM 840, ITLOS Reports 2012, 4
Dispute Regarding Navigational and Related Rights (Costa Rica v Nicaragua)
    [2009] ICJ Rep 213
East Timor (Portugal v Australia) [1995] ICJ Rep 90
Eritrea/Yemen Arbitration (First Stage: Territorial Sovereignty and Scope of
    Dispute) (9 October 1998) (2001) 22 RIAA 211, (2001) 40 ILM 900
Eritrea/Yemen Arbitration (Second Stage: Maritime Delimitation)
    (17 December 1999) (2001) 22 RIAA 335, (2001) 40 ILM 983
Fisheries Case (UK v Norway) [1951] ICJ Rep 116
Fisheries Jurisdiction Case (United Kingdom v Iceland) [1973] ICJ Rep 3
Frontier Dispute (Burkina Faso/Niger) [2013] ICJ Rep 44
Island of Palmas Case (Netherlands/USA) (Arbitral Award) (1928)
Jurisdiction of the Courts of Danzig (Beamtenabkommen) PCIJ Rep Series
    B No 15 (1928)
LaGrand Case (Germany v United States) [2001] ICJ Rep 466
Land, Island and Maritime Frontier Dispute (El Salvador/Honduras) [1992]
    ICJ Rep 351

Table of Cases

Legal Consequences of the Construction of a Wall in the Occupied Palestinian Territory (Advisory Opinion) [2003] ICJ Rep 136

Legal Status of Eastern Greenland (Denmark v Norway) PCIJ Rep Series A/B No 53 (1933)

Libyan American Oil Company (Liamco) v The Government of the Libyan Arab Republic (1977) 62 ILR 141

Maritime Boundary Arbitration in the Bay of Bengal between the People's Republic of Bangladesh and the Republic of India (Bangladesh v India) (2014)

Maritime Delimitation and Territorial Questions (Qatar v Bahrain) [2001] ICJ Rep 112

Maritime Delimitation in the Area between Greenland and Jan Mayen (Denmark v Norway) [1993] ICJ Rep 38

Maritime Delimitation in the Black Sea (Romania v Ukraine) [2009] ICJ Rep 61

Maritime Dispute (Peru v Chile) [2014] ICJ Rep 3

Mavrommatis Palestine Concessions, The (Greece v Great Britain) PCIJ Rep Series A No 2 (1924)

Mondev International Ltd v United States of America, ICSID (Additional Facility) Case No ARB(AF)/99/2 (11 October 2002) (2003) 42 ILM 85

North Sea Continental Shelf Cases (Federal Republic of Germany/Denmark, Federal Republic of Germany/Netherlands) [1969] ICJ Rep 3

Question of Jaworzina (Polish-Czechoslovakian Frontier) (Advisory Opinion) PCIJ Rep Series B No 8 (1923)

Questions of the Monastery of Saint Naoum (Albanian Frontier) (Advisory Opinion) PCIJ Rep Series B No 9 (1924)

Raibl-Societa Mineraria del Predil SpA v Italy (Raibl Claim) (19 June 1964) (1970) 40 ILR 260

Responsibilities and Obligations of States Sponsoring Persons and Entities with Respect to Activities in the Area (Advisory Opinion) (2011) ITLOS

Revision and Interpretation of the Judgment of 24 February 1982 in the Case Concerning the Continental Shelf (Tunisia/Libyan Arab Jamahiriya) [1985] ICJ Rep 192

Saipem SpA v The People's Republic of Bangladesh, ICSID Case No ARB/05/07 (Decision on Merits, 30 June 2009)

Sapphire International Petroleums Ltd v National Iranian Oil Company (Arbitral Award) (1967) 35 ILR 184

Saudi Arabia v Aramco (Arbitral Award) (1963) 27 ILR 116

Société Générale de Surveillance (SGS) v Republic of Philippines (Decision on Objections to Jurisdiction) (2004) 8 ICSID Rep 518

SS Lotus Case (France v Turkey) PCIJ Series A No 10 (1927)

Territorial and Maritime Dispute between Nicaragua and Colombia (Nicaragua v Colombia) [2012] ICJ Rep 624

xviii   *Table of Cases*

Texaco Overseas Petroleum Co (Topco) and California Asiatic (Calasiatic)
Oil Company v Government of the Libyan Arab Republic (Arbitral Award)
(1977) 53 ILR 389

CASES FROM REGIONAL COURTS

European Court of Human Rights

Bramelid and Malmström v Sweden (1982)
Fredin v Sweden (1991)
Loizidou v Turkey (1995)
Sporrong and Lönnroth v Sweden (1982)
Tre Traktörer Aktiebolag v Sweden (1989)
Zubani v Italy (1996)

Interamerican Court of Human Rights

Case of the Mayagna (Sumo) Awas Tingni Community v Nicaragua (2001)

African Commission on Human and Peoples' Rights

Media Rights Agenda v Nigeria (1998)

CASES FROM NATIONAL COURTS

Australia

Commonwealth, The v WMC Resources Ltd (1998)
Newcrest Mining (WA) Ltd v The Commonwealth (1997)

United Kingdom

Cook v Sprigg [1899] AC 572

USA

United States v Percheman 32 US 51 (1833)

Table of Treaties and Conventions

BILATERAL TREATIES AND AGREEMENTS

Accord relatif à la fixation de la ligne frontière entre la Perse et la Turquie (signed 23 January 1932)

Agreement between Austria and Yugoslavia Concerning the Immovable Property of Austrian Dual Owners in the Yugoslav Frontier Zone (with Final Protocol) (signed 19 March 1953)

Agreement between Belgium and France Relating to Frontier Workers (with Annexes) (signed 8 January 1949)

Agreement between Iceland and Norway on Fishery and Continental Shelf Questions (signed 28 May 1980)

Agreement between Italy and Yugoslavia Concerning the Delimitation of the Continental Shelf between the Two Countries in the Adriatic Sea (signed 8 January 1968)

Agreement between Qatar and Abu Dhabi on the Settlement of Maritime Boundaries and Ownership Islands (signed 20 March 1969)

Agreement between Sri Lanka and India on the Boundary in Historic Waters between the Two Countries and Related Matters (signed 26 and 28 June 1974)

Agreement between Sweden and Denmark on the Delimitation of the Continental Shelf and Fishing Zones (signed 9 November 1984)

Agreement between the Government of Argentina and the Government of Uruguay Relating to the Delimitation of the River Plate and the Maritime Boundary between Argentina and Uruguay (signed 19 November 1973)

Agreement between the Government of Australia and the Government of the Democratic Republic of Timor-Leste Relating to the Unitization of the Sunrise and Troubadour Fields (signed 6 March 2003)

Agreement between the Government of Australia and the Government of the Republic of Indonesia Relating to Cooperation in Fisheries (signed 22 April 1992)

Agreement between the Government of Brazil and the Government of Uruguay Relating to the Maritime Delimitation between Brazil and Uruguay (signed 21 July 1972)

Agreement between the Government of Canada and the Government of the French Republic on their Mutual Fishing Relations (signed 27 March 1972)

Agreement between the Government of Indonesia and the Government of Papua New Guinea Concerning the Maritime Boundary between the Republic of Indonesia and Papua New Guinea and Cooperation on Related Matters (signed 13 December 1980)

Agreement between the Government of the Commonwealth of Australia and the Government of the Republic of Indonesia Establishing Certain Seabed Boundaries (signed 18 May 1971)

Agreement between the Government of the French Republic and the Government of the Italian Republic on the Delimitation of the Maritime Boundaries in the Area of the Strait of Bonifacio (signed 28 November 1986)

Agreement between the Government of the Hellenic Republic and the Government of the Italian Republic for the Delimitation of the Continental Shelf (signed 24 May 1977)

Agreement between the Government of the Hellenic Republic and the Government of the Republic of Albania for the Delimitation of their Respective Continental Shelf and Other Maritime Zones (signed 27 April 2009)

Agreement between the Government of the Italian Republic and the Government of the Tunisian Republic Relating to the Delimitation of the Continental Shelf between the Two Countries (signed 20 August 1971)

Agreement between the Government of the Republic of Lithuania and the Government of the Republic of Belarus Concerning the Crossing Posts of the State Border (signed 18 July 1995)

Agreement between the Government of the Republic of Tunisia and the Government of the Italian Republic Concerning the Delimitation of the Continental Shelf between the Two Countries (signed 20 August 1971)

Agreement between the Government of the United Kingdom of Great Britain and Northern Ireland and the Government of the Kingdom of Norway Relating to the Delimitation of the Continental Shelf between the Two Countries (signed 10 March 1965)

Agreement between the Government of the United Republic of Tanzania and the Government of the People's Republic of Mozambique Regarding the Tanzania/Mozambique Boundary (signed 28 December 1988)

Agreement between the Government of the United Republic of Tanzania and the Government of the Republic of Seychelles on the Delimitation of the Maritime Boundary of the Exclusive Economic Zone and Continental Shelf (signed 23 January 2002)

Agreement between the Great Socialist People's Libyan Arab Jamahiriya and the Republic of Malta Implementing Article III of the Special Agreement and the Judgment of the International Court of Justice (signed 10 November 1986)

Agreement between the Kingdom of Saudi Arabia and the State of Kuwait Concerning the Submerged Area Adjacent to the Divided Zone (signed 2 July 2000)

Agreement between the Libyan Arab Socialist People's Jamahiriya and the Republic of Tunisia to Implement the Judgment of the International Court of Justice in the Tunisia/Libya Continental Shelf Case (signed 8 August 1988)

Agreement between the Netherlands and the Federal Republic of Germany Concerning Minor Frontier Traffic (signed 3 June 1960)

Agreement between the Republic of Cyprus and the Arab Republic of Egypt on the Delimitation of the Exclusive Economic Zone (signed 17 February 2003)

Agreement between the Republic of Slovenia and the Republic of Croatia on Border Traffic and Cooperation (signed 28 April 1997)

Agreement between the Socialist Republic of Vietnam and the People's Republic of China on the Delimitation of the Territorial Sea, Exclusive Economic Zone and Continental Shelf between the Two Countries in the Gulf of Tonkin (signed 25 December 2000)

Agreement between the United Kingdom and Portugal with Regard to the Northern Rhodesia-Angola Frontier (signed 18 November 1954)

Agreement between the United States of America and the Union of Soviet Socialist Republics on the Maritime Boundary (signed 1 June 1990)

Agreement between the United States of America and the United Mexican States Concerning Transboundary Hydrocarbon Reservoirs in the Gulf of Mexico (signed 20 February 2012)

Agreement between Yugoslavia and Greece Concerning Frontier Traffic (signed 18 June 1959)

Agreement Concerning the Sovereignty over the Islands of Farsi and Al-Arabiyah and the Delimitation of the Boundary Line Separating the Submarine Areas between Iran and Saudi Arabia (signed 24 October 1968)

xxii   *Table of Treaties and Conventions*

Agreement on Delimitation of Marine and Submarine Areas and Maritime Cooperation between the Republic of Colombia and the Republic of Haiti (signed 17 February 1978)

Agreement on Delimitation of the Continental Shelf between Iran and Saudi Arabia (signed 24 October 1968)

Agreement on Delimitation of the Maritime Boundaries between the Republic of Colombia and the Dominican Republic (signed 13 January 1978)

Agreement on Fishery Cooperation in the Tonkin Gulf between the Government of the People's Republic of China and the Government of Socialist Republic of Vietnam (signed 25 December 2000)

Agreement Relating to the Delimitation of the Continental Shelf between Greenland and Canada (signed 17 December 1973)

Agreement Relating to the Exploitation of the Frigg Field Reservoir and the Transmission of Gas Therefrom to the United Kingdom (signed between UK and Norway 10 May 1976)

Agreement Relating to the Exploitation of the Markham Field Reservoirs and the Offtake of Petroleum Therefrom (signed between UK and Netherlands 26 May 1992)

Agreement Relating to the Exploitation of the Statfjord Field Reservoirs and the Offtake of Petroleum Therefrom (signed between UK and Norway 16 October 1979)

Anglo-Irish Treaty of 1921 for the Establishment of the Boundary between Northern Ireland and the Rest of Ireland (signed 6 December 1921)

Boundary Agreement between Bahrain and Saudi Arabia (signed 22 February 1958)

Boundary Delimitation Treaty between the Republic of Venezuela and the Kingdom of the Netherlands (signed 31 March 1978)

Boundary Treaty between Colombia and Ecuador (signed 15 July 1916)

Boundary Treaty between the Kingdom of Nepal and the People's Republic of China (signed 5 October 1961)

Convention between Estonia and Latvia Regarding the Delimitation on the Spot of the Frontier between the Two States (signed 19 October 1920)

Convention between Latvia and Lithuania Regarding the Delimitation on the Spot of the Frontier between the Two States, and Also Regarding the Rights of the Citizens in the Frontier Zone, and the Status of Immovable Property Intersected by the Frontier Line (signed 14 May 1921)

Convention between the Austrian and Czechoslovak Republics Concerning the Delimitation of the Frontier between Austria and Czechoslovakia and Various Questions Connected Therewith (signed 10 March 1921)

Table of Treaties and Conventions xxiii

Convention between the Government of the French Republic and the Government of the Spanish State on the Delimitation of the Continental Shelves of the Two States in the Bay of Biscay (signed 29 January 1974)

Convention between the Government of the French Republic and the Government of the Spanish State on the Delimitation of the Territorial Sea and Contiguous Zone in the Bay of Biscay (signed 29 January 1974)

Convention between the Republic of Czechoslovakia and the Polish People's Republic Concerning Minor Frontier Traffic (signed 4 July 1959)

Convention between the United States and Mexico for the Elimination of the Bancos in the Rio Grande from the Effects of Articles I and II of the Treaty of 12 November 1884 (signed 20 March 1905)

Convention on Maritime Delimitation Agreement between the Government of His Most Serene Highness the Prince of Monaco and the Government of the French Republic (signed 16 February 1984)

Delimitation Agreement between Iran and Bahrain (signed 17 June 1971)

Delimitation Agreement between Iran and Oman (signed 25 July 1974)

Delimitation Agreement between Iran and Qatar (signed 20 September 1969)

Delimitation Agreement between Iran and Saudi Arabia (signed 24 October 1968)

Delimitation Agreement between the Commonwealth of the Bahamas and the Republic of Cuba (signed 3 October 2011)

Delimitation Agreement between the Republic of Estonia and the Kingdom of Sweden on the Delimitation of the Baltic Sea (signed 2 November 1998)

Delimitation Treaty between Australia and the Independent State of Papua New Guinea (signed 18 December 1978)

Delimitation Treaty between France and Germany (signed 14 August 1925)

Delimitation Treaty between the Government of the French Republic and the Government of the Republic of Venezuela (signed 17 July 1980)

Demarcation Convention between Argentina and Chile (signed 2 May 1904)

Franco-British Paris Convention on Certain Points Connected with the Mandates for Syria and the Lebanon, Palestine and Mesopotamia (signed 23 December 1920)

General Treaty between Germany and the Netherlands for the Settlement of Frontier Questions and Other Problems Outstanding between the Two Countries (signed 8 April 1960)

Heligoland–Zanzibar Treaty between the German Empire and the United Kingdom (signed 1 July 1890)

Israel-Jordan Peace Treaty (signed 26 October 1994)

Joint Development Agreement between Japan and the Republic of Korea (signed 30 January 1974)

xxiv *Table of Treaties and Conventions*

Joint Development Agreement between Kuwait and Saudi Arabia (signed 7 July 1965)

MoU between Thailand and Malaysia for the Establishment of a Joint Development Zone in the Gulf of Thailand (signed 21 February 1979) and Agreement for the Constitution of a Joint Authority (signed 30 May 1990)

MoU between the Government of the Republic of Indonesia and the Government of Australia Concerning the Implementation of a Provisional Fisheries Surveillance and Enforcement Arrangement (signed 29 October 1981)

MoU between the Government of the Republic of Indonesia and the Government of Australia Regarding the Operations of Indonesian Traditional Fishermen in Areas of the Australian Exclusive Economic Zone and Continental Shelf (signed 7 November 1974)

Peace Treaty of Fredrikshamn between Sweden and Russia (signed 17 September 1809)

Peace Treaty of the Pyrenees between France and Spain (signed 7 November 1659)

Protocol between France and Turkey Relative to the Surveillance and Fiscal Regime of the Frontier (signed 29 June 1929)

Protocol in Implementation of Article 6.2 of the Treaty between the Federal Republic of Nigeria and the Republic of Equatorial Guinea Concerning their Maritime Boundary (signed 3 April 2002)

Protocol of Peace, Friendship, and Boundaries between Ecuador and Peru (signed 29 January 1942)

Rodd Treaty between the United Kingdom and Ethiopia (signed 14 May 1897)

Treaty between Australia and the Democratic Republic of Timor-Leste Establishing Their Maritime Boundaries in the Timor Sea (signed 6 March 2018)

Treaty between Australia and the Independent State of Papua New Guinea Concerning Sovereignty and Maritime Boundaries in the Area between the Two Countries, Including the Area Known as Torres Strait, and Related Matters (signed 18 December 1978)

Treaty between Croatia and Bosnia and Herzegovina (signed 30 July 1999)

Treaty between Equatorial Guinea and Nigeria on Joint Exploration of Crude Oil, Especially at the Zafiro-Ekanga Oil Field Located at the Maritime Boundary of Both Countries (signed 3 April 2002)

Treaty between France and Germany Regarding the Delimitation of the Frontier (with Annexes, Protocol and Exchange of Notes) (signed 14 August 1925)

Treaty between Great Britain and Northern Ireland and Venezuela Relating to the Submarine Areas of the Gulf of Paria (signed 26 February 1942)

Table of Treaties and Conventions

Treaty between Nigeria and Sao Tome e Principe on the Joint Development of Petroleum and Other Resources in Respect of Areas of the Exclusive Economic Zone of the Two States (signed 21 February 2001)

Treaty between the Federal Republic of Nigeria and the Republic of Equatorial Guinea Concerning their Maritime Boundary (signed 23 September 2000)

Treaty between the Government of the United Kingdom and Northern Ireland and the Government of the Kingdom of Norway Relating to the Delimitation of the Continental Shelf between the Two Countries (signed 10 March 1965)

Treaty between the Government of the United Kingdom of Great Britain and Northern Ireland and the Government of the Republic of Honduras Concerning the Delimitation of the Maritime Areas between Cayman Islands and the Republic of Honduras (signed 4 December 2001)

Treaty between the Government of the United States of America and the Government of the United Mexican States on the Delimitation of the Continental Shelf in the Western Gulf of Mexico (signed 9 June 2000)

Treaty between the Kingdom of Denmark and the Federal Republic of Germany Concerning the Delimitation of the Continental Shelf under the North Sea (signed 28 January 1971)

Treaty between the Kingdom of Norway and the Russian Federation Concerning Maritime Delimitation and Cooperation in the Barents Sea and the Arctic Ocean (signed 15 September 2010)

Treaty between the Kingdom of the Netherlands and the Federal Republic of Germany Concerning the Course of the Common Frontier, the Boundary Waters, Real Property Situated near the Frontier, Traffic Crossing the Frontier on Land, and other Frontier Questions (signed 8 April 1960)

Treaty between the Kingdom of the Netherlands and the Federal Republic of Germany Concerning the Delimitation of the Continental Shelf under the North Sea (signed 28 January 1971)

Treaty between the Kingdom of the Netherlands and the Kingdom of Belgium on the Delimitation of the Territorial Sea (signed 18 December 1996)

Treaty between the People's Republic of China and the Socialist Republic of Vietnam on the Delimitation in the Beibu Gulf/Bac Bo Gulf (signed 25 December 2000)

Treaty between the Republic of Trinidad and Tobago and the Republic of Venezuela on the Delimitation of Marine and Submarine Areas (signed 18 April 1990)

xxvi   *Table of Treaties and Conventions*

Treaty between the United Kingdom and Iraq and Turkey Regarding the Settlement of the Frontier between Turkey and Iraq (with the Notes Exchanged) (signed 5 June 1926)

Treaty between Uruguay and Argentina Concerning the Rio de la Plata and the Corresponding Maritime Boundary (signed 19 November 1973)

Treaty Concerning Delimitation of Marine Areas and Maritime Cooperation between the Republic of Costa Rica and the Republic of Panama (signed 2 February 1980)

Treaty of Peace (Treaty of Trianon) between the Allied and Associated Powers and the Kingdom of Hungary (signed 4 June 1920)

Treaty of Saint Petersburg between Great Britain and Russia (signed 28 February 1925)

Treaty of Tordesillas between Spain and Portugal (signed 7 June 1494)

Treaty of Versailles between Germany and the Allied Powers (signed 28 June 1919)

Treaty on Delimitation between Colombia and Peru (signed 24 March 1922)

Treaty on Delimitation of Marine and Submarine Areas and Maritime Cooperation between the Republic of Colombia and the Republic of Costa Rica (signed 17 March 1977)

Treaty on Delimitation of Marine and Submarine Areas and Related Matters between the Republic of Panama and the Republic of Colombia (signed 20 November 1976)

Treaty on Delimitation of Marine and Submarine Areas between the Republic of Venezuela and the Dominican Republic (signed 3 March 1979)

Treaty on the State Border between the Republic of Croatia and Bosnia and Herzegovina (signed 30 July 1999)

Unitization Agreement between Venezuela and Trinidad and Tobago for the Exploitation and Development of Hydrocarbon Reservoirs of the Manakin-Cocuina Field (signed 16 August 2010)

MULTILATERAL TREATIES

African Charter on Human and Peoples' Rights (ACHPR) (signed 27 June 1981, entered into force 21 October 1986)

Agreement for the Implementation of the Provisions of the United Nations Convention on the Law of the Sea of 10 December 1982 Relating to the Conservation and Management of Straddling Fish Stocks and Highly Migratory Fish Stocks (signed 4 August 1995, entered into force 11 December 2001)

Table of Treaties and Conventions

Agreement Relating to the Implementation of Part XI of the 1982 Convention on the Law of the Sea of 10 December 1982 (signed 28 July 1994, entered into force 28 July 1996)

American Convention on Human Rights (ACHR) (signed 22 November 1969, entered into force 18 July 1978)

ASEAN-Australia-New-Zealand Free Trade Agreement (signed 27 February 2009)

Convention on Fishing and Conservation of the Living Resources of the High Seas (signed 29 April 1958, entered into force 20 March 1966) 559 UNTS 285

Convention on the Continental Shelf (signed 29 April 1958, entered into force 10 June 1964) 499 UNTS 311

Convention on the High Seas (signed 29 April 1958, entered into force 30 September 1962) 450 UNTS 11

Convention on the Territorial Sea and the Contiguous Zone (signed 29 April 1958, entered into force 10 September 1964) 516 UNTS 205

Energy Charter Treaty (ECT) (signed 17 December 1994, entered into force 16 April 1998)

European Convention on Human Rights (ECHR) (signed 4 November 1950, entered into force 3 September 1953)

International Covenant on Civil and Political Rights (signed 16 December 1966, entered into force 23 March 1976)

International Covenant on Economic, Social, Cultural Human Rights (signed 16 December 1966, entered into force 3 January 1976)

Montevideo Convention on the Rights and Duties of States (signed 26 December 1933, entered into force 26 December 1934) 165 LNTS 19

Nagoya Protocol on Access to Genetic Resources and the Fair and Equitable Sharing of Benefits Arising from their Utilization (ABS) to the Convention on Biological Diversity (signed 29 October 2010, entered into force 12 October 2014)

North American Free Trade Agreement (NAFTA) (signed 17 December 1992, entered into force 1 January 1994)

United Nations Charter (signed 26 June 1945, entered into force 24 October 1945) 1 UNTS XVI

United Nations Convention on the Law of the Sea (UNCLOS) (signed 10 December 1982, entered into force 16 November 1994) 1833 UNTS 3

Universal Declaration of Human Rights (UDHR) (signed 10 December 1948, entered into force 16 December 1948)

Vienna Convention on the Law of Treaties (VCLT) (signed 23 May 1969, entered into force 27 January 1980) 1155 UNTS 331

Other International Instruments

UN GENERAL ASSEMBLY RESOLUTIONS

UNGA Res 626 (VII) (21 December 1952) Right to exploit freely natural wealth and resources

UNGA Res 1803 (XVII) (14 December 1962) Permanent sovereignty over natural resources

UNGA Res 2158 (XXI) (25 November 1966) Permanent sovereignty over natural resources

UNGA Res 3067 (XXVIII) (16 November 1973) Reservation exclusively for peaceful purposes of the seabed and the ocean floor, and the subsoil thereof, underlying the high seas beyond the limits of present national jurisdiction and use of their resources in the interests of mankind, and convening of the Third United Nations Conference on the Law of the Sea

UNGA Res 3171 (XXVIII) (17 December 1973) Permanent sovereignty over natural resources

UNGA Res 3281 (XXIX) (12 December 1974) Charter of Economic Rights and Duties of States

ILC DOCUMENTS

Draft Articles on Diplomatic Protection (adopted 2006)

Draft Articles on Responsibility of States for Internationally Wrongful Acts (adopted 2001)

Draft Conclusions on Identification of Customary International Law (adopted 2018)

Other International Instruments xxix

STATE PROCLAMATIONS

Declaration of the Maritime Zone of Chile, Ecuador and Peru (Santiago Declaration) (18 August 1952)

Proclamation of Argentina on the Epicontinental Sea (5 December 1946)

Proclamations of US President Harry Truman on the policy of the United States with respect to the natural resources of the subsoil and the seabed of the continental shelf and with respect to coastal fisheries in certain areas of the high seas (28 September 1945)

NOTES EXCHANGED BETWEEN GOVERNMENTS

Notes exchanged between Brazil and Venezuela for the delimitation of their boundary (7 November 1929)

Notes exchanged between China and Burma for the making of the Sino-Burmese Boundary Treaty of 1 October 1960

Notes exchanged between China and Nepal for the making of the Sino-Nepalese Boundary Treaty of 5 October 1961

Notes exchanged between China and Pakistan for the making of the Sino-Pakistani Boundary Treaty of 3 March 1963

Notes exchanged between Italy and the Social Federal Republic of Yugoslavia regarding the creation of a joint fishing zone in the Gulf of Trieste (18 February 1983)

Notes exchanged between Poland and Czechoslovakia for the delimitation of their boundary (30 September and 1 October 1938)

Notes exchanged between the United Republic of Tanzania and Kenya concerning the delimitation of the territorial waters boundary between the two States (17 December 1975–9 July 1976)

REPORTS, CONFERENCE RECORDS

International Law Association, 'Statement of Principles Applicable to the Formation of General Customary International Law' (London Conference, 2000)

International Law Commission, 'Fragmentation of International Law: Difficulties Arising from the Diversification and Expansion of International Law: Report of the Study Group of the International Law Commission Finalized by Martti Koskenniemi' (13 April 2006) UN Doc A/CN.4/L.682

International Law Commission, 'Second Report on Succession in Respect of Matters other than Treaties' (18 June 1969) UN Doc A/CN.4/216/REV.1

International Law Commission, 'Survey of International Law in Relation to the Work of Codification of the International Law Commission: Preparatory work within the purview of article 18, paragraph 1, of the Statute of the International Law Commission (Memorandum submitted by the Secretary-General)' (10 February 1949) UN Doc A/CN.4/1/Rev.1

UNGA, 'Oceans and the Law of the Sea: Report of the Secretary-General' (25 November 2009) UN Doc A/64/66/Add.1

United Nations Conference on the Law of the Sea (Geneva 24 February–27 April 1958) Official Records, Summary Records of Meetings and Annexes, 13th Session

Abbreviations

ACmHPR	African Commission on Human and Peoples' Rights
AJIL	American Journal of International Law
ASEAN	Association of Southeast Asian Nations
ASIL	American Society of International Law
BIICL	British Institute of International and Comparative Law
CS	continental shelf
ECHR	European Convention on Human Rights
ECtHR	European Court of Human Rights
ECT	Energy Charter Treaty
EEZ	exclusive economic zone
GATT	General Agreement on Tariffs and Trade
IACHR	Inter-American Court of Human Rights
IBRU	International Boundaries Research Unit
ICJ	International Court of Justice
ICLQ	International Comparative Law Quarterly
ICSID	International Centre for Settlement of Investment Disputes
ILA	International Law Association
ILC	International Law Commission
ITLOS	International Tribunal for the Law of the Sea
JDA	joint development agreement
M	nautical mile(s) (as used by the International Hydrographic Organization)
NAFTA	North American Free Trade Agreement
NOC	national oil company
OGEL	Oil, Gas and Energy Law
OSCE	Organization for Security and Co-operation in Europe
PCA	Permanent Court of Arbitration
PSA	production sharing agreement

RECIEL	Review of European Community and International Environmental Law
TS	territorial sea
UN	United Nations
UNCLOS	United Nations Convention on the Law of the Sea 1982
UNGA	United Nations General Assembly
VCLT	Vienna Convention on the Law of Treaties
WTO	World Trade Organization
ZaöRV	Zeitschrift für ausländisches öffentliches Recht und Völkerrecht

1

Prolegomena

1.1 A NEW APPROACH TO INTERNATIONAL BOUNDARY-MAKING

The field of boundary-making is multi-disciplinary. Boundaries[1] were first studied by geographers, engineers, and commissioners concerned with the science of delimitation.[2] At the same time, boundaries have a significant place in the legal discourse.[3] The works of jurists contribute to the understanding of

---

[1] Although the terms 'boundary' and 'frontier' are often considered as synonyms and used interchangeably in the literature, they are distinct. As explained by boundary experts, 'frontiers are zones of varying widths' and were used in 'the political landscape centuries ago'. By contrast, the term 'boundary' is rather modern and denotes the specific lines established to divide the jurisdictions of states on land and at sea. V Prescott, *Political Frontiers and Boundaries* (Allen & Unwin 1987) 1; D Johnston, *Theory and History of Ocean Boundary-Making* (McGill-Queen's University Press 1988) 3, 226.

[2] See G Curzon, *Frontiers* (Clarendon 1908); T Holdich, *Political Frontiers and Boundary Making* (Macmillan 1916); C Fawcett, *Frontiers: A Study in Political Geography* (OUP 1918); P de La Pradelle, *La Frontière: Étude de Droit International* (Éditions Internationales 1928); S Boggs, *International Boundaries: A Study of Boundary Functions and Problems* (Columbia University Press 1940); S Jones, *Boundary-Making: A Handbook for Statesmen, Treaty Editors and Boundary Commissioners* (Carnegie Endowment for International Peace 1945); Prescott (n 1). The publications by Durham University's International Boundaries Research Unit (IBRU) are also of great importance.

[3] See A Cukwurah, *The Settlement of Boundary Disputes in International Law* (Manchester University Press 1967); E Luard, *The International Regulation of Frontier Disputes* (Thames & Hudson 1970); P Weil, *The Law of Maritime Delimitation: Reflections* (Grotius 1989); M Evans, 'Maritime Delimitation and Expanding Categories of Relevant Circumstances' (1991) 40 ICLQ 1; J Charney and R Smith (eds), *International Maritime Boundaries* (Brill 2002); N Antunes, *Towards the Conceptualisation of Maritime Delimitation* (Martinus Nijhoff 2003); D Freestone, R Barnes and D Ong (eds), *The Law of the Sea: Progress and Prospects* (OUP 2006); Y Tanaka, *Predictability and Flexibility in the Law of Maritime Delimitation* (OUP 2006); R Lagoni and D Vignes (eds), *Maritime Delimitation* (Brill 2006); T Cottier, *Equitable Principles of Maritime Boundary Delimitation* (CUP 2015); the ASIL publication *International Maritime Boundaries* (Martinus Nijhoff 1993–2016) vols 1–4 edited by J Charney and R Smith, vols 5–6 by D Colson and R Smith, vol 7 by C Lathrop.

1 Prolegomena

legal concepts related to delimitation and promote the peaceful settlement of international boundary disputes.[4]

This book offers a new approach to international boundary-making. It revisits the purpose and methods of delimitation in two ways. Firstly, it examines boundary-making from the perspective of non-state actors. Boundaries secure the co-existence not only of states with each other but also of states with non-state actors that hold interests in the area under delimitation. The presence of non-state actors in disputed areas, especially in contested waters, is ever-increasing. Therefore, it is important to map the place of private rights in the processes of boundary-making.

Secondly, the book provides a comparative analysis of land and maritime boundary-making. Although the subject matter of the book is maritime delimitation, the efficacy of the rules which govern this process is tested using the well-established norms of land delimitation. On the basis of a critical analysis of the legal framework governing maritime delimitation, the book makes recommendations for the evolution of international law of the sea.

1.2 BOUNDARIES REVISITED

International boundaries are as old as sovereign states.[5] They first emerged on land when states sought to determine the limits of their territorial dominion in relation to each other. At sea, international boundaries did not appear until the mid-twentieth century.[6]

The reasons for this delay were both legal and practical. The ocean has always been 'both a means of communication and a store of riches'.[7] But for centuries it

---

[4] This demonstrates that, despite their differences, law and science are complementary.

[5] The majority of scholars agree that the system of sovereign states emerged from the Peace of Westphalia in 1648. See L Gross, 'The Peace of Westphalia 1648–1948' (1948) 42 AJIL 20; P Stirk, 'The Westphalian Model and Sovereign Equality' (2012) 38 Review of International Studies 641, 641–42; A Cassese, *International Law in a Divided World* (Clarendon 1986) 34. According to others, however, the state as now understood first appeared in the fifteenth century. See D Raic, *Statehood and the Law of Self-Determination* (Brill Academic 2002) 20; M Wight, *Systems of States* (Leicester University Press 1977) 151; M Keen, *Medieval Europe* (Penguin 1991) 314ff; S Sassen, *Territory, Authority, Rights: From Medieval to Global Assemblages* (Princeton University Press 2006) 41.

[6] Until then, maritime delimitation dealt almost exclusively with the fixing of the outer limits of states' territorial waters (ie those directly adjacent to the shore). G Tanja, *The Legal Determination of International Maritime Boundaries: The Progressive Development of Continental Shelf, EFZ and EEZ Law* (Kluwer Law and Taxation 1990) xv, 1, 293.

[7] R-J Dupuy and D Vignes (eds), *A Handbook on the New Law of the Sea*, vol 1 (Martinus Nijhoff 1991) xlvi.

1.2 *Boundaries Revisited*

was considered to be open to all states for navigation and fishing.[8] States' offshore jurisdiction did not extend beyond three nautical miles from the coast, which made recourse to maritime boundaries relatively unnecessary.[9] In the course of time, events such as the need to extract natural resources from the ocean for reasons of energy security and economic development,[10] the decolonization and independence of numerous coastal nations,[11] and the codification of international law of the sea in official conventions,[12] led states to expand their maritime control to a much greater distance and establish international boundaries in the ocean.

Given its long history and application in different settings, the process of international boundary-making has undergone dramatic changes, which can be approached in various ways. The majority of studies refer to the evolution of boundaries from natural to artificial. Natural boundaries are those already fixed by nature (such as rivers, deserts, mountain crests or the shorelines of lakes and seas), and it is these that were mainly used in the past. By contrast, most modern boundaries can be described as artificial or conventional. They are marked by humankind, by means of stones, monuments or other means that do not follow the area's physical environment such as geometrical lines or parallels.[13]

The above classification is suited to studies in natural or political geography.[14] As a legal study, the present work suggests another taxonomy,

---

[8] Subject to the so-called 'freedom of the seas', a principle originally formulated by Hugo Grotius. See Chapter 2.

[9] V Prescott and C Schofield, *Maritime Political Boundaries of the World* (Martinus Nijhoff 2004) 215; Johnston (n 1) 7.

[10] See Proclamations of President Harry S. Truman, 'Policy of the United States with Respect to the Natural Resources of the Subsoil and the Seabed of the Continental Shelf', 'Policy of the United States with Respect to Coastal Fisheries in Certain Areas of the High Seas' (28 September 1945); Proclamation of Argentina on the Epicontinental Sea (5 December 1946); Declaration of the Maritime Zone of Chile, Ecuador, and Peru (18 August 1952) (Santiago Declaration).

[11] Between 1943 and 1973 alone, about seventy states achieved independence, fifty-five of which were coastal. F. Brown, 'Maritime Zones: A Survey of Claims' in R Churchill and others (eds), *New Directions in the Law of the Sea*, vol 3 (British Institute of International and Comparative Law 1973) 159.

[12] Initially through the Geneva Conventions of 1958: Convention on the Territorial Sea and the Contiguous Zone (signed 29 April 1958, entered into force 10 September 1964) 516 UNTS 205; Convention on the Continental Shelf (signed 29 April 1958, entered into force 10 June 1964) 499 UNTS 31; Convention on the High Seas (signed 29 April 1958, entered into force 30 September 1962) 450 UNTS 11; the Convention on Fishing and Conservation of the Living Resources of the High Seas (signed 29 April 1958, entered into force 20 March 1966) 559 UNTS 285. And later the United Nations Convention on the Law of the Sea (signed 10 December 1982, entered into force 16 November 1994) 1833 UNTS 3 (UNCLOS).

[13] See Boggs (n 2) 18–25; Jones (n 2) 7–8; Prescott (n 1) 63–80.

[14] Though not all geographers accept the division of boundaries into natural and artificial; see the works of Paul de La Pradelle, Sieger and Hartshorne cited in Boggs (n 2) 24.

4   *1 Prolegomena*

based on the legality of the ways in which boundaries are made. For many centuries, international boundaries were imposed unilaterally by forcible means and acts of political power. Today, however, the establishment of boundaries is a transactional legal process between the states concerned. This evolution of international boundary-making can be broken down into the following three phases.

Fifteenth and sixteenth centuries. During medieval times, the creation of boundaries was mainly based on acts of military or political supremacy. Quite often, boundaries would emerge from violent conflicts and long wars between powerful hegemonies. On other occasions, boundaries were established by imperial decrees and papal bulls on the basis of the discovery and symbolic annexation or occupation of *terra nullius*.[15] According to scholars, 'the medieval world did not have international boundaries as we understand them today' as 'authority over territorial spaces was overlapping and shifting'.[16] Unstable boundaries of this kind were often the source of conflicts between states rather than a construct that would consolidate international relations.[17]

Seventeenth to nineteenth centuries. The second phase of boundary-making was quite mixed. Some international delimitation treaties bilaterally establishing boundaries were signed but, overall, the majority of boundaries were still imposed unilaterally.[18] In Europe, the seventeenth century was marked by wars over land acquisition and territorial exchanges between the rulers of Westphalian states.[19] The creation of boundaries by arbitrary and forcible means continued on the continent for the next two centuries.[20] Outside Europe, the seventeenth century saw the start of the colonial era, which lasted until the 1900s. During that period, the majority of boundaries in America, Africa and Asia were

---

[15] S Sharma, *Territorial Acquisition, Disputes and International Law* (Martinus Nijhoff 1997) 38–39; E Milano, *Unlawful Territorial Situations in International Law: Reconciling Effectiveness, Legality and Legitimacy* (Martinus Nijhoff 2005) 81–83; Tanja (n 6) 2–3.

[16] M Zacher, 'The Territorial Integrity Norm: International Boundaries and the Use of Force' (2001) 55 International Organization 215, 216. See also G Clark, *The Seventeenth Century* (2nd edn, OUP 1961) esp ch 10.

[17] Zacher (n 16); H Bull, *The Anarchical Society* (Columbia University Press 1977) 34–37.

[18] G East, *The Geography Behind History* (Norton 1967) 98; Johnston (n 1) 7.

[19] S Korman, *The Right of Conquest: The Acquisition of Territory by Force in International Law and Practice* (Clarendon 1996) 7; G Clark, *Early Modern Europe from About 1450 to About 1720* (OUP 1972) 143.

[20] See the conflicts cited in Zacher (n 16) 217–19.

1.2 Boundaries Revisited

imposed by the European controlling powers in disregard of local rulers.[21]

Twentieth century to present. In the twentieth century, the making of boundaries became a strictly bilateral process. The settlement of two world wars, the end of colonialism, the formation of the League of Nations and its successor the United Nations and the development of international rules promoting interstate cooperation and maintaining international peace are some of the main explanations for this shift in the nature of boundary-making. Boundaries became the legitimate means of co-existence between states.

Under contemporary international law, boundaries can be established only through bilateral[22] and peaceful means.[23] The unilateral establishment of international boundaries is *ipso facto* void.[24] The vast majority of land and maritime boundaries are now established through treaties between the states concerned. This transactional process requires that 'two countries agree on a line and stick to it, as individuals agree on property lines'.[25] When no

---

[21] Milano (n 15); M Shaw, *Title to Territory in Africa: International Legal Issues* (Clarendon 1986) 27–58.

[22] *Case Concerning the Territorial Dispute (Libyan Arab Jamahiriya v Chad)* [1994] ICJ Rep 6, para 52: 'The fixing of a frontier depends on the will of the sovereign States directly concerned.' As added in *Delimitation of the Maritime Boundary in the Gulf of Maine Area (Canada v United States)* [1984] ICJ Rep 292, para 89, 'any delimitation must be effected by agreement between the States concerned, either by the conclusion of a direct agreement or, if need be, by some alternative method, which must, however, be based on consent'.

[23] UN Charter (signed 26 June 1945, entered into force 24 October 1945) 1 UNTS XVI, arts 2(3) and 33(1). The same is repeated in the law of the sea for maritime boundaries. See UNCLOS, preamble, arts 279–80. Although unlawful, aggression in connection with territorial claims has not entirely vanished, however (eg Turkish invasion of Cyprus in 1974; war between Israel and Arab States in 1948–49, 1956 and 1967; armed conflicts between Pakistan and Kashmir in 1965). See J Vasquez and M Henehan, 'Territorial Disputes and the Probability of War 1816–1992' (2001) 38 Journal of Peace Research 123; T Rider and A Owsiak, 'Border Settlement, Committee Problems, and the Causes of Contiguous Rivalry' (2015) 52 Journal of Peace Research 508; T Wright and P Diehl, 'Unpacking Territorial Disputes: Domestic Political Influences and War' (2016) 60 Journal of Conflict Resolution 645–669. No wars have yet taken place with regard to maritime boundaries (with the exception, perhaps, of the so-called Cod Wars, which were more akin to militarized conflicts than to actual wars). The dangerous tensions arising in the ocean that may threaten international stability are those concerning territorial sovereignty over islands (eg Sino-Japanese dispute over the Senkaku/Diaoyu islands in East China Sea; Sino-Vietnamese dispute over the Spratly islands in South China Sea).

[24] *Fisheries Case (United Kingdom v Norway)* [1951] ICJ Rep 116, 132: 'Although it is true that the act of delimitation is necessarily a unilateral act, because only the coastal State is competent to undertake it, the validity of the delimitation with regard to other States depends upon international law.' The same goes for land boundaries.

[25] S Jones 'Boundary Concepts in the Setting of Place and Time' (1959) 49 Annals of the Association of American Geographers 241, 251; Johnston (n 1) 7.

6 *1 Prolegomena*

agreement can be reached, states may resort to third bodies, such as international courts or tribunals.[26] Under no circumstances, though, can states resort to force, as that would breach their international duty to settle their disputes peacefully.

1.3 BOUNDARIES AND STATES

International law does not require that a state's boundaries be 'fully delimited and defined' for purposes of statehood.[27] A sovereign state exists even if its external boundaries are outstanding, unstable or actively challenged by another state.[28] Notwithstanding, international boundaries serve a number of practical and symbolic functions in the lives of states. On land, boundaries permit the exercise of states' territorial sovereignty and secure nations' self-sufficiency and territorial integrity.[29] At sea, boundaries are mainly associated with the economic welfare of states and the peaceful utilization of the oceans among nations.[30]

More importantly, 'Good fences make good neighbours'.[31] By definition, a boundary is '[a] line which marks the limits of an area'.[32] Both on land and at sea, international boundaries mark the limits of national jurisdiction between states. Within those limits, states exercise their authoritative powers (law-making, enforcement) over the things, persons and events situated in their domain.

This makes delimitation particularly important for land and maritime areas claimed by two (or more) neighbouring states, as happens when states challenge

---

[26] Adjudication and arbitration are the most popular third-party means of delimitation. States can also resort to mediation and conciliation, although these are rarely used. In a few cases, delimitation was effected by a boundary commission. For example, in *Decision Regarding Delimitation of the Border between Eritrea and Ethiopia* (2002) 25 RIAA 83, the commission comprised five arbitrators who performed delimitation on the basis of international law and the procedural rules of arbitration, although this amounted in essence to delimitation by an international tribunal.

[27] Questions of the Monastery of Saint Naoum (Albanian Frontier) (Advisory Opinion) PCIJ Rep Series B No 9 (1924) 10; *North Sea Continental Shelf Cases (Federal Republic of Germany/ Denmark, Federal Republic of Germany/Netherlands)* [1969] ICJ Rep 3, para 46. As stressed in *Deutsche Continental Shelf Gas-Gesellschaft v Polish State* (1929) PCIJ AD No 5, 14–15, '[w]hatever may be the importance of the delimitation of boundaries, one cannot go so far as to maintain that as long as this delimitation has not been legally effected the State in question cannot be considered as having any territory whatever'.

[28] J Crawford, *The Creation of States in International Law* (Clarendon 1979) 36–37.

[29] Boggs (n 2) 9–12.

[30] V Prescott, *The Maritime Political Boundaries of the World* (Methuen 1985) 1; Johnston (n 1) 42.

[31] A phrase spoken in Robert Frost's poem 'Mending Wall', R Frost, *North of Boston* (David Nutt 1914).

[32] <www.lexico.com/definition/boundary> accessed 7 February 2021.

1.4 BOUNDARIES AND NON-STATE ACTORS

the validity of a previous territorial arrangement[33] (typical on land) or when they disagree about the division of a previously undelimited space (typical in the ocean). In both cases, the establishment of international boundaries seeks to terminate the overlap of national claims by dividing the area in question between the states concerned.

Whether on land or at sea, and whether effected through a treaty or a third party, delimitation is inextricably intertwined with the interests of the states concerned. The process of delimitation always involves weighing and balancing the states' divergent interests with a view to reaching a result that will be workable for both sides.

But at the same time, the impact of international boundaries extends beyond the states' interests. It is common for there to be non-state actors residing or operating in land and maritime areas claimed by two states. Quite often, these natural or juridical persons hold private rights (eg for farming, grazing, exploration, fishing) granted by one or other of the states without the consent of the other.[34] On some occasions, those rights are granted at a time when the area is already the subject of controversy between the states, while on other occasions the interstate tension arises after the unilateral creation of private rights in a previously undelimited area. In both situations, though, the rights relate to a space claimed by two states.

As non-state actors, the holders of private rights are not parties to boundary disputes. These arise and are dealt with exclusively between States. However, the subsequent delimitation of the area in which private actors reside or operate can have a direct impact on their interests. If the area where private activities are carried on eventually remains with the state that originally controlled it, then the existing private rights will retain their status. On the other hand, if the area is redistributed to the other state, the private rights situated therein will be displaced, causing legal uncertainty for the interests of the private actors concerned.

The risk of reallocation is increasingly threatening private rights in contested waters. As much as 71 per cent of the earth's surface is covered by the

---

[33] This could be a boundary arrangement made by former colonial powers that was subsequently questioned by the colonized countries after gaining independence, or the limits of an empire or federation after its dissolution. The lines established by unilateral or forcible means were administrative or internal rather than international boundaries.

[34] See Chapter 2 for more on this practice.

8   *1 Prolegomena*

ocean and almost half of this is under the jurisdiction of coastal states.[35] However, only half of the world's maritime boundaries have been fixed.[36] During recent decades, the number of maritime boundary disputes has risen significantly, accompanied by the unilateral creation of private rights by the states involved.[37] While great efforts have been made in practice and jurisprudence to find equitable solutions for the states concerned, it is by no means certain that private interests find a place in the equation.

When investigating whether international law deals with the protection of private interests in contested waters, one must turn to the rules governing maritime delimitation as established by conventions on the law of the sea, delimitation treaties between states, the rulings of international courts or tribunals and custom.

Alone, however, an analysis of the rules of the sea would give only a snapshot of the place of private rights in maritime delimitation. In order to determine whether the interests of non-state actors are *effectively* protected in the ocean, one must consider how private rights ae treated by international boundary-making in general – that is, both on land and at sea. A comparison between land and maritime delimitation will show whether international law treats private rights in all settings in a coordinated manner or whether there are asymmetries between land and sea.

In light of the above, the book will answer the following questions:

– First, to what extent do private rights affect a boundary's course during land and maritime delimitation?
– Second, in what ways does international law preserve any reallocated private rights on land and at sea post delimitation?

1.5 HOW TO COMPARE LAND AND SEA?

Comparison is one of the most important research methods in law.[38] To compare is 'to put together several objects or several elements of one or more objects in order to examine the degrees of similarity so as to be able to

---

[35] H Tuerk, *Reflections on the Contemporary Law of the Sea* (Martinus Nijhoff 2012) 1; A Morgan, 'The New Law of the Sea: Rethinking the Implications for Foreign Jurisdiction and Freedom of Action' (1996) 27 Ocean Development and International Law 5, 22.

[36] I Karaman, *Dispute Resolution in the Law of the Sea* (Martinus Nijhoff 2012) 169; Prescott and Schofield (n 9) 217–18; H Monjur and others, 'Protracted Maritime Boundary Disputes and Maritime Laws' (2019) 2 Journal of International Maritime Safety, Environmental Affairs, and Shipping 89, 90.

[37] See Chapter 2.

[38] Maurice Adams, 'Doing What Doesn't Come Naturally. On the Distinctiveness of Comparative Law' in Mark Van Hoecke (ed), *Methodologies of Legal Research* (Hart Publishing 2011) 229:

1.5 How to Compare Land and Sea?

draw conclusions from them that the analysis of each of them alone would not necessarily have allowed one to draw'.[39] It is through systematic, comparative examination that one can acquire a thorough understanding of two or more legal concepts or mentalities.

For a comparison to be effective, it must be performed on like objects, as 'incomparables cannot be usefully compared'.[40] In law, the only elements that can be compared with each other are those that fulfil the same function.[41] At first glance, land and maritime delimitation may seem too distinct to be compared. Land delimitation is based on the premise that by law a particular territory can belong to only one state – the state that holds the stronger or more convincing title.[42] By contrast, maritime delimitation rests on the postulate that two or more states have an equal entitlement to the same area, which therefore must be divided between them on the basis of equity.[43]

In practice, however, the two delimitation processes are closely related. As stressed by the International Court of Justice (ICJ) in 1978, whether it is a land or a maritime boundary that is in question, 'the process is essentially the same, and inevitably involves the same element of stability and permanence'.[44] In both situations, the purpose of establishing an international boundary is to mark the limits of two contiguous jurisdictions in a final and peaceful manner.[45] As similarly expressed by scholars, '[t]he

'Comparison is inseparably connected with doing research in the humanities and social sciences. Nearly any claim we make as lawyers, as well as every distinction we draw, will implicitly or explicitly be set against another situation. A legal arrangement can only be qualified as satisfactory or good because there is another arrangement by which it can be measured; such an arrangement is never good in and of itself.' See also, J Smiths (ed), *Elgar Encyclopedia of Comparative Law* (Edgar Elgar 1998); M Van Hoecke (ed), *Epistemology and Methodology of Comparative Law* (Hart 2004); G Wilson, 'Comparative Legal Scholarship' in M McConville and WH Chui (eds), *Research Methods for Law* (Edinburgh University Press 2007) 87–103.

[39]   Definition by Y Chevrel, *La Littérature Comparée* (5th edn, Presses Universitaires de France 2006) 3, as translated by G Samuel, 'Comparative Law and Its Methodology' in Dawn Watkins and Mandy Burton (eds), *Research Methods in Law* (Routledge 2013) 101.

[40]   K Zweigert and H Kötz, *Introduction to Comparative Law* (Clarendon 1998) 34; M Graziadei, 'The Functionalist Heritage' in P Legrand and R Munday (eds), *Comparative Legal Studies: Traditions and Transitions* (CUP 2003) 102.

[41]   ibid.

[42]   *Island of Palmas Case (Netherlands v USA)* (Arbitral Award) (1928) 829; 838–39. See Chapter 2.

[43]   Weil (n 3) 91. See Chapter 2 for further analysis. The concept of equity is also analysed in Chapters 4 and 5. However, this does not mean that equity cannot apply in land delimitation. See *Case Concerning the Frontier Dispute (Burkina Faso v Republic of Mali)* [1986] ICJ Rep 554, 633.

[44]   *Aegean Sea Continental Shelf Case (Greece v Turkey)* [1978] ICJ Rep 3, 35–36.

[45]   *Case Concerning the Delimitation of Maritime Boundary between Guinea-Bissau and Senegal (Guinea-Bissau v Senegal)* (Award) (1989) para 63: 'An international frontier is a line formed by a succession of maximum points showing the limits of spatial validity of the rules of the

10   *1 Prolegomena*

motives for drawing boundaries on land and sea are identical' and 'the procedures by which States ... produce boundaries on land and sea have much in common'.[46] Therefore, it will be interesting to see whether the treatment of private rights is a matter on which the two delimitation processes converge or diverge.

Besides, the law of the sea has been largely governed by the principle of domination, according to which 'the land dominates the sea'.[47] This means that the powers that coastal states exercise in the ocean are derived from their sovereignty on land.[48] It also explains the application of certain land delimitation principles in maritime boundary-making.[49] The principal techniques now used in maritime delimitation, such as the median line/equidistance, were first developed by land geographers like Boggs, before being adopted by ocean-boundary experts.[50] Likewise, the configuration of the coast, which is a land feature, and the principle that the seabed is a natural prolongation of the state's land play a fundamental role in

> legal system of a State. The delimitation of the area of spatial validity of the State may refer to land, rivers or lake waters, the sea, the subsoil or the atmosphere ... From the legal point of view, there is no reason to establish different regimes according to the material element in which the limit is established.'

[46] Prescott (n 1) 24. Likewise Weil (n 3) 94: 'the process of maritime delimitation is and remains an exercise *sui generis* ... the dividing line to which it leads is undoubtedly very like a land boundary'. On the legal and functional similarities between land and maritime boundaries see also Tanja (n 6) 306. Perhaps the only difference is that, unlike many boundaries on land, no maritime boundary has ever been forced on a state by another state.

[47] *Fisheries Case* (n 24) 133; *North Sea Continental Shelf Cases* (n 27) para 96; *Aegean Sea Continental Shelf Case* (n 44) 36; *Maritime Delimitation in the Black Sea (Romania v Ukraine)* [2009] ICJ Rep 61, para 77.

[48] *North Sea Continental Shelf Cases* (n 27) para 96: 'The land is the legal source of the power which a State may exercise over territorial extensions to seaward.' *Aegean Sea Continental Shelf* (n 44) 36: '[I]t is solely by virtue of the coastal State's sovereignty over the land that rights of exploration and exploitation in the continental shelf can attach to it ... In short, continental shelf rights are legally both an emanation from and an automatic adjunct of the territorial sovereignty of the coastal State.'

[49] *Maritime Delimitation and Territorial Questions (Qatar v Bahrain)* [2001] ICJ Rep 40, para 185]; BB Jia, 'The Principle of the Domination of the Land over the Sea: A Historical Perspective on the Adaptability of the Law of the Sea to New Challenges' (2014) 57 German Yearbook of International Law 1; C Schofield, 'Defining the "Boundary" between Land and Sea: Territorial Sea Baselines in the South China Sea' in S Jayakumar, T Koh and R Beckman (eds), *The South China Sea Disputes and Law of the Sea* (Edward Elgar 2014).

[50] S Boggs, 'Problems of Water Boundary-Definition: Median Lines and International Boundaries Through Territorial Waters' (1937) 27 Geographical Review 445, 453–56; D Rothwell and T Stephens, *The International Law of the Sea* (Hart 2010) 385. Land geographers were first to suggest that the method of equidistance (which was primarily used for the delimitation of lakes and rivers) should extend to the delimitation of the maritime zones.

maritime delimitation.[51] Therefore, it is important to enquire whether the principles that regulate the place of private rights in land delimitation extend to ocean boundary-making too.

From the above it can be concluded that a comparative analysis of land and maritime delimitation is a legitimate undertaking. To perform this analysis, the book will compare delimitation treaties and rulings in both settings. Not only are these sources the principal means of boundary-making, they are also important for international law. Although international treaties are grounded on the principle of contractual freedom, they create solid state practices which may evolve into international custom.[52] Likewise, although *stare decisis* does not apply to international legal rulings, it is accepted that the decisions of international courts and tribunals on delimitation can crystallize into rules of international law.[53]

The systematic comparison underlying this book will be conducted by analysing the above sources in pairs based on their common functions. Thus, the book will compare the place of private rights first in land and maritime delimitation treaties[54] and then in land and maritime delimitation rulings.[55]

1.6 LIMITS ON RESEARCH

This book champions the comparison of land and maritime delimitation. In itself, this is a vast topic, whose breadth defies the confines of a single study. To overcome this challenge, the following limits have been placed on what will be examined.

First, it is not the purpose of this book to compare land and maritime delimitation *in toto* or *in abstracto*, but rather to focus on the different ways in which these two delimitation processes treat privately held rights in areas of overlapping sovereign claims. Any further similarities and differences between the two delimitation processes (eg in the treatment of geographical elements) may be briefly mentioned but will not be thoroughly discussed.

Second, the place of private rights in boundary-making can be approached from various epistemological perspectives (eg legal, economic, sociological,

---

[51] A Willis, 'From Precedent to Precedent: The Triumph of Pragmatism in the Law of Maritime Boundaries' (1986) 24 Canadian Yearbook of International Law 3; Y Tanaka, *The International Law of the Sea* (CUP 2012) 198–99.

[52] For an analysis, see Chapter 3, Section 3.4.1 and Chapter 4, Section 4.4.1.

[53] For an analysis, see Chapter 3, Section 3.4.2 and Chapter 4, Section 4.4.2.

[54] Chapter 3, Section 3.2 and Chapter 4, Section 4.2.

[55] Chapter 3, Section 3.3 and Chapter 4, Section 4.3.

anthropological). The book is concerned with the legal issues that may arise for non-state actors from the state practice of creating private rights in land and maritime areas of uncertain jurisdiction, as well as with the legal responses to those issues. As such, it will refer only to private rights created by states. On land, these are mainly ownership, housing, agricultural and mining rights. At sea, these are mainly rights for fishing and petroleum exploration, but also for scientific research. Any private rights that are not created by sovereign acts of states (eg the aboriginal rights of indigenous people) will not be analysed, unless it is important to refer to them for explanatory purposes.

Third, the book examines private rights from the perspective of international law. Although private rights are subject to the domestic rules of the granting state, the state's power to create such rights, be it on land or at sea, derives from international law. Also, the entire process of land and maritime delimitation, whether done through a treaty between the states concerned or through a third body, is profoundly international. All decisions made in relation to the boundary's location and the factors that affect those decisions are subject to international law. Likewise, the preservation of legally acquired private rights that have been reallocated post delimitation is a matter of international law.

Fourth, the book does not intend to discuss the role of private rights in the processes of boundary-making through the entire course of time. Rather, it will concentrate on the delimitation processes that have been developed from the twentieth century onwards. This choice is based on the following reasons.

As explained earlier, the expansion of state control in the ocean and the attendant need for maritime delimitation date from the twentieth century.[56] Likewise, the majority of modern international boundaries on land were established during the last 100 years or so.[57] Indeed, with the end of colonialism in Latin America, Africa and Asia the conclusion of two world wars and the dissolution of the former Soviet Union and Yugoslavia, many new states emerged, all seeking to establish their international boundaries.

Also, it was in the twentieth century that delimitation became a truly bilateral legal process.[58] In the Middle Ages, the vast majority of boundaries were unilaterally established by powerful rulers. In colonial times, boundaries

---

[56] See Section 1.2.

[57] D Carter and H Goemans, 'The Making of the Territorial Order: New Borders and the Emergence of Interstate Conflict' (2011) 65 International Organization 275–309; Organization for Security and Co-operation in Europe (OSCE), 'Applied Issues in International Land Boundary Delimitation/Demarcation Practices' (2011) <www.osce.org/cpc/85263?download=true> accessed 20 March 2020.

[58] See Section 1.2.

were also arbitrarily imposed by European hegemonies which exercised control over the then known world. During the twentieth century, however, it became apparent that boundaries could be established only through transactional processes, rather than by forcible or arbitrary means. The controversial boundary-making practices of the past were eventually replaced by legal treaties freely concluded between sovereign states and by sophisticated rulings delivered by international courts and tribunals.

1.7 BOOK PLAN

The book is structured as follows:

Chapter 2 broaches a preliminary – yet fundamental – legal issue, which is the creation of private rights in areas of uncertain jurisdiction. Do states possess the same competence to create private rights in delimited and undelimited spaces? The chapter begins by discussing the creation of private rights by states in general. It refers to the types and nature of the private rights most commonly granted on land and at sea. Then, it examines whether the lack of clearly established boundaries prohibits or otherwise hinders states from granting private rights in land and maritime spaces that are also claimed by other states. This will determine whether private rights in disputed areas are legitimate or not.

Chapter 3 examines the role of private rights in the process of land and maritime delimitation. By analysing a series of delimitation treaties and rulings, the chapter investigates whether the presence of private rights in land and maritime areas of overlapping claims can affect the course of international boundaries. A comparative analysis of the two delimitation processes reveals that this impact is significant on land but almost absent in the ocean. Hence, the risk of reallocation is greater for offshore private rights in the first place.

Chapter 4 investigates the way in which international law treats any reallocated private rights post delimitation. More specifically, the chapter examines whether private rights will vanish upon their reallocation on land or at sea and what legal mechanisms are available in international law to protect those rights against imminent discharge. A comparative analysis between the two settings reveals that reallocated private rights have a greater chance of surviving on land than at sea post delimitation.

Chapter 5 synthesizes the findings of the previous two chapters. Significant asymmetries exist between land and maritime delimitation as far as the treatment of private rights is concerned, and this has serious legal implications for non-state actors and for international law in general. Against this background, the chapter examines whether the unbalanced treatment of private rights on land and at sea is justified on legal grounds. The study concludes that this asymmetry is not satisfactorily justified, stressing the need for an equilibrium in the treatment of private rights in land and maritime delimitation.

Chapter 6 addresses the problem revealed by the foregoing findings. Based on the observation that private rights are protected more effectively on land, the chapter explains what legal changes can be effected in the framework of maritime delimitation to increase the protection of private rights in the ocean.

Chapter 7 summarizes the main findings of the book and the lessons that maritime delimitation can draw from land with a view to achieving greater coherence in the protection of non-state actors' rights in both settings.

2

Private Rights in Areas of Uncertain Jurisdiction

2.1 INTRODUCTION

One of the main manifestations of a state's authoritative powers on land and at sea is the granting of private rights to individuals and legal persons situated in its domain. The creation of private rights in areas with fixed international boundaries does not cause any particular problems of international law for states. The presence of boundary lines marks the extent of the granting state's jurisdiction in a clear-cut way, separating it from the jurisdiction of its neighbours. This often leads scholars to maintain that boundaries are a prerequisite for a state to exercise its authoritative powers on land and at sea.[1]

If that is the case, then how is it that states grant private rights in undelimited spaces, especially in areas of overlapping national claims? What are the features and the nature of those rights? And more importantly, are they valid or void?

A two-step process will be followed in answering these questions. First, the chapter will discuss the creation of private rights by states in general. It will begin by describing states' powers on land and at sea and then examine the types of private rights most commonly granted in those settings and the legal nature of those rights. Next, the chapter will focus on the creation of private rights in areas of overlapping national claims, analysing the causes of such overlap on land and at sea, in turn. It will then consider whether the lack of fixed boundaries restricts the competence of states to create private rights in land and maritime spaces.

The findings reached in each section reveal that the absence of fixed international boundaries does not affect the powers of states to create private rights on land or at sea, even in areas claimed by two or more parties. Rather,

---

[1] See V Adami, *National Frontiers in Relation to International Law* (T Behrens tr, OUP 1927) 3; P Blyschak, 'Offshore Oil and Gas Projects amid Maritime Border Disputes: Applicable Law' (2013) 6 Journal of World Energy Law and Business 210, 211.

16   2 *Private Rights in Areas of Uncertain Jurisdiction*

the states' competence to create private rights in areas of uncertain jurisdiction rests on a bona fide claim to legal title. Although this claim may be rebutted or reduced by the establishment of an international boundary, the private rights will be legitimate and active.

2.2 STATE POWERS ON LAND AND AT SEA: SOVEREIGNTY VIS-À-VIS SOVEREIGN RIGHTS

The existence and lives of states are inextricably intertwined with land.[2] Every sovereign state possesses a part of the earth's surface, which comprises the mainland, any lakes and rivers on its surface, the air space above it and the subsoil below it.[3]

In international law the above land areas are collectively designated state territory.[4] It is where a state's population resides and where the state applies its full powers of sovereignty by exercising its jurisdiction to prescribe and enforce.[5] Also, with very few exceptions around the world, a state's sovereignty covers ownership of the natural resources situated in the subsoil (*in situ*) of its territory.[6] The inalienable right of states to freely explore, develop and

---

[2]   Montevideo Convention on the Rights and Duties of States (signed 26 December 1933, entered into force 26 December 1934) 165 LNTS 19, art 1: 'The State as a person of international law should possess the following qualifications: (a) a permanent population; (b) a defined territory; (c) government; and (d) capacity to enter into relations with other States.' However, the term 'defined' does not mean that a state's territory must be delimited by means of international boundaries. J Crawford, *The Creation of States in International Law* (Clarendon 1979) 36–37. See also *Questions of the Monastery of Saint Naoum (Albanian Frontier)* (Advisory Opinion) PCIJ Rep Series B No 9 (1924) 10; *Deutsche Continental Shelf Gas-Gesellschaft v Polish State* (1929) PCIJ AD No 5,14–15; *North Sea Continental Shelf Cases (Federal Republic of Germany v Denmark, Federal Republic of Germany v Netherlands)* [1969] ICJ Rep 3, para 46.

[3]   According to the Roman doctrine *cuius est solum, eius est usque ad coelum et ad inferos'* (whoever owns the soil owns it all the way to Heaven and all the way to Hell). A significant number of states also possess insular formations in the ocean, such as islands, islets, rocks and reefs. However, these fall outside the scope of the present study.

[4]   I Brownlie, *Principles of Public International Law* (8th edn, OUP 2012) 115.

[5]   According to the rules *quidquid est in territorio, est etiam de territorio* and *qui in territorio meo est, etiam meus subditus est* (whatever person or thing is on or enters a territory is the subject of that territory). L Oppenheim, *International Law: A Treatise*, vol 1 (6th edn, Longmans 1947) 408–409. For an analysis of prescriptive and enforcement jurisdiction, see F Mann, 'The Doctrine of Jurisdiction in International Law' (1964) 111 Collected Courses of the Hague Academy of International Law 1, 13; M Shaw, *International Law* (6th edn, CUP 2008) 645.

[6]   Such exceptions are found in the United States and Germany. In the United States petroleum underground belongs to the (public or private) landowner. See B Taverne, *An Introduction to the Regulation of the Petroleum Industry: Laws, Contracts and Conventions* (Martinus Nijhoff 1994) 11. The German Federal Mining Law defines mineral resources as all mineral substances – solid, liquid or gaseous (except for water) – occurring in natural sediments or accumulations (deposits) onshore as well as offshore. Mineral resources are further classified as

2.2 State Powers on Land and at Sea

dispose of their natural wealth for the good of their people is established in a number of UN resolutions and recognized as a fundamental principle of international law.[7]

The ocean is also important in the lives of states. However, their powers at sea – in contrast to land – have greatly evolved over time. For centuries, the ocean was considered too immense to be enclosed and appropriated by nations.[8] The only part of the seas that came under state control was a 3-M coastal belt known as the territorial sea (TS). Possession of this maritime zone was based on the customary rule of 'cannon shot', according to which 'territorial sovereignty ends where the power of arms (cannons) ends'.[9]

The picture changed radically in the mid-twentieth century.[10] The occurrence of the two world wars instilled a belief that states needed to turn to the

---

bergfrei or *grundeigen*. Only mineral resources classified as *grundeigen* go with the land and are protected as ownable private property. Mineral resources classified as *bergfrei* are freely available for mining. They include metals like iron, gold, copper, coal, geothermal energy and salt. Mineral resources in the continental shelf are also classified as *bergfrei*. Other natural resources, such as basalt lava, quartz and clay, are classified as *grundeigen*. Through this classification, the Federal Mining Law denies landowners access to resources categorized as *bergfrei*, which are regarded as goods over which no one has ownership. They may, however, be exploited, subject to permission from the relevant authorities. A Ronne, 'Public and Private Rights to Natural Resources and Differences in their Protection?' in A McHarg and others (eds), *Property and the Law of Natural Resources* (OUP 2010) 118.

[7] See UNGA Res 626 (VII) (21 December 1952) Right to Exploit Freely Natural Wealth and Resources; UNGA Res 1803 (XVII) (14 December 1962) Permanent Sovereignty over Natural Resources; UNGA Res 2158 (XXI) (25 November 1966) Permanent Sovereignty over Natural Resources; UNGA Res 3171 (XXVIII) (17 December 1973) Permanent Sovereignty over Natural Resources; UNGA Resolution 3281 (XXIX) (12 December 1974) Charter of Economic Rights and Duties of States. Although UN resolutions are not legally binding, their continuous application by states may form rules of customary law. See M Öberg, 'The Legal Effects of Resolutions of the UN Security Council and General Assembly in the Jurisprudence of the ICJ' (2006) 16 European Journal of International Law 879–906.

[8] A conception originally expressed by Hugo Grotius in *Mare Liberum Sive De Jure Quod Batavis Competit ad Indicna Commercia Dissertatio* (Elzevier 1609) *The Freedom of the Seas, Or, The Right which Belongs to the Dutch to Take Part in the East Indian Trade* (R Van Deman Magoffin tr, OUP 1916). According to Grotius, the sea is 'not susceptible of occupation' because it can 'neither easily be built upon nor enclosed' (Freedom of the Seas 28–31, see also 37–38, 50–51).

[9] This rule, attributed to Cornelius van Bynkershoek and dating from 1702, remained valid during next two centuries. W Walker, 'Territorial Waters: The Cannon Shot Rule' (1945) 22 British Yearbook of International Law 210; 211–13; L Brilmayer and N Klein, 'Land and Sea: Two Sovereignty Regimes in Search of a Common Dominator' (2001) 33 Journal of International Law and Politics 703, 717.

[10] The following lines describe this change in a humorous, yet accurate manner:

> Good gracious, dear Grotius,
> Your law is atrocious,
> Your *mare liberum* must end.

2 Private Rights in Areas of Uncertain Jurisdiction

ocean for living and non-living natural resources.[11] During the same period, the end of colonialism in Latin America, Africa and Asia marked the birth of numerous coastal nations seeking access to the ocean for the purposes of economic development.[12] Against this background, a significant number of littoral states asserted national claims to the waters and the subsoil beyond the TS, up to a distance of 200 nautical miles (M) offshore.[13]

Responding to the unilateral proclamations of such states, the 1958 Convention on the Continental Shelf was the first international treaty to expand national jurisdiction over the seabed.[14] It was not until 1982, however, that the expansion of state control in the ocean was completed with the United Nations Convention on the Law of the Sea (UNCLOS).[15] Pursuant to this treaty, every littoral state is entitled to a 12-M TS, a 200-M exclusive economic

> The cannon shot rule
> Is a rule for a fool
> In these days of the ICBM.
> Van Bynkershoek's wishes
> Aren't good for the fishes
> When everyone has his own fleet.
> Economists smirk
> At McDougal and Burke
> 'Cause their freedom's a right to deplete.
> The maritime powers
> Have long had their hours
> In using the Ocean for free …
> Dear Grotius, my gracious!
> The oceans aren't spacious,
> They're nothing but coastal states' lakes!
>
> *F Christy, 'Ode to the Grotian Ocean'*

Quoted in R Friedheim, *Negotiating the New Ocean Regime* (University of South Carolina Press 1992) 17–19.

[11] RJ Dupuy and D Vignes (eds), *A Handbook on the New Law of the Sea*, vol 1 (Martinus Nijhoff 1991) 3–4.

[12] Between 1943 and 1973 alone, some seventy states gained independence, fifty-five of which were coastal states. E Brown, 'Maritime Zones: A Survey of Claims' in R Churchill and others (eds), *New Directions in the Law of the Sea*, vol 3 (British Institute of International and Comparative Law 1973) 159.

[13] eg Proclamations of US President Harry Truman on the policy of the United States with respect to the natural resources of the subsoil and the seabed of the continental shelf and with respect to coastal fisheries in certain areas of the high seas (28 September 1945); Proclamation of Argentina on the Epicontinental Sea (5 December 1946); Declaration of the Maritime Zone of Chile, Ecuador and Peru (Santiago Declaration) (18 August 1952).

[14] Convention on the Continental Shelf (signed 29 April 1958, entered into force 10 June 1964) 499 UNTS 31, arts 1–2.

[15] UNCLOS (signed 10 December 1982, entered into force 16 November 1994) 1833 UNTS 3.

2.2 State Powers on Land and at Sea

zone (EEZ) and a continental shelf (CS) extending to 200 M and, in certain circumstances, up to 350 M from the coast.[16]

According to legal theory and case law, the TS, CS and EEZ are institutions so well established that they are part of customary international law[17] Thus, all coastal states are entitled to them, including even those that have not signed or ratified the conventions of the sea. The legal upshot of this is that almost 40 per cent of the world's ocean space is now under the jurisdiction of states.[18] Yet, the legal regimes and states' rights that apply within each maritime zone are significantly different.

The TS is an essential appurtenance of every coastal state's land territory.[19] This has two consequences. First, the possession of this zone is not subject to a previous claim. In the words of Sir Arnold McNair,

> To every State whose land territory is at any place washed by the sea, international law attaches a corresponding portion of maritime territory consisting of what the law calls territorial waters (and in some cases national waters in addition). International law does not say to a State: 'You are entitled to claim territorial waters if you want them.' ... The possession of this territory is not optional, not dependent upon the will of the State, but compulsory.[20]

Second, the coastal state possesses powers of full sovereignty within this zone. But in contrast to land and internal waters (eg bays and ports), where the state is free to prohibit entry by foreigners, the state's sovereignty in the TS is subject to the right of innocent passage by foreign ships.[21] By imposing this limitation,

---

[16] ibid, arts 3, 57, 76 respectively. Article 33(1) UNCLOS establishes a further maritime belt, the so-called contiguous zone, which extends to a maximum of twenty-four nautical miles from a state's baseline. In essence, it serves as a buffer zone in which a state may exercise the control necessary to prevent and punish any infringement of its customs, fiscal, immigration or sanitary laws and regulations. The zone is part of the EEZ (if the coastal state has laid claim to an EEZ) or the high seas (if it has not) and therefore will not be examined separately in this study.

[17] On the status of the TS, see *Fisheries Case (UK v Norway)* [1951] ICJ Rep 116, Dissenting Opinion of Judge McNair 48. On the CS, see *North Sea Continental Shelf Cases* (n 2) para 19. On the EEZ, see Case Concerning the Continental Shelf (Tunisia/Libyan Arab Jamahiriya) [1982] ICJ Rep 18, para 34; *Delimitation of the Maritime Boundary in the Gulf of Maine Area (Canada v United States)* [1984] ICJ Rep 292, para 94. See also Y Tanaka, *International Law of the Sea* (CUP 2012) 84, 125, 133; R Churchill and V Lowe, *The Law of the Sea* (3rd edn, Manchester University Press 1999) 160–61.

[18] A Morgan 'The New Law of the Sea: Rethinking the Implications for Foreign Jurisdiction and Freedom of Action' (1996) 27 Ocean Development and International Law 5, 22.

[19] *Arbitral Award in the Matter of Delimitation of a Certain Part of the Maritime Boundary between Norway and Sweden (Grisbådarna Case) (Norway v Sweden)* (1909) 11 RIAA 147–66.

[20] *Fisheries Case* (n 17) Dissenting Opinion of Judge McNair 48.

[21] A foreign vessel's passage is innocent if it is 'not prejudicial to the peace, good order or security of the coastal State'. UNCLOS, arts 17, 19.

the law of the sea seeks to strike a balance between the national interests of littoral states in the sea belt adjacent to their coasts and the need for the international community to have access to these waters for navigational purposes.[22] Also, as on land, the state owns all the natural resources (living and non-living) that are located in its TS to an unlimited depth.[23]

The CS comprises the seabed and subsoil of the submarine areas that extend beyond a coastal state's TS as a natural prolongation of the land territory to the outer edge of the CS margin or to a distance of 200 M from the baseline.[24] The breadth of this zone can be extended to 350 M from the baseline upon a successful application by the coastal state to the Commission on the Limits of the Continental Shelf.[25] A state does not wield full sovereignty within its CS but instead possesses lesser (sovereign) rights for the purposes of exploration and development of the natural resources (eg oil, gas, minerals) that lie in the seabed and subsoil.[26] This is because, although an extension of land, the CS is not part of the state's territory.[27] Coastal states do not own the CS as they do land. If they did, this would encourage 'a new form of colonial competition among the maritime nations' and possibly jeopardize freedom of the high seas.[28]

---

[22] M McDougal and W Burke, 'Crisis in the Law of the Sea: Community Perspectives versus National Egoism' (1958) Yale Law Journal 67539–40; S Ghosh, 'The Legal Regime of Innocent Passage through the Territorial Sea' in H Caminos (ed), *Law of the Sea* (Ashgate 2001) 37.

[23] L Oppenheim, *International Law* (8th edn, Longmans 1955) 462; R Lagoni, 'Oil and Gas Deposits across National Frontiers' (1979) 73 AJIL 215, 216.

[24] UNCLOS, art 76(1). States can choose between the distance criterion and the natural prolongation when defining their CS. Note that there is a difference between the legal concept of the CS and the physical phenomenon as referred to by geographers. See *Case Concerning the Continental Shelf (Tunisia/Libyan Arab Jamahiriya)* (n 17) paras 46–47. Without wishing to undermine the scientific approach preferred by geographers, the present work refers to the legal, not the geographical, conception of the CS.

[25] UNCLOS, art 76(5)–(8). The first states to apply for an extended CS were the Russian Federation, Brazil and Canada. At the time of writing, the commission had received 77 applications, listed at <www.un.org/depts/los/clcs_new/commission_submissions.htm> accessed 20 March 2020.

[26] UNCLOS, art 77(1). It is estimated that 87 per cent of the world's known submarine oil deposits fall within states' 200-M CS. C Schofield, 'Parting the Waves: Claims to Maritime Jurisdiction and the Division of Ocean Space' (2012) 1 Penn State Journal of Law and International Affairs 40, 46.

[27] 'While the concept of sovereignty is inherent in the relationship between a State and its territory and, by a logical process of extension, between a State and its Territorial Sea, it does not apply to the relationship of a coastal State to its Continental Shelf. Territorial sovereignty is an absolute and exclusive power which a State exercises over its territory. It is inconceivable that power of the same nature should be exercised over areas which do not form part of the territorial domain.' United Nations Conference on the Law of the Sea (Geneva 24 February–27 April 1958) Official Records,: Summary Records of Meetings and Annexes, 13th Session, 16.

[28] President Johnson at a UN General Assembly meeting in 1966, quoted in M Nordquist (ed), *United Nations Convention on the Law of the Sea 1982: A Commentary*, vol 1 (Martinus Nijhoff 1985) 3.

2.2 State Powers on Land and at Sea

Hence, the powers of a coastal state within its CS are significantly reduced *ratione materiae* compared to the powers that the same state possesses on its land and in its TS. Territorial sovereignty is all-encompassing, as it includes all sorts of authoritative powers that the state may exercise over persons, things and events within its domain. By contrast, a state's jurisdiction over the CS is merely 'functional', as it is limited to operations of an economic nature such as exploration of natural resources in the seabed.[29]

Nonetheless, as on land and in the TS, the state's rights within its CS are inherent and exclusive.[30] This means, firstly, that the state's right to explore and exploit the natural wealth of its CS does not depend on a good claim or occupation.[31] Rather, the natural resources of this zone are the preserve of the coastal state, regardless of the usage to which they may be put.[32] Secondly, if the state does not avail itself of its own rights in the CS, no one else can do so without the state's express consent.[33]

By contrast, the ocean floor beyond the CS and its natural resources fall outside the limits of national jurisdiction. This part of the seabed, which is known as the 'Area', belongs to all mankind and can be explored only by special permission granted by an international committee (the International Seabed Authority). The above categorization is expressly enshrined in part XI UNCLOS.[34] However, the idea that the seabed beyond the CS cannot be appropriated by states, as it would expose the ocean to the risk of colonization, was expressed as early as 1966, when President Lyndon Johnson stressed that

> under no circumstances, we believe, must we ever allow the prospects of rich harvest and mineral wealth to create a new form of colonial completion among the maritime nations. We must be careful to avoid a race to grab and to hold the lands under the high seas. We must ensure that the deep sea and the ocean bottoms are, and remain, the legacy of all human beings.[35]

---

[29] B Oxman, 'The Territorial Temptation: A Siren Song at Sea' (2006) 100 AJIL 100 830, 836.

[30] UNCLOS, art 77(3).

[31] ibid.

[32] C Redgwell, 'Property Law Sources and Analogies in International Law' in A McHarg and others (eds), *Property and the Law of Natural Resources* (OUP 2010) 109; R Higgins, *Problems and Process: International Law and How We Use It* (Clarendon 1994) 138.

[33] UNCLOS, art 77(2).

[34] ibid, arts 133(a), 136–38.

[35] Quoted in S Amerasinghe, 'The Third United Nations Conference on the Law of the Sea' in M Nordquist (ed), *United Nations Convention on the Law of the Sea 1982: A Commentary*, vol 1 (Martinus Nijhoff 1985) 3.

2 Private Rights in Areas of Uncertain Jurisdiction

Finally, the EEZ comprises the seabed and the superjacent water column within a maximum distance of 200 M from the state's baseline.[36] Like the CS, the EEZ is a zone of functional jurisdiction.[37] Here, instead of full sovereignty, coastal states possess lesser rights (jurisdiction) for the conduct of certain economic activities such as the exploration and exploitation of natural resources, the production of energy from water, currents and winds, and the construction of artificial islands, offshore structures and installations.[38]

Again as in the CS, a state's rights in the EEZ are exclusive, which means that no one else can exercise them without the state's consent. But in contrast to the CS and the TS, possession of the EEZ is not inherent but optional. In order to exercise the above-mentioned rights, a state must first lay claim to the EEZ on the basis of a national law or declaration.[39] To date, over 100 of the world's 152 littoral states have successfully laid claim to an EEZ.[40] This means that 90–95 per cent of the world's fisheries are now under national jurisdiction.[41]

The waters beyond the EEZ are known as the high seas and fall beyond the limits of national jurisdiction.[42] This part of the ocean is not amenable to any form of state (or private) appropriation on account of the principle of freedom of the high seas. Under the existing framework established by UNCLOS, the high seas are open to lawful and peaceful use by all states, whether coastal or land-locked.[43] As a result, all states have freedom of navigation, fishing and overflight in this part of the ocean, as well as the freedom to lay submarine cables and pipelines and to conduct scientific research there.[44]

In sum, the authoritative rights which states possess on land and at sea are divergent and multi-dimensional, ranging from full sovereignty on the one

---

[36] UNCLOS, art 55. If a state's CS measures 200 M, it coincides with the EEZ. If it extends beyond 200 M, it covers the seabed beyond that point, but not the water column above it, which is considered part of the high seas.

[37] M Gavouneli, *Functional Jurisdiction in the Law of the Sea* (Martinus Nijhoff 2007) 68–69; B Kwiatkowska, *The 200 Mile Exclusive Economic Zone in the Law of the Sea* (Martinus Nijhoff 1989) 4–5; J Kraska, *Maritime Power and the Law of the Sea* (OUP 2011) 142.

[38] UNCLOS, art 56. The same article also places certain responsibilities on states relating to the preservation and management of natural resources.

[39] Tanaka (n 17) 127; Morgan (n 18) 11.

[40] S Ebbin, AF Hoel and AK Sydnes, *A Sea Change: The Exclusive Economic Zone and Governance Institutions for Living Marine Resources* (Springer 2005) xi.

[41] ibid.

[42] If a state has not claimed an EEZ, the high seas are adjacent to its TS.

[43] UNCLOS, arts 87–89.

[44] Provided these freedoms are exercised with due regard for the interests of other states. UNCLOS, art 87.

2.3 Private Rights on Land and at Sea

hand (on land and in the TS) to lesser sovereign rights on the other (in the CS and the EEZ).

2.3 PRIVATE RIGHTS ON LAND AND AT SEA: GENERAL FEATURES

Whether in the form of full sovereignty or lesser sovereign rights, a state's jurisdiction over its territory and maritime zones is undeniable. On the basis of this power, the state grants private rights (directly or indirectly) to physical or legal persons that reside or wish to operate within its domain.

2.3.1 Types of Private Rights

States create various types of private rights depending on where they are located. On land and islands, the rights they grant consist mainly of ownership titles to land parcels, concessions for various economic and commercial activities (eg hunting, fishing in lakes and rivers, mining of coal and minerals, extraction of other natural resources, construction of industrial units), leases (for housing, farming and grazing purposes) and permits for the installation of wires or pipelines.

The creation and regulation of those rights are subject to the granting state's national laws, such as its constitution and parliamentary acts or royal decrees.[45] For example, a state may create derivative ownership titles to land, which can be acquired by private actors in accordance with the conditions laid down in the state's planning or land law. This process usually includes the submission of an application to the competent public authority and the payment of a fee. Once all legal conditions have been satisfied, the applicant receives a legal title (eg ownership deed, permit to construct buildings on a plot) which is recorded in a public register.

---

[45] It is beyond the scope of this study to analyse such domestic laws, examples of which are the UK Game Licences Act 1860; the UK Agriculture Act 1947; the Japanese Mining Law No 289 of 1950; the UK Mines (Working Facilities and Support) Act 1966; the German Federal Mining Law of 1980; the Constitution of the Federative Republic of Brazil (the Union) of 1988 (amended in 1996); the Scottish Agricultural Holdings Act 1991; the Polish Hunting Law of 1995; the Canadian Land Act 1996, the Mozambican Land Law of 1997; the Australian Land Administration Act 1997; the Latvian Forest Law of 2000; the Namibian Forest Law of 2001; the French Mining Code of 2011; the Dutch Mining Law of 2002; and the Danish Consolidated Act No 889 of 2007 on the Use of the Danish Subsoil. See also, C Blackhall, *Planning Law and Practice* (Cavendish 2005); L Christy and others (eds), *Forest Law and Sustainable Development* (World Bank 2007), esp chs 1 and 2 on land law and water resources; E Dietsche 'Sector Legal Frameworks and Resource Property Rights' in R Dannreuther and W Ostrowski (eds), *Global Resources* (Springer 2013) 159–84.

24   2 *Private Rights in Areas of Uncertain Jurisdiction*

For the mining of resources situated in the state's subsoil or the conduct of hunting activities in state-owned areas such as forests and valleys, the public authorities award licences to interested private actors upon compliance with certain legal requirements (eg in relation to public health and safety or environmental protection) and the payment of a fee or royalty.

In maritime areas, the private rights created by states are also numerous but are mostly limited to concessions and leases for the conduct of economic or commercial activities (eg fishing, exploration and extraction of petroleum, minerals or other natural resources) or for the conduct of scientific operations (eg locating hydrocarbon reservoirs, preserving marine resources), or permits for the installation of submarine cables (eg for telecommunications purposes) or pipelines (eg for energy purposes).

The creation and regulation of offshore private rights are also subject to a state's domestic laws.[46] For example, for the exploitation of hydrocarbons situated in the state's CS, the competent authorities issue permits to the interested private actors, which, depending on the activities concerned, may be an exploratory or a drilling permit. The form of the permit and how it is granted will depend on the state's domestic petroleum regime. In some jurisdictions, like the United Kingdom and Norway, a licence is awarded to the most successful applicant through the conduct of bidding rounds.[47] In other systems, like Nigeria and Kenya, the permit takes the form of a contract awarded directly by the state, such as a production sharing agreement or

---

[46]   It is beyond the scope of this study to analyse such, examples of which are the US Outer Continental Shelf Lands Act 1953; China's 1982 Regulation on the Exploitation of Offshore Petroleum Resources in Cooperation with Foreign Enterprises 1982; Canada's Fisheries Act 1985; Kenya's Petroleum (Exploration and Production) Act (Cap 308) 1986; Australia's Fish Resources Management Act 1994 and Pearling Act 1990; Law No 2289/1995 of the Hellenic Republic on prospecting, exploration and exploitation of hydrocarbons and other provisions; Norway's (Petroleum) Law No 72 of 1996; the Brazilian Petroleum Law No 9478 of 1997; the UK Petroleum Act 1998; the UK Marine and Coastal Access Act 2009; the Danish Continental Shelf Law No 1101 of 2005; the Scottish Aquaculture and Fisheries Act 2013; the Cypriot Marine Scientific Research Regulation No 577 of 2014; Mexico's 1976 Requirements Applicable to Marine Scientific Research Projects Carried Out by Foreign Nationals in the Territorial Sea, on the Continental Shelf and in the Exclusive Economic Zone; the Gabonese Law No 9/84 Establishing an Exclusive Economic Zone of 200 Nautical Miles and Note on Rules Governing Marine Scientific Research Activities; and the 1988 Regulations for Marine Scientific Research in the Maritime Zones of the Republic of Maldives. See also J Sprankling, *The International Law of Property* (OUP 2014) 158, 168; Ebbin, Hoel and Sydnes (n 40) esp ss II and III on national and regional activities in the EEZ; Churchill and Lowe (n 17) 407–08.

[47]   Which bidder is successful will depend on various factors (eg highest monetary offer, efficiency of the company's proposed work plan, compliance with regional health and safety and environmental regulations). See K Dam, *Oil Resources: Who Gets What How?* (University of Chicago Press 1976) 6–7.

2.3 Private Rights on Land and at Sea

a service contract concluded between the government (or the state's national oil company) and the private oil company.[48]

Another activity in the ocean of importance to private actors is fishing. Fish are essential to all nations, be it for human consumption or as processed animal feed, oil or fertilizer.[49] In general, free-swimming fish are not owned by anyone, including coastal states. Ownership is acquired only after the fish have been caught and brought into the individual's possession.[50] Notwithstanding, a person needs to be licensed by a state to enter its TS or EEZ for the purpose of fishing, otherwise it will be infringing the state's national jurisdiction. A fishing licence is awarded in accordance with the state's domestic rules and after payment of a fee. When awarding fishing licences, a coastal state is subject to the restrictions laid down in UNCLOS[51] and other regional or international law instruments[52] concerning limits on catches to avoid over-exploitation.

Finally, a smaller but increasing number of private operations at sea relate to scientific research. Marine research is important to humans in many ways. It is the means by which oil and gas reservoirs essential for meeting states' energy needs can be detected and new living species vital to the preservation of the marine environment discovered.[53] It also uncovers micro-organisms and genetic resources in the seabed and the water column for use in biochemistry, medicine and the cosmetics industry.[54]

UNCLOS allows every coastal state to authorize and perform scientific research within its maritime zones.[55] But as with all operations, the conduct of scientific research by a private actor within a state's maritime spaces requires a licence from the competent authorities in the coastal state. The awarding of this licence is governed by the state's domestic regulations and subject to payment of a fee. Again, when exercising its rights in relation to scientific research, the coastal state is also subject to certain duties imposed by

---

[48]   Taverne (n 6) 20–29.

[49]   Churchill and Lowe (n 17) 281.

[50]   ibid.

[51]   UNCLOS, arts 56(1), 61, 62.

[52]   eg EU directives and regulations or the Common Fisheries Policy of the EU.

[53]   L Kimball, *International Ocean Governance: Using International Law and Organizations to Manage Marine Resources Sustainably* (IUCN 2001) 8.

[54]   For an analysis, see David Leary and others, 'Marine Genetic Resources: A Review of Scientific and Commercial Interest' (2009) 33 Marine Policy 183; E Tsioumani, 'Discussion of Marine Genetic Resources' (2007) 37 Environmental Policy and Law 366, 366–68; M Vierros and others, 'Who Owns the Ocean? Policy Issues Surrounding Marine Genetic Resources' (2016) 25 Limnology and Oceanography Bulletin 29.

[55]   UNCLOS, arts 245–46.

2 Private Rights in Areas of Uncertain Jurisdiction

UNCLOS[56] and other instruments of international law[57] to ensure the conservation and sustainable use of marine resources.

2.3.2 Nature of Private Rights

Despite their differences, private rights on land and at sea have two main features in common. First, they are of a contractual[58] or mixed contractual/regulatory nature.[59] The contractual character of the rights results from the fact that they are based on an agreement between the state and a private actor.[60] The state consents to grant the specific right for a fixed or unlimited period of time and the natural or juridical person who is the licensee makes a monetary contribution in return, in the form of either a one-off payment or periodic fees or royalties. It is common for the agreement to contain a dispute resolution clause, as is normally the case with contracts.[61] The regulatory character of the rights results from the fact that they are subject to state regulation and control. For example, the right-holder may have specific obligations towards the state and the community, the breach of which can entail serious legal consequences such as the infliction of an administrative penalty, the attribution of civil or criminal liability, or the revocation of the granted right.[62]

---

[56]   ibid, arts 249ff.

[57]   Nagoya Protocol on Access to Genetic Resources and the Fair and Equitable Sharing of Benefits Arising from their Utilization (ABS) to the Convention on Biological Diversity (signed 29 October 2010, entered into force 12 October 2014).

[58]   eg production sharing agreements, service contracts.

[59]   This is the characterization scholars give in particular to oil concessions granted in the UK and in other jurisdictions with a similar petroleum licensing system. See T Daintith, *The Legal Character of Petroleum Licences: A Comparative Study* (Dundee University Press 1981) 9; T Daintith, G Willoughby and A Hill, *United Kingdom Oil and Gas Law* (3rd edn, Sweet & Maxwell 2000) 1–323; G Gordon, 'Petroleum Licensing' in G Gordon, J Paterson and E Usenmez, *Oil and Gas Law: Current Practices and Emerging Trends* (2nd edn, Dundee University Press 2011) 72–73. Construction permits granted by states on land and other state acts imposing regulatory obligations on private actors can be similarly characterized.

[60]   Depending on the governing law, the agreement may be verbal or in writing and the contract may be recorded in a public register or ratified by the parliament. The fact that one of the parties to the agreement is a state should not be thought to imply that the agreement is a treaty, which by definition are concluded between states (or sometimes international organizations). On the contractual nature of an agreement between a state and a private actor, see *Libyan American Oil Company (Liamco) v Government of the Libyan Arab Republic* (1977) 62 ILR 141, 169; *Saudi Arabia v Aramco* (Arbitral Award) (1963) 27 ILR 117, 161; *Texaco Overseas Petroleum Co (Topco) and California Asiatic (Calasiatic) Oil Company v Government of the Libyan Arab Republic* (Arbitral Award) (1977) 53 ILR 389, 463–68.

[61]   Gordon (n 59).

[62]   ibid.

2.3 *Private Rights on Land and at Sea*

Second, private rights on land and at sea are of proprietary nature. In all legal systems, ownership is the most comprehensive real right that a person may hold in relation to a thing (eg a specific parcel of land, its appurtenances, a house).[63] It provides the holder with the absolute and exclusive right to use that thing, to collect the fruits of it, and to dispose of or even destroy it. The subordinate, non-ownership rights that a state creates are also of proprietary nature in most legal systems. A concession or licence is essentially a usufruct,[64] lease[65] or *profit-à-prendre*,[66] which allows its holder to use a thing that belongs to someone else for a certain period of time and to acquire title to its fruits or the products extracted from it.[67] A permit to install wires or pipelines is akin to the property right of servitude or easement,[68] which grants a person the right to enter into or use another person's property.

The proprietary nature of the above-mentioned rights is affirmed also in international law. In principle, private rights are governed by domestic rules. Over the years, however, a number of developments in international law, mainly in the areas of human rights and investment, have established the proprietary nature of certain rights (regardless of their characterization in domestic law) in order to protect them against various forms of state interference, such as eminent domain and uncompensated expropriation.

In particular, the European Court of Human Rights (ECtHR) has confirmed the proprietary nature of ownership (over tangible and incorporeal things), licences, usufruct, leases and similar contractual rights with economic

---

[63] For civil law jurisdictions, see Article 544 of the French Civil Code; Article 903 of the German Civil Code; Articles 973 and 1000 of the Greek Civil Code; Article 2 of the General Principles of Civil Law of the People's Republic of China and Article 64 of the 2007 Property Law of the People's Republic of China, although Chinese law does not recognize private ownership in land but provides only for a right of usufruct; Article 206 of the Japanese Civil Code; Article 211 of the Korean Civil Code. On English law, see H Lawson and B Rudden, *The Law of Property* (3rd edn, Clarendon 2002) 68–71, 90–91. On US law, see Restatement of Law of Property as Adopted and Promulgated by the American Law Institute (Washington DC, 9 May 1936) 25–26. On Scottish law, see D Spier, *Law Essentials: Property Law* (Dundee University Press 2008) 2–3. On Islamic law, see J Schacht, *An Introduction to Islamic Law* (Clarendon 1964) 141.

[64] This is the term used in civil law jurisdictions.

[65] This is the term used in US and Scottish law.

[66] This is the term used in English law.

[67] An rare case in which an oil concession was considered not to be of a proprietary nature was *The Commonwealth v WMC Resources Ltd* (1998) 72 ALJR 280 in Australia. However, in *Newcrest Mining (WA) Ltd v The Commonwealth* (1997) 71 ALJR 1346, the High Court of Australia had recognized the proprietary nature of mineral leases. For an analysis, see M Crommelin, 'The Legal Character of Resource Titles' (1998) 17 Australian Mining and Petroleum Law Journal 57–70. The author would like to thank Professor Tina Hunter Soliman for her input.

[68] These are the terms used respectively in civil law and common law.

28   *2 Private Rights in Areas of Uncertain Jurisdiction*

value.[69] A similar approach has been adopted by the Inter-American Court of Human Rights (IACHR) and the African Commission on Human and Peoples' Rights (ACmHPR).[70] Likewise, a natural or legal person's ownership of tangible or incorporeal things, as well as mining leases, concessions for the exploration of natural resources and similar contractual rights of commercial value, have been recognized as property interests in numerous international investment treaties[71] and arbitral awards.[72]

A question that may arguably arise is whether a state's sovereign rights within its CS and EEZ – as distinct from the full sovereignty (ownership) it possesses over its land and TS – are sufficient for the creation of private property rights.[73] There is no clear answer in statutory or case law. In the literature, however, it is widely agreed that the powers which the international law of the sea grants to coastal states allow them to confer non-ownership rights (eg petroleum and fishing licences or leases, permits for the installation of pipelines and wires in the seabed) on private actors in exchange for consideration. Although not as comprehensive as ownership, these are akin to usufruct or *profit-à-prendre*, which makes them property (or quasi-property) rights.[74]

---

[69] See *Sporrong and Lönnroth v Sweden* (1982) Series A no 52; *Bramelid and Malmström v Sweden* App nos 8588/79, 8589/79 (ECtHR, 12 October 1982); *Tre Traktörer Aktiebolag v Sweden* (1989) 13 EHRR 309; *Fredin v Sweden* (1991) 13 EHRR 784; *Loizidou v Turkey* (1995) Series A no 310; *Zubani v Italy* (1996) 32 EHRR 14. See also K Reid, *A Practitioner's Guide to the European Convention on Human Rights* (4th edn, Sweet & Maxwell 2011) 681–90; L Sermet, *The European Convention on Human Rights and Property Rights* (Human Rights Files No 11 rev, Council of Europe 1998) <www.echr.coe.int/LibraryDocs/DG2/HRFILES/DG2-EN-HRFILES-11%281998%29.pdf> accessed 20 March 2020.

[70] See *Case of the Mayagna (Sumo) Awas Tingni Community v Nicaragua* (IACHR, 31 August 2001); *Media Rights Agenda v Nigeria* (ACmHPR, 31 October 1998), cited in Sprankling (n 46) 34.

[71] See Energy Charter Treaty (signed 17 December 1994, entered into force 16 April 1998) art 1(6); North American Free Trade Agreement (NAFTA) (signed 17 December 1992, entered into force 1 January 1994) art 1139; ASEAN-Australia-New-Zealand Free Trade Agreement (signed 27 February 2009) art 2(c)(vi).

[72] See *Raibl-Societa Mineraria del Predil SpA v Italy (Raibl Claim)* (19 June 1964) (1970) 40 ILR 260, 277–80; *Amoco International Finance Corp v Government of the Islamic Republic of Iran, National Iranian Oil Company, National Petrochemical Company and KHARG Chemical Company Ltd* (14 July 1987) 15 Iran–USCTR 189, 220. See also Sprankling (n 46) 36–37; G Christie, 'What Constitutes a Taking of Property?' (1962) British Yearbook of International Law 307, 316–17; G Aldrich, 'What Constitutes a Taking of Property? The Decisions of the Iranian-United States Claims Tribunal' (1994) AJIL 88(4) 585–610.

[73] A person cannot at law create rights that exceed those they already possess. Hydrocarbons in the seabed are not under the full ownership of coastal states, yet neither are they entirely ownerless (*res nullius*). Under the international law of the sea, the rights of coastal states over such resources are limited to exploration and exploitation.

[74] See P Cameron, *Property Rights and Sovereign Rights: The Case of the North Sea Oil* (Academic Press 1983) 51; D Renman, *Markets Under the Sea? A Study of the Potential Private Property Rights in the Seabed* (Institute of Economic Affairs 1984) 38–41; F Penick,

2.4 *Private Rights in Areas of Overlapping Claims* 29

The most important consequence of characterizing a private right as a property right or interest is its enforceability *erga omnes*. This concept comes from Roman law and is generally used to mean that rights or obligations produce their effects vis-à-vis everyone. That is in contrast to contract law, where a right can be enforced only against a party to the contract (*inter partes*) and no other. Hence, the holder of a property right cannot be prevented from exercising it by anyone else. This includes other private actors but also the state that created the private right in the first place.[75]

2.4 THE CREATION OF PRIVATE RIGHTS IN LAND AND MARITIME AREAS OF OVERLAPPING SOVEREIGN CLAIMS

The remarks made in Sections 2.2 and 2.3 about a state's power to create private rights on land and at sea apply unproblematically in areas that clearly fall within the granting state's jurisdiction – that is, delimited areas. By contrast, the lack of clearly defined boundaries creates uncertainty over which state may exercise jurisdiction within an area of overlapping national claims. It could be thought that this would generally deter states from granting private rights in such areas of uncertain jurisdiction.

However, this assumption is far from true. The present study reveals that a significant number of private rights have been granted in land and maritime spaces claimed by two (or sometimes more) states.[76] An indicative and non-exhaustive list of examples, compiled by the author, can be found in the Table 1.

As the table shows, the private rights granted are mainly associated with agricultural activities, fishing and exploration of natural resources. In some cases, these rights were granted by one of the states involved,[77] while in others each state acted without the other's consent.[78] On some occasions, the area where the private rights were granted was the subject of a pre-existing dispute

---

'The Legal Character of the Right to Explore and Exploit the Natural Resources of the Continental Shelf' (1985) 22 San Diego Law Review 765; 768; A Jennings, *Oil and Gas Exploration Contracts* (Sweet & Maxwell 2002) 2; A Scott, *The Evolution of Resource Property Rights* (OUP 2008) pts II and III; Sprankling (n 46) 168; R Shotton (ed), *Use of Property Rights in Fisheries Management* (Food and Agricultural Organization of the United Nations 2000) 39–46, 53–56.

[75] Unless the exercise of the private right is contrary to a legal rule or public policy.

[76] Information gleaned from the exchanges between the parties involved before international courts or arbitral tribunals and from the literature.

[77] eg Australia/East Timor; Bangladesh/India; Cameroon/Nigeria; Ghana/Ivory Coast; Kenya/Somalia.

[78] eg Canada/USA; Eritrea/Yemen; India/Pakistan; France/UK.

TABLE 1 *Examples of private rights granted in land and maritime areas of overlapping national claims*

Location of overlapping claims	Private rights granted by one or more states
Argentina/Chile	Land titles
Australia/East Timor (Timor Gap)	Concessions for fishing, offshore petroleum operations
Australia/Indonesia (Timor Gap)	Concessions for offshore petroleum operations
Bangladesh/India (Bay of Bengal)	Concessions for fishing
Bangladesh/Myanmar (Bay of Bengal)	Concessions for fishing, offshore petroleum operations
Barbados/Trinidad and Tobago	Concessions for fishing, offshore petroleum operations
Belgium/Netherlands	Land titles, housing leases
Cameroon/Nigeria (Bakassi Peninsula, Lake Chad, maritime space)	Agricultural rights, concessions for petroleum operations
Canada/France (St Pierre and Miquelon archipelago)	Concessions for fishing, petroleum operations
Canada/USA (Gulf of Maine)	Concessions for fishing, offshore petroleum operations
China/Japan (East China Sea)	Concessions for fishing, offshore petroleum operations
China/North Korea/South Korea (Yellow Sea)	Concessions for fishing, offshore petroleum operations
China/Philippines (South China Sea)	Concessions for fishing, offshore petroleum operations
Denmark/Norway (Jan Mayen)	Concessions for fishing
El Salvador/Honduras (land area, Gulf of Fonseca)	Land titles, land concessions
Eritrea/Ethiopia	Concessions for land use and mineral activities, licences for associated communications facilities
Eritrea/Yemen (Red Sea)	Licences for fishing, construction of fish processing plant, hotel and lighthouse, conduct of scientific, commercial and tourist activities, radio signal transmission, concessions for offshore petroleum operations
Germany/Denmark/Netherlands (North Sea)	Concessions for offshore petroleum operations

(continued)

2.4 *Private Rights in Areas of Overlapping Claims* 31

TABLE 1 (*continued*)

Location of overlapping claims	Private rights granted by one or more states
Ghana/Côte d'Ivoire (East Atlantic Ocean)	Concessions for offshore petroleum operations
Guinea/Guinea-Bissau (East Atlantic Ocean)	Concessions for fishing, offshore petroleum operations
Guyana/Suriname (West Atlantic Ocean)	Concessions for offshore petroleum operations
Guyana/Venezuela (Atlantic Ocean)	Concessions for offshore petroleum operations
India/Pakistan (Great Rann of Kutch)	Licences for agricultural, grazing and fishing activities
Iran/Kuwait/Saudi Arabia (Persian Gulf)	Concessions for offshore petroleum operations
Israel/Lebanon (East Mediterranean Sea)	Concessions for offshore petroleum operations
Israel/Palestine (West Bank, Gaza Strip)	Housing, agricultural rights
Libya/Malta	Concessions for offshore petroleum operations
Newfoundland and Labrador/Nova Scotia	Concessions for offshore petroleum operations
Nicaragua/Colombia (Caribbean Sea)	Permits for the collection of coconuts, extract of guano and lime phosphate, fishing, conduct of scientific research operations
Nicaragua/Costa Rica (Caribbean Sea)	Concessions for offshore petroleum operations
Nicaragua/Honduras (Caribbean Sea, Bobel Cay, Savanna Cay, Port Royal Cay, South Cay)	Licences for fishing, concessions for offshore petroleum operations, construction of antennas on islands
Nigeria/Equatorial Guinea (Gulf of Guinea)	Concessions for offshore petroleum operations
Norway/Denmark (Eastern Greenland)	Concessions for trade, hunting, fishing, mining
Norway/Sweden (Grisbådarna banks)	Concessions for fishing
Qatar/Bahrain (Arabian/Persian Gulf)	Concessions for land, fishing rights, pearling and gypsum activities, offshore petroleum operations
Romania/Ukraine (Black Sea)	Concessions for offshore petroleum operations
Somalia/Kenya (West Indian Ocean)	Concessions for offshore petroleum operations

(*continued*)

2 Private Rights in Areas of Uncertain Jurisdiction

TABLE 1 (*continued*)

Location of overlapping claims	Private rights granted by one or more states
Tunisia/Libya (Mediterranean Sea)	Concessions for fishing, offshore petroleum operations
UK/France (Anglo-French Channel in Atlantic Ocean)	Concessions for fishing, offshore petroleum operations

between the neighbouring states,[79] while on others the dispute over the undelimited area arose after the private rights had been unilaterally granted.[80] That said, the moment when the private rights were created (before or after the emergence of the boundary dispute) is of little relevance. Without fixed boundaries, any area between two states can be a source of potential overlapping claims. Sooner or later uncertainty may arise as to which state owns the area, and private rights are likely to be involved given that states may invoke pre-existing private rights as evidence of control over the area, or they may grant new rights to create a new territorial or sovereign claim. In both situations, private rights will eventually be at issue in areas of overlapping national claims.

It is easy to understand why states undertake such unilateral acts. Firstly, the creation of private rights in contested areas is a way for the competing states to bolster their claims against each other. The presence of private rights may be used as evidence (especially in land disputes) of the claimant's jurisdiction in the area in question or of the boundary's exact location under the doctrines of effective occupation or acquiescence and estoppel.[81] Secondly, by creating private rights, states improve the economic and living conditions for people residing in the area of overlapping claims. Thirdly, the granting of exploratory (eg petroleum, mining) rights over natural resources may provide states with a source of income and help them to cover their own and other states' energy needs.

The above explains why states are generally not deterred from granting private rights in undelimited areas, even where there is an ongoing land or maritime dispute with their neighbours. Yet, does this mean that states possess

---

[79] eg Cameroon/Nigeria; China/Philippines (South China Sea); China/Japan (East China Sea).
[80] eg Belgium/Netherlands; Germany/Denmark/Netherlands; Guyana/Suriname; Ghana/Ivory Coast; Kenya/Somalia.
[81] See Chapter 3.

2.4 *Private Rights in Areas of Overlapping Claims* 33

the legal competence to create private rights in areas of uncertain jurisdiction? To address this question, the subsections below will first describe how a situation of overlapping national claims arises on land and at sea, and then, examine whether the lack of fixed boundaries affects the states' legal competence to create private rights in land and maritime areas of overlapping claims.

2.4.1 *The Cause of Overlapping Land and Maritime Claims*

A situation of overlapping land claims emerges when two (or more) states assert that they possess sovereignty over the same land. Such overlap may occur in one of two ways: each state may claim that the entire area in question belongs to its own domain, without asserting a specific boundary; or the two states may each propose a different boundary line for the same area, resulting in a portion of that area being claimed by both sides. For scholars, the two situations are distinct: the first concerns the attribution of territory, while the latter pertains only to the boundary's location.[82] According to international case law, however, this is not a difference of substance but 'a difference of degree as to the way the operation in question is carried out'.[83] In both situations, the dispute can be successfully settled through the process of delimitation.

As on land, a situation of overlapping claims in the ocean arises when two states assert that the same portion of the seabed or the water column is under their national control. However, the reasons that cause an overlap of claims in the ocean are significantly different than on land. An overlap of territorial claims emerges from the behaviour of the states concerned – that is, their competing assertions with regard to territorial allocation or the boundary's location. By contrast, an overlap of maritime claims is the outcome of two purely objective factors: one legal, the other geographical.[84]

The legal factor is the right of every coastal state to possess a 12-M TS, a 200-M CS and a 200-M EEZ. All coastal states are vested with this right under international law by virtue of their territorial sovereignty and equality.[85]

---

[82] See A Allot, 'Boundaries and the Law in Africa' in C Widstrand (ed), *African Boundary Problems* (Brill 1969) 9; F Kratochwil and others, *Peace and Disputed Sovereignty: Reflections on Conflict over Territory in International Law and Relations* (University Press of America 1985) 1.

[83] *Case Concerning the Frontier Dispute (Burkina Faso v Republic of Mali)* [1986]) ICJ Rep 554, 563. See also *Island of Palmas Case (Netherlands v USA)* (Arbitral Award) (1928) 838–40.

[84] P Weil, *The Law of Maritime Delimitation: Reflections* (Grotius 1989) 48.

[85] *Case Concerning the Continental Shelf (Libyan Arab Jamahiriya v Malta)* [1985] ICJ Rep 13, para 46. This confirms the principle that land dominates the sea.

2 *Private Rights in Areas of Uncertain Jurisdiction*

The geographical factor is the physical proximity that by nature exists between most neighbouring states with opposite or adjacent coasts and which commonly causes the prolongations of their respective domains in the ocean to abut and overlap.[86] This overlap between the states' legal entitlements to the same maritime space leads to a conflict of claims over the extent of each state's jurisdiction in that area.

To separate their overlapping entitlements in the ocean, states need to establish a boundary line through the process of delimitation. The boundary line will essentially fix the limit of each state's jurisdiction over the shared maritime space by reducing the legal entitlements of both sides.[87] Unlike land delimitation, there will be no winner: each state will receive a portion of the disputed maritime area, although it may be significantly smaller than what it originally claimed.

2.4.2 *The Legal Competence of States to Create Private Rights in Areas of Overlapping Claims*

To create private rights on land, a state must first possess sovereignty over the territory in question; otherwise, it will be acting *ultra vires*. Customarily, territorial sovereignty is acquired by virtue of a title.[88] The title consists of the legal and factual elements on the basis of which a certain territory is deemed to belong to a state.[89] It is the means (both the evidence and the source) by which a state can exercise its public powers over a part of the earth's surface in an absolute manner and to the exclusion of any other state.[90]

A land title is acquired through various acts of the state. Classic international law identifies five main ways in which title may be acquired: occupation of *terra nullius*; prescription after effective possession for a long time; cession or transfer of territory by treaty; accession; and conquest.[91] Cession is

---

[86] According to Brownlie, 'there is no coastal State in the world that does not have an overlapping maritime zone with at least one other State'. J Crawford, *Brownlie's Principles of Public International Law* (8th edn, OUP 2012) 281.

[87] That is why, according to Weil, 'delimitation means amputation'. Weil (n 84) 48. Likewise, G Tanja, *The Legal Determination of International Maritime Boundaries: The Progressive Development of Continental Shelf, EFZ and EEZ Law* (Kluwer Law and Taxation 1990) xvi, expressing the view that delimitation 'means restriction'.

[88] *Island of Palmas* (n 83) 838–39.

[89] M Shaw, *Title to Territory in Africa: International Legal Issues* (Clarendon 1986) 490.

[90] *Island of Palmas* (n 83) 838–39.

[91] Oppenheim (n 5) 498.

2.4 *Private Rights in Areas of Overlapping Claims* 35

described in the literature as a derivative mode of acquisition, while the other four are considered as original modes of acquisition.[92]

The above classification has been criticized by modern scholars as unsound for various reasons.[93] For one thing, it appears to be too absolute, as there is no rule in international law stating that these are the sole modes of acquisition. On the contrary, the issue of territorial sovereignty is extremely complex and requires the application of many international law principles. This is clear from relevant case law. Although international judges acknowledge that title can be acquired in various ways, they refrain from qualifying the above five modes of acquisition as exclusive or orthodox.[94]

Secondly, the use of private law concepts in public international law might be inappropriate. As stressed by Jennings, the five modes of acquisition mentioned above are essentially based upon the methods of transferring private property *inter vivos* under civil (Roman) law. Even if these methods were applicable in the sphere of public international law, they could not apply where a new state is concerned, as they presuppose that the state exists already.[95]

Another point of disagreement among theorists is the legality of the afore-mentioned modes of acquisition as a prerequisite for their effectiveness.[96] For example, conquest is one of the oldest means of acquiring territory. However, its lawfulness is seriously questioned by many scholars as it disregards the prohibition on the use of force in interstate relations under international law.[97] For others, although the use of force is unlawful, conquest is nonetheless effective as a means of acquiring territory.[98] And in-between are those who believe that the title created by conquest is valid but imperfect, and as such

---

[92] ibid.

[93] R Jennings, *The Acquisition of Territory in International Law* (Manchester University Press 1963) 6–7; I Brownlie, *Principles of Public International Law* (7th edn, OUP 2008) 127; D O'Connell, *International Law* (Stevens & Sons 1965) 405.

[94] eg *Island of Palmas* (n 83) 839.

[95] Jennings (n 93) 7.

[96] See S Sharma, *Territorial Acquisition, Disputes and International Law* (Martinus Nijhoff 1997) 145–46.

[97] Jennings (n 93) 54–56; F. Milano, *Unlawful Territorial Situations in International Law: Reconciling Effectiveness, Legality and Legitimacy* (Martinus Nijhoff 2005) 101–107. See also M McMahon, *Conquest and Modern International Law: The Legal Limitations on the Acquisition of Territory by Conquest* (Kraus Reprint 1975). According to others, this principle applies only in the case of illegal war, not war conducted in the context of self-defence. G Schwarzenberger, 'Title to Territory: Response to a Challenge' (1957) 51 AJIL 308, 314.

[98] H Kelsen, *Principles of International Law* (Lawbook Exchange 1952) 214.

must be followed by a treaty of cession or an act of recognition by the international community to produce its effects.[99]

In contrast to these theoretical positions, the legality of the means of acquiring title is treated with greater flexibility in international case law. In many cases, international courts have affirmed that the prima facie lawful title of one state may eventually be rejected as ineffective or as inferior to that of the other state.[100] In others, it was decided that even a doubtful or prima facie unlawful title can be legitimized in international law by virtue of acquiescence or lasting possession of a territory that was previously under the sovereignty of another state.[101]

The above suggests that territorial sovereignty can be created and proven by title irrespective of the conditions under which the title has been acquired. This means that a state's claim to sovereignty over a given territory is essentially an assertion of title to that area. The validity of this claim will be subject to proof of the existence of title. In other words, an assertion of title itself creates a presumption of the existence of territorial sovereignty. Depending on the legal and factual circumstances of the case in question, the lawfulness of the claimed title may prima facie already have been established or it may be established at a later stage. In either case, the title will successfully create a presumption of territorial sovereignty for the state asserting it.[102]

In land areas of overlapping claims, both states claim sovereignty (ie title) over the same territory. However, it is an axiom of international law that territorial sovereignty belongs to one state only – the state that holds the better or stronger title.[103] This situation of overlapping titles will be resolved once the process of delimitation is completed. The fixing of an international boundary

---

[99] Q Wright, 'The Stimson Note of January 7, 1932' (1932) 26 AJIL 342; Schwarzenberger (n 97) 314, 318–19. Jennings (n 93) 62 also supports international recognition of title acquired by force, but considers that it is the act of recognition, not the act of force, that creates the title.

[100] *Island of Palmas* (n 83) 839, 846; *Case Concerning the Frontier Dispute (Burkina Faso v Republic of Mali)* (n 83) para 63.

[101] *Arbitration between India and Pakistan for the Indo-Pakistan Western Boundary (Rann of Kutch) (India v Pakistan)* (1968) 440; *Case Concerning Kasikili/Sedudu Island (Botswana v Namibia)* [1999] ICJ Rep 1045, 1105; *Question of Jaworzina (Polish-Czechoslovakian Frontier)* (Advisory Opinion) PCIJ Rep Series B No 8, 20 (1923). See also E Luard, *The International Regulation of Frontier Disputes* (Thames & Hudson 1970) 19.

[102] The opposite would mean that without boundaries there is no sovereignty or statehood, which would be absurd.

[103] *Island of Palmas* (n 83) 838. See also Weil (n 84) 91: 'Land delimitation rests basically on the principle that sovereignties may not overlap and that a given area must therefore inevitably belong by law to one or other of the States in question. In the event of a dispute, the right course . . . is to determine which of the parties has produced the more convincing proof of title to the disputed area.'

2.4 Private Rights in Areas of Overlapping Claims

(through a treaty or a third body) will enable each state to mark the limits of its own territorial sovereignty and recognize the powers of its neighbour on the other side of the boundary.[104]

Delimitation does not in itself create territorial sovereignty, however; it is the title that does this. Delimitation will simply put an end to the clash between the states' respective claims to the same territory. Until that happens, no rule of international law prevents a state from relying on the presumption of territorial sovereignty resulting from its assertion of title. This is notwithstanding the fact that the presumption may eventually be rebutted if the title is successfully challenged as unlawful or the other state's title prevails as more convincing.

A question arises as to whether the losing state can retrospectively be held responsible under international law for breaching the winning state's territorial sovereignty through the acts it conducted unilaterally pending delimitation, including the granting of private rights in the area of overlapping claims. This seems plausible in principle but is very rare in practice. Firstly, unless invoked by the parties, the question of state responsibility and reparation for a violation of state sovereignty falls beyond the scope of boundary delimitation.[105] So far, very few states have made such claim in a boundary dispute.[106] And more strikingly, international courts are reluctant to proceed with or accept such claims.[107] Secondly, the acting state's claim to title establishes the bona fide nature of its acts in the undelimited area. To be held responsible for breaching its neighbour's sovereignty pending

---

[104] A Cukwurah, *The Settlement of Boundary Disputes in International Law* (Manchester University Press 1967) 29.

[105] See E Milano and I Papanicolopulu, 'State Responsibility in Disputed Areas on Land and at Sea' (2011) 71 ZaöRV 589, explaining that 'an ex post facto characterisation of a territorial situation as "adverse occupation" will not automatically lead to a determination of State responsibility for wrongful occupation or for acts related to the occupation prohibited under international law'.

[106] eg *Case Concerning the Land and Maritime Boundary between Cameroon and Nigeria (Cameroon v Nigeria: Equatorial Guinea Intervening)* [2002] ICJ Rep 303; *Territorial and Maritime Dispute between Nicaragua and Colombia (Nicaragua v Colombia)* [2012] ICJ Rep 624; *Certain Activities Carried Out by Nicaragua in the Border Area (Nicaragua v Costa Rica)* [2015] ICJ Rep 665.

[107] In *Case Concerning the Land and Maritime Boundary between Cameroon and Nigeria* (n 106) 452–53, for example, the ICJ considered that as Cameroon's territorial claim was successful, there was no need to examine its request regarding the international responsibility of Nigeria for its unilateral acts in the disputed area pending delimitation. The only case to have affirmed such responsibility was *Certain Activities Carried Out by Nicaragua in the Border Area (Nicaragua v Costa Rica)* (n 106) 42. However, the lack of a concrete precedent makes it difficult to ascertain the legal requirements for state responsibility in disputed areas. See Milano and Papanicolopulu (n 105) 589.

2 Private Rights in Areas of Uncertain Jurisdiction

delimitation, the author state must have acted mala fide.[108] This could only be the case if the acting state knew from the beginning that the disputed area belonged to the other state by virtue of a valid title.[109] Consequently, any private rights which have been granted by a state acting in good faith in the undelimited area are legally valid.[110]

In sum, the above points demonstrate that the lack of fixed boundaries does not prohibit or otherwise restrict the powers of states in areas of overlapping claims on land. The fact of claiming a bona fide title to the territory in question, gives a state the capacity to create private rights therein, even if that area is subsequently reallocated to another state. Hence, any unilaterally granted private rights will be valid.

Things are not much different at sea, where the exercise of state powers also requires title. In this case, the title will describe the criteria upon which a state is empowered to exercise its rights and jurisdiction over its maritime zones.[111] However, two important differences exist between a territorial and a maritime title.

First, a maritime title is not acquired by virtue of the state's acts. Rather, international law of the sea vests such title in every coastal state as an extension of its sovereignty on land.[112] Second, in a maritime area of overlapping claims each of the states involved possesses a title.[113] But in contrast to land, where only one title can prevail, both maritime titles are legitimate. The subsequent establishment of a maritime boundary through the process of delimitation will not seek to allocate the entire area to the state that holds the better or stronger title – as the titles held by both states are equal – but rather to divide the shared maritime space between the parties.[114]

---

[108]   See Milano (n 97) 133–53.

[109]   eg a treaty in force.

[110]   This is borne out by the fact that international courts and tribunals take those rights into consideration in land delimitation cases. See Chapters 3 and 4. However, whether performance of those rights will be impossible after reallocation (if the area is reallocated to the other state) is a separate issue appertaining to frustration, as pointed out in Chapters 3 and 5.

[111]   Weil (n 84) 48; Tanaka (n 17) 134.

[112]   Convention on the Territorial Sea and the Contiguous Zone (signed 29 April 1958, entered into force 10 September 1964) 516 UNTS 205, arts 1, 24; Convention on the Continental Shelf, art 2; UNCLOS, arts 2, 56, 77.

[113]   According to the rules of the law of the sea embodied in the instruments cited in n 115.

[114]   Weil (n 84) 92: 'Far from assuming that there can be only one title to a given area, [maritime delimitation] postulates the existence of two equally valid titles in competition with one another over the same area. It is not a question of which proof is more or less convincing, which title is the weightier, but of requiring from each of the parties with these equally well-founded titles a reasonable sacrifice such as would make possible a division of the area of overlap.' For a similar position in case law, see *North Sea Continental Shelf Cases* (n 2) para

2.4 Private Rights in Areas of Overlapping Claims

Despite the above differences between situations of overlapping national claims on land and at sea, there are also some important similarities. As on land, the states' powers in the ocean are not created by boundaries, but only from the possession of title.[115] The subsequent establishment of a maritime boundary will merely terminate the conflict between the states' claims to the same area. Until that happens, international law allows each state to rely on its legal entitlement in that space – regardless of the fact that this might be curtailed when the maritime boundary is fixed.[116]

This begs the question of whether the state that has unilaterally granted private rights in the shared maritime space pending delimitation can retrospectively be held responsible for breaching international law in the event that the area is redistributed to its neighbour. This question covers two separate issues.

The first is whether the acting state can be held responsible for breaching its neighbour's exclusive sovereign rights in the disputed maritime area. Case law considers this as unlikely – although on the basis of somewhat divergent legal reasoning. In *Aegean Sea* (a case preceding UNCLOS), the ICJ initially took the view that 'seismic exploration of natural resources of the continental shelf without the consent of the coastal State might, no doubt, raise a question of infringement of the latter's exclusive right of exploration'.[117] But in the end it was held that the unilateral conduct of seismic surveys in the disputed area was unlikely to cause irreparable harm to the other state's sovereign rights.

The issue was also raised in the more recent case of *Ghana/Côte d'Ivoire*. In the provisional measures order of 2015, it was considered that 'the acquisition and use of information about the resources of the disputed area would create a risk of irreversible prejudice to the rights of Côte d'Ivoire should the Special Chamber, in its decision on the merits (delimitation), find that Côte d'Ivoire has rights in all or any part of the disputed area'.[118] The judges were particularly concerned that such a change in the status quo would not be reversible

---

20: '[T]he process of [maritime] delimitation is essentially one of drawing a boundary between areas which already appertain to one or other of the States affected.'

[115] For a definition of maritime title, see Weil (n 84) 48.

[116] Given that maritime delimitation means 'amputation' or 'restriction' in the words of, respectively, Weil (n 84) and Tanja (n 87).

[117] *Aegean Sea Continental Shelf Case (Greece v Turkey)* (Order on Request for the Indication of Interim Measures of Protection, 11 September 1976) para 31.

[118] *Dispute Concerning Delimitation of the Maritime Boundary between Ghana and Côte d'Ivoire in the Atlantic Ocean (Ghana v Côte d'Ivoire)* (Provisional Measures, ITLOS Order of 25 April 2015) para 95.

40   2 *Private Rights in Areas of Uncertain Jurisdiction*

with compensation.[119] Yet, a different decision was made in the delimitation judgment of 2017. As highlighted by the Special Chamber of ITLOS,

> [I]n a case of overlap both States concerned have an entitlement to the relevant continental shelf (as well as to the Territorial Sea and Exclusive Economic Zone) on the basis of their relevant coasts. Only a decision on delimitation establishes which part of the continental shelf under dispute appertains to which of the claiming States. This means that the relevant judgment gives one entitlement priority over the other. . . .
>
> [T]he consequence of the above is that maritime activities undertaken by a State in an area of the continental shelf which has been attributed to another State by an international judgment cannot be considered to be in violation of the sovereign rights of the latter if those activities were carried out before the judgment was delivered and if the area concerned was the subject of claims made in good faith by both States.[120]

According to this latter approach, the question of interference in a state's sovereign rights is determined by the legal entitlements that international law confers on the parties concerned pending delimitation, not by the nature of their unilateral acts. Until such time as an international boundary is established, both states have a legitimate entitlement to the contested region.[121] In these circumstances, it would be legally groundless to retrospectively accuse a state of having violated its neighbour's sovereign rights.

The second issue is whether the acting state can be held responsible for breaching the twin obligations that Articles 74(3) and 83(3) UNCLOS impose on states pending delimitation of the EEZ and the CS: the positive obligation to negotiate with a view to entering into 'provisional arrangements of a practical nature';[122] and the negative obligation 'not to jeopardise or hamper the reaching of the final [delimitation] agreement'. What little case law there is on the matter confirms that this is possible but not unavoidable. These two provisions of UNCLOS were interpreted in *Guyana/Suriname*, where the arbitral tribunal distinguished between those activities that had a permanent physical impact on the marine environment (ie drilling) and those that did not (eg seismic surveys), and pointed out that unilaterally engaging in the former

---

[119]   ibid, paras 89–91.

[120]   *Dispute Concerning Delimitation of the Maritime Boundary between Ghana and Côte d'Ivoire in the Atlantic Ocean (Ghana/Côte d'Ivoire)* (ITLOS Judgment 2017) paras 591–92.

[121]   Given that states rely on the maritime zones to which they are entitled under the law of the sea. A state would be responsible, however, if it acted beyond such zones.

[122]   eg a provisional boundary agreement, a joint development agreement or a mutual restraint agreement (moratorium).

2.4 Private Rights in Areas of Overlapping Claims 41

activities could jeopardize or hamper the final delimitation agreement.[123] By contrast, seismic surveys (and, potentially, fishing or scientific research activities) could be conducted unilaterally in the disputed area.[124] That said, the acting state could nevertheless violate the obligation to negotiate in good faith with its neighbour under Articles 74(3) and 83(3) regardless of the nature of the activities performed. Such liability could arise if the state that is acting unilaterally has refused to participate in negotiations or respond to the other state's proposals.[125] However, such state will escape liability if it has invited the other party to negotiate or informed it of its intentions or has offered to share the financial benefits of its activities in the disputed area.[126] Also, as recently held in *Ghana/Côte d'Ivoire*, the objecting state is barred from invoking a violation of the obligation to negotiate if it has never requested its neighbour to take part in negotiations.[127]

Hence, a state that has unilaterally granted private rights in a disputed maritime space may breach either, both or neither of its obligations under UNCLOS. The answer will depend on the nature of the operations performed unilaterally and the conditions under which they are performed. The law of the sea does not impose an absolute prohibition on states exercising their sovereign rights pending delimitation. As explained in case law, 'the parties' ability to pursue economic development in the disputed area during a boundary dispute' should not be stifled, 'as the resolution of such disputes will typically be a time-consuming process'.[128] In other words, Articles 74(3) and 83(3) do not block the powers of states in the disputed maritime area.[129] States have full possession of those powers – and the legal competence to create private rights in the shared maritime space – under the general

---

[123] *Arbitration between Guyana and Suriname (Guyana v Suriname)* (2007) para 470. This was in line with the distinction made by the ICJ in *Aegean Sea*.

[124] This matter is quite debatable. It could be argued that any unilateral activity (such as the conduct of seismic surveys or even fishing) in the disputed area could potentially aggravate the dispute or jeopardize the final delimitation agreement, especially where the disputes are enduring or heavily politicized. According to Professor Churchill, however, such activities 'in the undelimited area would probably not 'jeopardise or hamper', but taking enforcement measures against the vessels of another party to the delimitation dispute probably would'. British Institute of International and Comparative Law, *Obligations of States in Undelimited Maritime Areas*: Report of Conference Held on 22 July 2016 (BIICL 2016) 13.

[125] *Arbitration between Guyana and Suriname* (n 123) pars 473–77.

[126] ibid, paras 476–77.

[127] *Dispute Concerning Delimitation of the Maritime Boundary between Ghana and Côte d'Ivoire in the Atlantic Ocean* (Judgment) (n 120) para 628.

[128] *Arbitration between Guyana and Suriname* (n 123) [470].

[129] Milano and Papanicolopulu (n 105) 612.

2 Private Rights in Areas of Uncertain Jurisdiction

provisions of UNCLOS and customary law.[130] Placing a legal prohibition on state activities pending delimitation would prejudice the states' sovereign rights.

Consequently, any private rights which have been granted by the acting state in the undelimited area are legally valid. Even a potential violation of Articles 74(3) and 83(3) by the acting state will not affect the legal status of private rights situated therein. The obligations which UNCLOS imposes in those provisions are procedural, not substantive.[131] Their purpose is to regulate the states' relations in contested waters, not to prohibit the creation of private rights by either party. The cause of a potential violation of those obligations would not be the private rights themselves but the fact that the state granted those rights without meeting the procedural conditions laid down in UNCLOS. Hence, although a breach of those obligations may give rise to state responsibility under the Draft Articles on Responsibility of States for Internationally Wrongful Acts,[132] it will not affect the legal status of the private rights that have been created – for their creation is not prohibited by international law.[133]

The above points demonstrate that the lack of fixed boundaries in the ocean does not inhibit coastal states from exercising their powers in the

---

[130] ibid.

[131] A procedural obligation applies in transitional situations and lasts only for a limited time. Such obligations secure the due process of a legal procedure (eg maritime delimitation) and the peaceful relations between the states involved. By contrast, a substantive obligation requires states to abstain from a specific act *ipso facto* prohibited by law. These obligations are permanent and as such burden states at all times. Examples are the obligation not to use force under Article 2(4) of the UN Charter and the obligations that stem from *jus cogens* (eg prohibition of aggression or genocide). See M Pappa, 'Private Oil Companies Operating in Contested Waters and International Law of the Sea: A Peculiar Relationship' [2018] 1 OGEL <www.ogel.org>.

[132] Draft Articles on Responsibility of States for Internationally Wrongful Acts (adopted 2001) arts 1–2. Things are somewhat unclear as regards reparation for such a breach. In principle, this may range from mere declaratory relief to restitution or compensation. See Draft Articles 31–37. In practice, though, international courts and tribunals are likely to award only declaratory relief.

[133] See Pappa (n 131). This explains why no international court or tribunal has ever ordered a unilaterally acting state to revoke any previously granted private rights in the disputed area. At best, states can be ordered (by means of provisional measures) to refrain from granting any new rights until the dispute has been settled. In *Dispute Concerning Delimitation of the Maritime Boundary between Ghana and Côte d'Ivoire in the Atlantic Ocean* (Provisional Measures) (n 118) paras 99–100, Ghana was ordered simply to refrain from granting new petroleum permits until final delimitation. The Special Chamber observed that the suspension of ongoing petroleum operations 'would entail the risk of considerable financial loss to [the acting state] and its concessionaires', which would therefore 'cause prejudice to the rights claimed by [the acting state] and create an undue burden on it'.

shared maritime space. The only condition is that the states act within the extremities of their entitled maritime zones.[134] The jurisdiction of each state within these zones is not conditional or dormant pending delimitation, but legitimate and active. As such, it can be exercised at all times and irrespective of the presence of maritime boundaries. In the words of Professor Weil,

> [W]hen the maritime projections of two States meet and overlap, each of them must inevitably forego the full enjoyment of the maritime jurisdiction it could have claimed had it not had the geographical misfortune to find its appropriation in conflict with that of its neighbour.[135]

In sum, when a maritime space is claimed by two neighbouring states, each of the parties involved has the legal competence to create private rights therein, provided those rights are located within a maximum distance of 200 M from the coast.[136] Conversely, no legal competence exists for areas beyond the legal limits of the states' entitled maritime zones. In this respect, the powers of states at sea are no different from those on land. Likewise, the legal status of private rights in both settings is irrelevant to the lawfulness of the granting state's behaviour. Even if that state is held responsible for a violation of international law, such rights will be legally valid.

2.5 CONCLUSIONS

The land and (to the maximum extent of 350 M) the ocean constitute the spatial framework within which states exercise their authoritative powers. On land, a state's powers are all-encompassing and take the form of full sovereignty. At sea, the state possesses full sovereignty within its TS, and lesser (sovereign) rights within its CS and EEZ.

One of the main expressions of a state's land and maritime jurisdiction is the granting of private rights to the natural or legal persons that reside or wish to operate in its domain. These rights allow their holders to enter the state's land and maritime areas and to engage in a range of legal and economic activities in an exclusive manner.

When a state's jurisdiction is delimited through clearly established boundaries, the creation of private rights does not pose any particular problems

---

[134] ie 12 M for the TS, and 200 M for the CS and the EEZ.

[135] Weil (n 84) 3. See also Tanja (n 87) xv–xvi.

[136] That is the legal breadth of the CS and the EEZ. As already mentioned, according to Article 76(6) UNCLOS, the breadth of the CS can extend to 350 M. However, the vast majority of states possess a 200-M CS.

under international law. By contrast, the creation of those rights in undelimited areas can be a source of considerable controversy when the same territorial or maritime space is concurrently claimed by two (or more) states. Are these rights legitimate?

To address this question, the chapter undertook a comparative analysis of the legal competence of states to create private rights in delimited and disputed areas. Revisiting the relationship between international boundaries and state powers, it has dispelled the uncertainty over the status of private rights in spaces without fixed international boundaries.

Whether on land or at sea, the creation of private rights by states depends not on the presence of international boundaries but rather on a bona fide assertion of title to the area of interest. Title is the legal means from which a state derives the power to perform its functions within a certain area of land or maritime space in an absolute and exclusive manner. By contrast, delimitation seeks to mark the limits of two states' contiguous jurisdictions, not to create or activate their authoritative powers.

Arguably, the presence of international boundaries facilitates the exercise of state powers, but under no circumstances are boundaries the source of those powers. Delimitation merely separates the states' overlapping claims. Until that happens, each of the concerned states may rest on the claim that the area in question belongs to it by virtue of title – even if its original claim is subsequently rebutted or reduced after the boundary is fixed.

In other words, the lack of fixed boundaries does not prohibit states from exercising their powers in areas of overlapping national claims. Consequently, any private rights granted therein are active and legitimate. The possibility of the area in which a state has created private rights eventually passing to the other state post delimitation, or of the acting state retrospectively being held liable for breaching any international rules pending delimitation, are important legal issues but do not reduce the legal competence of states to create private rights on land and at sea.

Given their legitimacy, private rights in areas of overlapping national claims should be taken into account in the legal framework on international boundary-making. The following chapters will examine, in turn, the extent to which this is the case on land and at sea.

3

The Divergent Role of Private Rights in Land and Maritime Delimitation

3.1 INTRODUCTION

Chapter 2 explained that states possess the legal capacity to create private rights in undelimited land and maritime spaces. This chapter probes the role of those rights in the actual processes of land and maritime delimitation. In particular, it asks, to what extent do private rights affect the boundary's course on land and at sea?

To address this question, the study performs a comparative analysis by pairs. First, it compares the impact of private rights in land and maritime delimitation treaties. Then it compares their impact in land and maritime delimitation rulings.

A synthesis of the findings reached reveals that private rights have a significant and far-reaching effect on land delimitation, while their effect on maritime delimitation is minimal or non-existent. This asymmetry has important implications for private actors operating in contested waters and for international law in general.

3.2 DELIMITATION BY TREATY

The vast majority of existing boundaries on land and at sea have been established by treaties concluded between the states concerned.[1] There are many reasons why agreements are preferable to delimitation judgments or arbitral awards. A bilateral agreement allows states to keep the matters at issue under

---

[1] According to UN records, several hundreds of treaties on land and maritime delimitation have been signed, whereas delimitation judgments and arbitral awards number only a few dozen. For delimitation treaties, see <https://treaties.un.org/pages/lononline.aspx?clang=_en>, <https://treaties.un.org/pages/AdvanceSearch.aspx?tab=CN&clang=_en> accessed 20 March 2020. For judicial decisions and arbitral awards, see <www.icj-cij.org/en/list-of-all-cases>, <https://pca-cpa.org/en/cases/>, <www.itlos.org/cases/list-of-cases/> accessed 20 March 2020.

46   3 *Private Rights in Land and Maritime Delimitation*

their control. The parties may agree on whatever boundary line they prefer and take into account factors (legal or non-legal) that might be deemed inadmissible by an international court or tribunal. In addition, a delimitation agreement allows both sides to join the negotiating table not as competitors but as equal players. There will be no winner or loser at the end of discussions, even if one side eventually retracts from its original position in a spirit of compromise.[2]

The number of boundary treaties signed to date runs into hundreds, and more are still to be concluded. A comprehensive list of land delimitation treaties signed from the twentieth century onwards can be found in Clive Parry's Consolidated Treaty Series[3] and the Treaty Series of the League of Nations and its successor the United Nations.[4] Also, Ian Brownlie's *African Boundaries: A Legal and Diplomatic Encyclopaedia* is a useful source for delimitation treaties that have settled boundaries in Africa.[5] Maritime agreements are mainly to be found in the United Nations Treaty Series.[6] Also, more than 130 maritime delimitation treaties are extensively analysed in a voluminous collection entitled *International Maritime Boundaries*, published by the American Society of International Law.[7]

An analysis of each and every delimitation treaty concluded during the past two centuries would be impracticable. However, it is not only the size of the corpus that makes their study difficult. Even when the final text of a treaty is publicly available and an official English translation exists, the preparatory materials often remain secret. Fortunately, a number of states have disclosed their exchanges of diplomatic notes or parliamentary records, revealing the factors that weighed on their decisions over the location and course of their international boundaries. But until such time as the preparatory materials for all delimitation treaties become publicly available, our knowledge of the precise reasons for state decisions will remain incomplete.

---

[2] V Prescott, *Political Frontiers and* Boundaries (Allen & Unwin 1987) 58–63; I Karaman, *Dispute Resolution in the Law of the Sea* (Martinus Nijhoff 2012) 184; A Oude Elferink, 'International Law and Negotiated and Adjudicated Maritime Boundaries: A Complex Relationship' (2015) 48 German Yearbook of International Law 1, 5–7; D Johnston, *Theory and History of Ocean Boundary-Making* (McGill-Queen's University Press 1988) 233.

[3] Parry's collection, published by Oceana in 1969 covers the early twentieth century.

[4] The League of Nations and UN collections cover all treaties from the twentieth century to date; see <https://treaties.un.org/pages/lononline.aspx?clang=_en>, <https://treaties.un.org/pages/A dvanceSearch.aspx?tab=CN&clang=_en> accessed 20 March 2020.

[5] University of California Press 1979.

[6] Available at <https://treaties.un.org/pages/AdvanceSearch.aspx?tab=CN&clang=_en> accessed 20 March 2020.

[7] Volumes 1–4 were edited by Jonathan Charney and Robert Smith, volumes 5 and 6 by David Colson and Robert Smith and volume 7 by Coalter Lathrop.

3.2 *Delimitation by Treaty* 47

An additional challenge for the researcher is the lack of delimitation rules to be followed by states when making their boundary agreements. It is important to mention that, in the case of maritime delimitation, the conventions of the sea call on states to act on the basis of equity when fixing their boundaries.[8] Yet, whether on land and at sea, international law refrains from imposing a fixed delimitation method. As a result, each land and maritime delimitation treaty has its particularities, which are shaped by the historic, economic and socio-political background, the signatories' relations and the role of practitioners and other experts in its making.

The challenges identified above would have been a deterrent to undertaking the present study had its purpose been to provide an exhaustive list of delimitation treaties and all factors affecting the course of the boundaries they define.[9] However, this book does not pretend to have such a broad scope. Rather, its purpose is to identify the trends that emerge from current state delimitation practices in relation to private rights, and to assess whether they are apt to give rise to customary rules. A practical way of identifying those trends is to examine the role of private rights during the various phases of delimitation. A close look at land and maritime delimitation treaties reveals that the process of boundary-making consists of three distinct phases.

In land treaties, those three phases are allocation, delimitation and demarcation.[10] Allocation is the initial division of the territory in question between the states concerned.[11] Delimitation is the precise definition of the boundary's course in the treaty's text.[12] Demarcation is the actual marking of the boundary line on the terrain.[13]

---

[8] Convention on the Territorial Sea and the Contiguous Zone (signed 29 April 1958, entered into force 10 September 1964) 516 UNTS 205, art 12; Convention on the Continental Shelf (signed 29 April 1958, entered into force 10 June 1964) 499 UNTS 311, art 6; United Nations Convention on the Law of the Sea, (UNCLOS) (signed 10 December 1982, entered into force 16 November 1994), 1833 UNTS 3, arts 15, 74, 83.

[9] That would be the case if the study were a treatise on delimitation agreements or if it applied an empirical (quantitative) research method.

[10] These terms were introduced by one of the most prominent publicists in boundary studies, Stephen Barr Jones. See S Jones, *Boundary-Making: A Handbook for Statesmen, Treaty Editors and Boundary Commissioners* (Carnegie Endowment for International Peace 1945) 5. Before Jones, Paul de La Pradelle had referred to those stages as preparation, decision and execution; see P de La Pradelle, *La Frontière: Étude de Droit International* (Éditions Internationales 1928) 73. There is also a fourth stage, called administration, which is concerned with the official measures taken to maintain a boundary and will not be discussed in this study.

[11] Jones (n 10) 5.

[12] ibid.

[13] ibid.

48   3 *Private Rights in Land and Maritime Delimitation*

In maritime treaties, three comparable (although not entirely identical) phases can be distinguished – namely, negotiation, delimitation and demarcation.[14] Negotiation is the states' presentation of their respective positions with a view to working out an agreement on how the area should be divided up.[15] Delimitation has the same meaning as on land.[16] Demarcation is also the materialization of the boundary line, typically on maps or digital records and less frequently by physical means on the surface of the sea.[17]

Given the similarity between the phases underlying land and maritime delimitation treaties, it seems justified to analyse them together. However, as the following paragraphs will show, there are also some important differences between land and maritime treaties concerning the delimitation methods applied by states on land and at sea, as well as the impact of private rights on the boundary's course.

3.2.1 *The Significant Role of Private Rights in Land Delimitation Treaties*

In the past, land boundary-making was mainly carried out by geographic and geometric means, respectively based on features of physical geography (eg mountain and water crests, rivers) or astronomic lines (eg meridians, straight lines or parallels).[18] But in the twentieth century it became apparent that the establishment of land boundaries needed to reflect human and economic factors, such as the interests of individuals in the area under delimitation. Gradually, private rights began to play a significant role in land treaties, seen in all three stages (allocation, delimitation, demarcation) of boundary-making. The following subsections will analyse this trend in detail.

---

[14]   These phases emerge from the texts of maritime delimitation treaties and from the literature. See all volumes of *International Maritime Boundaries*; D Anderson, 'Negotiating Maritime Boundary Agreements: A Personal View' in R Lagoni and D Vignes (eds), *Maritime Delimitation* (Martinus Nijhoff 2006); H Srebro, *International Boundary Making* (International Federation of Surveyors 2013) 23ff; G Esch (ed), *Marine Managed Areas: Best Practices for Boundary Making* (Coastal Services Center 2006) 22; cf Prescott (n 2) 23.

[15]   Anderson (n 14).

[16]   ibid; Srebro (n 14).

[17]   Esch (n 14); S Nichols, *Tidal Boundary Delimitation* (University of New Brunswick 1996) 4; G Tanja, *The Legal Determination of International Maritime Boundaries: The Progressive Development of Continental Shelf, EFZ and EEZ Law* (Kluwer Law and Taxation 1990) xvii, 292.

[18]   An analysis of those methods falls outside the scope of the present study. See J Reeves, 'International Boundaries' (1944) 38 AJIL 533–45; S Boggs, *International Boundaries: A Study of Boundary Functions and Problems* (Columbia University Press 1940) 157–64.

3.2.1.1 The Importance of Private Rights in Boundary Allocation

During this initial phase, states negotiate over the general location of their mutual boundary. This process is heavily politicized.[19] It commences with the exchange of the parties' proposals in relation to the boundary in question and concludes with an alignment or compromise between the expressed positions.

States do not come to the negotiating table alone, however. A team of technical experts, such as boundary engineers, geodesists, cartographers, computer scientists and legal consultants, accompany each party during this process, providing accurate data and useful information about the area to be delimited.[20] The contribution of those experts is continuous – from the commencement of bargaining to the definitive marking of the boundary on the terrain and accompanying boundary administration.[21]

During this process, states invoke a series of factors, including their own and their nationals' historical, economic and socio-political interests in the discussed area. The preparatory materials that have been disclosed in relation to delimitation treaties and the observations of leading scholars show that the rights of individuals (eg housing, agricultural, grazing, mining) in land areas play a significant role in boundary allocation.

As an example, one may cite the boundary established between China and Burma in 1960, where the dwelling and economic rights of individuals were extensively considered by the states during the allocation process.[22] Likewise, the very titles and the preambles of the delimitation agreements between Latvia and Lithuania in 1921[23] and between Germany and the Netherlands in 1960[24] point to the important role private rights played in the conclusion of those treaties.

---

[19] Prescott (n 2) 11; Jones (n 10) 5–6.

[20] R Adler, *Geographical Information in Delimitation, Demarcation, and Management of International Land Boundaries* (Boundary and Territory Briefing 3(4), IBRU 2000) 2–3.

[21] ibid.

[22] According to the notes exchanged between China and Burma for the making of the Sino-Burmese Boundary Treaty of 1 October 1960, it was agreed that certain villages would be exchanged so that they would not be administered partly by China and partly by Burma. See also M Maung, 'The Burma-China Boundary Settlement' (1961) 1 Asian Survey 38, 42–43.

[23] Convention between Latvia and Lithuania Regarding the Delimitation on the Spot of the Frontier between the Two States, and Also Regarding the Rights of the Citizens in the Frontier Zone, and the Status of Immovable Property Intersected by the Frontier Line (signed 14 May 1921).

[24] Treaty between the Netherlands and the Federal Republic of Germany Concerning the Course of the Common Frontier, the Boundary Waters, Real Property Situated near the Frontier, Traffic Crossing the Frontier on Land, and other Frontier Questions (signed 8 April 1960).

On some occasions, the private actors concerned have even been invited to participate in the allocation process. This was the case in Europe after each world war. When Hungary and Yugoslavia decided to allocate their new boundaries, they first heard the views of landowners, farmers and residents in the areas under delimitation.[25] Similarly, in Upper Silesia, the Saar Territory and Schleswig, the dwellers and mineral workers in those regions were invited to vote on the allocation of the new boundaries between Germany and its neighbours.[26] In those situations, the land was distributed 'according to the wishes of the affected population, rather than by a decision of central government'.[27]

Of course, this does not mean that private rights affect the allocation process in every delimitation treaty, nor that they are the only factors to do so.[28] In rare cases, like China's agreements with Nepal and Pakistan, the rights of people situated near the proposed boundary were actively discussed by governments in their diplomatic correspondence, but it appears that it was the states' strategic and political interests in the areas that ultimately had the greatest bearing on allocation.[29]

The majority of treaties examined nonetheless show that private rights do affect states' decisions on boundary allocation. Also, no situations have been found in which existing private rights were not mentioned at all during the negotiation of land delimitation treaties.[30] This clearly demonstrates that private rights are of great importance during the initial stage of land boundary-making.

---

[25] D Cree, 'Yugoslav-Hungarian Boundary Commission' (1925) 65 Geographical Journal 89–110; Prescott (n 2) 187.

[26] For example, Article 88 of the Treaty of Versailles, signed 28 June 1919, states that 'regard will be paid to the wishes of the inhabitants as shown by the vote, and to the geographical and economic conditions of the locality' (see also art 47). See Jones (n 10) 31–33; N Berdichevsky, *The German-Danish Border: A Successful Resolution of an Age-Old Conflict or its Redefinition?* (Boundary and Territory Briefing 2(7), IBRU 1999). Of course, heeding local interests is not without problems. For example, some interpretative issues arose when a similar provision was inserted in Article 12 of the Anglo-Irish Treaty of 1921 appointing a commission to establish the boundary between Northern Ireland and the rest of Ireland. In the end, the article was construed in a restrictive manner. See K Rankin, 'The Role of the Irish Boundary Commission in the Entrenchment of the Irish Border: From Tactical Panacea to Political Liability' (2008) 34 Journal of Historical Geography 422–47.

[27] Berdichevsky (n 26) 14.

[28] For example, the nationality and the language of the people residing in the area in question may also matter, although, according to Jones, the correlation between boundaries and these factors is not well established. Jones (n 10) 25–28.

[29] See notes exchanged between China and Burma for the making of the Sino-Burmese Boundary Treaty of 1 October 1960 and between China and Pakistan for the making of the Sino-Pakistani Boundary Treaty of 3 March 1963.

[30] Even if, in the end, they did not affect the boundary's location.

3.2.1.2 The Importance of Private Rights in Boundary Delimitation

Once treaty negotiations have successfully allocated the land in question, the next step is to define the boundary line – a process known as delimitation. This process is more technical and precise than allocation, but more complex as well. The delimited boundary may coincide with the line decided upon during allocation, or it may depart to greater or lesser extent from that line. This will depend on the chosen method of delimitation. The present study has found that two delimitation methods prevailed during the last two centuries: one based on factors of human geography, and the other on existing administrative lines. In both situations, private rights play a significant role.

DELIMITATION BASED ON FACTORS OF HUMAN GEOGRAPHY The first method which became popular in twentieth century for the delimitation of land boundaries is the anthropogeographic method.[31] According to this method, which was widely used to delimit land boundaries in the twentieth century, delimitation should be based on elements of human geography, such as the interests of the people situated in the area.

On some occasions, private interests were considered so important that the international boundary coincided exactly with the property lines of local farms and houses. For instance, that was the case with the boundaries fixed between Hungary, Romania and Czechoslovakia in 1920[32] and between Czechoslovakia and Poland in 1938.[33]

On other occasions, the boundary lines initially agreed upon were adjusted during delimitation, so that dwellers' estates astride the borderline would not be partitioned – as in the case of Germany's boundaries with Poland in 1919,[34] Demark in 1920[35] and France in 1925.[36] The same goes for the boundary established between China and Nepal in 1961,[37] and for Turkey's boundaries with Persia (Iran) and Iraq established respectively in 1932 and 1965.[38]

---

[31] Boggs (n 18) 26–27; Jones (n 10) 94–95.

[32] Treaty of Trianon between the Allied and Associated Powers and Hungary (signed 4 June 1920). See G Motta, *Less than Nations: Central-Eastern European Minorities after WWI*, vol 1 (Cambridge Scholars 2013) 347.

[33] Notes exchanged between Poland and Czechoslovakia for the delimitation of their boundary (30 September and 1 October 1938). See also Boggs (n 18) 104.

[34] Treaty of Versailles; Boggs (n 18) 102–103; Jones (n 10) 95.

[35] Danish-German referendum of 10 February 1920; Prescott (n 2) 191.

[36] Delimitation Treaty between France and Germany (signed 14 August 1925).

[37] Boundary Treaty between the Kingdom of Nepal and the People's Republic of China (signed 5 October 1961); Prescott (n 2) 232. Private rights did not affect the allocation phase, however.

[38] Accord relatif à la fixation de la ligne frontière entre la Perse et la Turquie (signed 23 January 1932); Treaty between the United Kingdom and Iraq and Turkey Regarding the

52   3 *Private Rights in Land and Maritime Delimitation*

Sometimes, the boundary as originally allocated was moved dozens of kilometres to avoid disturbing existing local interests, as was the case between Syria and Palestine in 1920.[39]

DELIMITATION BASED ON PRE-EXISTING ADMINISTRATIVE LINES The second delimitation method used in modern times was to follow pre-existing administrative or internal lines and upgrade them to international boundaries.[40] This method has its roots in the doctrine of *uti possidetis* (from the Latin maxim *uti possidetis, ita possideatis*, meaning 'as you possess, so you may possess'), which is a basic principle of international law.[41]

This doctrine was first applied to the newly formed states of Latin America at the end of colonialism. To avoid being considered as *terrae nullius*, the independent states adopted the lines that had previously been established by the colonial powers. Examples include the boundary established between the Dominican Republic and Haiti in 1929, which followed the administrative lines previously set by Spain and France,[42] and the boundaries between Ecuador with Peru and between Brazil, Guyana and Bolivia, which largely followed the limits of the previous Spanish and Portuguese domains.[43]

The application of the *uti possidetis* principle gradually expanded to include the former colonies of Africa and Asia.[44] For instance, the international boundary between Angola and Namibia follows the same course as the administrative line established by the Portuguese and German powers in

Settlement of the Frontier between Turkey and Iraq (with the Notes Exchanged) (signed 5 June 1926); Boggs (n 18) 148–52.

[39] Franco-British Paris Convention on Certain Points Connected with the Mandates for Syria and the Lebanon, Palestine and Mesopotamia (signed 23 December 1920). See H Srebro and M Shoshany, 'Towards a Comprehensive International Boundary Making Model' (2006) <www.fig.net/resources/proceedings/fig_proceedings/fig2006/papers/ts63/ts63_01_srebro_sh oshani_0293.pdf> accessed 3 April 2021.

[40] O Bakhashab, 'The Legal Concept of International Boundary' (1996) 9 Economy and Administration 29; Organization for Security and Co-operation in Europe (OSCE), 'Applied Issues in International Land Boundary Delimitation/Demarcation Practices' (2011) <www.osce.org/cpc/85263?download=true> accessed 20 March 2020.

[41] That the intangibility of frontiers is a firmly established principle of international law was first affirmed by the ICJ in *Case Concerning the Frontier Dispute (Burkina Faso/Republic of Mali)* [1986] ICJ Rep 554, para 20.

[42] Treaty for the Frontier Delimitation between the Dominican Republic and Haiti (signed 21 January 1929).

[43] Boggs (n 18) 79–80; Jones (n 10) 13.

[44] In 1964, the Organization of African Unity Assembly of Heads of State and Government called upon member states 'to respect the borders existing on their achievement of national independence'. See African Union Border Programme (AUBP), *Delimitation and Demarcation of Boundaries in Africa* (2013) 9 <www.peaceau.org/uploads/au2013-en-delim-a-demar-of-bound-gen-iss-a-studies-elec2.pdf> accessed 20 March 2020.

3.2 *Delimitation by Treaty*

1886, while the administrative line between the Egyptian Chadivate and the Ottoman Empire became the international boundary between Egypt and Palestine in 1906.[45] Similarly, Burma's agreements with Pakistan in 1964 and India in 1967 upgraded the former limits of the British administrative areas to international boundaries.[46]

The practice of following previous lines is of great practical benefit.[47] For one thing, it preserves the long-existing status quo between the parties concerned. By creating a climate of certainty and stability, it minimizes the risk of armed conflict between the states over their mutual boundary.[48] In addition, the perpetuation of former internal boundaries upholds the rights and interests long acquired by residents on the borderline.[49] The preservation of pre-existing internal lines in land delimitation treaties has also been hailed by boundary experts for respecting anthropogeographic factors (eg private properties, land rights, infrastructure) and long-established local conditions.[50]

Because of these advantages, the practice of following pre-existing lines in delimitation treaties applies to this day.[51] Although colonialism is now a bygone era, the dissolution of the Union of Soviet Socialist Republics (Soviet Union) and the Socialist Federate Republic of Yugoslavia has given rise to many new states in modern times.[52] When negotiating their international boundaries in the 1990s, these new states agreed to preserve the internal limits of the former republics in compliance with the *uti possidetis* norm. Hence, the international boundaries of Croatia in 1999 follow the

---

[45] Srebro and Shoshany (n 39) 6.

[46] Prescott (n 2) 232–33.

[47] OSCE (n 40). That is not to say that the application of *uti possidetis* has been problem-free. In some situations, bitter boundary disputes broke out between newly independent states over the legality of the pre-existing colonial boundaries and ended up before international courts and tribunals (eg *Case Concerning Territorial and Maritime Dispute between Nicaragua and Honduras in the Caribbean Sea (Nicaragua v Honduras)* [2007] ICJ Rep 659; *Land, Island and Maritime Frontier Dispute (El Salvador/Honduras)* [1992] ICJ Rep 351).

[48] OSCE (n 40).

[49] ibid.

[50] ibid 14–15. On some occasions, the treaty allowed for modifications of the pre-existing line to ease or improve the conditions under which people in the border area lived. See Treaty between Croatia and Bosnia and Herzegovina (signed 30 July 1999) art 3.

[51] According to an empirical study, it is the method that prevails in modern boundary-making. See D Carter and H Goemans 'The Making of the Territorial Order: New Borders and the Emergence of Interstate Conflict' (2011) 65 International Organization.

[52] ibid. See also M Shaw, 'The Heritage of States: The Principle of *Uti Possidetis Juris* Today' (1996) 67 British Yearbook of International Law 75; Shaw, 'Peoples, Territorialism and Boundaries' (1997) 8 European Journal of International Law 478; OSCE (n 40).

54   3 *Private Rights in Land and Maritime Delimitation*

country's pre-existing administrative lines with Bosnia and Herzegovina and Serbia.[53] Likewise, the international boundary between Lithuania and Belarus follows the previous administrative lines of the Soviet period.[54]

In sum, both of the modern delimitation methods pay considerable attention to private rights situated in land areas under consideration. That said, there have also been situations where private rights had a limited or no impact on the delimitation process, but they are very few in number. Examples include the treaties between the United States and Mexico in 1905,[55] Germany and France in 1925,[56] France and Turkey (for the border in Syria) in 1929,[57] Belgium and France in 1949,[58] and Israel and Jordan in 1994.[59] In those exceptional situations, it appears that an alignment of the boundary with the existing private rights was either unnecessary (eg due to the rarity of existing private rights or their long distance from the border)[60] or impracticable (eg when it was agreed that the boundary line would follow a river).[61]

Despite such exceptions, it is evident that the importance private rights in land boundary-making were seen to have in the allocation phase continues in the main stage of delimitation, too.

3.2.1.3 The Importance of Private Rights in Boundary Demarcation

The final step in land boundary-making is to transpose the verbal and graphical definition of the boundary from the treaty text to the surface of the land.[62] To achieve that, members of the boundary commission mark the boundary on

---

[53]   Treaty on the State Border between the Republic of Croatia and Bosnia and Herzegovina (signed 30 July 1999). See OSCE (n 40) 13.

[54]   Agreement between the Government of the Republic of Lithuania and the Government of the Republic of Belarus Concerning the Crossing Posts of the State Border (signed 18 July 1995). See OSCE (n 40) 14.

[55]   Convention between the United States and Mexico for the Elimination of the Bancos in the Rio Grande from the Effects of Articles I and II of the Treaty of 12 November 1884 (signed 20 March 1905).

[56]   Treaty between France and Germany Regarding the Delimitation of the Frontier (with Annexes, Protocol and Exchange of Notes) (signed 14 August 1925).

[57]   Protocol between France and Turkey Relative to the Surveillance and Fiscal Regime of the Frontier (signed 29 June 1929).

[58]   Agreement between Belgium and France Relating to Frontier Workers (with Annexes) (signed 8 January 1949).

[59]   Israel-Jordan Peace Treaty (signed 26 October 1994).

[60]   As in the above-mentioned examples of France/Turkey and France/Belgium.

[61]   eg As in the above-mentioned examples of US/Mexico and Israel/Jordan.

[62]   Ron Adler, *Positioning and Mapping International Land Boundaries* (Boundary and Territory Briefing 2(1), IBRU 1995) 10.

3.2 *Delimitation by Treaty*   55

the ground with pillars, posts or beacons. In general, demarcation is not mandatory for the completion of boundary-making, but its role is of great practical importance. By making their boundaries visible on the terrain, states seek to avoid future conflicts with their neighbours and to prevent encroachment by foreigners.[63]

The present study observes that private rights have an equally significant role in this phase, too. In principle, demarcation follows the course of the boundary line as defined in the delimitation treaty. However, it is possible for the boundary commissioners to discover that this definition disregards certain realities of the terrain or the interests of people situated in the borderline area.[64] To avoid the practical and legal problems that may arise in such situations, delimitation treaties often contain a special clause empowering the boundary commissioners to deviate from the defined line.[65]

Such provisions were inserted in the Argentina-Chile convention of 1904,[66] the Colombia-Ecuador treaty of 1916,[67] the Colombia-Peru treaty of 1922,[68] the Estonia-Latvia treaty of 1920[69] and the convention between Latvia and Lithuania of 1921.[70] More recent examples are found in the 1960 treaty

---

[63] Although not mandatory, demarcation has been recognized as important by judges and scholars. See *Case Concerning the Temple of Preah Vihear (Cambodia v Thailand)* [1962] ICJ Rep 6. See also A Cukwurah, *The Settlement of Boundary Disputes in International Law* (Manchester University Press 1967) 78 ('demarcation is the crux of all boundary making'); T Holdich, *Political Frontiers and Boundary Making* (Macmillan 1916) 211 ('to the demarcator belongs the real romance of the work').

[64] Holdich (n 63) 208:

> [I]t is in this process [of demarcation] that disputes usually arise, and weak elements in the treaties or agreements are apt to be discovered. Important features are found in unexpected positions, and a thousand points of local importance crop up which could never have been taken into account by the delimitators, whose definitions leave them unconsidered and unadjusted.

[65] As stressed by Jones (n 10) 5, 'demarcation is not solely an engineering task, for almost inevitably there are fine decisions on site to be made', while according to Holdich (n 63) 212, 'the demarcator is the best judge of the local situation and, nine cases out of ten, his advice will have to be taken'.

[66] Demarcation Convention between Argentina and Chile (signed 2 May 1904).

[67] Boundary Treaty between Colombia and Ecuador (signed 15 July 1916).

[68] Treaty of Delimitation between Colombia and Peru (signed 24 March 1922).

[69] Convention between Estonia and Latvia Regarding the Delimitation on the Spot of the Frontier between the Two States (signed 19 October 1920).

[70] Convention between Latvia and Lithuania Regarding the Delimitation on the Spot of the Frontier between the Two States, and Also Regarding the Rights of the Citizens in the Frontier Zone, and the Status of Immovable Property Intersected by the Frontier Line (signed 14 May 1921).

56   3 *Private Rights in Land and Maritime Delimitation*

between the Netherlands and Germany[71] and the 1999 delimitation treaty between Croatia and Bosnia-Herzegovina.[72]

Under most treaties, the commissioners have only minimal power to deviate from the delimited line, although the demarcators are generally allowed considerable discretion in choosing the methods that will lead to the desired result.[73] An example is in the Ecuador-Peru protocol of 1942, which empowered the commissioners to perform any acts 'as they may consider advisable in order to adjust the line' to local realities.[74] A similar arrangement was made between Brazil and Venezuela in 1929,[75] and between the United Kingdom and Portugal for Rhodesia's boundary in 1954.[76]

Again, this does not mean that all delimitation treaties allow the boundary to be adjusted at the demarcation stage. Typically, a deviation clause is a last resort, used to preserve dwelling or farming rights on small land parcels that would be intersected by the boundary. But such a provision is omitted when larger areas of land (eg forests, valleys, extensive fields) are redistributed from one state to another, as a substantial deviation would contradict the states' will concerning the boundary's location.[77]

Nonetheless, here too, as in the preceding phases of allocation and delimitation, the impact of private rights on demarcation is significant and extensive. It can therefore be said that private rights have a consistently important role at all stages of concluding land delimitation treaties.

3.2.2 *The Restricted Role of Private Rights in Maritime Delimitation Treaties*

An analysis of maritime delimitation treaties reveals that the role of private rights in the comparable phases of ocean boundary-making (negotiation, delimitation, demarcation) is much smaller by comparison.

---

[71] General Treaty between Germany and the Netherlands for the Settlement of Frontier Questions and Other Problems Outstanding between the Two Countries (signed 8 April 1960).

[72] Treaty on the State Border between the Republic of Croatia and Bosnia and Herzegovina (signed 30 July 1999).

[73] Jones (n 10) 57–60.

[74] Protocol of Peace, Friendship, and Boundaries between Ecuador and Peru (signed 29 January 1942) art 9.

[75] Exchange of Notes between Brazil and Venezuela for the delimitation of their boundary (7 November 1929) para 12.

[76] Agreement between the United Kingdom and Portugal with Regard to the Northern Rhodesia-Angola Frontier (signed 18 November 1954) art 2(3).

[77] eg agreements between United States and Mexico (n 55); France and Germany (n 56); Belgium and France (n 58).

3.2 Delimitation by Treaty

3.2.2.1 The Moderate Role of Private Rights in Boundary Negotiation

The first stage in the making of a maritime delimitation treaty consists of the states' exchanges on their respective positions with a view to reaching a boundary agreement. Just like the allocation stage on land, the negotiation process at sea is heavily politicized.[78] Here too, the parties receive the assistance of consultants and technical experts, which continues until the delimitation treaty is signed.[79]

Another similarity with the allocation process on land is that each of the negotiating states invokes considerations related to its own and its nationals' interests in the maritime area under discussion. These include the fishing and petroleum exploratory rights of private actors. The disclosed diplomatic and parliamentary reports and the preambles to some of the delimitation treaties show that private interests are often raised by the states involved.[80] As examples, one may cite the agreements between Australia and Indonesia in 1971,[81] Brazil and Uruguay in 1972,[82] Argentina and Uruguay in 1973,[83] Colombia and Panama in 1976, Colombia and Haiti in 1978,[84] Iceland and Norway in 1980,[85] France and Monaco in 1984[86] and Denmark and Sweden in 1984.[87]

But as this study observes, the actual impact of private rights on the progress and the outcome of negotiations is rather mixed. On some occasions, the presence of private rights encourages the negotiating parties to commence the bargaining process and determines how the shared maritime space is divided.

---

[78] Prescott (n 2) 82–106.

[79] Johnston (n 2) 27; D Anderson, *Modern Law of the Sea: Selected Essays* (Martinus Nijhoff 2008) 414.

[80] Statistically, the greater part of those interests relate to fishing. See B Kwiatkowska, 'Economic and Environmental Considerations in Maritime Boundary Delimitations' in J Charney and L Alexander (eds), *International Maritime Boundaries*, vol 1 (Martinus Nijhoff 1993) 81–84.

[81] Agreement between the Government of the Commonwealth of Australia and the Government of the Republic of Indonesia Establishing Certain Sea-Bed Boundaries (signed 18 May 1971).

[82] Agreement between the Government of Brazil and the Government of Uruguay Relating to the Maritime Delimitation between Brazil and Uruguay (signed 21 July 1972).

[83] Agreement between the Government of Argentina and the Government of Uruguay Relating to the Delimitation of the River Plate and the Maritime Boundary between Argentina and Uruguay (signed 19 November 1973).

[84] Agreement on Delimitation of the Maritime Boundaries between the Republic of Colombia and the Dominican Republic (signed 13 January 1978).

[85] Agreement between Iceland and Norway Concerning Fishery and Continental Shelf Questions (signed 28 May 1980).

[86] Convention on Maritime Delimitation Agreement between the Government of His Most Serene Highness the Prince of Monaco and the Government of the French Republic (signed 16 February 1984).

[87] Agreement between Sweden and Denmark on the Delimitation of the Continental Shelf and Fishing Zones (signed 9 November 1984).

58   3 *Private Rights in Land and Maritime Delimitation*

That is particularly the case when both states have granted private rights in the area – hence, they both have an interest in securing those rights during negotiations. For example, in the resource-rich North Sea, delimitation between the surrounding states has reportedly been affected by the petroleum licence-holders, as the establishment of clear maritime boundaries would provide investors with a secure title over the explored areas.[88] Likewise, it is reported that in the Persian Gulf oil companies encouraged states to negotiate delimitation agreements in the 1960s and 1970s.[89] In those situations, the presence of private rights in the areas under delimitation affected the initial division of the shared waters between the states concerned.

On the other hand, when only one of the states concerned has awarded private rights in the shared maritime area and has done so without its neighbour's consent, the presence of those rights tends to have exactly the opposite effect on the negotiation process. On many occasions, such unilateral behaviour has stalled discussions between the two states involved, as was the case between Guyana and Suriname, Kenya and Somalia, Ghana and Côte d'Ivoire, and Bangladesh and Myanmar. In all of these cases, previous negotiations broke down after the granting of private rights by one side.[90] On other occasions, the unilateral granting of private rights in the shared maritime space has even created a climate of hostility, to the point of almost sparking armed conflict between the formerly negotiating states. Examples include the tension between China and Japan in the East China Sea or between China and Vietnam in the South China Sea, which increase dramatically whenever fishing or oil exploratory vessels from one of the states enter the shared waters without the other state's consent.[91]

---

[88]   For an excellent analysis, see A Oude Elferink, *The Delimitation of the Continental Shelf between Denmark, Germany and the Netherlands: Arguing Law, Practicing Politics?* (CUP 2013) 77, 98, 142 (esp quoted letters between oil companies and governments). See also P Birnie and C Mason, 'Oil and Gas: the International Regime' in C Mason (ed), *The Effective Management of Resources: The International Politics of the North Sea* (Nichols 1979) 25; A Kemp, *The Official History of North Sea Oil and Gas*, vol 1 *The Growing Dominance of the State* (Routledge 2012) 2–9; N Smith, *The Sea of Lost Opportunity: North Sea Oil and Gas, British Industry and the Offshore Supplies Office* (Elsevier 2011) 23–25; J Wils and E Neilson, *The Technical and Legal Guide to the UK Oil and Gas Industry* (Aberlour 2007) 17–21.

[89]   Delimitation Agreement between Iran and Saudi Arabia (signed 24 October 1968); Delimitation Agreement between Iran and Qatar (signed 20 September 1969); Delimitation Agreement between Iran and Bahrain (signed 17 June 1971); Delimitation Agreement between Iran and Oman (signed 25 July 1974). For an analysis, see A Razavi, *Continental Shelf Delimitation and Related Maritime Issues in the Persian Gulf* (Martinus Nijhoff 1997) 161.

[90]   In each case, the boundary question was eventually referred to a judicial body.

[91]   See US Council on Foreign Relations, 'Global Conflict Tracker' <www.cfr.org/interactives/global-conflict-tracker#!/conflict/tensions-in-the-east-china-sea> accessed 20 March 2020.

3.2 *Delimitation by Treaty*

The reasons why private rights tend to have a negative impact on maritime boundary negotiations might be political or economic.[92] But, as this study observes, there is also a legal explanation for this negative effect. As seen earlier, Articles 74(3) and 83(3) UNCLOS impose two procedural obligations on states during the delimitation process.[93] According to these twin provisions, each state must negotiate in good faith with its neighbour and behave in a way that does not jeopardize or hamper the reaching of the final delimitation agreement. It is recalled that the unilateral granting of private rights in the shared maritime space pending delimitation could be deemed a breach of the above duties causing the acting state to be held responsible for an internationally wrongful act – even if that state ultimately retains the area in question.[94]

Hence, if the presence of private rights in a maritime area under delimitation is a source of tension between the states concerned, it is hard to see how those private interests could have a positive impact on the negotiating process. No state would be disposed to allow the private rights unilaterally granted by its neighbour to affect the division of the shared maritime space.

In sum, although private rights are often raised by states during boundary negotiations, their impact on the division of the shared maritime space is significantly more limited than at the corresponding stage of land boundary-making.

3.2.2.2 The Limited Role of Private Rights in Boundary Delimitation

When negotiations are successful and the parties agree on the boundary's location, the next step is to precisely define its course in the delimitation treaty. Whether existing private rights can affect this process depends on the chosen delimitation method. To that extent, there is little difference from the process on land. However, closer analysis reveals that private rights have a far more limited effect on the boundary's course in maritime treaties.

---

[92] According to Prescott (n 2) 156, the presence, or even the suspicion, of natural resources in the area in question complicates boundary negotiations, as each state will wish to secure access to them. The same can be said of states' conflicting navigation and military interests in disputed maritime spaces of strategic importance.

[93] See Chapter 2.

[94] See Chapter 2. See also *Arbitration between Guyana and Suriname (Guyana v Suriname)* (2007) 152ff; British Institute of International and Comparative Law, 'Obligations of States under Articles 74(3) and 83(3) of UNCLOS in respect of Undelimited Maritime Areas' (conference report 2016) 6–39; F. Milano and I Papanicolopulu, 'State Responsibility in Disputed Areas on Land and at Sea' (2011) 71 ZaöRV 587, 608–36; M Pappa, 'Private Oil Companies Operating in Contested Waters and International Law of the Sea' [2018] 1 OGEL <www.ogel.org>.

60   3 *Private Rights in Land and Maritime Delimitation*

Throughout history of ocean boundary-making, two delimitation methods have prevailed: equidistance (or the median line) and equitable principles.[95] According to the first method, the boundary line is made of a series of points which are equally distant from the states' base points.[96] According to the second method, the construction of the boundary line is based on various circumstances and factors that lead to an equitable solution.[97]

Despite their apparent differences, the two delimitation methods are considered to be closely interrelated as they both aim for an equitable result.[98] That is why the conventions of the sea refrain from treating one or other of the methods as dominant for purposes of maritime boundary delimitation. Certain provisions of those conventions make explicit reference to the median line,[99] but this does not make equidistance an exclusive or mandatory method of maritime delimitation.[100] Any delimitation method can apply, insofar as it brings a fair result.

DELIMITATION BASED ON EQUIDISTANCE Studies on state practices have shown that the principle of equidistance is a much older method of delimitation than that of equitable principles and more widely applied in maritime delimitation treaties.[101] An early instance of its application was the 1809 treaty between Russia and Sweden, which established the median line for the delimitation of the Bay of Bothnia and the Aaland Sea.[102] Other examples include the 1965 treaty between the United Kingdom and Norway,[103] the 1971 agreement

---

[95]   Other methods (eg bisector) are also available, but rarely used.

[96]   Y Tanaka, *International Law of the Sea* (CUP 2012) 186–215.

[97]   ibid.

[98]   *Maritime Delimitation and Territorial Questions (Qatar v Bahrain)* [2001] ICJ Rep 112, para 231; Y Tanaka, *Predictability and Flexibility in the Law of Maritime Delimitation* (OUP 2006) 109, 123–26.

[99]   Convention on the Territorial Sea and the Contiguous Zone, art 12(1); Convention on the Continental Shelf, art 6; UNCLOS, art 15.

[100] *North Sea Continental Shelf Cases (Federal Republic of Germany/Denmark, Federal Republic of Germany/Netherlands)* [1969] ICJ Rep 51, para 81; *Case Concerning the Continental Shelf (Libyan Arab Jamahiriya/Malta)* [1985] ICJ Rep 13, para 44.

[101] It is reported that almost 90 per cent of existing maritime delimitation treaties have applied equidistance. V Prescott and C Schofield, *The Maritime Political Boundaries of the World* (2nd edn, Martinus Nijhoff 2013) 238. See also Tanaka (n 98) 20; R Churchill and V Lowe, *The Law of the Sea* (3rd edn, Manchester University Press 1999) 197.

[102] Peace Treaty of Fredrikshamn between Sweden and Russia (signed 17 September 1809).

[103] Treaty between the Government of the United Kingdom and Northern Ireland and the Government of the Kingdom of Norway Relating to the Delimitation of the Continental Shelf between the Two Countries (signed 10 March 1965).

between Tunisia and Italy,[104] the 1980 treaty between Costa Rica and Panama,[105] the Tanzania's agreements with Mozambique in 1988 and the Seychelles in 2002,[106] and the 2003 agreement between Cyprus and Egypt.[107]

The main reason why this method is so popular is that it lends a high degree of objectivity and predictability to the process of delimitation.[108] Each state can foresee the outcome of delimitation by calculating the portion of the shared maritime space that it will eventually receive by equidistance. The method's appeal is also explained by the ease with which the median line can be constructed, compared to any other line or curve.[109]

Attractive though the method may be, its strict application leaves some important elements out of the delimitation process, including any islands and low-tide elevations, natural resources and factors of human geography that may be present in the area. To address the inconveniences caused by its strict application, states often agree to re-draw the median line in the light of the above-mentioned factors. This happens particularly where there are large insular features that generate their own maritime zones and base points.[110]

On the other hand, deviations from the original median line are rarely made on non-geographical grounds, such as the presence of exploratory or fishing rights in the boundary area. A rare exception was the 1958 treaty between Bahrain and Saudi Arabia, where a third of the maritime boundary departed from the median line as originally agreed in order to make it coincide with the limits of the important *Fasht Abu Sa'afah* oil field that was under exploration.[111] A similar deviation occurred in the 1969 delimitation treaty

---

[104] Agreement between the Government of the Republic of Tunisia and the Government of the Italian Republic Concerning the Delimitation of the Continental Shelf between the Two Countries (signed 20 August 1971).

[105] Treaty Concerning Delimitation of Marine Areas and Maritime Cooperation between the Republic of Costa Rica and the Republic of Panama (signed 2 February 1980).

[106] Agreement between the Government of the United Republic of Tanzania and the Government of the People's Republic of Mozambique Regarding the Tanzania/ Mozambique Boundary (signed 28 December 1988); Agreement between the Government of the United Republic of Tanzania and the Government of the Republic of Seychelles on the Delimitation of the Maritime Boundary of the Exclusive Economic Zone and Continental Shelf (signed 23 January 2002).

[107] Agreement between the Republic of Cyprus and the Arab Republic of Egypt on the Delimitation of the Exclusive Economic Zone (signed 17 February 2003).

[108] See *North Sea Continental Shelf Cases* (n 100) para 23.

[109] Anderson (n 14) 127.

[110] Prescott (n 2) 154.

[111] Boundary Agreement between Bahrain and Saudi Arabia (signed 22 February 1958). See Ian Townsend-Gault, 'Offshore Boundary Delimitation in the Arabian/Persian Gulf in D Johnston and P Saunders, *Ocean Boundary Making: Regional Issues and Developments* (Croom Helm 1988) 210–11.

62   3 *Private Rights in Land and Maritime Delimitation*

between Qatar and the United Arab Emirates, where bends were added to the median line to avoid encroaching on existing oil wells.[112] More impressively, the boundary established between Iran and Saudi Arabia in 1968 followed a zigzag course to avoid the partition of existing oil concessions and the structures of operators.[113] Also, in the delimitation treaty between Italy and Tunisia in 1971, it is explicitly stated that the CS boundary follows the limits of the Tunisian fishery zone, which had been in place since 1963.[114]

Nonetheless, the number of delimitation treaties in which existing private rights had no impact on the boundary's course is much greater. For example, petroleum concessions situated in or near the boundary area played no role in the delimitation agreements between Greece and Italy in 1977, Greece and Albania in 2009,[115] and Kuwait and Saudi Arabia in 2000.[116] Likewise, the maritime boundary agreed between Australia and Timor Leste in 2018 did not follow the pre-existing petroleum permits in the shared waters.[117] Nor did private fishing rights have any impact on the boundary agreements between Canada and France (Saint-Pierre and Miquelon) in 1972,[118] Argentina and Uruguay in 1973,[119] Sri Lanka and India in 1974,[120] Kenya and Tanzania in 1976,[121] Italy and

[112] Agreement between Qatar and Abu Dhabi on the Settlement of Maritime Boundaries and Ownership Islands (signed 20 March 1969). Townsend-Gault (n 111) 214.

[113] Agreement on Delimitation of the Continental Shelf between Iran and Saudi Arabia (signed 24 October 1968). Townsend-Gault (n 111) 213; Kwiatkowska (n 80) 91.

[114] Agreement between the Government of the Italian Republic and the Government of the Tunisian Republic Relating to the Delimitation of the Continental Shelf between the Two Countries (signed 20 August 1971). Kwiatkowska (n 80) 84.

[115] Agreement between the Government of the Hellenic Republic and the Government of the Italian Republic for the Delimitation of the Continental Shelf (signed 24 May 1977); Agreement between the Government of the Hellenic Republic and the Government of the Republic of Albania for the Delimitation of their Respective Continental Shelf and Other Maritime Zones (signed 27 April 2009). The delimitation treaty between Greece and Albania was unilaterally revoked by Albania as inequitable. The two states are currently negotiating a new maritime boundary.

[116] Agreement between the Kingdom of Saudi Arabia and the State of Kuwait Concerning the Submerged Area Adjacent to the Divided Zone (signed 2 July 2000).

[117] Treaty between Australia and the Democratic Republic of Timor-Leste Establishing their Maritime Boundaries in the Timor Sea (signed 6 March 2018).

[118] Agreement between the Government of Canada and the Government of the French Republic on their Mutual Fishing Relations (signed 27 March 1972).

[119] Agreement between the Government of Argentina and the Government of Uruguay Relating to the Delimitation of the River Plate and the Maritime Boundary between Argentina and Uruguay (signed 19 November 1973).

[120] Agreement between Sri Lanka and India on the Boundary in Historic Waters between the Two Countries and Related Matters (signed 26 and 28 June 1974).

[121] Notes exchanged between the United Republic of Tanzania and Kenya concerning the delimitation of the territorial waters boundary between the two states (17 December 1975–9 July 1976).

3.2 *Delimitation by Treaty*

Yugoslavia in 1983,[122] France and Monaco in 1984,[123] or France and Italy in 1986,[124] although they were reportedly raised by the states concerned during negotiations.[125]

DELIMITATION BASED ON EQUITABLE PRINCIPLES The alternative method of equitable principles, brings various factors into play in the process of delimitation. Typically, they relate to states' coastal geography, the presence of islands in the area under delimitation, the parties' navigation rights and natural resources (hydrocarbons, fish) known or suspected to be present in the area. This method has been applied in many treaties, including those between the Netherlands (Antilles) and Venezuela in 1978,[126] the Dominican Republic and Venezuela in 1979,[127] France and Venezuela in 1980,[128] and Tunisia and Libya in 1988.[129]

The method of equitable principles is more flexible than equidistance, as it allows for a case-by-case arrangement. Therefore, it could be assumed that private rights play a predominant role in treaties that have favoured this particular method of delimitation.

In practice, however, that has been observed on only a handful of occasions. Other factors, such as coastal geography, are generally considered to be more important. One of the rare exceptions is the treaty between Trinidad and Tobago and Venezuela in 1990, where regard was had to the existing oil fields and concessions in the area when tracing three out of the four boundary

---

[122] Notes exchanged between Italy and the Social Federal Republic of Yugoslavia regarding the creation of a joint fishing zone in the Gulf of Trieste (18 February 1983). See G Blake and D Topalovic, 'The Maritime Boundaries of the Adriatic Sea' (Maritime Briefing 1(8), IBRU 1996) 3.

[123] Convention on Maritime Delimitation between the Government of His Most Serene Highness the Prince of Monaco and the Government of the French Republic.

[124] Agreement between the Government of the French Republic and the Government of the Italian Republic on the Delimitation of the Maritime Boundaries in the Area of the Strait of Bonifacio (signed 28 November 1986).

[125] See the preambles of the aforesaid treaties and the notes exchanged between the governments. See also Kwiatkowska (n 80) 83.

[126] Boundary Delimitation Treaty between the Republic of Venezuela and the Kingdom of the Netherlands (signed 31 March 1978).

[127] Treaty on the Delimitation of Marine and Submarine Areas between the Republic of Venezuela and the Dominican Republic (signed 3 March 1979).

[128] Delimitation Treaty between the Government of the French Republic and the Government of the Republic of Venezuela (signed 17 July 1980).

[129] Agreement between the Libyan Arab Socialist People's Jamahiriya and the Republic of Tunisia to Implement the Judgment of the International Court of Justice in the Tunisia/Libya Continental Shelf Case (signed 8 August 1988).

64   3 *Private Rights in Land and Maritime Delimitation*

sectors.[130] Likewise, the 1980 agreement between Iceland and Norway determining fisheries jurisdiction gave consideration above all to the dependence of Iceland and its nationals on fishing activities. As a consequence, Iceland was entitled to a 200-M economic zone at the expense of Norway.[131] More recently, in the 2001 treaty between Honduras and the United Kingdom delimiting the Cayman Islands area it was explicitly stated that the boundary's course would be affected by the parties' long-standing fishing interests and oil concessions in the Caribbean Sea.[132]

The majority of treaties applying the method of equitable principles, however, are not affected by such considerations. For example, in Germany's 1971 treaties with Denmark and the Netherlands, the oil concessions previously awarded by the Danish and Dutch authorities had no impact on the boundary's course.[133] Nor did Australia's oil concessions have any effect on its boundary agreement with Papua New Guinea in 1978.[134] In the Dutch-Belgian agreement of 1996, a gravel concession that was previously issued by the Netherlands likewise had no effect on the outcome of delimitation.[135] And there is no evidence that the long-standing fishing rights of private actors in the

---

[130] Treaty between the Republic of Trinidad and Tobago and the Republic of Venezuela on the Delimitation of Marine and Submarine Areas (signed 18 April 1990). See Kwiatkowska (n 80) 92–93.

[131] Agreement on Fishery and Continental Shelf Questions between Iceland and Norway (signed 28 May 1980) – although it was not truly a delimitation treaty. S Rolston and T McDorman, 'Maritime Boundary Making in the Arctic Region' in D Johnston and P Saunders, *Ocean Boundary Making: Regional Issues and Developments* (Croom Helm 1988) 33–34.

[132] Treaty between the Government of the United Kingdom of Great Britain and Northern Ireland and the Government of the Republic of Honduras Concerning the Delimitation of the Maritime Areas between Cayman Islands and the Republic of Honduras (signed 4 December 2001).

[133] Treaty between the Kingdom of Denmark and the Federal Republic of Germany Concerning the Delimitation of the Continental Shelf under the North Sea (signed 28 January 1971); Treaty between the Kingdom of the Netherlands and the Federal Republic of Germany Concerning the Delimitation of the Continental Shelf under the North Sea (signed 28 January 1971). It should be pointed out, first, that the method of equitable principles was indicated by the ICJ in 1969 after the parties had requested it to determine the principles upon which the boundary delimitation should be based (prior to which Denmark and the Netherlands had favoured equidistance and followed the median line when issuing their permits), and second, that the Court announced a non-exhaustive list of factors that states should consider during delimitation, which referred to the unity of any hydrocarbon deposits discovered by states after delimitation but not to the existing oil concessions.

[134] Treaty between Australia and the Independent State of Papua New Guinea Concerning Sovereignty and Maritime Boundaries in the Area between the Two Countries, Including the Area Known as Torres Strait, and Related Matters (signed 18 December 1978).

[135] Treaty between the Kingdom of Netherlands and the Kingdom of Belgium on the Delimitation of the Territorial Sea (signed 18 December 1996).

3.2 *Delimitation by Treaty* 65

Gulf of Tonkin affected the boundary between China and Vietnam in 2000, even though fishing was reportedly the main reason for this delimitation agreement.[136]

The above demonstrates that, regardless of the chosen delimitation method (equidistance or equitable principles), private rights have much less influence on the delimitation process in maritime boundary treaties than in land boundary treaties

3.2.2.3 The Absence of Private Rights in Boundary Demarcation

The physical marking of boundaries in the ocean is typically omitted as unfeasible or unnecessary.[137] Rather, what qualifies as demarcation here is drawing the boundary on a map or inserting it in a geographical information system.[138]

An exception was the 1942 treaty between Great Britain and Venezuela delimiting the submarine areas in the Gulf of Paria. In that instance, a mixed commission was appointed 'to take all necessary steps to demarcate the lines ... by means of buoys or other visible methods on the surface of the sea or on the land as the case may be'.[139] A similar provision was included in the 1990 delimitation treaty between Venezuela and Trinidad and Tobago.[140]

But no matter how demarcation is conducted, there is no evidence that it has been or is likely to be affected by existing private rights. No delimitation treaties or literature sources report such an effect. That is in stark contrast to the impact private rights have on the demarcation of land boundaries.

In sum, Section 3.2 has demonstrated that the role of private rights differs between land and maritime delimitation treaties. The Section 3.3 will examine whether this difference is also found in land and maritime delimitation rulings by international courts and tribunals.

---

[136] Agreement between the Socialist Republic of Vietnam and the People's Republic of China on the Delimitation of the Territorial Sea, Exclusive Economic Zone and Continental Shelf between the Two Countries in the Gulf of Tonkin signed 25 December 2000). On the negotiating background, see Z Keyuan, 'The Sino-Vietnamese Agreement on Maritime Boundary Delimitation in the Gulf of Tonkin' (2005) 36 Ocean Development and International Law 13.

[137] Anderson (n 14) 141.

[138] Esch (n 14) 22.

[139] Treaty between Great Britain and Northern Ireland and Venezuela Relating to the Submarine Areas of the Gulf of Paria (signed 26 February 1942) art 4.

[140] ibid, art 5.

66   3 *Private Rights in Land and Maritime Delimitation*

3.3 DELIMITATION BY A COURT OR TRIBUNAL

Given the prevalence of delimitation treaties, the number of delimitation judgments and arbitral awards is relatively small.[141] That said, there are far more relating to the sea than to land, and their number is constantly rising.[142] The present study identifies two main reasons for this trend.

First, the fact that land disputes are concerned with questions of sovereignty and territorial integrity makes states reluctant to refer a case to a third body for fear of losing the dispute's control. In comparison, states' conflicting interests in the ocean are narrower than on land, as they primarily concern access to natural resources and navigation, rather than sovereignty and statehood.[143]

Second, many (if not most) maritime boundary disputes are caused by ambiguity in the applicable provisions of the conventions of the sea, especially UNCLOS.[144] As confirmed by judicial authorities, these provisions have been 'consciously designed to decide as little as possible', representing a compromise between the divergent delimitation methods (equidistance, equitable principles) adopted by states.[145] Consequently, it is not unusual for the interpretation and application of those provisions to give rise to disputes, many of which end up before international courts or tribunals.

Although delimitation rulings (as opposed to delimitation treaties) remain limited in number, they are worth analysing for the light they shed on the practices followed by international judicial bodies. That said, the purpose of

---

[141]   While some hundreds of delimitation treaties have been signed, fewer than fifty cases in all have been submitted to third parties for the delimitation of land and maritime boundaries. The cases can be found on the websites of the International Court of Justice (ICJ) <www.icj-cij.org/en/list-of-all-cases>, the Permanent Court of Arbitration (PCA) <https://pca-cpa.org/cases/> and the International Tribunal for the Law of the Sea (ITLOS) <www.itlos.org/cases/list-of-cases/> all accessed 20 March 2020.

[142]   T Cottier, *Equitable Principles of Maritime Boundary Delimitation* (CUP 2015) 271: 'Next to the jurisprudence of the World Trade Organization (WTO) since 1995 and the settlement of investment disputes both within and outside the International Convention for the Settlement of Investment Disputes (ICSID Convention), maritime boundary delimitation amounts to the most important field of litigation in contemporary public international law.' As observed by Oude Elferink (n 2) 5, only 6.5 per cent of maritime boundaries delimited between 1925 and 1990 were fixed by international courts or tribunals – a figure that increased to 16.3 per cent for the period 2003–2011. See also J Charney, 'Introduction' in J Charney and L Alexander (eds), *International Maritime Boundaries*, vol 1 (Martinus Nijhoff 1993) xxvii–xxx.

[143]   On the differences between sovereignty and sovereign rights, see Chapter 2.

[144]   In the majority of maritime delimitation cases, each state adopts a different delimitation method or a different interpretation of the relevant provisions of the conventions of the sea – mainly due to the failure of international law of the sea to establish a fixed delimitation method.

[145]   *Eritrea/Yemen Arbitration (Second Stage: Maritime Delimitation)* (2001) 40(4) ILM 983, para 116.

this study is not to analyse every land and maritime delimitation case in detail, for each one is a *unicum*, born of a particular set of facts and decided on its particular merits.[146] It is rather to identify trends in the treatment and importance international case law accords to private rights in the context of boundary-making. Before these trends are analysed, however, some preliminary observations must be made about land and maritime delimitation rulings.

First, whether in land or maritime delimitation cases, the way in which private rights are raised is always the same. For an argument or a particular circumstance to be considered by an international court or tribunal, it must be brought to the judges' attention. Given that non-state actors possess no *locus standi* in international forums,[147] only the disputing states are in a position to bring forward the matter of private rights.

Second, a delimitation judgment is concerned only with issues that are relevant to the dispute (eg territorial sovereignty, the boundary's location or method of establishment). Therefore, private rights can be invoked by the disputing states only in support of their boundary claims.

Third, the lack of a predetermined delimitation method noted in relation to delimitation treaties applies also to land and maritime delimitation rulings. However, this does not mean that delimitation rulings are made arbitrarily or that they follow no rules whatsoever. Like all international judgments, delimitation rulings are based on the sources and rules of public international law.[148] In maritime delimitation cases, judges are additionally guided by the conventions of the sea.[149] Therefore, only matters with a legal bearing are admissible in a delimitation case, and all claims submitted (including the presence of private rights in the disputed area) must be examined by judges through the lens of international law.

The above similarities between land and maritime delimitation rulings justify analysing them together. But, as the following paragraphs will reveal, there are also important differences concerning the applicable delimitation processes and the impact of private rights on the boundary's course.

---

[146] *Dispute Concerning Delimitation of the Maritime Boundary between Guinea and Guinea-Bissau (Guinea v Guinea-Bissau)* (1985) 24 ILM 252, para 89.

[147] ICJ Statute, arts 34(1), 62(1); PCA Rules 2012, art 17(5); ITLOS Rules, art 31(1). That said, ITLOS allows non-state entities to access its proceedings in certain situations (ie exploration of the area (UNCLOS, pt XI), or where all parties agree to confer jurisdiction on ITLOS (ITLOS Statute, art 20(2)), but not in delimitation cases.

[148] ICJ Statute, art 38.

[149] Convention on the Territorial Sea and the Contiguous Zone, art 12; Convention on the Continental Shelf, art 6; UNCLOS, arts 15, 74, 83.

68   3 *Private Rights in Land and Maritime Delimitation*

3.3.1 *The Significant Role of Private Rights in Land Delimitation Rulings*

When hearing a land boundary dispute, the competent court or tribunal first examines whether a delimitation treaty is already in place. If a valid agreement is found to exist, the judges will comply with it.[150] In that case, it is unlikely that any other factors will determine or affect the boundary's course, unless the circumstances dictate otherwise.[151]

If no boundary agreement exists (which is the case in many disputes), the judges will examine whether the factors invoked by the states may weight in their decision-making. Typically, these factors concern the states' conduct in the disputed area, including the granting and regulation of private rights (eg through deeds of land ownership, licences for farming, grazing, fishing in rivers or lakes). Such acts are in some cases invoked by only one of the states,[152] while in others both sides rely on them.[153] Whether or not the claims are accepted depends on the quality of evidence produced. Notwithstanding, an analysis of case law reveals that private rights have a significant impact on land delimitation rulings in three main ways.[154]

3.3.1.1 Private Rights in Support of *Uti Possidetis*

As explained earlier, states that were formerly colonies or belonged to a federation tend to upgrade their previous administrative boundaries to

---

[150] *Case Concerning the Territorial Dispute (Libyan Arab Jamahiriya/Chad)* [1994] ICJ Rep 6, paras 75–76; *Case Concerning the Land and Maritime Boundary between Cameroon and Nigeria (Cameroon v Nigeria; Equatorial Guinea Intervening)* [2002] ICJ Rep 303, para 68; *Case Concerning the Frontier Dispute (Benin/Niger)* [2005] ICJ Rep 90, paras 77, 141; *Frontier Dispute (Burkina Faso/Niger)* [2013] ICJ Rep 44, para 78.

[151] See *Temple of Preah Vihear* (n 63). Although a delimitation treaty had been signed between Siam and France in 1904 and the frontier had been fixed by a commission, a dispute arose between Thailand and Cambodia over the boundary's course at Preah Vihear. Cambodia successfully relied on subsequent state conduct in the area under the doctrine of acquiescence.

[152] eg *Cameroon v Nigeria* (n 150).

[153] eg *Libyan Arab Jamahiriya/Chad* (n 150).

[154] There have been land delimitation cases in which the role of private rights has been recognized without explicit reference to *uti possidetis*, acquiescence or *effectivités*. In the *Abyei Area* case (concerning delimitation effected by a boundary commission) the arbitral tribunal remarked that 'it was reasonable to find out where people lived, where they took their cattle, and where they shared grazing and water with other people'; that 'traditional rights acquired by populations within the Abyei Area ... will not be affected by the Tribunal's boundary delimitation'; that '[b]y their very nature, boundary delimitation decisions must be capable of practical implementation, requiring on occasion deference to geographical necessities'; and that 'pre-existing rights may result in spatial adjustments when delimiting boundaries'. *Arbitration Regarding the Delimitation of the Abyei Area between the Government of Sudan and the Sudan People's Liberation Movement/Army* (2009) paras 598, 752, 692, 754.

3.3 *Delimitation by a Court or Tribunal* 69

international boundaries upon gaining independence, on the basis of the doctrine of *uti possidetis*.[155] This doctrine is also widely applied in land delimitation cases.[156] As repeatedly acknowledged by courts, the transformation of administrative boundary lines into international frontiers is a 'general principle which is logically connected with the phenomenon of obtaining independence', as its effect is to 'freeze the territorial title' to protect sovereignty.[157]

If the parties in the case wish delimitation to be performed on the basis of *uti possidetis* but cannot agree as to the boundary's exact location, then the presence of private rights in the area can be used as valuable evidence of their claims.

For example, in *El Salvador/Honduras*, such evidence consisted of the land titles the Spanish Crown had granted to individuals during colonial times.[158] The lines of these titles formed a provincial boundary, which, according to the judges, should become the international boundary between the states. Likewise, in *Croatia v Slovenia* the cadastral districts containing housing and farming rights that the authorities of the two sides had granted to individuals at the time of the former Socialist Federal Republic of Yugoslavia were deemed 'a *prima facie* indication' of the independent states' land boundary.[159] Hence, delimitation was largely aligned with the limits of private properties situated in the municipal cadastral districts.

In sum, the judicial practice of upgrading previous administrative lines to land boundaries promotes stability and complies with the rules of international law. More importantly, it respects pre-existing private rights in the disputed area, securing them against reallocation.

3.3.1.2 Private Rights in Support of Acquiescence

Of course, not all states are former colonies or in the past had administrative boundaries that can be upgraded to international boundaries. The boundary must therefore be determined by the judges. Private rights can be of great importance in such situations, as they may indicate the boundary's exact location under the legal doctrines of acquiescence and estoppel.[160] These

---

[155] See Section 3.2.1.2.
[156] eg *Burkina Faso/Republic of Mali* (n 41) para 23; *El Salvador/Honduras* (n 47) 386–87.
[157] *Burkina Faso/Republic of Mali* (n 41); *Arbitration between the Republic of Croatia and the Republic of Slovenia (Croatia v Slovenia)* (2017) para 256.
[158] *El Salvador/Honduras* (n 47) 388–89.
[159] *Croatia v Slovenia* (n 157) *passim.*
[160] Although distinct concepts, acquiescence (tacit recognition of a situation) and estoppel (precluding a state from making a claim that is inconsistent with its previous conduct in connection therewith) are essentially two expressions of the same principle. See R Jennings,

70   3 *Private Rights in Land and Maritime Delimitation*

doctrines adhere to the general principle of consistency, according to which a state must 'maintain towards a given factual or legal situation an attitude consistent with that which it was known to have adopted with regard to the same circumstances on previous occasions'.[161]

Based on the above, international judges have systematically affirmed that a boundary can be established not only by an explicit agreement between the states concerned but also by tacit recognition, which qualifies as acquiescence.[162] Tacit recognition exists when a state adopts a passive stance (eg does not protest) towards its neighbour's sovereign acts (eg creation of private rights) along the claimed boundary line.[163] The importance of acquiescence is not limited to its role in evidencing the boundary's location but extends into the sphere of substantive law, as it creates title for the invoking state.[164]

As stressed in the *Temple of Preah Vihear* and *Rann of Kutch* cases, the tacit acceptance of a state's sovereign acts by its neighbour creates an environment of stability and finality, akin to that arising from an explicit boundary agreement.[165] A subsequent objection by the acquiescing state is precluded (estopped) as being contradictory to its previous position and detrimental to its relationship with its neighbour.[166] The acquiescing state's behaviour is not subject to any particular conditions of duration, but the state must have remained passive before the case goes to litigation. As explained by Judge Alfaro, '[p]assiveness in front of given facts is the most general form of

---

> The Acquisition of Territory in International Law (Manchester University Press 1963) 45; H Thirlway, 'The Law and Procedure of the International Court of Justice: Part Two' (1990) 62 British Yearbook of International Law 30. See also Judge Fitzmaurice in *Temple of Preah Vihear* (n 63) 62.

[161]   I McGibbon, 'Estoppel in International Law' (1958) 7 ICLQ 468, 512; E Luard, *The International Regulation of Frontier Disputes* (Thames & Hudson 1970) 182.

[162]   *Question of Jaworzina (Polish-Czechoslovakian Frontier)* (Advisory Opinion) PCIJ Rep Series B No 8 (1923) 20; *Temple of Preah Vihear* (n 63) 21, 39ff (Separate Opinion of Judge Alfaro, who provides an excellent analysis of the doctrine of acquiescence citing various international precedents); *Arbitration between India and Pakistan for the Indo-Pakistan Western Boundary (Rann of Kutch) (India v Pakistan)* (1968) 71ff, 346, 440–54.

[163]   In accordance with the principle *qui tacet consentire videtur, si loqui debuisset ac potuisset* (one who is silent when they ought to have spoken and was able to is taken to agree).

[164]   *Temple of Preah Vihear* (n 63) 39; *Rann of Kutch* (n 162) 450; Jennings (n 160) 50.

[165]   *Temple of Preah Vihear* (n 63) 34; *Rann of Kutch* (n 162) 449–450.

[166]   In accordance with the principle *venire contra factum proprium non valet* (no one may set themselves in contradiction to their own previous conduct). G Schwarzenberger, 'Title to Territory: Response to a Challenge' (1957) 51 AJIL 308, 316: 'The pliability of recognition as a general device of international law makes recognition an eminently suitable means for the purpose of establishing the validity of a territorial claim in relation to other States. However weak a title may be, and irrespective of any other criterion, recognition estops the State which has recognized the title from contesting its validity at any future time.'

3.3 *Delimitation by a Court or Tribunal*

acquiescence or tacit consent. Failure of a State to assert its right ... can only mean abandonment to that right."[167]

Consequently, a line determined according to the private rights that have been granted by a state in the disputed area may constitute a valid boundary line if it has not elicited any reaction from the other state before the commencement of dispute settlement proceedings.

3.3.1.3 Private Rights in Support of *Effectivités*

The third, and most common, legal basis on which private rights affect a delimitation ruling is the doctrine of *effectivités*. This refers to the effective exercise of a state's authoritative powers over a specific territory,[168] and it is mainly invoked when a state asserts that it possesses sovereignty over the entire disputed area, as opposed to claiming a specific boundary line.

As explained earlier, land delimitation rests on the principle that a specific territory can belong to only one state – the state possessing the stronger title.[169] In numerous cases, international courts have affirmed that, in the absence of a title (eg a delimitation treaty), the execution of authoritative acts by a state, such as the granting of private rights in the disputed area, is as good as title.[170] The only requirements are an intention on the part of the state to act *à titre de souverain* (as a sovereign) and a manifestation of its exercise of authority.[171] Exercise of authority can manifest as political, administrative or military control over the area in question, or the exploration of natural recourses.[172]

---

[167] *Temple of Preah Vihear* (n 63) 38 (Separate Opinion of Judge Alfaro).

[168] *Nicaragua v Honduras* (n 47).

[169] See Chapter 2, Section 2.4.

[170] The importance of the principle of effective possession (or effective jurisdiction) has been systematically recognized by international judges since the nineteenth century. See *Arbitration Concerning the Definite Fixing of the Italian-Swiss Frontier at the Place Called Alpe de Cravairola (Italy/Switzerland)* (1874) 150ff; *Island of Palmas Case (Netherlands/USA)* (Arbitral Award) (1928) 839; *Burkina Faso/Mali* (n 41) para 63; *Rann of Kutch* (n 162) 547ff; *Case Concerning Kasikili/Sedudu Island (Botswana/Namibia)* [1999] ICJ Rep 1045, 1094; *Cameroon v Nigeria* (n 150) 353. See also, Case Concerning Sovereignty over Certain Frontier Land *(Belgium/Netherlands)* (1959) ICJ Rep 209, 229; *Libyan Arab Jamahiriya/Chad* (n 150) paras 75–76, where the principle of effective possession was acknowledged by the judges, although it was not discussed in detail, as a valid treaty was found to exist.

[171] *Legal Status of Eastern Greenland (Denmark v Norway)* (1933) PCIJ Rep Series A/B No 53 (1933) 45–46; *El Salvador/Honduras* (n 47) 388–99. Also, whether the state is acting in good or bad faith is irrelevant; L Oppenheim, *International Law: A Treatise*, vol 1 (6th edn, Longmans 1947) 527.

[172] N Hill, *Claims to Territory in International Law and Relations* (OUP 1945) 156–57; Y Blum, *Historic Titles in International Law* (Springer 1965) 101, 110, 118, cited in BT Sumner,

72   3 *Private Rights in Land and Maritime Delimitation*

No specific duration is required, but the acts in question must be of a public rather than a purely private nature.[173]

As stressed in *Eritrea/Yemen (First Stage)*, the mere conduct of a private activity (eg fishing) by a state's nationals in the disputed area does not in itself suggest the presence of state sovereignty. To be evidence of that, the activity must be accompanied by state regulations (eg licensing, control, enforcement).[174] As similarly stressed in *Botswana v Namibia*, the occupation of the disputed area by a native tribe and the conduct of agricultural or grazing activities by its members prior to the establishment of any public administration in that region are purely private, not sovereign, acts.[175] However, these private acts can create title if subsequently ratified by the invoking state.[176]

Hence, insofar as the rights of private actors in the disputed area are subject to state control – be it at the time of their creation or upon subsequent ratification by public authorities – they can establish sovereignty for the invoking state. Once the criteria of *effectivités* are met, the invoking state can claim possession of a title, which is valid *erga omnes*.[177] When both states rely on private rights existing in the same area, the court's decision will be made on the basis of the more convincing evidence.[178]

The application of *effectivités* also extends to the delimitation of bays. Although located in the ocean, bays are considered as internal waters and, as such, they are part of the land held by states. Hence, the regulation of private rights in those waters can constitute an entitlement to sovereignty for the invoking party, as was affirmed in *Croatia v Slovenia* in connection with the regulation of fishing and other private activities by the states in the Bay of Piran.[179]

To conclude, this section has confirmed that private rights play an equally important role in land delimitation rulings as they do in land delimitation treaties.

'Territorial Disputes at the International Court of Justice' (2004) 53 Duke Law Journal 1779, 1788.

[173] *El Salvador/Honduras* (n 47) 399. See also Schwarzenberger (n 166) 316.

[174] *Eritrea/Yemen Arbitration (First Stage: Territorial Sovereignty and Scope of Dispute)* (2001) 40(4) ILM 900, paras 313–16. See also *Case Concerning Sovereignty over Pulau Ligitan and Pulau Sipadan (Indonesia/Malaysia)* [2002] ICJ Rep 625, 685; *Nicaragua v Honduras* (n 47) 688; *Territorial and Maritime Dispute between Nicaragua and Colombia (Nicaragua v Colombia)* [2012] ICJ Rep 624, 656ff.

[175] *Botswana/Namibia* (n 170) 1105–106.

[176] ibid.

[177] *Island of Palmas* (n 170) 840; Schwarzenberger (n 166) 322.

[178] *Rann of Kutch* (n 162); *Eritrea/Yemen* (n 174); *El Salvador/Honduras* (n 47).

[179] *Croatia v Slovenia* (n 157) 273–79.

3.3.2 *The Restricted Role of Private Rights in Maritime Delimitation Rulings*

As in land disputes, the judges in maritime cases first examine whether a boundary agreement is already in place. But as the history of boundary-making is much newer in the ocean, such agreements are rarely found.[180] Hence, in most cases, judges construct the boundary line *de novo* or determine the principles of delimitation to be subsequently followed by the states involved.

As on land, states invoke various factors to sway the court's decision, including the presence of private rights in the disputed area. But compared to land rulings, the effect of private rights in maritime cases is much reduced. The present study observes that this has not always been the case, for courts' attitudes towards private rights shifted dramatically in the middle of the twentieth century.

3.3.2.1 The Importance of Private Rights in Early Delimitation Cases

Before the adoption of the first conventions of the sea in 1958, delimitation rulings were very few in number and only concerned the TS. Subscribing to the view that the TS is a land appurtenance, courts would apply land delimitation principles to this maritime space.

For example, in the famous *Grisbådarna Case* of 1909 between Norway and Sweden,[181] it was initially suggested that the boundary should follow a perpendicular line. However, as observed by the tribunal, that would be inconsistent with certain factors of human geography. In particular, a perpendicular line would cut across the Grisbådarna fishing banks, where Swedish nationals possessed almost exclusive rights to lobster fishing. Under this division, those private rights were threatened with reallocation to Norway. The panel pointed out that

> it is a well established principle of the law of nations that the state of things that actually exists and has existed for a long time should be changed as little as possible;
>
> this principle is especially applicable in the case of private interests which, once disregarded, cannot be effectively preserved by any manner of sacrifice on the part of the Government of which the parties are subjects.[182]

---

[180] eg *Cameroon v Nigeria* (n 150) for the first part of the maritime boundary; *Maritime Dispute (Peru v Chile)* [2014] ICJ Rep 3, where it was held that a maritime boundary existed (before 1954) by virtue of a tacit agreement between the parties on a distance of 80 M.

[181] *Arbitral Award in the Matter of Delimitation of a Certain Part of the Maritime Boundary between Norway and Sweden (Grisbådarna Case) (Norway v Sweden)* (1909) 11 RIAA 147,

[182] Unofficial English translation <www.worldcourts.com/pca/eng/decisions/1909.10.23_Norway_v_Sweden.pdf> accessed 28 February 2021, 6.

74   3 *Private Rights in Land and Maritime Delimitation*

To avoid redistributing the private rights in question, the tribunal decided to adjust the boundary line in compliance with the principle *quieta non movere*, awarding the Grisbådarna bank to Sweden.

In the *Fisheries Case* of 1951, the ICJ likewise paid special attention to the private fishing licences that had been granted by Norway in the waters claimed by the United Kingdom. In a dictum almost lifted from a land delimitation judgment, the Court found that the long-standing and regulatory nature of those licences gave Norway jurisdiction over the disputed waters. As explained by the judges, the fishing rights that those concessions had vested in Norway's inhabitants were not only vital to peoples' needs but they also attested to the ancient and peaceful usage of the area by Norway.[183] To preserve those private rights and the status quo in the disputed area, the Court decided in favour of Norway.

3.3.2.2 The Judicial Shift in Modern Delimitation Cases

Interestingly, the role of private rights in maritime delimitation started to decrease in the following decades with the establishment of the CS and the EEZ and the ensuing rise in the number of cases referred to international courts and tribunals.

1960S–1980S: PRIVATE RIGHTS IN EQUITABLE PRINCIPLES Broadly speaking, the period between the 1960s and 1980s was governed by the Geneva Conventions of 1958. During that period, international case law displayed a preference for the method of equitable principles.[184] Under this method, delimitation is affected by any factors that may lead to an equitable result. As generally noted by judges, there is no exhaustive list of, or limit to, those factors.[185] On the contrary, they 'evolve from physical, mathematical, historical, political, economic or other facts . . . and from the characteristics peculiar to the region'.[186]

In practice, however, the factors recognized by courts during this period related mainly to coastal geography while those unrelated to geography

---

[183] *Fisheries Case (UK v Norway)* [1951] ICJ Rep 116, 142–43.
[184] See *North Sea Continental Shelf Cases* (n 100); *Case Concerning the Continental Shelf (Tunisia/Libyan Arab Jamahiriya)* [1982] ICJ Rep 18; and other cases cited in this section. An exception was *Libyan Arab Jamahiriya/Malta* (n 100), where the method of corrective equidistance was applied.
[185] *North Sea Continental Shelf Cases* (n 100) para 93. See also *Delimitation on the Continental Shelf between the United Kingdom of Great Britain and Northern Ireland and the French Republic (UK v France)* (Arbitral Award) (1977) paras 83–84.
[186] *Guinea v Guinea-Bissau* (n 146) para 89.

3.3 *Delimitation by a Court or Tribunal*

were treated with great scepticism. In the words of Collins and Rogoff, the tendency in maritime delimitation decisions at that time 'may be viewed as a progression of attempts to reduce the factors that may be considered' in the delimitation process.[187]

In particular, international courts have systematically rejected private fishing activities in the disputed area, on the grounds that they are purely economic factors extraneous to delimitation. As explained by judges, it is not the purpose of delimitation to refashion geography or compensate states for nature's inequalities.[188] Therefore, economic factors cannot affect the boundary's course, unless ignoring them would have 'catastrophic repercussions' for the livelihood of a state's population.[189]

Although it is true that the principle of distributive justice does not apply in maritime delimitation, the courts' reasoning is dubious for two main reasons. First, without a clear definition of the term 'catastrophic', it is unclear what justification there was for disregarding fishing rights in past cases. The potential reallocation of fishing rights caused by maritime delimitation may have serious (if not 'catastrophic') economic consequences for the persons affected if the absorbing state refuses to preserve them.[190] Hence, it is puzzling why judges rejected those factors as irrelevant to delimitation.

Second, it is overly simplistic to dismiss private fishing rights as purely resource-related or economic factors. Aside from their relation to natural resources and their importance for the people's economic needs, private fishing rights are predominantly legal factors. They are granted by states pursuant to their domestic rules and create a legal relationship between the granting state and the right-holder. The rejection of such active rights during the delimitation process and their subsequent reallocation may have serious legal implications, similar to those identified in *Grisbådarna* and *Fisheries* cases.[191] There were admittedly some early delimitation cases in which

---

[187] E Collins and M Rogoff, 'The Gulf of Maine Case and the Future of Ocean Boundary Delimitation' (1986) 38 Maine Law Review 1, 39.

[188] *North Sea Continental Shelf Cases* (n 100) para 91; *Libyan Arab Jamahiriya/Malta* (n 100) para 46.

[189] *Delimitation of the Maritime Boundary in the Gulf of Maine Area (Canada/ United States)* [1984] ICJ Rep 292, 341–42; *Libyan Arab Jamahiriya/Malta* (n 100) 41, 46; *Guinea v Guinea-Bissau* (n 146) 302.

[190] One of the most prominent scholars who first objected to the practice of courts of rejecting economic and other non-geographical factors as irrelevant to maritime delimitation was Malcolm Evans. See M Evans, 'Maritime Delimitation and Expanding Categories of Relevant Circumstances' (1991) 40 ICLQ 1; Evans, 'Maritime Boundary Delimitation: Where Do We Go from Here?' in D Freestone, R Barnes and D Ong (eds), *The Law of the Sea: Progress and Prospects* (OUP 2006) 156–59.

[191] These implications are discussed in Section 3.4.

76   3 *Private Rights in Land and Maritime Delimitation*

international courts showed great sensitivity towards private fishing rights, but that stance was abandoned in subsequent cases.

Much the same can be said of the treatment of oil concessions in the disputed area during this period. Like fishing rights, they were disregarded as irrelevant to delimitation.[192] In the famous *North Sea Continental Shelf Cases*, the judges initially stressed that the need to keep deposits unified is a factor to which states should give consideration during pre-delimitation negotiations.[193] However, the panel eventually decided that this was not a special circumstance that should affect the boundary's course, as the 'question of natural resources is less one of delimitation than of eventual exploitation'.[194] As a result, the private oil concessions granted by Denmark and the Netherlands and for which they had followed the course of the median line were ignored. Having rejected the method of equidistance, the Court found it unnecessary to pay any attention to the (median) line traced by the oil permits.[195]

In other cases, it was held that a line of permits could not be treated as a boundary line, unless its presence was 'consistent' and 'unequivocal'.[196] However, it remains unclear what exactly was meant by this, as the line of concessions invoked as a basis for the boundary line was dismissed without any indication of what legal elements would have made its presence consistent and unequivocal. It may therefore be questioned whether the decision to reject this factor was well founded.

By way of exception, the only occasion when concessions mattered in maritime delimitation was in *Tunisia/Libyan Arab Jamahiriya* in 1982.[197] In that case, the Court accepted that the circumstances which can affect the process of delimitation are not limited to geography but can also include the conduct of states in the area, as well as their historic rights and economic interests. In relation to state conduct, particular attention was paid to the line of petroleum permits and oil wells which existed in the disputed area. According to the judges, that line was a de facto maritime limit and therefore had to be followed during the process of delimitation. Hence, the Court relied heavily on the line of adjoining concessions when determining the boundary's

---

[192]   *Gulf of Maine* (n 189) 309–12; *Libyan Arab Jamahiriya/Malta* (n 100) 29; *Guinea v Guinea-Bissau* (n 146) paras 122–24. See also R Meese, 'The Relevance of the Granting of Oil Concessions in a Maritime Delimitation: The Jurisprudence of the International Court of Justice' [2003] 2 OGEL <www.ogel.org>.
[193]   *North Sea Continental Shelf Cases* (n 100) 51.
[194]   ibid 45–46, 12.
[195]   ibid 24–46 67–85 (Separate Opinion of Judge Jessup).
[196]   *Gulf of Maine* (n 189) 309–12; *Libyan Arab Jamahiriya/Malta* (n 100) 29.
[197]   *Tunisia/Libyan Arab Jamahiriya* (n 184).

3.3 *Delimitation by a Court or Tribunal* 77

course. The decision was treated as an untimely departure from existing case law and the judges were strongly criticized by their colleagues for assuming an activist role and failing to follow the approach taken in previous cases.[198]

To avoid the risk of a similar reaction, courts in subsequent cases adopted a consistently harsh approach towards oil concessions.[199] A characteristic example is the *Gulf of Maine*, a case largely concerned with Canadian oil concessions in waters claimed by the United States. While the judges initially acknowledged that the United States 'showed a certain imprudence in maintaining silence after Canada had issued the first permits', they eventually concluded that an 'attempt to attribute to such silence ... legal consequences taking the concrete form of an estoppel, seems to be going too far'.[200] However, the fact that the Court rejected a line of concessions that had been respected by the United States for eight continuous years, after accepting one that had lasted for six years in the case between Tunisia and Libya, raises serious concerns over the criteria applied by international judges in making their decisions on state conduct.

The judges' strict stance on oil concessions was maintained in *Libyan Arab Jamahiriya v Malta*, leading to a legal paradox. Although, when delimiting the CS, the ICJ was initially prepared to take into account those factors which are 'pertinent to the institution of the continental shelf as it has developed within the law',[201] it refused to consider the parties' oil concessions in the disputed area. In so doing, it appeared unfortunately to overlook the fact that petroleum exploration has been the driving force behind the establishment of the CS under international law, and the *raison d'être* for the delimitation of this maritime zone.[202]

---

[198] See dissenting opinions of Judges Gros, Evensen and Oda. See also Cottier (n 142) 284.

[199] This stance has been criticized in the literature for ignoring the fact that the establishment of maritime boundaries is inextricably linked to the exploration of natural resources by states. Access to the ocean's resources (and primarily petroleum) was the *raison d'être* of Truman proclamation and the subsequent fixing of the limits of maritime zones in UNCLOS. It is also observed that the process of maritime delimitation is usually initiated in areas that are rich, or believed to be rich, in hydrocarbons (eg North Sea, Arab Gulf). After all, 'a Continental Shelf without natural resource is of no legal or economic value in international law to the concerned States'. Joy Ejegi, 'What Are the Mechanisms for Resolving Disputes between Countries with Transboundary Resources? A Closer Examination' [2005] 2 OGEL <www.ogel.org>.

[200] *Gulf of Maine* (n 189) paras 140–48.

[201] *Libyan Arab Jamahiriya/Malta* (n 100) para 48.

[202] It is clear from the Truman proclamation, as well as the proclamations of the CS of other States in the mid-twentieth century, that one of the main reasons for the establishment of this maritime zone was coastal states' access to hydrocarbons in the seabed. See Proclamation of US President Harry Truman on the policy of the United States with respect to the natural

78   3 *Private Rights in Land and Maritime Delimitation*

According to some judges and scholars, this strict stance taken towards oil concessions situated in disputed areas seeks to prevent states from extending claims in the CS through the doctrine of *effectivités*.[203] Although this doctrine is widely accepted in land delimitation, it does not apply in the ocean. The reason is that all coastal states possess rights in the CS *ipso facto* and *ab initio* – so the existence of such rights does not depend on their being claimed or on occupation.[204]

This justification is not entirely convincing. Firstly, the fear of occupation of the seabed is not real, as both states possess a legal entitlement in the shared area pending delimitation.[205] As explained in this study, delimitation is not the source of states' authoritative powers in the ocean – these exist already under international law.[206] Its effect is rather to give priority to one of the two vying titles. The presence of private fishing or petroleum rights in the region can inform this decision.

Secondly, delimitation rests on the principle of state consent, which is the legal basis of acquiescence and estoppel. There is no apparent reason why these doctrines should not apply in maritime cases which involve private rights like petroleum permits. Of course, that is not to say that all lines of oil concessions should be upgraded to maritime boundaries. However, the unchallenged presence of petroleum permits in the shared maritime area before the initiation of judicial proceedings should qualify as tacit agreement between the states concerned regarding the boundary's location. In the words of Professor Evans, in boundary delimitation there are times when state 'actions speak louder than words' and therefore they should be given greater attention by the judges.[207]

1990S–PRESENT: PRIVATE RIGHTS IN CORRECTIVE EQUIDISTANCE The period from 1990s onwards displays some differences compared to its predecessor. UNCLOS, adopted by almost all states, replaced the Geneva Conventions of 1958. Also, the method of equitable principles was superseded

---

      resources of the subsoil and the seabed of the continental shelf (28 September 1945); Proclamation of Argentina on the Epicontinental Sea (5 December 1946); Declaration of the Maritime Zone of Chile, Ecuador and Peru (Santiago Declaration) (18 August 1952). See also Chapter 2.

[203] *Tunisia/Libyan Arab Jamahiriya* (n 184) 318–19 (Dissenting Opinion of Judge Evensen); P Weil, *The Law of Maritime Delimitation: Reflections* (Grotius 1989) 92; Tanaka (n 96) 211.

[204] *North Sea Continental Shelf Cases* (n 100) para 19.

[205] Provided their claims are based on the rights vested in them by international law.

[206] See Chapter 2.

[207] M Evans, *Relevant Circumstances and Maritime Delimitation* (Clarendon 1989) 220.

3.3 Delimitation by a Court or Tribunal

by that of modified equidistance.[208] This method consists of three steps: first, a provisional equidistance line is first drawn; next, the judges examine whether any circumstances justify shifting it; and lastly, the judges perform a disproportionality test to make sure that there is no significant inequality between the areas awarded to the states concerned. This method has been hailed in both scholarship and case law as a guarantee of objectivity and predictability in maritime delimitation.[209] As a consequence, it is resolutely applied by courts 'unless there are compelling reasons that make it unfeasible' in a particular case.[210]

Yet, the disregard for private rights in maritime delimitation continued and became almost standard practice in modern cases. When applying corrective equidistance, judges only take account of geographical factors, such as the concavity or convexity and the length of the states' coasts, or the presence of islands in the area. Non-geographical factors, on the other hand, are rejected almost by reflex.

For example, judges continue to treat fishing activities as extraneous 'economic' factors irrelevant to delimitation, unless doing so would cause 'catastrophic' repercussions for the people in the area.[211] But, as in previous cases, they fail to explain the exact meaning of this condition.

To date, the only case in which fishing rights have affected maritime delimitation is *Jan Mayen* in 1993. At first, the factors invoked by the parties in relation to security, the size of their population and their socio-economic interests in the disputed area were rejected by the Court as irrelevant. However, particular attention was paid to the fishing activities of the states' nationals. The Court acknowledged that the fishing of capelin was vital to the livelihood and the well-being of the states' populations. It also observed that

---

[208] See *Qatar v Bahrain* (n 98); *Guyana v Suriname* (n 94); *Maritime Delimitation in the Black Sea (Romania v Ukraine)* [2009] ICJ Rep 61; *Dispute Concerning Delimitation of the Maritime Boundary between Bangladesh and Myanmar in the Bay of Bengal (Bangladesh/Myanmar)* (2012) 51 ILM 840, ITLOS Reports 2012, 4; *Croatia v Slovenia* (n 157); *Dispute Concerning Delimitation of the Maritime Boundary between Ghana and Côte d'Ivoire in the Atlantic Ocean (Ghana/Côte d'Ivoire)* (Judgment) (2017) ITLOS.

[209] *Libyan Arab Jamahiriya/Malta* (n 100) para 45; Tanaka (n 98) 123; S Jiuyong, 'Maritime Delimitation in the Jurisprudence of the International Court of Justice' (2010) 9 Chinese Journal of International Law 271.

[210] *Romania v Ukraine* (n 208) [116]. Such an exception was *Nicaragua v Honduras* (n 47), where the parties' complex geographical situation and the presence of third states in the area favoured the old geometric bisector method.

[211] *Eritrea/Yemen* (n 145) 346ff; *Arbitration between Newfoundland and Labrador and Nova Scotia (Newfoundland and Labrador v Nova Scotia)* (2002) 61; *Arbitration between Barbados and Trinidad and Tobago (Barbados v Trinidad and Tobago)* (2006) Award 73; *Arbitration in the Bay of Bengal (Bangladesh v India)* (2014) 124.

80   3 *Private Rights in Land and Maritime Delimitation*

the provisional median line would attribute to Norway the whole area of the parties' overlapping fishing claims. To avoid this inequitable result, the Court shifted the line eastwards so that Denmark received a larger part of the area than it would have done if the original median line had been followed.[212]

Although a majority decision of fourteen to one, the ruling was strongly criticized by panel members themselves (both dissenting and non-dissenting) and by scholars for departing from previous decisions on the role of non-geographical factors in maritime delimitation and for 'sending strong echoes of distributive justice'.[213]

To avoid similar criticism, courts never again allowed private fishing rights to affect a boundary's course.[214] According to the view that currently prevails among judges, the presence of such rights in contested waters and the drawing of an international boundary are entirely independent of each other.[215] Even when those rights are long-standing and clearly threatened with reallocation, they are considered as mere economic factors that have no effect on the boundary's course.[216]

Yet, as explained above, it is problematic and hardly justified to treat fishing rights as a 'resource-related' or purely 'economic' – as opposed to a legal – factor. International case law's disregard for private fishing rights often sparks reactions from local communities. An example is the objection of Colombian fishermen towards the 2012 delimitation ruling of the ICJ in *Nicaragua v Colombia*.[217]

---

[212]   *Case Concerning Maritime Delimitation in the Area between Greenland and Jan Mayen (Denmark v Norway)* [1993] ICJ Rep 38, 72ff.

[213]   See Declaration of Vice-President Oda Separate Opinions of Judges Schwebel and Weeramantry and Dissenting Opinion of Judge Fischer; R Churchill, 'The Greenland-Jan Mayen Case and its Significance for the International Law of Maritime Boundary Delimitation' (1994) 9 International Journal of Marine and Coastal Law 1, 21–22; G Politakis, 'The 1993 Jan Mayen Judgment: The End of Illusions?' (1994) 41 Netherlands International Law Review 1.

[214]   It could be thought that the delimitation judgment between Peru and Chile departs from this trend. In this case, the ICJ acknowledged that a maritime boundary already existed (before 1954 or so) for part of the disputed area by virtue of a tacit agreement between the parties. This agreement stemmed from, inter alia, the parties' diplomatic statements and their fishing and law enforcement activities in the area. However, state conduct was considered by judges only at the beginning of the decision, which concerned the presence of a boundary agreement. By contrast, no weight was attached to private rights (eg as relevant factors) during the actual delimitation process, which concerned the boundary's course. Besides, four dissenting judges expressed doubts about the existence of a tacit agreement. *Peru v Chile* (n 180) Dissenting Opinion of Judges Xue, Gaja, Bhandari and Judge ad hoc Orrego Vicuna.

[215]   *Eritrea/Yemen* (n 145) paras 109–10.

[216]   ibid, paras 47–74.

[217]   M Aznar, 'The Human Factor in Territorial Disputes' in M Kohen and M Hebie (eds), *Research Handbook on Territorial Disputes in International Law* (Edward Elgar 2018) 291.

3.3 *Delimitation by a Court or Tribunal*

With regard to oil concessions, judges maintain that a line of existing permits cannot be taken into account in delimitation proceedings, unless it constitutes a tacit agreement between the states as to the boundary's exact location.[218] This would appear to suggest that a line of concessions can affect the boundary's course on the basis of acquiescence. However, in none of those cases have courts indicated what legal requirements must be met for a tacit boundary agreement to exist. Despite the great number of disputes involving oil permits, no court has ever thoroughly explained why such an agreement was not found to be in place.

Absent a clear explanation as to what constitutes a tacit agreement, the repeated rejection of private permits from the process of delimitation is not based on convincing legal reasons but rather on the judges' desire to follow previous case law. This means that a line of concessions risks being rejected even if it would qualify as an indication of the boundary's location under the doctrine of acquiescence.

For example, in the *Eritrea/Yemen Arbitration (Second Stage: Maritime Delimitation)*, while it was initially acknowledged that the presence of oil concessions could militate in favour of following the median line in the disputed area, in the end it was concluded that the purpose of delimitation is not to promote petroleum operations but to define enduring boundaries.[219] Hence, even if the method of equidistance could be used, the boundary was constructed on the basis of geometry rather than the line of concessions coinciding with equidistance.

Likewise, in *Guyana v Suriname*, although the tribunal acknowledged that the disputed area had a high concentration of petroleum activities, as both parties had been granting oil concessions between 1977 and 2004, it chose to follow the 'marked reluctance of international courts and tribunals to accord significance to the oil practice of parties in the determination of the delimitation line'.[220] Although the application of equidistance led to a result that largely matched the line of Guyana's permits in the disputed area, it cut through one of the state's eastern oil blocks.[221] This effect could have been

---

[218] Delimitation of Maritime Areas between Canada and the French Republic *(St Pierre et Miquelon)* (Arbitral Award) (1992) paras 89–91; *Newfoundland and Labrador v Nova Scotia* (n 211) para 3.4; *Cameroon v Nigeria* (n 150) para 304; *Barbados and Trinidad v Tobago* (n 211) paras 361–64; *Nicaragua v Honduras* (n 47) paras 247, 253–58; *Nicaragua v Colombia* (n 174) 705; *Romania v Ukraine* (n 208) para 198. See also Meese (n 192).

[219] *Eritrea/Yemen* (n 145) 354–55.

[220] *Guyana v Suriname* (n 94) 122–25.

[221] See 'CGX Energy Pleased with Guyana/Suriname Resolution' (*Rigzone*, 21 September 2007) <www.rigzone.com/news/oil_gas/a/50517/cgx_energy_pleased_with_guyanasuriname_resolution/> accessed 31 March 2021.

82   3 *Private Rights in Land and Maritime Delimitation*

avoided if oil concessions were recognized by international jurisprudence as factors that could shift or adjust the provisional equidistance line.

A much stricter approach towards oil permits was adopted in the delimitation case between Ghana and Côte d'Ivoire in 2017. The applicant state, Ghana, claimed that the maritime boundary with its neighbour in the West Atlantic Ocean should be based on equidistance. As evidence, Ghana invoked a series of oil permits that both states had granted to oil companies during the previous fifty years and which had followed the equidistance principle without any protest from either side.[222] The claimant argued that the long-standing presence of this concession line was a tacit boundary agreement of the kind that could affect maritime delimitation according to case law.[223]

The Special Chamber of ITLOS accepted that delimitation should be effected by the well-established method of equidistance. However, it based its decision on reasons of geometry and coastal geography, rejecting the evidence put forward by Ghana in support of the presence of a tacit agreement. Although the judges observed that both sides' permits conformed to equidistance, they concluded that 'oil practice, no matter how consistent it may be, cannot in itself establish the existence of a tacit agreement on a maritime boundary'.[224] Rather, these acts were simply 'the manifestation of the caution exercised by the Parties' pending delimitation.[225] It added that '[t]o equate oil concession limits with a maritime boundary would be equivalent to penalizing a State for exercising such caution and prudence'.[226] Hence, although the boundary which the Special Chamber drew was almost identical to the line claimed by Ghana, and although all of Ghana's active oil permits in the disputed area were eventually secured from reallocation, their protection was incidental rather than purposeful.

To comply with previous case law, the Special Chamber ruled out the possibility of legally valid private rights having any role in maritime delimitation, even if those rights were clear evidence of equidistance.[227] The generalization that oil practice could not qualify as tacit agreement took the reluctance with which case law treated private exploratory rights to an even higher level, eliminating any chance of those rights affecting maritime

---

[222]   *Ghana/Côte d'Ivoire* (n 208) 21ff, 33ff.
[223]   ibid 40ff.
[224]   ibid, para 215.
[225]   [ibid, quoting *Sovereignty over Pulau Ligitan and Pulau Sipadan (Indonesia/Malaysia)* [2002] ICJ Rep 625, 664, para 79.
[226]   ibid, para 225.
[227]   ibid, paras 211–28, 468–79.

delimitation. It remains to be seen whether international courts will maintain this stance in subsequent cases, but in the meantime states can be expected to be more cautious about basing their boundary claims on oil concessions.

It is regrettable that a wish to avoid criticism should have led judges to follow the previous practice of rejecting non-geographical factors, given that this may be to the detriment of legally valid private rights. Again, that is not to say that all concession lines in disputed waters should play a role in delimitation. But in certain cases, these legal factors should be accepted by courts, either as evidence of the boundary's location or as factors that can shift the course of the provisional equidistance line.

In sum, the above observations show that in maritime delimitation rulings, as in maritime delimitation treaties, private rights have little impact, irrespective of the chosen delimitation method (equitable principles, equidistance) or applicable convention on the law of the sea (Geneva Conventions 1958, UNCLOS).

3.4 ASSESSMENT OF STATE AND JUDICIAL PRACTICE

Whether in interstate treaties or judicial rulings, private rights play a differing role in land and maritime delimitation. While they have an increasingly important place on land, their role in the ocean is becoming evermore reduced or even absent. This antithesis has an impact on international law and private interests, which is analysed in the following paragraphs.

3.4.1 *Absence of an International Custom on Land and at Sea*

This chapter has demonstrated that there is a consistent state practice of protecting private rights on land against potential reallocation caused by delimitation. A question that arises is whether this practice can give rise to a rule of customary law.

It is widely accepted in legal theory (and has so far never been denied in case law) that bilateral treaties can contribute to the formation of custom concerning certain matters of a general nature, such as the application of a specific delimitation method.[228] A similar case could be made for the role of private rights in delimitation, provided the two constituent elements of custom

---

[228] I Brownlie, *Principles of Public International Law* (7th edn, OUP 2008) 13; H Thirlway, *The Sources of International Law* (OUP 2014) 72; R Baxter, 'Treaties and Customs' (1970) 129 Collected Courses of the Hague Academy of International Law 24, 81. A similar claim is made in relation to maritime delimitation treaties. See Tanaka (n 98) 132.

84   3 *Private Rights in Land and Maritime Delimitation*

(general state practice and *opinio juris*) are present.[229] The evidence allowing their presence to be confirmed or denied will be discussed below.[230]

Firstly, to qualify as a custom, state practice must be sufficiently widespread and representative.[231] Overall, there is no rule of thumb as to what practice meets this criterion, as circumstances may vary between cases. According to legal theory and case law, the state practice does not need to be universal; rather, it must be followed by a substantial number of states without protest from others.[232] Whether the concerned states are 'major' or 'minor' international powers is also irrelevant, for all sovereign states are equal in international law.[233] If, however, the acts constituting the practice 'are divergent to the extent that no pattern of behaviour can be discerned, no general practice (and thus no corresponding rule of customary international law) can be said to exist'.[234]

The examples mentioned in this chapter, show that a great number of states all over the world have established their land boundaries in a way that secures the rights of individuals against reallocation and given that there is no evidence of state protest against this practice, it can be argued that the element of generality is met.

Secondly, for it to acquire the status of a custom, state practice must also be characterized by consistency. It may be difficult to prove such a vague element. According to the ICJ, neither 'complete consistency' nor 'absolute

---

[229]   International Law Commission (ILC), Draft Conclusions on Identification of Customary International Law, with Commentaries (2018) 123; *North Sea Continental Shelf Cases* (n 100) para 77; *Libyan Arab Jamahiriya/Malta* (n 100) para 27.

[230]   The evidence discussed here corresponds to that generally relied on by international courts and tribunals – though with a degree of discretion – to ascertain the existence of a custom. As observed in legal scholarship, 'the [ICJ] has no single approach to the formation of customary international law. This conclusion applies both to the evidence invoked by the Court and the actual methods employed in the process of finding of new customary rules.' B Schlütter, *Developments in Customary International Law: Theory and the Practice of the International Court of Justice and the International Ad Hoc Criminal Tribunals for Rwanda and Yugoslavia* (Brill 2010) 168.

[231]   ILC (n 229) 136.

[232]   Article 38(1)(b) ICJ Statute refers not to 'universal practice' but to 'general practice'. As stressed by the International Law Association (ILA) Committee on the Formation of Customary International Law, 'given the inherently informal nature of customary law, it is not to be expected, neither is it the case, that a precise number or percentage of States is required'. ILA, 'Statement of Principles Applicable to the Formation of General Customary International Law' (London Conference, 2000) 25. See also *Fisheries Jurisdiction Case (United Kingdom v Iceland)* [1974] ICJ Rep 3, 23–26; *North Sea Continental Shelf Cases* (n 100) 42; Brownlie (n 228) 8.

[233]   J Grant, *International Law Essentials* (Dundee University Press 2010) 17.

[234]   ILC (n 229) 137.

3.4 Assessment of State and Judicial Practice

rigorous conformity' is required.[235] Rather, the practice in question should be 'a constant and uniform usage' without much 'fluctuation and discrepancy' in the performance thereof.[236]

To confirm the presence of this element, one should ideally examine all land delimitation treaties signed from the twentieth century onwards – a task that goes beyond the limits of this study. However, the mere number of land delimitation treaties that reportedly respect private rights, compared to those that do not, can be perceived as evidence of consistency.

The question of duration needs clarifying. In the past, it was maintained that only practices that had been followed 'since time immemorial' or for 'over 100 years' could constitute a custom.[237] However, that is no longer the case. Arguably, 'some period of time must elapse for a general practice to emerge', as 'there is no such thing as instant custom'.[238] But no particular duration is required, provided that the state practice is widespread and consistent. The ICJ's judgment in the *North Sea Continental Shelf Cases* shows how quickly a state practice can become an international custom.[239] As the Court insisted, 'the passage of only a short period of time is not necessarily, or of itself, a bar to the formation of a new rule of customary international law'.[240]

Finally, the most important element of custom is *opinio juris* (*sive necessitatis*), or the fact that the practice in question is accepted by states as law.[241] This is what distinguishes custom from mere usage (non-binding state practice) or habit.[242] In general, the element of legal conviction may be quite problematic, as it is not until the conviction is formed that a customary rule

---

[235] *Case Concerning Military and Paramilitary Activities in and against Nicaragua (Nicaragua v United States of America)* [1986] ICJ Rep 14, para 186. See also *Fisheries Case* (n 183) 131.

[236] *Asylum Case (Columbia v Peru)* [1950] ICJ Rep 266, 276–77.

[237] Grant (n 233) 16; Brownlie (n 228) 7.

[238] ILC (n 229) 138.

[239] Until 1958 (when the Convention on the Continental Shelf was concluded), case law took the position that coastal states had no exclusive right to the natural resources of the CS, as these resources were open to appropriation by any state. Only eleven years later (in 1969), the ICJ affirmed that this right existed and was part of customary international law.

[240] *North Sea Continental Shelf Cases* (n 100) para 74.

[241] ICJ Statute, art 38(1)(b); *North Sea Continental Shelf Cases* (n 100) para 77. See also ILC (n 229) 139: *Opinio juris* 'is to be distinguished from other, extralegal motives for action, such as comity, political expediency or convenience: if the practice in question is motivated solely by such other considerations, no rule of customary international law is to be identified. ... Seeking to comply with a treaty obligation as a treaty obligation, much like seeking to comply with domestic law, is not acceptance as law for the purpose of identifying customary international law: practice undertaken with such intention does not, by itself, lead to an inference as to the existence of a rule of customary international law.'

[242] ILC (n 229) 126.

86   *3 Private Rights in Land and Maritime Delimitation*

comes into being.[243] As explained in the literature, however, acceptance of a certain practice as law does not necessarily mean that states feel that they are bound by an existing legal obligation.[244] Rather, *opinio juris* denotes that a certain practice is regarded by states as conforming to a useful and desirable rule – a rule that should exist.[245]

Yet the most challenging issue is how to prove this subjective element. Proof requires evidence of the states' intention to consider a particular practice as law, irrespective of whether this practice displays the elements of generality and consistency. There is no fixed line on the form such evidence should take. This has led scholars like Kelsen and Guggenheim to maintain that it is 'almost impossible' to identify the intention of states for purposes of proving the existence of custom.[246] Nonetheless, evidence of *opinio juris* can be in the form of, inter alia, public statements and official publications by states (eg maps), diplomatic correspondence, court decisions and treaty provisions.[247]

In delimitation treaties, the will of states to protect private rights from reallocation is reflected in the provisions on the boundary's location and its turning points, as well as in the provisions empowering the boundary commissioners to shift the line's originally agreed course. But whether states perceive this practice as law, rather than as an act of courtesy or morality, cannot be easily proven, unless they explicitly express this view in the treaty's text or its preparatory materials (*travaux préparatoires*) – as indeed happened in many of the land delimitation treaties discussed in this chapter.[248]

According to the learned jurist and international judge Hersch Lauterpacht, however, the difficulty of identifying *opinio juris* can be surmounted through a 'flexible interpretation' of the notion. As he explained, specific state behaviour 'pursued uniformly and constantly' may give rise to custom, 'provided that there is no clear intention to deny it the element of obligation'.[249] In this light, even acts of 'neighbourliness, reasonableness and accommodation, may, in

---

[243] See J Kammerhofer, 'Uncertainty in the Formal Sources of International Law: Customary International Law and Some of Its Problems' (2004) 15 European Journal of International Law 523.

[244] H Thirlway, *International Customary Law and Codification* (Sijhoff 1972) 53–54; Thirlway (n 160) 43. See also A D'Amato, *The Concept of Custom in International Law* (Cornell University Press 1971) 51.

[245] ibid.

[246] H Kelsen, 'Théorie du Droit International Coutumier' (1939) 1 Revue International de la Théorie du Droit 253, 264–66; P Guggenheim , *Traité de Droit International Public* (Librairie Georg 1953) 46–48, both cited in D'Amato (n 244) 52.

[247] ILC (n 229) 140.

[248] See Section 3.2.1.1.

[249] E Lauterpacht (ed), International Law: Being the Collected Papers of Hersch Lauterpacht, vol 1 (CUP 1970) 63.

3.4 Assessment of State and Judicial Practice

the interest of international stability and good faith, assume the complexion of binding international custom'.[250] As similarly stressed by Judge Tanaka in the *North Sea Continental Shelf Cases*, instead of trying to identify the subjective motives of states, greater attention should be given to the necessity of such a customary rule in the international community.[251] The same could be said of the practice of upholding private rights in land delimitation treaties.

The above analysis suggests that the systematic protection of private rights in land delimitation treaties is a potential source of (or at least contributes to the creation of) a customary rule, by which states will be bound when entering into a delimitation agreement.

The same cannot be said of the ocean. Firstly, the number of maritime boundaries that were actually designed or shifted in accordance with private rights is relatively small in relation to the total number of delimitation agreements that involve private rights. By contrast, a large number of treaties completely passed over the redistributing impact of the agreed boundary on existing private rights.

Secondly, even in cases where a maritime boundary was eventually adjusted, that was done mainly for economic rather than legal reasons. For example, the main reason why states have in the past agreed that their boundary should follow an existing oil concession was to avoid wasteful exploitation by keeping the deposit unified, rather than to secure their contractual relation with the operator. Likewise, fishing rights were upheld mainly to promote the states' economic development rather than secure the private interests in question.

Thirdly, the petroleum rights that have affected maritime delimitation were not always held by private actors.[252] On many occasions, operations were conducted by national oil companies (NOCs).[253] NOCs can be holders of commercial interests,[254] but also act as agents of their home states. In this light, it is unclear whether the attention paid to petroleum permits was aimed at protecting existing private interests or promoting the national and political interests of the home states.

---

[250] ibid 64.

[251] Dissenting Opinion 176.

[252] ibid.

[253] eg the companies operating in the Middle East. Even in the North Sea, companies like BP were still under state ownership or control at the time of delimitation.

[254] A Rawlings, 'The Rise of the National Oil Company: Implications for International Oil Companies' [2015] 6 OGEL <www.ogel.org>; S Marzuki, 'The Dynamism of Joint Operating Agreements Involving National Oil Companies' [2013] 4 OGEL <www.ogel.org>; M Kanervisto and F Pereira, 'National Oil Companies Operating in Upstream Petroleum Projects and Participating in Joint Operating Agreements' [2013] 4 OGEL <www.ogel.org>.

88   3 *Private Rights in Land and Maritime Delimitation*

The above suggests that, in contrast to land, there is no established state practice of protecting private rights against potential reallocation at sea. Despite the great (and ever-increasing) presence of private rights in contested waters, their impact on delimitation treaties is restricted and inconsistent. This hinders the creation of a customary rule obliging states to take account of private rights in maritime delimitation treaties.

The fact that state practice diverges in different settings can be criticized for legal and practical reasons. Although land boundaries are inextricably linked to issues of sovereignty and statehood, their creation is not linked solely to the interests of states; it can also be of benefit to the rights and needs of non-state actors situated in the area under delimitation. Yet, states pay little or no attention to private interests when making their maritime boundaries, even though these lines are *ipso facto* linked to operations traditionally conducted by non-State actors, such as fishing or petroleum exploration. Ultimately, the disparity between state practice on land and at sea hinders the establishment of a common customary rule that would oblige states to respect private rights in both settings.

3.4.2 *Absence of Coherent Case Law on Land and at Sea*

Aside from state practice, the position taken in case law towards private rights is also important for international law. It is recalled that Article 38(1) of the ICJ Statute, which enumerates the sources of international law, lists judicial decisions as 'a subsidiary means for the determination of international law'.[255] The drafting of this provision (and its almost identically worded predecessor in the Statute of the Permanent Court of Justice) provoked scepticism about the inclusion of judicial decisions in the sources of international law.[256] Yet, the rising number of judicial bodies and their importance in the international legal order have given case law a 'systemic role' in scholarship and practice.[257] Although not a formal source of law (as are international treaties, custom and general principles

---

[255] The listed sources of international law are: international treaties, custom, general principles of law, judicial decisions and the teachings of the most highly qualified publicists. However, it is argued that this list is not restrictive and that 'the drafting of Article 38 ... was not an act of creation, but of recording: Article 38 in itself is not the sources of sources.' Thirlway (n 228) 6, 10.

[256] M Andenas and JR Leiss, 'The Systemic Relevance of "Judicial Decisions" in Article 38 of the ICJ Statute' (2017) 77 ZaöRV 907, 925.

[257] ibid.

3.4 Assessment of State and Judicial Practice

of law), international judgments and arbitral awards qualify as material sources providing evidence of the existence of legally binding rules.[258] Hence, a question that arises is whether the case law of international courts and tribunals can mandate the protection of private rights in land and maritime delimitation.

In answering that question, consideration must first be given to whether jurisprudence affects the development of international law. At first glance, this might seem unlikely. International rules are generally made by states (by signing an international convention, following a specific practice that may evolve into international custom, or accepting a certain principle as an international rule).[259] On the contrary, judicial rulings are primarily concerned with the identification and interpretation of the international rules created by states.[260] What is more, the rule of *stare decisis* does not apply in international case law.[261] An international court or tribunal is free to depart from a previous ruling and follow its own approach.

However, this does not mean that international case law has no influence on international law, whether general or customary. As stressed in legal scholarship, the ICJ is 'fully capable' of making 'a valuable contribution both to the settlement of disputes and to the development of international law'.[262] In addition to performing its primary function of 'determining and clarifying' existing law, case law sheds 'fresh light on the considerations and principles on which the law is based in a manner to suggest the path for future development'.[263] Hence, '[t]he generation of legal normativity in the course

---

[258] Tanaka (n 96) 11, 18: 'The formal sources refer to the source from which the legal rule derives its legal validity, while material sources denote the provenance of the substantive content of the rule.' Yet, as stressed by Andenas and Leiss (n 256) 928, 'this two-level construction does not imply that judicial decisions share no features at all with the (formal) legal sources listed in (a)–(c) [of Article 38(1) ICJ Statute]'.

[259] G Guillaume, 'The Use of Precedent by International Judges and Arbitrators' (2011) 2 Journal of International Dispute Settlement 5.

[260] ibid.

[261] The rule of precedent applies in domestic (common) law. During the drawing up of the 1899 and 1907 conventions establishing the Permanent Court of Arbitration, consideration was given to expanding *stare decisis* in international law to allow controversial legal issues to be settled on the basis of previous decisions. However, when the Statute of the Permanent Court of International Justice (the predecessor of the ICJ) was drafted in 1922, it was made clear that 'judicial decisions state but do not create law'. Guillaume (n 259) 8.

[262] H Waldock, 'The International Court of Justice as Seen from the Bar and Bench' (1983) 54 British Yearbook of International Law 1, 4. See also A Alvarez-Jimenez, 'Methods for the Identification of Customary International Law in the International Court of Justice's Jurisprudence: 2000–2009' (2011) 60 ICLQ 681; 682–685.

[263] Waldock (n 262) 4.

90   3 *Private Rights in Land and Maritime Delimitation*

of international adjudication should be understood as judicial lawmaking and as an exercise of public authority'.[264]

The law-making capacity of international courts and tribunals is particularly evident in the context of delimitation, operating through the crystallization and development of the principles applying to the establishment of international boundaries.[265] This is for three main reasons.

Firstly, both on land and at sea, international law provides no fixed delimitation method. Rather, it is the judges hearing the case who will determine the exact location of the boundary by identifying the applicable international rules. That is clear in land delimitation cases, where international courts and tribunals have consistently clarified the role of *effectivités* or acquiescence in establishing title over a disputed territory.[266] Indeed, '[f]ar from being treated as a subsidiary source of international law, the judgments and opinions (of international courts) are treated as authoritative pronouncements of the current state of international law'.[267] Likewise, it is judicial rulings, rather than a convention or other source of law, that highlight the importance of stability and finality in international boundary-making.[268]

Even in the case of maritime delimitation, where the conventions of the sea do provide some guidance as to the outcome of delimitation, these rules are so indeterminate that they create great confusion as to which boundary line is the most suitable in a particular situation.[269] It is again judges and

---

[264]   A von Bogdandy and I Venzke, 'Beyond Dispute: International Judicial Institutions as Lawmakers' in A von Bogdandy and I Venzke (eds), *International Judicial Lawmaking: On Public Authority and Democratic Legitimation in Global Governance* (Springer 2012) 4.

[265]   See M Shaw, 'The International Court of Justice and the Law of Territory' in C Tams and J Sloan (eds), *The Development of International Law by the International Court of Justice* (OUP 2013); V Lowe and A Tzanakopoulos, 'The Development of the Law of the Sea by the International Court of Justice' in Tams and Sloan (eds), *The Development of International Law by the International Court of Justice* (OUP 2013); R Jennings, 'What Is International Law and How Do We Tell It When We See It?' (1981) 37 Annuaire Suisse de Droit International 59, 68; T Ginsburg, 'Bounded Discretion in International Judicial Lawmaking' (2004) 45 Virginia Journal of International Law 631; Tanaka (n 96) 214. As observed by Weil (for maritime delimitation), 'the legal conquest of maritime delimitation is not the work of either treaty or custom but of the courts which, far from being a subsidiary source of international law, here play the role of a primary and direct source of law, even if they have chosen modesty to ascribe the credit to customary law'. Weil (n 203) 8. As added by another learned scholar, 'it is not inaccurate to consider the impressive line of maritime boundary decisions as forming a common law in the classic sense'. J Charney, 'International Maritime Boundary Delimitation' (1994) 88 AJIL 227, 228.

[266]   R Higgins, *Problems and Process: International Law and How We Use It* (Clarendon 1994) 202.

[267]   ibid.

[268]   ibid.

[269]   That is why, according to jurisprudence, every delimitation case is a unicum.

3.4 *Assessment of State and Judicial Practice*

arbitrators who put an end to this uncertainty by interpreting the existing rules and identifying those state practices that can found new rules. That is particularly evident in the development of the three-step method of corrective equidistance.[270]

Secondly, although each ruling refers to a specific case, international courts and tribunals regularly cite previous decisions to support their judgements. This consistency among decisions creates a 'persuasive precedent' which, although not binding upon judges, can be influential for future cases.[271]

Thirdly, delimitation rulings can affect state practice – and therefore contribute to the development of international custom.[272] Judicial rulings bind only the states involved.[273] It is, however, common for third states (that were not parties to a decided case) to consider themselves bound by the legal principles they affirm through the force of custom. For example, states often invoke past delimitation rulings upholding certain customary norms to support their claims.[274] Even in delimitation treaties, where parties are free to apply any delimitation method, states tend to treat equidistance as a method dictated by case law on the basis of custom.

Having explained the influence that case law can have on international law in general, it remains to be seen whether it can create or evince a rule enjoining the protection of private rights during delimitation.

With regard to land delimitation cases, it was observed that private rights could determine the boundary's course through the doctrines of *uti possidetis*, acquiescence and *effectivités*. In those situations, private rights are secured against reallocation. The systematic consideration of private rights by courts and tribunals may create a persuasive precedent for their protection in future delimitation cases. It may also enhance the (already existing) state practice of upholding private rights in land delimitation treaties.

A strikingly opposing trend is observed in maritime delimitation cases, where private rights are unlikely to have an impact on the final ruling. As already noted, the judicial stance towards private rights in maritime delimitation has not always been so harsh. In early cases, where boundary-making was limited to the TS, international courts found it almost natural to follow the

---

[270] See *Qatar v Bahrain* (n 98) and other subsequent delimitation cases discussed earlier in this chapter.

[271] Guillaume (n 259) 9–12. The term 'persuasive precedent' is used in the literature in relation to the decisions of the ECtHR, but it can extend by analogy to the decisions of international courts. See F. Kirk, *EU Law* (Pearson Education 2012) 35.

[272] Alvarez-Jimenez (n 262) 683–85.

[273] ICJ Statute, art 59; ITLOS Statute, art 33; PCA Rules 2012, art 34.

[274] This often occurs in relation to states' obligations pending delimitation under Articles 74(3) and 83(3) UNCLOS or in the application of equidistance in delimitation.

92   3 *Private Rights in Land and Maritime Delimitation*

rules that applied in land delimitation. Hence, judges felt that international law imposed on them an obligation to take account of private rights during maritime delimitation and to preserve them from potential reallocation.

Things changed radically in the mid-twentieth century when judicial delimitation expanded to all maritime zones. Despite the absence of a fixed delimitation method in international law, courts made a serious attempt to standardize the delimitation process and the factors that affected their decisions. Although this lent a high degree of objectivity and predictability to the process of delimitation, it was at the expense of private interests. In almost every case during the last fifty years, courts have relied solely on factors of coastal geography for the delimitation of maritime boundaries. In contrast to land delimitation cases, private rights were treated as subordinate factors which could not affect the course of a maritime boundary.

Such systematic rejection of private rights in maritime disputes opened the way to their reallocation. This study has identified several instances where a reallocation of active private rights resulted from the stance taken by an international court or tribunal,[275] and it is to be expected that the same may occur in future cases.[276] The almost standard practice of judges disregarding private rights in maritime delimitation creates a 'precedent' cautioning against the consideration of private rights in subsequent cases.

This may in turn impact on state practice. States may consider that the protection of private rights at sea is not required by international law. This

---

[275] *North Sea Continental Shelf Cases* (n 100); *Tunisia/Libyan Arab Jamahiriya* (n 184); *Libyan Arab Jamahiriya/Malta* (n 100); *Gulf of Maine* (n 189); *Eritrea/Yemen* (n 145); *Guinea v Guinea-Bissau* (n 146); *Cameroon v Nigeria* (n 150); *Guyana v Suriname* (n 94); *Newfoundland and Labrador v Nova Scotia* (n 211). Two points are worth noting here. First, the vast majority of reallocated private rights are related to petroleum operations (rather than to fishing or scientific research). This may be because petroleum exploration is one of the main reasons why maritime boundary disputes end up in international courts. Second, the cases of reallocation identified in this study exclude those situations where the affected oil blocks did not belong to any company at the time of delimitation (as in the case of Myanmar's oil blocks AD-11, 12, 13, 14, which passed to Bangladesh post delimitation, or Nicaragua's oil blocks, which were subsequently awarded to Honduras) and oil blocks that were explored by a national oil company while delimitation was under way (as was the case with the massive Olimpiskiyi field in the Black Sea, which was explored by a Ukrainian State company and passed to Romania post delimitation).

[276] For example, it is foreseeable that a relocation of existing private rights will occur in the upcoming delimitation judgment between Kenya and Somalia if the ICJ applies the equidistance method without giving effect to the existing oil permits in the disputed area. On this case, see M Pappa, 'The Impact of Judicial Delimitation on Private Rights Existing in Contested Waters: Implications for the Somali-Kenyan Maritime Dispute' (2017) 61 Cambridge Journal of African Law 393.

would ultimately intensify the existing trend in maritime delimitation treaties, where states pay little or no attention to private rights in contested waters.

The asymmetry in how judicial authorities treat private rights in land and maritime disputes attests to a significant fragmentation in international case law, the effect of which is to hinder the establishment of a general rule that would apply in all delimitation cases. That is rather problematic, especially in the so-called mixed cases, where the same court or tribunal is requested to delimit both the land and the maritime boundaries of two states on the basis of international law. Although judges have affirmed that when it comes to maritime delimitation 'the land dominates the sea',[277] the rules which apply in these two settings are significantly different. Land delimitation is concerned with the legal context within which it takes place, whereas maritime delimitation is more technical and rigid.

Arguably, not all land delimitation principles need apply in the ocean. However, the purpose and the nature of delimitation is the same in both settings. Both on land and at sea, delimitation seeks to set the limits of two states' contiguous jurisdictions. In both situations, the establishment of international boundaries is based on the principles of stability and finality. Unless the concerned states decide otherwise, a boundary is established in order to remain in place for ever.

For judges of the sea, the concept of stability explains why geographical factors are so important in the process of delimitation. Unlike other factors (eg natural resources), the features of physical geography are permanently present. However, this argument is never employed by courts in land delimitation. In those cases, judges rely not on factors of physical geography but only on purely legal factors to determine the boundary's course.

If the courts hearing maritime disputes wish to rely solely on geographical factors, they should simply close the list of circumstances to be considered during delimitation. But so long as this list remains open, it is plausible that any factor (including private rights present in the disputed area) can affect a maritime boundary's course. The exclusion of private rights from maritime delimitation rests on judicial choice, not on a rule of international law.

3.4.3 *Implications for Non-State Actors*

Most importantly, the fact that similar rights are treated differently on land and at sea has legal and practical implications for non-state actors with interests in areas under delimitation. When they are taken into consideration in fixing the

---

[277] *North Sea Continental Shelf Cases* (n 100) para 96.

boundary's location (which is more often the case on land than at sea), private rights remain in their original position post delimitation. But when they do not, as it is typically the case in the ocean, private rights are threatened with redistribution from one state to another as a result of the boundary's settlement.

This means that the chances of private rights surviving are significantly greater in land delimitation than in maritime delimitation. Upon its transfer from state A to state B, the redistributed maritime area and any private rights therein will no longer fall under the jurisdiction of the state which originally controlled the area and created those rights.

In terms of private law, this change of circumstances is so fundamental that it can extinguish the legal relationship existing between state A and the right-holder on the grounds of frustration or impossibility of performance.[278] At the very least, this creates great uncertainty for individuals who already possess fishing, exploratory or scientific rights in contested waters. It may also deter private actors from investing large sums of money in resource-rich maritime areas with unsettled or disputed boundaries.

The secondary position private rights possess in both maritime delimitation treaties and rulings cultivates the impression that offshore private rights are 'second-class' rights compared to their counterparts on land. Ultimately, this may lead to the assumption that offshore private rights are not worthy of protection by international law.

3.5 CONCLUSIONS

Land and maritime delimitation have many similarities, but the way they treat private rights is not one of them. A comparative analysis of delimitation treaties and rulings in both settings has demonstrated that the role of private rights is much stronger in land than in ocean boundary-making.

With regard to delimitation treaties, it has been observed that private rights are much better placed on land than at sea. The number of boundaries that have been affected by private rights is far greater on land. Also, in land delimitation treaties the impact of private rights is equally strong at all three stages of boundary-making – namely, allocation, delimitation and demarcation. On the contrary, the effect of private rights in maritime delimitation treaties is moderate in the negotiation process and minimal or none in the delimitation and demarcation of the boundary line.

---

[278] Provided the requirements laid down in the law governing the right, which is normally the law of the granting state, are met (eg a frustrating event must be unforeseeable and supervening). See Pappa (n 276).

3.5 Conclusions

With regard to delimitation rulings, the treatment of private rights is also better on land than at sea. The number of cases which have been affected by the presence of private rights is significantly greater in the context of land delimitation. By contrast, although private rights were quite important in early maritime delimitation cases, they became overshadowed by geographical factors in later judgments and arbitral awards.

Hence, although private rights exist in both settings (land and sea), they are perceived differently in each. When it comes to land delimitation, these rights are treated as purely legal factors. In striking contrast, delimitation in the ocean is more akin to a mathematical exercise. It treats private rights as mere economic or non-geographical factors, which makes their rejection almost instinctive.

The asymmetry characterizing the treatment of private rights on land and at sea creates a tension within the sphere of public international law.

Firstly, it prevents the creation of a common state practice for the protection of private rights in the context of land and maritime delimitation. The important role private rights possess in land delimitation treaties could contribute to the creation of a customary rule that would oblige states to consider those factors when establishing their boundaries. Unfortunately, the same cannot be said of private rights in maritime delimitation treaties.

Secondly, the different treatment of private rights in land and maritime delimitation rulings signifies that international jurisprudence is severely fragmented. The systematic recognition of private rights in land delimitation cases creates a strong (persuasive) precedent for their protection in future disputes. It may also instil in states a greater sense of obligation to consider private rights when entering into their boundary agreements. On the contrary, the systematic rejection of private rights in maritime delimitation cases prevents the development of case law that would prescribe the protection of private rights at sea. This in turn hinders the establishment of a general delimitation rule applicable across the board in land and maritime cases.

Finally, from a pragmatic point of view, the inferior place that private rights possess in maritime delimitation creates great uncertainty for private actors over the fate of their interests in waters claimed by two states. The potential extinction of active private rights due to a subsequent delimitation treaty or ruling may be extremely harmful (if not devastating) for their holders' economic and legal interests. It is important to examine whether this challenge is reversible – that is, whether a reallocated private right can survive post delimitation. This is the question addressed in Chapter 4.

4

The Uneven Preservation of Reallocated Private Rights on Land and at Sea

4.1 INTRODUCTION

When regard is had to private rights during delimitation, they remain under the granting state's jurisdiction; but when this is not the case, they may pass under another state's control. The question that then arises is, can reallocated private rights still be preserved post delimitation on land and at sea?

To answer this question, the chapter examines the various mechanisms available in international law for accommodating reallocated private rights in each setting. First, it compares the conventional mechanisms employed by states in the context of land and maritime delimitation. Next, it compares the mechanisms relied on by courts and tribunals in land and maritime delimitation cases.

A synthesis of the findings reached shows that the preservation of reallocated private rights is more systematic and effective on land than in the ocean. This asymmetry has important implications for offshore private interests and for international law in general.

4.2 CONVENTIONAL MECHANISMS OF PROTECTION

In general, the fact that private rights play an important role in land delimitation treaties secures against redistribution. Insofar as they determine or otherwise affect the boundary's course, private rights will remain under the granting state's control.

On some occasions, though, the reallocation of private rights is inevitable.[1] However, a close analysis of those situations reveals that a number of

---

[1] As when the existing private rights are too far from the boundary, or when the states agree that the boundary line shall follow a geographical feature like a river or a mountain crest. See Chapter 3.

sophisticated mechanisms are employed by states to preserve the reallocated private rights on land post delimitation. These mechanisms are of a conventional nature, as they are agreed between the states concerned. In some situations, the delimitation treaty provides that the state to which the territory in question will be transferred is required to respect in a fair and unprejudiced manner any private rights in that territory. This provision is known as a grandfather clause.[2] On other occasions, a separate agreement is made between states during or post delimitation, allowing private actors who reside on one side of the boundary to continue enjoying rights (eg working, farming) in areas which have been transferred to the other side of it.

Such conventional mechanisms are also available in the context of maritime delimitation. A reallocated private right can be preserved either through a grandfather clause contained in the maritime delimitation treaty or through a separate cooperation agreement concluded between the neighbouring states post delimitation.

The presence of similar conventional mechanisms for land and sea allows them to be analysed jointly. At first glance, it may be assumed that the use and efficacy of those mechanisms is similar in both settings. That is not the case though. An analysis of primary sources reveals that the preservation of private rights subject to reallocation is more systematic and effective on land than in the ocean, where private rights tend more frequently to undergo reallocation.

4.2.1 *The Systematic Employment of Conventional Mechanisms on Land*

The systematic protection of reallocated private rights by states on land stems both from the employment of grandfather clauses in delimitation treaties and from the conclusion of cooperation agreements between states post delimitation.

4.2.1.1 The Widespread Use of Grandfather Clauses in Land Delimitation Treaties

The vast majority of land delimitation treaties that cause a reallocation of private rights contain a grandfather clause. This clause is mainly concerned with the protection of ownership and other property rights of individuals who have been displaced as a result of the delimited territory being transferred to

---

[2] The term 'grandfather clause' is not found in official documents such as delimitation treaties, but is used by lawyers and technical experts to describe a clause which preserves a pre-existing status quo (eg private rights) in the area under delimitation.

another state. Quite often, this provision regulates the effect on a displaced person's nationality, too. But on most occasions, the protection of the affected private rights is independent of a potential change in the right-holder's nationality.

An early example of a grandfather clause is found in the territorial arrangement between the USA and Mexico of 1905.[3] In particular, it was agreed that the residents of certain land parcels which were redistributed from one state to the other would be free to choose between retaining the citizenship of the county to which their property originally belonged or acquiring the nationality of the absorbing state. In either case, it was ensured that any reallocated property rights would be inviolably respected post delimitation as if they belonged to citizens of the absorbing state.[4]

The grandfather clause was also widely employed in Europe after the extensive territorial changes caused by the two world wars. An example is found in the delimitation treaty concluded between Germany and France in 1925.[5] Although certain areas were ceded from France to Germany, it was agreed that the rights of French people in those areas (including ownership and lease contracts) would remain unaffected post delimitation.[6] In addition, a series of tax and other privileges were granted to the owners of agricultural or forestal estates and mills in the affected French communes.[7]

A similar arrangement was made between Germany and the Netherlands in 1960.[8] While certain Dutch areas passed to Germany, it was agreed that Dutch dwellers would receive authorization for unlimited residence in the Federal Republic of Germany.[9] Likewise, the acquired rights of Dutch natural and legal persons domiciled in those areas would be respected by the German authorities post delimitation.[10]

Another interesting arrangement was made between Israel and Jordan in 1994.[11] Although certain territorial areas passed under Jordan's sovereignty, it

---

[3] Convention between the United States and Mexico for the Elimination of the Bancos in the Rio Grande from the Effects of Articles I and II of the Treaty of 12 November 1884 (signed 20 March 1905).

[4] ibid, art IV.

[5] Treaty between France and Germany Regarding the Delimitation of the Frontier (with Annexes, Protocol and Exchange of Notes) (signed 14 August 1925).

[6] ibid, arts 4, 32.

[7] ibid, arts 48, 50.

[8] General Treaty between Germany and the Netherlands for the Settlement of Frontier Questions and other Problems Outstanding between the Two Countries (Treaty of Settlement) (signed 8 April 1960).

[9] ibid, art 9.

[10] ibid, art 13.

[11] Israel-Jordan Peace Treaty (signed 26 October 1994).

was agreed that the private land ownership rights and other property interests of Israeli people would remain unaffected for twenty-five years, with the protection being automatically renewed for the same length of time unless the parties agreed otherwise.[12]

Likewise, when the Austro-Yugoslavian boundary was settled, a special arrangement was made between the two parties, allowing the Austrian dual owners residing permanently in the Yugoslav frontier zone to retain title to the immovable property they formerly held in that area.[13]

Of course, that is not to say that a grandfather clause is found in every land delimitation treaty that has caused a reallocation of private rights. When the redistribution concerns a small land parcel or part of a private estate (eg a farm), it may alternatively be agreed that the private property affected will be acquired by the absorbing state through the means of compensated expropriation or eminent domain.[14] In that case, the reallocated private right will cease to exist post delimitation, but its holder will receive monetary compensation for their loss. However, it is observed that states generally prefer to uphold reallocated private rights post delimitation rather than expropriate them. This arrangement is more practical and less costly than the alternative of expropriation, which requires a thorough investigation of title and an estimation of the affected property's value.[15]

From the above, it can be seen that states prioritize the preservation of reallocated rights on land. Although the alternative of compensated discharge is also available, states generally prefer to keep reallocated rights alive post delimitation, accommodating the interests of the non-state actors concerned.

4.2.1.2 The Widespread Conclusion of State Cooperation Agreements on Land

On some occasions, private actors do not permanently reside in the redistributed territory but possess working or other economic rights in it. In those situations, a cooperation arrangement, known as a minor frontier traffic agreement, can be made between states, allowing such people to cross the border on a daily basis and exercise their displaced rights unhindered.

---

[12] ibid, annex I.
[13] Agreement between Austria and Yugoslavia Concerning the Immovable Property of Austrian Dual Owners in the Yugoslav Frontier Zone (with Final Protocol) (signed 19 March 1953).
[14] S Jones, *Boundary-Making: A Handbook for Statesmen, Treaty Editors and Boundary Commissioners* (Carnegie Endowment for International Peace 1945) 44–47.
[15] ibid.

Such an arrangement was made between Austria and the former Czechoslovakia in 1921.[16] It was agreed that the inhabitants of the Austrian communes in the border area would enjoy the freedom to cross the boundary and to transport the products of the soil and cattle-raising industry free of duties and without any need for export licences. They were accorded the freedom to cross the border for work purposes given that they would return to their homes on the other side of the boundary on the same day.[17] Also, the residents of the border area retained the right to use the produce of the land and forests 'which they have enjoyed from time immemorial'.[18]

These arrangements became very popular in Europe in the mid-twentieth century with the establishment of new boundaries after the two world wars. For example, a similar agreement was made between Belgium and France in 1949 for Belgian and French nationals who were domiciled on one side of the boundary but had to cross it daily for work in the industrial, commercial or agricultural sector. To continue exercising those rights, a person would receive one of four different types of permit (temporary, ordinary, ordinary permanent or permanent).[19]

A similar arrangement was made between the former Czechoslovakia and Poland in 1959 to facilitate the boundary crossings by residents of towns in the frontier area and short stays on the other side for family, employment or agricultural purposes.[20] Likewise, a frontier traffic agreement was concluded between the former Yugoslavia and Greece in 1959,[21] and between Germany and the Netherlands in 1960.[22]

Because of its practicality, the system of frontier traffic was also applied outside Europe. An example was the arrangement made between France and Turkey in 1929, which allowed the dwellers of the frontier zone between Turkey and Syria the freedom to cross the boundary without the payment of fees for the purposes of farming and grazing.[23]

---

[16] Convention between the Austrian and Czechoslovak Republics Concerning the Delimitation of the Frontier between Austria and Czechoslovakia and Various Questions Connected Therewith (signed 10 March 1921).

[17] ibid, pt III.

[18] ibid, pt VI, art 1.

[19] Agreement between Belgium and France Relating to Frontier Workers (with Annexes) (signed 8 January 1949) arts 1–3.

[20] Convention between the Republic of Czechoslovakia and the Polish People's Republic Concerning Minor Frontier Traffic (signed 4 July 1959).

[21] Agreement between Yugoslavia and Greece Concerning Frontier Traffic (signed 18 June 1959).

[22] Agreement between the Netherlands and the Federal Republic of Germany Concerning Minor Frontier Traffic (signed 3 June 1960).

[23] Protocol between France and Turkey Relative to the Surveillance and Fiscal Regime of the Frontier (signed 29 June 1929).

4.2 Conventional Mechanisms of Protection

Typically, the duration of such freedom is long (ie for as long as the private rights in question last). On rare occasions, though, this freedom may last for only a few years. For example, the agreement between Latvia and Lithuania of 1921 provided that the owners of immovable properties (eg farms) that were intersected by the boundary line could cross the border for agricultural purposes for only two years post delimitation. They then had to liquidate the part situated on the other side of the line or let it be expropriated by the absorbing state in return for compensation, so that all their rights would be located on one side of the border.[24]

In sum, the frequent inclusion of a grandfather clause in land delimitation treaties and the great number of cooperation agreements concluded between states post delimitation demonstrate that the preservation of reallocated private rights on land – whether relating to residence or simply work and economic activities – ranks as a high priority for states.

4.2.2 The Restricted Employment of Conventional Mechanisms at Sea

In contrast to land, the extent to which states accommodate reallocated private rights in the ocean is much more limited. This can be seen both in the infrequent use of grandfather clauses in maritime delimitation treaties and in the rarity of cooperation agreements between states post delimitation.

4.2.2.1 The Limited Use of Grandfather Clauses in Maritime Delimitation Treaties

A grandfather clause may be used in maritime delimitation treaties for the purposes of accommodating private fishing rights in the transboundary area. Reference may be made to the delimitation treaty between Sri Lanka and India of 1974, where it was explicitly stated that the Indian fishermen operating in waters that subsequently passed to Sri Lanka would be free to continue their activities in the same area.[25] A similar arrangement was made between Canada and France for the protection of French fishing rights in Saint-Pierre and

---

[24] Convention between Latvia and Lithuania Regarding the Delimitation on the Spot of the Frontier between the Two States, and Also Regarding the Rights of the Citizens in the Frontier Zone, and the Status of Immovable Property Intersected by the Frontier Line (signed 14 May 1921) art 7.

[25] Agreement between Sri Lanka and India on the Boundary in Historic Waters between the Two Countries and Related Matters (signed 26 and 28 June 1974) art 5.

102   4 *Uneven Preservation of Reallocated Private Rights*

Miquelon in 1972,[26] and between Kenya and Tanzania in 1976 for the reciprocal recognition of the fishing licences and practices of the indigenous people of each state.[27]

A grandfather clause may also be used for the protection of offshore petroleum rights in the transboundary area. Such provision was made in Germany's delimitation treaties with the Netherlands and with Denmark in 1971. It is recalled that some oil blocks that the Dutch and Danish authorities had awarded to private operators for exploration purposes prior to maritime delimitation were intersected by the final boundary.[28] To accommodate the concessionaires' interests in the redistributed areas, it was agreed that Germany would grant the same permits to the companies concerned.[29]

An equally interesting provision is found in the delimitation treaty between Australia and Papua New Guinea of 1978.[30] In particular, it was agreed that Australia's former licensees would be granted new petroleum permits by Papua New Guinea on terms that would be no less favourable than those provided under Papua New Guinea law for any other permit-holder.[31] In addition, Article 12 of the same treaty is concerned with the preservation of traditional fishing rights in the protected zone of the Torres Strait. A similar provision on the preservation of traditional or customary fishing rights is found in the delimitation treaty concluded between Indonesia and Papua New Guinea in 1980.[32]

In 1996, Belgium and the Netherlands agreed that a Dutch concession held by a company for the dredging of sand and gravel in an area which became

---

[26]   Agreement between the Government of Canada and the Government of the French Republic on their Mutual Fishing Relations (signed 27 March 1972).

[27]   Notes Exchanged between the United Republic of Tanzania and Kenya concerning the delimitation of the territorial waters boundary between the two states (17 December 1975–9 July 1976) art 3.

[28]   See Chapter 3.

[29]   Treaty between the Kingdom of Netherlands and the Federal Republic of Germany Concerning the Delimitation of the Continental Shelf under the North Sea (signed 28 January 1971) art 4, annex 2; Treaty between the Kingdom of Denmark and the Federal Republic of Germany Concerning the Delimitation of the Continental Shelf under the North Sea (signed 28 January 1971) art 4, annex 2.

[30]   Treaty between Australia and the Independent State of Papua New Guinea Concerning Sovereignty and Maritime Boundaries in the Area between the Two Countries, Including the Area Known as Torres Strait, and Related Matters (signed 18 December 1978).

[31]   ibid, art 5.

[32]   Agreement between the Government of Indonesia and the Government of Papua New Guinea Concerning the Maritime Boundary between the Republic of Indonesia and Papua New Guinea and Cooperation on Related Matters (signed 13 December 1980) art 5.

4.2 Conventional Mechanisms of Protection

Belgian would be respected by Belgium for five years and then renewed for the same company under similar conditions.[33]

From the above, it can be concluded that the number of maritime delimitation treaties containing grandfather clauses is considerable. This might give the impression that the protection of reallocated private rights at sea is as effective as on land. However, it would be wrong to think so, for three main reasons.

Firstly, the employment of grandfather clauses in the ocean is significantly more restricted than on land. Given the number of maritime delimitation treaties which have caused a reallocation of private rights, the proportion of agreements that contain a grandfather clause is very small. Indeed, about one-third of existing maritime delimitation treaties make no provisions at all for accommodating private rights in the transboundary area.[34] For example, in the delimitation treaty signed between Greece and Albania in 2009, it was agreed that the existing petroleum concessions would remain in force for each side only within the confines of the boundary that was established.[35] On the other hand, no reference was made to the status of permits that extended across the agreed boundary. Likewise, in the delimitation treaty concluded between the United States and the former Soviet Union in 1990, no provision was made for the preservation of the transboundary marine fisheries that pre-existed in the Bering Sea.[36] What is striking in those situations is not only the omission of a grandfather clause from the maritime delimitation treaties but also the absence of any remedy or compensation post delimitation for the holders of the private interests affected.[37]

Secondly, on many occasions the grandfather clause was inserted to preserve traditional private rights that pre-existed in the area rather than to

---

[33] Treaty between the Kingdom of the Netherlands and the Kingdom of Belgium on the Delimitation of the Territorial Sea (signed 18 December 1996). See also E Franckx, 'Belgium and the Netherlands Settle their Last Frontier Disputes on Land as well as at Sea' [1998] Revue Belge de Droit International 338, 378–92; J Charney and R Smith (eds), *International Maritime Boundaries*, vol 4 (Martinus Nijhoff 2002) 2927.

[34] D Colson, 'The Legal Regime of Maritime Boundary Agreements' in J Charney. and L Alexander (eds), *International Maritime Boundaries*, vol 1 (Martinus Nijhoff 1993) 54.

[35] Agreement between the Government of the Hellenic Republic and the Government of the Republic of Albania for the Delimitation of their Respective Continental Shelf and Other Maritime Zones (signed 27 April 2009) art 3.

[36] Agreement between the United States of America and the Union of Soviet Socialist Republics on the Maritime Boundary (signed 1 June 1990). See also E Hey, *The Regime for the Exploitation of Transboundary Marine Fisheries Resources* (Martinus Nijhoff 1989) 2.

[37] In contrast to land, no publicly available information suggests that compensation has been granted to the holders of absorbed offshore private rights (eg on the basis of expropriation). The author contacted the parties (states, non-state actors) involved in the above situations but received no response with regard to this matter.

104   4 *Uneven Preservation of Reallocated Private Rights*

accommodate any commercial or industrial private rights.[38] Usually, the protection of traditional fishing, hunting or gathering rights is dictated by a regional custom.[39] In that case, the insertion of a grandfather clause in the delimitation treaty is an act of domestic rather than international law.

Thirdly, it is more common for maritime delimitation treaties to employ mineral clauses or general/best effort provisions on cooperation.[40] A mineral clause provides that if the boundary cuts through a reservoir of mineral resources, the states concerned will enter into an agreement providing for those reserves to be exploited jointly.[41] A general/best effort clause is more abstract and provides that the states concerned will cooperate in various sectors (eg fishing, petroleum exploration, scientific research, protection of the environment) post delimitation, as opposed to actually preserving any affected private rights.[42]

One reason why such provisions outnumber grandfather clauses might be that states find them more practical to apply than enforcing private rights against another state. The pressure imposed on the absorbing state to recognize the private rights which its neighbour had unilaterally created in the shared maritime space – perhaps in breach of Articles 74(3) and 83(3)

---

[38] eg agreements between Sri Lanka and India, Papua New Guinea and Australia, and Kenya and Tanzania. This is in contrast to land, where post-delimitation arrangements are primarily concerned with the preservation of commercial private rights.

[39] For example, Australian legislation on aboriginal fishing rights explicitly refers to the protection of traditional fishing rights in the waters between Australia and Papua New Guinea. See Australian Law Reform Commission, 'The Recognition of Aboriginal Customary Laws' (ALRC Report 31, 1986) s 35.

[40] It is estimated that about two-thirds of the existing maritime delimitation treaties contain such provisions. Colson (n 34); D Colson and R Smith (eds), *International Maritime Boundaries*, vol 5 (Martinus Nijhoff 2005) 3624–25.

[41] See Agreement between the Government of the United Kingdom of Great Britain and Northern Ireland and the Government of the Kingdom of Norway Relating to the Delimitation of the Continental Shelf between the Two Countries (signed 10 March 1965) art 4; Agreement between Italy and Yugoslavia Concerning the Delimitation of the Continental Shelf between the Two Countries in the Adriatic Sea, (signed 8 January 1968) art 2; Treaty between Uruguay and Argentina Concerning the Rio de la Plata and the Corresponding Maritime Boundary (signed 19 November 1973) art 43; Agreement between the Hellenic Republic and the Italian Republic on the Delimitation of the Respective Continental Shelf Areas of the Two States (signed 24 May 1977) art 2; Treaty between the Federal Republic of Nigeria and the Republic of Equatorial Guinea Concerning their Maritime Boundary (signed 23 September 2000) art 6; Treaty between the Kingdom of Norway and the Russian Federation Concerning Maritime Delimitation and Cooperation in the Barents Sea and the Arctic Ocean (signed 15 September 2010) art 5.

[42] eg Treaty on Delimitation of Marine and Submarine Areas and Maritime Cooperation between the Republic of Colombia and the Republic of Costa Rica (signed 17 March 1977) art 3.

4.2 *Conventional Mechanisms of Protection*

UNCLOS[43] – could increase the underlying interstate tension and undermine the preservation of the affected rights. Instead, the insertion in the delimitation treaty of a more abstract clause requiring states to cooperate after delimitation, without specific reference to the reallocated private rights, might be more acceptable to the absorbing state.

Despite the frequent presence of mineral clauses in maritime delimitation treaties, their efficacy can be questioned for various reasons. In principle, the subject matter of a mineral clause is limited to mineral and petroleum resources and does not extend to other private activities like fishing or scientific research. To protect private rights in non-petroleum operations, it would be preferable for states from the outset to include in their delimitation treaty a general/best effort clause or a special provision referring to mineral and non-petroleum rights alike.[44]

It is also worth highlighting that the mineral and the general/best effort clauses are 'largely political window dressing'.[45] Their abstract language suggests that they are used mainly to promote the states' political relations rather than to serve as a legal shield for the protection of non-state actors' rights. If states were more concerned about accommodating private interests, then grandfather clauses would systematically be employed in maritime delimitation treaties.

Besides, the wording of a mineral or general/best effort clause usually refers to future situations (eg the future discovery of transboundary reservoir or the future development of living resources) rather than existing ones, which gives such clauses more of a programmatic than a resolutive purpose.[46] On some occasions, the general/best effort clause even provides that states will cooperate to determine the possible existence of transboundary resources, but will refrain from actually granting private rights within a certain distance of the

---

[43] On these provisions, see Chapters 2 and 3.

[44] eg Treaty between the Kingdom of Norway and the Russian Federation Concerning Maritime Delimitation and Cooperation in the Barents Sea and the Arctic Ocean (signed 15 September 2010), which includes both a mineral clause in Article 5 and a separate clause for state cooperation in the context of fishing in Article 4; Treaty between the People's Republic of China and the Socialist Republic of Vietnam on the Delimitation in the Beibu Gulf/Bac Bo Gulf (signed 25 December 2000), which contains a mineral clause in Article VII and a cooperation clause in relation to fishing in Article VIII.

[45] Colson (n 34) 54.

[46] eg Agreement Relating to the Delimitation of the Continental Shelf between Greenland and Canada (signed 17 December 1973) arts III–V; Convention between the Government of the French Republic and the Government of the Spanish State on the Delimitation of the Continental Shelves of the Two States in the Bay of Biscay (signed 29 January 1974) art 4. See V Becker-Weinberg, *Joint Development of Hydrocarbon Deposits in the Law of the Sea* (Springer 2014) 58.

established boundary.[47] This clearly reflects a lack of interest in promoting private activities in the transboundary maritime area on the part of the states.

More importantly, the mere insertion of a mineral clause or a general/best effort clause does not *ipso facto* secure any private rights that may exist in the transboundary area. The preservation of those rights requires that the states concerned enter into a cooperation agreement post delimitation. But as Section 4.2.2.2 will reveal, only a small number of such agreements have been signed. The only obligation which mineral and general/best effort clauses impose on states is to negotiate in good faith and exchange information about the deposits straddling the boundary; there is no obligation to actually reach a cooperation agreement.[48]

To conclude, although the grandfather clause is available to states for the purpose of accommodating reallocated private rights both on land and at sea, its effectiveness in these two settings is far from equal. The observations made in Sections 4.2.1.1 and 4.2.1.2, reveal that the use of this mechanism is more systematic on land. At sea, states generally prefer to employ other contractual clauses designed more to promote the governments' political relations than to preserve any reallocated private rights.

4.2.2.2 The Limited Conclusion of State Cooperation Agreements at Sea

Even when not mentioned in a maritime delimitation treaty, the preservation of reallocated private rights at sea is still possible if states voluntarily agree to cooperate post delimitation. For example, states may choose to enter into a separate agreement to jointly explore the transboundary area and accommodate any private rights therein.

When the boundary intersects a hydrocarbon deposit that is already being exploited by one side, the states concerned may decide to conclude a unitization agreement. In the literature, the latter is described as 'the joint, coordinated operation of an oil and gas reservoir underlying the delimited boundary between two States as a single deposit'.[49] This practice enables states

---

[47] eg Treaty between the Government of the United States of America and the Government of the United Mexican States on the Delimitation of the Continental Shelf in the Western Gulf of Mexico (signed 9 June 2000) art 4. See also Agreement Concerning the Sovereignty over the Islands of Farsi and Al-Arabiyah and the Delimitation of the Boundary Line Separating the Submarine Areas between Iran and Saudi Arabia (signed 24 October 1968) art 4.

[48] Colson (n 34) 55; Becker-Weinberg (n 46) 49; R Lagoni, 'Oil and Gas Deposits across National Frontiers' (1979) 73 AJIL 215, 233–39.

[49] T Wälde and others, 'International Unitisation of Oil and Gas Fields: The Legal Framework of International Law, National Laws, and Private Contracts' [2007] 2 OGEL <www.ogel.org>; A Bastida and others, 'Cross-Border Unitisation and Joint Development Agreements: An

4.2 Conventional Mechanisms of Protection

to keep the existing operator(s) in the area and to ensure that each side retains its full rights in the natural resources of the seabed.

Perhaps the two most emblematic examples are the North Sea agreements between the United Kingdom and Norway on the unitization of the Frigg gas field in 1976 and the unitization of the Statfjord oil reservoirs in 1979.[50] Another unitization agreement was signed between the United Kingdom and the Netherlands in 1992,[51] while three other examples are those between Nigeria and Equatorial Guinea in 2002,[52] Venezuela and Trinidad and Tobago in 2010[53] and the USA and Mexico in 2012.[54] More recently, Australia and Timor Leste agreed on unitization, as the boundary established in March 2018 resulted in much of the Sunrise gas field being redistributed in favour of Timor.[55]

When the delimited area is rich in fish, it may be that states enter a fisheries agreement post delimitation. An example is the agreement between Italy and the former Yugoslavia in 1983, which, in order to preserve the traditional fishing rights of the local inhabitants, established a common fishing zone in the area straddling the pre-existing maritime boundary in the Gulf of Trieste.[56] A similar arrangement was made between Slovenia and Croatia in 1997

International Law Perspective' (2007) 29 Houston Journal of International Law 355, 358. Unitization was first used in the United States for the exploitation of oil reservoirs that straddled the boundaries of several private lands; its use was subsequently extended to the exploitation of reservoirs straddling international boundaries.

[50] Agreement Relating to the Exploitation of the Frigg Field Reservoir and the Transmission of Gas Therefrom to the United Kingdom (signed 10 May 1976); Agreement Relating to the Exploitation of the Statfjord Field Reservoirs and the Offtake of Petroleum Therefrom (signed 16 October 1979).

[51] Agreement Relating to the Exploitation of the Markham Field Reservoirs and the Offtake of Petroleum Therefrom (signed 26 May 1992).

[52] Protocol in Implementation of Article 6.2 of the Treaty between the Federal Republic of Nigeria and the Republic of Equatorial Guinea Concerning their Maritime Boundary (signed 3 April 2002); Treaty between Equatorial Guinea and Nigeria on Joint Exploration of Crude Oil, Especially at the Zafiro-Ekanga Oil Field Located at the Maritime Boundary of Both Countries (signed 3 April 2002).

[53] Unitization Agreement between Venezuela and Trinidad and Tobago for the Exploitation and Development of Hydrocarbon Reservoirs of the Manakin-Cocuina Field (signed 16 August 2010).

[54] Agreement between the United States of America and the United Mexican States Concerning Transboundary Hydrocarbon Reservoirs in the Gulf of Mexico (signed 20 February 2012).

[55] Treaty between Australia and the Democratic Republic of Timor-Leste Establishing Their Maritime Boundaries in the Timor Sea (signed 6 March 2018) art 7.

[56] Notes exchanged between Italy and the Social Federal Republic of Yugoslavia regarding the creation of a joint fishing zone in the Gulf of Trieste (signed 18 February 1983). See G Blake and D Topalovic, 'The Maritime Boundaries of the Adriatic Sea' (Maritime Briefing 1(8), IBRU 1996) 3.

108   *4 Uneven Preservation of Reallocated Private Rights*

concerning the Adriatic Sea.[57] In 2000, China and Vietnam also signed a fisheries agreement for the Gulf of Tonkin.[58]

The above examples are certainly significant but relatively few in number compared to the quantity of maritime delimitation treaties that have caused a reallocation of private rights. To date, only a small number of unitization and fisheries agreements have been signed around the world.[59]

Also, the effectiveness of those mechanisms is debatable for various reasons. On many occasions, states entered into cooperation agreements to accommodate traditional private rights (eg relating to fishing) rather than preserve commercial rights.[60] On others, the purpose of the cooperation agreement was to enhance the states' political relations or promote sustainable use of their shared marine resources, rather than accommodate private rights pre-existing in the transboundary area.[61]

In many situations, the unitization agreement did not even concern reallocated private rights, as the permits for the exploration of petroleum were granted by states after the boundary was settled.[62] What worried states on those occasions was the threat to the unity of a hydrocarbon deposit discovered post delimitation which straddled the boundary. In those cases, unitization was the only practical way for states to proceed with and optimize exploitation of the discovery.[63]

---

[57] Agreement between the Republic of Slovenia and the Republic of Croatia on Border Traffic and Cooperation (signed 28 April 1997). See M Grbec, *The Extension of Coastal State Jurisdiction in Enclosed or Semi-Enclosed Seas: A Mediterranean and Adriatic Perspective* (Routledge 2014) 177.

[58] Agreement on Fishery Cooperation in the Tonkin Gulf between the Government of the People's Republic of China and the Government of Socialist Republic of Vietnam (signed 25 December 2000).

[59] Compare this with the number of cooperation agreements concluded by states during delimitation, mentioned below. However, it is not the purpose of the present study to provide an exhaustive list of cooperation agreements but rather to analyse the trends discernable in state practice.

[60] eg agreements made in the Adriatic Sea.

[61] As expressly stated in the preamble to the Gulf of Tonkin fisheries agreement between China and Vietnam (n 58). Optimization of the exploration of a shared gas deposit was also the reason why Australia and Timor Leste inserted a unitization clause in their delimitation treaty. The two states were already conducting joint operations in the area before delimitation.

[62] eg the United Kingdom's North Sea unitization agreements with Norway and the Netherlands. P Cameron, 'Cross-Border Unitisation in the North Sea' [2007] 2 OGEL <www.ogel.org>. Although private rights were in place when the unitization agreement was signed, they had been granted post delimitation, so the question of reallocation did not arise.

[63] J Woodlife, 'International Unitisation of an Offshore Gas Field' (1997) 26 ICLQ 338, 339; F Botchway, 'The Context of Trans-Boundary Energy Resource Exploitation: The Environment, the State and the Methods' [2004] 3 OGEL <www.ogel.org>.

4.2 *Conventional Mechanisms of Protection*

Even when unitization clearly involves reallocated private rights, states are under no obligation, nor do they find it easy, to conclude an agreement to this effect. Although it might be thought that the presence of a clearly established boundary (as agreed by states in a delimitation treaty) would facilitate state cooperation post delimitation, the conclusion of an agreement at that stage is not without its problems.[64] States must return to the negotiating table and may even have to abandon their original resource claims in order to reach a cooperation agreement. Without a strong political will and a spirit of compromise on both sides, new tensions may arise dooming the negotiations to failure.

Also, as observed earlier in relation to the grandfather clause in maritime delimitation treaties, it may be difficult for the absorbing state to recognize a private right that was unilaterally created by its neighbour in breach of its procedural obligations pending delimitation. Unless the states already entertain amicable relations or a large deposit is discovered in the transboundary area, they may have next to no incentive to conclude a unitization agreement.

By contrast, the vast majority of cooperation agreements at sea are concluded between states *pending* delimitation and take the form of joint development and joint fishing agreements.[65] There are two main reasons for this.

[64] On the merits and challenges of state cooperation post delimitation, see I Townsend-Gault, 'Zones of Cooperation in the Oceans: Legal Rationales and Imperatives' in MH Nordquist and JN Moore (eds), *Maritime Border Diplomacy* (Martinus Nijhoff 2012).

[65] Both unitization and joint development agreements allow states to explore their resources in common. However, whereas a unitization agreement covers a delimited area, a joint development agreement records the arrangements made between two states to develop and share the agreed proportions of the resources discovered 'within a geographic area whose sovereignty is disputed' (ie an undelimited area). Bastida (n 49) 359. According to the present study, at least twenty joint development agreements have been signed – eg Joint Development Agreement between Kuwait and Saudi Arabia (signed 7 July 1965); Joint Development Agreement between Japan and the Republic of Korea (signed 30 January 1974); MoU between Thailand and Malaysia for the Establishment of a Joint Development Zone in the Gulf of Thailand (signed 21 February 1979) and Agreement for the Constitution of a Joint Authority (signed 30 May 1990); Treaty between Nigeria and Sao Tome e Principe on the Joint Development of Petroleum and Other Resources in Respect of Areas of the Exclusive Economic Zone of the Two States (signed 21 February 2001). For joint fishing agreements, see MoU between the Government of the Republic of Indonesia and the Government of Australia Regarding the Operations of Indonesian Traditional Fishermen in Areas of the Australian Exclusive Economic Zone and Continental Shelf (signed 7 November 1974); MoU between the Government of the Republic of Indonesia and the Government of Australia Concerning the Implementation of a Provisional Fisheries Surveillance and Enforcement Arrangement (signed 29 October 1981); Agreement between the Government of Australia and the Government of the Republic of Indonesia Relating to Cooperation in Fisheries (signed 22 April 1992).

First, agreements made pending delimitation are of a temporary nature, as they apply only until such time as the boundary's location is finally settled. They allow states to shelve the boundary question and cooperate without prejudice to each other's sovereign claims.[66] Although this arrangement will not terminate their disagreement over the boundary, it will enable states to exercise their sovereign and economic rights (eg relating to fishing, petroleum exploration) in a spirit of compromise and in a manner that secures any existing private interests in the shared area. In the words of Anderson,

> [T]he solution of a joint area may be second best to an agreed boundary; but a joint area may well be better than seeing a dispute remain unresolved and possibly grow more serious. The governments may prefer a compromise to a defeat in litigation. An effective treaty providing for joint development may allow the industry to work and produce benefits for many years in an area which would otherwise have remained blighted by dispute over jurisdiction. 'Half a loaf is better than no bread', as the saying goes.[67]

On the other hand, it may be more difficult for states to return to the negotiating table after their boundary has been delimited, as their interests may no longer coincide or the operator appointed by one state may not be to the other state's liking.[68]

Second, the conclusion of a cooperation arrangement pending delimitation is also encouraged by Articles 74(3) and 83(3) UNCLOS. It is recalled that these twin provisions require that states, 'in a spirit of understanding and cooperation, shall make every effort to enter into provisional arrangements of a practical nature and, during that transitional period, not to jeopardize or hamper the reaching of the final agreement' for the delimitation of their EEZ and CS. Although states are not obliged to actually reach a provisional arrangement, the breach of their procedural duty to negotiate pending

---

[66] It is common for a joint development agreement to contain a 'without prejudice' clause, according to which nothing in the signed agreement shall be interpreted as a change to the states' original sovereign claims in the shared area. Of course, that is not to say that joint development agreements are always easy to conclude. See C Schofield, 'No Panacea? Challenges in the Application of Provisional Arrangements of a Practical Nature' in MH Nordquist and JN Moore (eds), *Maritime Border Diplomacy* (Martinus Nijhoff 2012); J Gao, 'Joint Development in the East China Sea: Not an Easier Challenge than Delimitation' (2008) 23 International Journal of Marine and Coastal Law 39.

[67] D Anderson, 'Strategies for Dispute Resolution: Negotiating Joint Agreements' in G Blake and others (eds), *Boundaries and Energy: Problems and Prospects* (Kluwer Law International 1998) 475.

[68] For instance, the constitution of the absorbing state may prohibit foreign investments. On the practical difficulties raised by unitization, see Townsend-Gault (n 64) 113, 118.

4.2 Conventional Mechanisms of Protection

delimitation may make them liable for an internationally wrongful act.[69] Also, it is widely believed that the obligation of states to cooperate pending delimitation constitutes a rule of customary law.[70] Hence, the thought that unilateral operations in the shared area would breach this rule can lead states to reach a cooperation agreement during delimitation.

By contrast, Articles 74(3) and 83(3) UNCLOS do not require states to cooperate post delimitation. A general requirement for states to cooperate does exist under Article 123 UNCLOS, but it applies only to states bordering enclosed or semi-enclosed seas and concerns sustainability and environmental issues rather than the preservation of pre-existing private rights. This has led many scholars to maintain that there is no obligation for states to cooperate in the ocean post delimitation,[71] which would suggest that any cooperation agreements signed post delimitation are only products of good will.

Of course, it could be argued that such an obligation exists under Article 3 of the 1974 UN Charter of Economic Rights and Duties of States, which provides that '[i]n the exploitation of natural resources shared by two or more countries, each State must co-operate on the basis of a system of information and prior consultations in order to achieve optimum use of such resources without causing damage to the legitimate interest of others'.[72]

Resolutions of the UN General Assembly normally serve as mere recommendations and as such are not legally binding instruments. However, it is accepted that they carry legal weight as evidence of *opinio juris* testifying to

---

[69] See Chapter 2.

[70] An analysis of this issue falls outside the scope of this book. For a comprehensive account of the different opinions on this matter, see W Onorato and I Shihata, 'The Joint Development of International Petroleum Resources in Undefined and Disputed Areas' (1996) 11 ICSID Review 299; D Ong, 'Joint Development of Common Offshore Oil and Gas Deposits: "Mere" State Practice or Customary International Law?' (1999) 93 AJIL 771; I Townsend-Gault, 'Offshore Petroleum Joint Development Agreements: Functional Instruments? Compromise? Obligation?' in Gerald Blake and others (eds), *The Peaceful Management of Transboundary Resources* (Springer 1995) 69; T Cottier, *Equitable Principles of Maritime Boundary Delimitation* (CUP 2015) 367; V Becker-Weinberg, *Joint Development of Hydrocarbon Deposits in the Law of the Sea* (Springer 2014) 202.

[71] C Robson, 'Transboundary Petroleum Reservoirs: Legal Issues and Solutions' in Gerald Blake and others (eds), *The Peaceful Management of Transboundary Resources* (Springer 1995) 8; M Miyoshi, 'The Basic Concept of Joint Development of Hydrocarbon Resources in the Continental Shelf (1988) 3 International Journal of Estuarine and Coastal Law 1, 8–9; R Churchill and V Lowe, *The Law of the Sea* (3rd edn, Manchester University Press 1999) 200; Bastida (n 49) 375–80.

[72] UNGA Resolution 3281 (XXIX) (1974) UN Doc A/9030.

4 Uneven Preservation of Reallocated Private Rights

the presence of customary norms.[73] Although the resolution referred to above was shunned by 'most of the industrialized Western States',[74] Article 3 was adopted unanimously. To that extent, it could be argued that states bear an obligation to cooperate post delimitation in order to ensure optimum exploitation of their natural resources.

However, uncertainty reigns over what constitutes a breach of this obligation. Although there is currently some knowledge (albeit limited) about what can constitute a breach of the obligation to cooperate pending delimitation,[75] the same cannot be said of the situation post delimitation. In the absence of clarification from scholarship or case law, it is difficult to determine under what circumstances states may be found in breach of their obligation to cooperate post delimitation. To condemn a state for simply failing to

---

[73] MD Öberg, 'The Legal Effects of Resolutions of the UN Security Council and General Assembly in the Jurisprudence of the ICJ' (2006) 16 European Journal of International Law 879

[74] The states that voted against the Charter were Belgium, Denmark, Germany, Luxemburg, the United Kingdom and the United States. Austria, Canada, France, Ireland, Israel, Italy, Japan, the Netherlands, Norway and Spain abstained. The reference to 'industrialized' states does not mean that they alone create customary norms, as all sovereign states are equal under international law. However, it could be argued that in certain contexts, as in this resolution concerning the exploration of natural resources, some states may influence the decisions of others. M Shaw, *International Law* (8th edn, CUP 2017) 59: '[I]t is inescapable that some States are more powerful and influential than others and that their activities should be regarded as of greater significance. This is reflected in international law so that custom may be created by a few States, provided those States are intimately connected with the issue at hand, whether because of their wealth and power or because of their special relationship with the subject-matter of the practice . . . Law cannot be divorced from politics or power and this is one instance of that proposition.' A Kaczorowska, *Public International Law* (4th edn, Routledge 2010) 38: '[I]f a large number of States representing the major political, legal and socio-economic systems follow a particular practice and expect it to be binding, it will become a customary rule.' An example of developed or industrialized states having helping to create customary international law is the contribution made by the former Soviet Union and the United States to the development of space law. B Cheng, *Studies in International Space Law* (OUP 1997) 126–46. See also B Lepard, *Customary International Law: A New Theory with Practical Applications* (CUP 2010). According to other scholars, however, the reference to industrialized states may be a useful means of determining whether the requirement of state practice is met, but should be regarded as a rule, as states' interests may differ. N Petersen, 'The Role of Consent and Uncertainty in the Formation of Customary International Law' (2011) 4 Max Planck Institute for Research on Collective Goods 1, 3–4; M Byers, 'Power, Obligation, and Customary International Law' (2001) 11 Duke Journal of Comparative and International Law 81, 84.

[75] eg in *Arbitration between Guyana and Suriname (Guyana v Suriname)* (2007), where Guyana was found responsible for breaching Articles 74(3) and 83(3) UNCLOS as it chose to perform unilateral acts rather than to cooperate with its neighbour pending delimitation. However, according to case law, only those unilateral acts that have a permanent impact on the seabed (eg drilling) constitute such a breach. See Chapter 2.

cooperate with its neighbour after a successful delimitation might be a severe restriction of its sovereignty.[76] Only those unilateral acts that clearly harm the other state or the environment should qualify as breach. Without a clear framework as to what constitutes a breach of the obligation to cooperate post delimitation, states do not have the same legal reasons to enter into a cooperation agreement post delimitation as they do pending delimitation.

A final point should be made about the reasons why states generally decide to conclude a cooperation agreement in the ocean. Whether pending or post delimitation, such agreements are mainly signed with a view to promoting the states' interests in a certain maritime space.[77] By definition, a unitization agreement is concluded to preserve the unity of a hydrocarbon deposit that straddles a maritime boundary (as splitting it may reduce its economic value) and to prevent each state from siphoning off fugacious resources from its neighbour's part of the shared CS.[78] Similarly, a joint development mechanism is aimed at preventing states from infringing each other's sovereign rights or causing tension in the shared maritime space.[79] And the main purpose of a fisheries agreement is no different – that is, to provide states with equitable access to the living resources they share and to ensure that those resources will be exploited in a sustainable manner.[80]

Arguably, these cooperative state arrangements may end up accommodating private rights in the region in question, but, unlike arrangements on land,

---

[76] P Cameron, 'The Rules of Engagement: Developing Cross-Border Petroleum Deposits in the North Sea and the Caribbean' (2006) ICLQ 559, 583, according to whom a state may proceed with unilateral operations in the transboundary area as long as it respects the unity of the deposit and applies good oil practice. See also G Sanchez and R McLaughlin, 'The 2012 Agreement on the Exploitation of Transboundary Hydrocarbon Resources in the Gulf of Mexico: Confirmation of the Rule or Emergence of a New Practice?' (2015) 37 Houston Journal of International Law 681, 708–09.

[77] H Fox and others, *Joint Development of Offshore Oil and Gas: A Model Agreement for States for Joint Development with Explanatory Commentary* (British Institute of International and Comparative Law 1989) 33; Bastida (n 49) 357–58, 378–80; Becker-Weinberg (n 70) 69, adding that cooperation agreements also facilitate the exchange of technology and know-how between states.

[78] See Wälde (n 49); Ong (n 70) 778–79; I Townsend-Gault, 'The Frigg Gas Field: Exploitation of an International Cross-Boundary Petroleum Field' (1979) 3 Marine Policy 302, 303; J Ejegi, 'What Are the Mechanisms for Resolving Disputes between Countries with Transboundary Resources? A Closer Examination' [2005] 2 OGEL 2 (5)1 <www.ogel.org>.

[79] According to leading scholars, the 'rule of capture' (which in the past applied systematically applied in the United States) allowing the owner of a land parcel to extract oil and gas from it even if these resources have been drained by another person's land has no place in international law. W Onorato, 'Apportionment of an International Common Petroleum Deposit' (1968) 17 ICLQ 85, 101; Miyoshi (n 71) 5–6; Lagoni (n 48); Fox (n 77) 34.

[80] That is usually stipulated in the preamble to those agreements. See the Gulf of Tonkin agreement between China and Vietnam (n 58).

there is no convincing evidence that the protection of private rights is the main motive for concluding cooperation agreements in the ocean. While cooperation agreements on land explicitly refer to the preservation of private rights affected by delimitation, their counterparts at sea highlight the importance of good relations between the states involved.[81]

To conclude, this section has shown that states are less intent on accommodating reallocated private rights in the ocean than on land. Although similar conventional mechanisms are available to states in both settings, they are less frequently employed at sea. And even when states make use of such mechanisms in the ocean, the reasons for, and the outcome of, their use are significantly different than on land. Section 4.3 will examine the attitudes of judicial bodies towards reallocated private rights on land and at sea.

4.3 JUDICIAL MECHANISMS OF PROTECTION

As seen in Chapter 3, private rights play an important role in land delimitation rulings as conclusive evidence of which state possesses sovereignty over the disputed territory or where the boundary should lie. In those situations, private rights are protected from reallocation. But even when the reallocation of private rights is inevitable (eg when a valid boundary is found to be in place), judges tend to indicate to the disputing states the legal means of ensuring that private interests are preserved after delimitation.

These legal means are also available in the context of maritime delimitation. The judges of the sea, like those of the land, may advise the states to cooperate post delimitation in order to preserve any displaced private interests. Hence, in theory, the preservation of reallocated private rights can be achieved equally in land and maritime delimitation cases, as nothing precludes judges from advising states to cooperate. In practice, however, a great disparity is observed between land and maritime rulings.

4.3.1 *Extensive Preservation of Reallocated Private Rights in Land Delimitation Rulings*

The number of land delimitation rulings that have led to the reallocation of private rights is relatively small. But even in those few cases, judges paid particular attention to preserving the private interests affected by the delimitation.

---

[81] See the texts and titles of agreements cited in this section.

4.3 Judicial Mechanisms of Protection

An example is the *El Salvador/Honduras* judgment of 1992.[82] In this case, the ICJ relied heavily on the presence of private rights to prove the existence of *effectivités*. As the judges remarked:

> It cannot be excluded, however, that . . . the situation may arise in some areas whereby a number of the nationals of the one Party will, following the delimitation of the disputed sectors, find themselves living in the territory of the other, and property rights apparently established under the laws of the one Party will be found to have been granted over land which is part of the territory of the other.[83]

To prevent the damaging effect of such inevitable reallocation of private rights, the judges advised the two states to cooperate closely. It was suggested that special measures be employed by the parties to take account of this situation, 'in full respect for acquired rights, and in a humane and orderly manner'.[84]

In particular, the Court encouraged the establishment of a joint boundary commission 'to study and propose solutions for the human, civil and economic problems which may affect their compatriots, once the frontier problem has been resolved'.[85] The parties accepted the judgment and stressed that priority would be given to the human aspect when implementing it. As a consequence, an agreement was struck in 1998 allowing the displaced people to choose their nationality and secure their existing rights regardless of their ethnicity.[86]

Another example is the ICJ's 1999 ruling in the case between Namibia and Botswana concerning the delimitation of the Chobe river and the status of the Kasikili/Sedudu Island situated therein.[87] The ruling favoured Botswana, as a valid delimitation treaty was found to be in place. However, the nationals of Namibia were recognized as having long-established interests in the redistributed area in terms of fishing and navigation. To safeguard those interests post delimitation, the Court stated that:

> The nationals of Namibia, and vessels flying its flag, are entitled to, and shall enjoy, a treatment equal to that accorded by Botswana to its own nationals

---

[82] *Land, Island and Maritime Frontier Dispute (El Salvador/Honduras)* [1992] ICJ Rep 351.

[83] ibid, para 66.

[84] ibid.

[85] ibid.

[86] See A Llamzon, 'Jurisdiction and Compliance in Recent Decisions of the International Court of Justice' (2008) 815 European Journal of International Law 815, 826; C Paulson, 'Compliance with Final Judgments of the International Court of Justice since 1987' (2004) 98 AJIL 434, 437.

[87] *Case Concerning Kasikili/Sedudu Island (Botswana/Namibia)* [1999] ICJ Rep 1045.

and to vessels flying its own flag. Nationals of the two States, and vessels, whether flying the flag of Botswana or of Namibia are, therefore, subject to the same conditions as regards navigation, fishing and environmental protection.[88]

The ruling was accepted by both sides.

A similar dictum is found in the 2002 delimitation judgment on the land and maritime boundary between Cameroon and Nigeria.[89] The Court did not construct the land boundary *de novo*, as it accepted that delimitation had already been effected by a series of agreements signed by the former colonial powers, which favoured Cameroon.[90] However, that boundary line cut through villages and land parcels that were previously under Nigerian control. The judges considered that they had no power to modify an already delimited line to avoid a reallocation effect. Instead, they advised the states to cooperate when implementing the judgment to ensure that the rights and interests of the local populations were respected.[91]

Despite the disputants' violent past relations, they both accepted the judgment. To implement it as smoothly as possible, they established a mixed boundary commission along with two sub-commissions, one of which was tasked with the demarcation of the boundary and the other with ensuring that the rights of the affected populations were protected. Although demarcation of this long boundary has been extremely time consuming, the work of the second sub-commission was quickly accomplished. A team of experts in property law, human rights and sociology worked closely with local populations, showing great sensitivity to their interests, and reported its suggestions to the boundary commission.[92]

The continuity of private rights on land was also discussed in the *Abyei Area* case, which concerned a delimitation previously effected by a boundary commission. While acknowledging that 'a transfer of territory has an effect on the people who inhabit it',[93] the arbitral tribunal stressed that this should not prejudice any private rights situated therein:

---

[88] ibid, para 103.

[89] *Case Concerning the Land and Maritime Boundary between Cameroon and Nigeria (Cameroon v Nigeria; Equatorial Guinea Intervening)* [2002] ICJ Rep 303.

[90] ibid, para 68.

[91] ibid, paras 107, 123.

[92] For an update on the mixed commission's work, see <https://unowas.unmissions.org/camer oon-nigeria-mixed-commission> accessed 20 March 2020. On the sub-commissions' tasks, see G Oduntan, *International Law and Boundary Disputes in Africa* (Routledge 2015) 233–34.

[93] *Arbitration Regarding the Delimitation of the Abyei Area between the Government of Sudan and the Sudan People's Liberation Movement/Army* (2009) para 545.

4.3 *Judicial Mechanisms of Protection*

The jurisprudence of international courts and tribunals as well as international treaty practice lend additional support to the principle that, in the absence of an explicit prohibition to the contrary, the transfer of sovereignty in the context of boundary delimitation should not be construed to extinguish traditional rights to the use of land (or maritime resources).[94]

[T]he PCIJ confirmed that the transfer of sovereignty over a particular territory does not extinguish private rights pertaining to the use of that territory: 'Private rights acquired under existing law do not cease on a change of sovereignty,' the PCIJ held, adding that it was unreasonable to assume that 'private rights acquired from the State as the owner of the property are invalid as against a successor in sovereignty'.[95]

A more recent example of judicial protection of reallocated private rights is found in the delimitation award rendered in the boundary dispute between Croatia and Slovenia in 2017.[96] It is recalled that delimitation was here mainly based on the limits of the pre-independence cadastral districts.[97] Although the tribunal explained that it had to establish a legal boundary on the basis of international law – as opposed to one based solely on practical considerations of physical or human geography – it noticed that certain parts of the established line would affect the local people's interests.[98] To secure those interests from the consequences of reallocation, the judges gave the states the option to either 'agree on an adjustment' of the boundary line 'or to find other ways to resolve those problems in a spirit of friendly cooperation'.[99]

The above examples show that international case law attaches importance to accommodating reallocated private rights on land. Although the task of international courts and tribunals is limited to deciding on the boundary's location, judges and arbitrators go a step further in advising states to cooperate post delimitation with a view to preserving the private interests affected.

4.3.2 *Limited Preservation of Reallocated Private Rights in Maritime Delimitation Rulings*

As seen in Chapter 3, the systematic rejection of private rights as irrelevant to maritime delimitation rulings opens the door to their reallocation. Although

---

[94] ibid, para 753.
[95] ibid, para 755.
[96] *Arbitration between the Republic of Croatia and the Republic of Slovenia (Croatia v Slovenia)* (2017).
[97] See Chapter 3.
[98] *Croatia v Slovenia*, Award, paras 357, 565.
[99] ibid, para 565.

118   *4 Uneven Preservation of Reallocated Private Rights*

there have been numerous cases in which such reallocation did occur, little or no attention was paid to preserving displaced private interests post delimitation in those cases. At best, judges sometimes advised the disputants to cooperate post delimitation, but with a view to promoting their national interests rather than for the purpose of accommodating the private rights affected by the delimitation.

An example can be found in the famous *North Sea Continental Shelf Cases*. It is recalled that the ICJ's rejection of equidistance affected the Dutch and Danish petroleum permits situated in the boundary area.[100] But even though those permits were at the core of Germany's boundary dispute with Denmark and the Netherlands, the Court made no reference to the status of the private rights involved. It did advise the states to cooperate, but for a different reason. For the judges, cooperation was important, not so much for the preservation of existing private rights post delimitation but rather for maintaining the unity of hydrocarbon deposits that straddled the maritime boundary and for ensuring that the oil profits were shared equitably between the states concerned.[101] It should be mentioned that the states did eventually agree to preserve the contractors' rights in the transboundary area, but they did so, not by entering into a unitization agreement, as the Court had urged them to do, but rather by inserting a grandfather clause in their subsequent delimitation treaties.

Another example comes is the *Eritrea/Yemen* arbitration.[102] It is recalled that the private fishing and petroleum rights in the disputed area did not affect the tribunal's decision on the boundary's location.[103] Interestingly, though, it paid attention to the rights of artisanal fishermen in the disputed areas during the first stage of the award, which was concerned with territorial questions. According to the tribunal, the fishing private rights that had existed in the Red Sea since time immemorial had to be respected by states regardless of the outcome of their international dispute. Hence, although certain islands were awarded to Yemen, the latter was requested to respect the traditional fishing rights of Eritrea's nationals in the surrounding waters as if they were its own nationals.[104]

---

[100] See Chapter 3.

[101] *North Sea Continental Shelf Cases (Federal Republic of Germany/Denmark, Federal Republic of Germany/Netherlands)* [1969] ICJ Rep 51, paras 97–99. See Separate Opinion of Judge Jessup, 79–81, stating that the existing private rights should not be rendered 'null and void' post delimitation and encouraging the parties to conclude a unitization agreement.

[102] *Eritrea/Yemen Arbitration (Second Stage: Maritime Delimitation)* (17 December 1999) (2001) 22 RIAA 335.

[103] ibid 354–55.

[104] *Eritrea/Yemen Arbitration (First Stage: Territorial Sovereignty and Scope of Dispute)* (9 October 1998) (2001) 22 RIAA 211, paras 525–26.

The tribunal clarified that the preservation of those traditional fishing rights was not based on international law but on a system of 'private justice', or the so-called *lex pescatoria*, which is essentially a local custom maintained by those participating in fishing.[105] This implied that the industrial or commercial private rights that fell outside the sphere of this custom would remain unprotected. The tribunal's reliance on a local custom raises concerns about the sources of law on which the award was founded.[106] It would have been more judicious to base the protection of fishing rights on the doctrine of acquired rights, which is part of international law.[107]

In relation to offshore oil concessions affected by the boundary line, the tribunal referred to the importance of state cooperation with a view to the joint exploration of petroleum resources.[108] But, as in the *North Sea Continental Shelf Cases*, this suggestion was based on the economic benefits that would accrue to the states from keeping the hydrocarbon deposits unified rather than on accommodating existing private rights affected by the boundary's course.

Things were not much different in the maritime boundary dispute between Guinea and Guinea-Bissau.[109] According to the case facts, the oil companies operating in the area had some influence on the states' decision to request judicial delimitation.[110] However, the tribunal's decision to base delimitation solely on geographical factors led to the displacement of existing oil permits. Once again, no reference was made to the status of the private rights thus affected. As in previous cases, the parties were advised to cooperate in the transboundary area in order to promote their economic interest in petroleum exploitation rather than secure existing private rights.[111] In 1986, the states announced that they would cooperate, although there is no evidence that an agreement was subsequently concluded.[112]

An interesting situation arose in the case between Tunisia and Libya.[113] It is recalled that the ICJ relied heavily on the line of existing petroleum

---

[105] ibid, para 340.

[106] N Antunes, 'The 1999 Eritrea-Yemen Maritime Delimitation Award and the Development of International Law' (2001) 50 International and Contemporary Law Quarterly 299, 308.

[107] The doctrine of acquired rights is discussed in Section 4.4.1.

[108] *Eritrea/Yemen* (n 102) paras 84–86.

[109] *Dispute Concerning Delimitation of the Maritime Boundary between Guinea and Guinea-Bissau (Guinea v Guinea-Bissau)* (1985) 24 ILM 252.

[110] R Pietrowski, 'Introductory Note' to the Delimitation Award (1985) 24 ILM 252. See also J Frynas, *Foreign Investment and International Boundary Disputes in Africa: Evidence from the Oil Industry* (Occasional Papers Series No 9, African Studies Centre 2000).

[111] *Guinea v Guinea-Bissau* (n 109) paras 121–23.

[112] Pietrowski (n 110).

[113] *Case Concerning the Continental Shelf (Tunisia/Libyan Arab Jamahiriya)* [1982] ICJ Rep 18.

concessions in the disputed area.[114] However, the coordinates of Libya's concessions were miscalculated by the Court, causing an overlap with Tunisia's permits. In 1984, Tunisia filed an application for revision, asking the ICJ to correct the concession points. However, its claim was rejected on the grounds that these overlaps were caused unintentionally.[115] No reference, however, was made to the protection of the rights of the contractors thereby affected. The delimitation judgment was eventually implemented in 1988. To resolve the problem of the overlapping oil concessions, a joint venture was set up between states enabling operations in the transboundary area to be jointly financed and performed.[116] There was no advice from the Court on this matter, so the conclusion of this agreement can only be attributed to the states' political will to overcome the disadvantages judicial delimitation had caused to their and their contractors' interests.

In some cases, judges took it almost for granted that states would cooperate post delimitation in conducting joint transboundary operations. This was the case in the *Gulf of Maine* dispute.[117] It is recalled that the parties' petroleum and fishing activities in the disputed area played no role in the Court's judgment.[118] The judges acknowledged that delimitation would cause certain areas to pass from one state to the other, but no reference was made to the status of the private rights that pre-existed in those areas.[119] In a strikingly brief comment, the Court simply referred to the parties' 'long tradition of friendly and fruitful co-operation in maritime matters', expressing its conviction that they would be once more able to 'surmount any difficulties and take the right steps to ensure the positive development of their activities' in the domains of fishing and hydrocarbon exploration.[120] But, given the tense relations existing between the states at the time, there was no ensuing cooperation aimed at preserving those private interests.[121]

---

[114] See Chapter 3.
[115] *Revision and Interpretation of the Judgment of 24 February 1982 in the Case Concerning the Continental Shelf (Tunisia v Libyan Arab Jamahiriya)* [1985] ICJ Rep 192. See also Cottier (n 70) 284.
[116] See Cottier (n 70) 285; M Miyoshi, *The Joint Development of Offshore Oil and Gas in Relation to Maritime Boundary Delimitation* (Maritime Briefing 2(5), IBRU 1999) 34.
[117] *Delimitation of the Maritime Boundary in the Gulf of Maine Area (Canada/ United States)* [1984] ICJ Rep 292.
[118] ibid 341, 342 paras 140–48.
[119] ibid, paras 238–39.
[120] ibid, para 240.
[121] The only sign of cooperation between the two states was the conclusion of a fisheries agreement in 1990. However, the purpose of this agreement was not to protect private interests but to mitigate over-exploitation of the transboundary area by both sides. E Pudden and

4.3 Judicial Mechanisms of Protection

In most cases, moreover, judges did not even suggest that the states cooperate in the transboundary area. A typical example is the dispute between Libya and Malta.[122] It is recalled that in this case the Court ruled out the consideration of non-geographical factors in the disputed maritime area.[123] As a result, the boundary cut through a series of oil blocks that were being explored by Malta's concessionaire. Yet, no recommendation was made to the states to cooperate post delimitation. Although implemented in 1986, the judgment did not allay the tensions between Libya and Malta over the oil blocks in the transboundary area, which frustrated any attempt at cooperation.[124]

A similar stance was taken by the judges in the land and maritime boundary dispute between Cameroon and Nigeria.[125] For those interested in the status of reallocated private rights post delimitation, this judgment is a real puzzle. It is recalled that in the first part of the judgment, which was concerned with land delimitation, the Court expressly requested the parties to cooperate so that the private rights of local inhabitants would be preserved after the boundary's settlement.[126] Surprisingly, though, it adopted a different position in the second part of its judgment, which was concerned with the delimitation of the maritime boundary between the two states. The Court disregarded non-geographical factors during delimitation, including Nigeria's oil concessions in the disputed waters.[127] As a consequence, the privately held concessions in three Nigerian oil blocks were affected by the boundary line.[128]

Despite the concerns expressed by Nigeria about the challenges likely to be raised by the redistribution of their concessions to Cameroon, the judges made no reference at all to state cooperation post maritime delimitation. The problems that the Court's passive stance would cause became clear when the

---

D VanderZwaag, 'Canada-USA Bilateral Fisheries Management in the Gulf of Maine: Under the Radar Screen' (2007) 16 RECIEL 36.

[122] *Case Concerning the Continental Shelf (Libyan Arab Jamahiriya/Malta)* [1985] ICJ Rep 13.

[123] ibid 29, 41, 46.

[124] Agreement between the Great Socialist People's Libyan Arab Jamahiriya and the Republic of Malta Implementing Article III of the Special Agreement and the Judgment of the International Court of Justice (signed 10 November 1986). On the continuing tension between Libya and Malta, see 'Border Dispute Blocks Heritage's Progress in Malta' (Means Borders, 23 June 2011) <http://menasborders.blogspot.co.uk/2011/06/border-dispute-blocks-heritages.html> accessed 20 March 2020.

[125] Judgment (2002) ICJ.

[126] Judgment [107]; [123].

[127] *Cameroon v Nigeria* (n 89) para 304.

[128] Specifically, 33 per cent of OPL230, 8 per cent of OPL98 and 8 per cent of OPL224 passed to Cameroon. See C Schofield and C Carleton, 'Technical Consideration in Law of the Sea Dispute Resolution' in A Oude Elferink and D Rothwell (eds), *Oceans Management in the 21st Century: Institutional Frameworks and Responses* (Brill 2004) 247.

122   *4 Uneven Preservation of Reallocated Private Rights*

states constituted the mixed boundary commission to implement the judgment.[129] Several significant controversies arose between the two sides during that phase, which can hardly have been unexpected given that the parties had not decided – or even been encouraged to decide – whether (and how) they could cooperate post delimitation in the exploration of the affected oil blocks. This demonstrates that judicial delimitation is not a panacea to all problems linked to maritime boundaries. International courts can settle long and complex boundary disputes in a conclusive and peaceful manner; yet there are times when their decisions may create new tensions between the parties, turning state cooperation into a thorny process or mere wishful thinking.

The circumstances were somewhat similar in the arbitration between Newfoundland and Labrador and Nova Scotia.[130] Although the award was rendered by a regional tribunal, it closely followed international case law on maritime delimitation. The panel's disregard of non-geographical factors led to a situation where one of Nova Scotia's active petroleum permits straddled the boundary as fixed by the tribunal.[131] Again, like previous rulings, the award made no reference to state cooperation or any other means of protecting the private interests affected by the boundary.[132]

A more recent case concerning private permits was the arbitration between Guyana and Suriname.[133] Although of great significance for the international law of the sea, as it established states' obligations in boundary disputes, it did little to protect private rights affected by maritime delimitation. Once again, the lack of attention to non-geographical factors resulted in the boundary cutting through one of Guyana's oil blocks that was explored by a private oil company.[134] Although only a small part of the block passed to Suriname, the award could have suggested ways of preserving the existing private interests in the transboundary area (eg through unitization). Unfortunately, however, the tribunal remained passive on that matter, and so did the states post delimitation.

---

[129]   G Oduntan, 'Modalities for Post Boundary Dispute, Cross Border JPZs/Unitisation Upstream Hydrocarbon Exploitation in the Gulf of Guinea?' [2009] 4 OGEL <www.ogel.org>.

[130]   *Arbitration between Newfoundland and Labrador and Nova Scotia (Newfoundland and Labrador v Nova Scotia)* (2002).

[131]   ibid, para 3.4, though the award was generally accepted by both sides. See Nova Scotia, 'Nova Scotia Says Boundary Decision Paves Way for Oil and Gas Activity' (2 April 2002) <https://novascotia.ca/news/release/?id=20020408002> accessed 20 March 2020.

[132]   For a critical commentary on the case, see R Meese, 'The Arbitration between Newfoundland and Labrador and Nova Scotia Concerning Portions of the Limits of their Offshore Areas: The Relevance of the Conduct of the Parties in Maritime Delimitation' [2003] 5 OGEL <www.ogel.org>.

[133]   *Guyana v Suriname* (n 75).

[134]   ibid 122–25.

In sum, the above examples show that the determination of international courts and tribunals to secure reallocated private rights after land delimitation does not extend to maritime cases. Although a much larger number of delimitation rulings have led to the reallocation of private rights at sea than on land, and even though judges have the power to advise states to cooperate post delimitation in both settings, displaced private interests are more effectively protected in land cases.

4.4 ASSESSMENT OF STATE AND JUDICIAL PRACTICE

As this chapter has demonstrated, the preservation of reallocated private rights on land and at sea is uneven. While states and judicial bodies are eager to accommodate reallocated private interests on land, their stance is different when it comes to offshore private rights. The implications of this asymmetry are discussed below.

4.4.1 *Absence of an International Custom on Land and at Sea*

Although it does not happen very often, private rights on land may end up on the opposite side of the boundary after delimitation. This does not mean, however, that those rights will cease to exist upon reallocation.

Many land delimitation treaties provide that the private rights affected by the delimitation shall be respected by the absorbing state. The need to maintain the legal cohesion between the private right and its holder prevails over the acquiring state's authority to exercise its powers of eminent domain and terminate the absorbed right.

When a region in which private rights are held is transferred to another state but the private actors remain in their country of origin, a special interstate agreement may allow individuals to cross the border and continue enjoying those rights just as they did before delimitation. In that case, the separation of private rights from their holders caused by land delimitation will be merely physical, not legal. The underlying principle is that private rights and their holders constitute a legal unit which should not be disturbed by the establishment of land boundaries.

This would seem to testify to the existence of a firm state practice of preserving reallocated private rights on land post delimitation. The next step is to ascertain whether this practice can help establish an international custom by satisfying the requirements of generality and *opinio juris*.[135]

---

[135] The analysis in this section is similar to that in Chapter 3, Section 3.4.1.

124   *4 Uneven Preservation of Reallocated Private Rights*

This study has found that the preservation of reallocated private rights on land is a widespread and standard practice. As seen in Section 4.2.1, conventional means (special clauses inserted in delimitation treaties, cooperation agreements made by states post delimitation) have been employed by a great number of states from all over the world without protest from other states.

As for consistency, this presupposes identifying all delimitation treaties and agreements that provide for the preservation of reallocated private rights post delimitation – a task that falls outside the scope of this book. However, the mere fact that uses of conventional mechanisms to preserve reallocated private rights greatly outnumber situations in which such rights were liquidated or extinguished by the absorbing state is a clear sign of consistency in the state practice of accommodating private rights affected by land delimitation.

To qualify as *opinio juris*, the preservation of reallocated private rights on land must be regarded as legal obligation by states. Even if they do not expressly say so, this practice is clearly based on the doctrine of acquired rights (*droits acquis*),[136] which has its roots in the fourteenth century and has been recognized ever since in legal theory and case law as a fundamental principle of international law protecting private rights from unlawful acts of state interference, such as expropriation or arbitrary discharge.[137] According to this doctrine, a private right is protected against interference not only by the state that created but also by any successor state. Therefore, when a state absorbs the territory of another, it has a duty to respect any private rights in that territory, as the opposite would 'threaten or otherwise destroy the continuity of the international legal order'.[138]

---

[136]   As evidenced by the terminology used (eg 'acquired rights', 'vested rights') in state agreements and judicial rulings. See examples analysed in this chapter.

[137]   E de Vattel, *The Law of Nations or the Principles of Natural Law, Applied to the Conduct and to the Affairs of Nations and of Sovereigns* (trans of 1758 edn by C Fenwick, Carnegie Institution of Washington 1916) bk III, ch XIII, 200–201; KS Sik, 'The Concept of Acquired Rights in International Law: A Survey' (1977) 24 Netherlands International Law Review 120. However, it is worth mentioning that the juridical enforcement of acquired rights has its roots in domestic law. See the famous US case *United States v Percheman* (1833) 32 US 51 and the English case *Cook v Sprigg* (1899) AC 572. But see International Law Commission, 'Second Report on Succession in Respect of Matters other than Treaties' (18 June 1969) UN Doc A/CN.4/216/REV.1, 72, where Mohammed Bedjaoui, Special Rapporteur of the ILC, rejects the doctrine of acquired rights in international law as controversial and problematic: 'If such rights were maintained, all human societies would be paralysed.'

[138]   H Lauterpacht, *Private Sources and Analogies of International Law* (Longmans Green 1927) 129. Two important points must be made here. First, territorial transfer is different from a mere change in a state's government, as it entails a change in sovereignty. Second, the extent of the territorial transfer is irrelevant where the private rights were granted by the predecessor state in the area subsequently absorbed by the successor state. See D O'Connell, *State Succession in Municipal and International Law* (CUP 1967) 3ff, 237–38.

4.4 *Assessment of State and Judicial Practice*

The underlying legal reason for this effect is that private law survives a change of sovereignty whereas public law does not.[139] The only conditions that must be fulfilled for private rights to be protected in such circumstances is that they have been 'properly vested' in a natural or legal person by the predecessor state and that they are of 'an assessable monetary value'.[140] A right is properly vested when it has been legally acquired under the rules of the granting state. That is not the case with rights that are void *ab initio* (eg rights that have been granted by a state *ultra vires*) or rights subject to a condition that has not been met (imperfect rights).[141] As regards monetary value, it is accepted that the term refers mainly to property rights, both *in rem* (eg property rights in land) and *in personam* (rights arising from concessions or other contracts).[142] On the other hand, commercial privileges with no financial value cannot qualify as acquired rights.[143]

Based on the above, any private rights that meet those requirements will not become void after delimitation, even though they will pass under foreign jurisdiction. Of course, that is not to say that the rights will be eternally immune to the absorbing state's interference. Upon their transfer to the other state, the rights will become subject to that state's national laws (regulations, taxation, etc.), which may eventually affect their status.[144] However, any annulment of a properly vested private right will place an international law obligation on the absorbing state to compensate the affected right-holder or to grant them a new right of equivalent value.[145] The opposite (ie the uncompensated lapse of an acquired right) would 'fall short of the international standard of civilized society, because it violates the sense of equity of the civilized world, on which its deepest legal convictions rest, which is at the root of all legislation on expropriation, and which has been ratified by a long international custom'.[146]

---

[139] O'Connell (n 138) 104; Amos Hershey, *The Essentials of International Public Law and Organization* (2nd edn, Macmillan 1927) 224.

[140] O'Connell (n 138) 245–47.

[141] ibid.

[142] P Lalive, 'The Doctrine of Acquired Rights' in M Bender (ed), *Rights and Duties of Private Investors Abroad* (International and Comparative law Center 1965) 183; 'Boundary Disputes between States: The Impact on Private Rights' (1969) 69(1) Columbia Law Review 129.

[143] A licence for a public dispensary falls into this category. O'Connell (n 138) 246.

[144] J-L Brierly, 'Règles Générales du Droit de la Paix' (1936) 58 Collected Courses of the Hague Academy of International Law 5, 65.

[145] A Hershey, 'The Succession of States' (1911) 5 AJIL 296; 'Boundary Disputes between States' (n 142) 144; C Dupuis, 'Règles Générales du Droit de la Paix' (1930) 32 Collected Courses of the Hague Academy of International Law 1, 163.

[146] G Kaeckenbeeck, 'The Protection of Vested Rights in International Law' (1936) 17 British Yearbook of International Law 16.

The above analysis suggests that the state practice of preserving reallocated private rights on land post delimitation can establish (or at least contribute to the creation of) a customary rule binding upon any states that find themselves in a similar position. What remains to be examined is whether the same applies in the context of maritime delimitation.

This study has shown that conventional mechanisms, such as grandfather clauses or cooperation agreements concluded post delimitation, are also available for the purpose of accommodating offshore private rights affected by delimitation. However, these mechanisms have been employed far less at sea than on land.

With regard to the grandfather clause, it appears that states are generally reluctant to include such a provision in their maritime delimitation treaties. The pressure it puts on the absorbing state to recognize a foreign private right that has been unilaterally created by its neighbour discourages the employment of grandfather clauses.

States seem to consider the conclusion of a separate cooperation agreement a more attractive option. But, as already observed, they prefer to sign such agreements during, rather than after, delimitation. And even when they decide to conclude a cooperation agreement once the boundary has been settled, they are mainly driven by the wish to promote their own economic interests than by concern to protect the private rights that have been affected by the boundary. In that case, the preservation of private rights is consequential, if not incidental.

The above suggests that a firm state practice of preserving reallocated private rights, as identified on land, does not exist at sea. Even if one considers the criteria of duration and generality to be met (considering that conventional mechanisms for the preservation of offshore private rights have been in place since the mid-twentieth century), the element of consistency in state practice is clearly lacking, as states have on many occasions done nothing to accommodate the private rights affected by delimitation.

More importantly, the fact that conventional mechanisms are employed by states to promote their own interests rather than to protect the private rights affected shows that the element of *opinio juris* is lacking in state practice in the ocean. That is particularly striking, as it contradicts the doctrine of acquired rights analysed above. The difference in the attitudes of states towards onshore and offshore private rights affected by delimitation raises the question of whether the doctrine of acquired rights applies in the ocean as it does on land.

4.4 *Assessment of State and Judicial Practice*

State succession has not been definitively defined in legal theory.[147] Reference is most frequently made to the Vienna Convention on Succession of States in respect of Treaties, which describes state succession as 'the replacement of one State by another in the responsibility for the international relations of territory'.[148] As explained by O'Connell, this replacement may be effected by various means, including 'violent annexation, peaceful cession, revolution or emancipation of subject regions or extensive territorial resettlements'.[149] In all these situations, 'one State ceases to rule in a territory, while another takes its place'.[150]

One could argue that the redistribution of a maritime area from one state to another does not qualify as state succession, for it does not entail a change in sovereignty (unless it concerns the TS) but is simply a transfer of sovereign rights. It is true that the CS and the EEZ – which is where offshore private rights are most commonly found – are not part of state territory as they do not fall under a coastal state's sovereignty.[151] Be that as it may, they nonetheless fall under the state's control for the purposes indicated by the international law of the sea. Hence, no matter which maritime zone is concerned (TS, CS or EEZ), the redistributed part of the ocean and any private rights therein will pass under the jurisdiction (prescriptive, enforcement, judicial) of the absorbing state after delimitation. If anything, this effect is similar to that produced on land.

Besides, even if it is accepted that the reallocation of the CS or the EEZ does not qualify as state succession *stricto sensu*, the protection of legally vested rights[152] nonetheless follows under international law.[153] As emphatically stressed by the Permanent Court of International Justice in the seminal *German Settlers* case:

> Even those who contest the existence in international law of a general principle of State succession do not go so far as to maintain that that private

---

[147] Various approaches can be found. See O'Connell (n 138) 3–35; M Craven, *The Decolonization of International Law: State Succession and the Law of Treaties* (OUP 2007) 11–12.

[148] Vienna Convention on Succession of States in respect of Treaties (signed 23 August 1978, entered into force 6 November 1996) 1946 UNTS 3, art 2(1)(b).

[149] O'Connell (n 138) 1–2.

[150] ibid.

[151] See Chapter 2.

[152] As seen in Chapter 2, an offshore private right is legally vested if located within the granting state's claimed maritime zones, even if this area is concurrently claimed by another state.

[153] See *Certain Questions Relating to Settlers of German Origin in the Territory Ceded by Germany to Poland (German Settlers)* PCIJ Rep Ser B No 6 (1923) 36; *The Mavrommatis Palestine Concessions (Greece v United Kingdom)* PCIJ Rep Ser A No 2 (1924); *Certain German Interests in Polish Upper Silesia (Germany v Poland)* PCIJ Rep Ser A No 7 (1926) 42.

128   *4 Uneven Preservation of Reallocated Private Rights*

rights including those acquired from the State as the owner of the property are invalid as against a successor in sovereignty.[154]

As added in another part of this judgment, the opposite contention 'is based on no principle and would be contrary to an almost universal opinion and practice'.[155]

For all the above reasons, this study finds that the doctrine of acquired rights should apply at sea, as it does on land for cases of territorial redistribution between states. Insofar as the preservation of reallocated private rights in the ocean is inconsistent and haphazard, it contradicts the corresponding state practice on land and hinders the establishment of a customary rule obliging states to accommodate those rights in all settings.

4.4.2 *Absence of Coherent Case Law on Land and at Sea*

Having assessed the practice of states towards reallocated private rights and its significance in international law, this study will now evaluate the line taken in international case law.

It might be thought that since delimitation cases are exclusively concerned with state interests in the disputed area, any reference by judicial bodies to the interests of non-state actors is unwarranted or even prohibited. However, that is not entirely correct. When deciding a dispute (whether on delimitation or on any other issue), judicial bodies are required to apply the rules and principles of international law in general. One of those principles is the protection of acquired rights against state interference in the event of territorial changes.

As this study has observed, the reallocation of private rights is rare in land delimitation rulings. Unless otherwise dictated by the case facts (eg the existence of a valid boundary treaty), the presence of private rights in the disputed territory tends to determine the boundary's course. But even in the few cases in which the reallocation of private rights has proved unavoidable, judges have affirmed that the rights in question should be preserved by the absorbing state. The decision to protect those rights is neither an act of discretion nor a display of judicial activism. Rather, it signals observance of the doctrine of acquired rights, which is a general principle of international law.

Despite the absence of *stare decisis* in international case law, the court practice protecting private interests on land post delimitation creates a precedent which may influence similar cases in the future. In addition, the judicial trend of encouraging states to cooperate post delimitation for the

---

[154] *German Settlers* (n 153) 36.
[155] ibid. See also *Upper Silesia* (n 153) 22–24, 40.

purpose of accommodating private interests can only reinforce the existent (and already extensive) state practice of preserving reallocated private rights on land through conventional mechanisms.

Unfortunately, the same argument cannot be made for maritime delimitation cases. In most rulings, courts make no reference whatsoever to the status of existing private rights that would change hands post delimitation. Departing from the practice followed in land delimitation cases, the judges of the sea omit to advise states about the steps that should be taken post delimitation to accommodate any private interests thus affected. Of course, states can always reach a cooperation agreement themselves after delimitation. But without minimum guidance from judicial authorities, the prospect of two former disputants reaching a cooperation agreement seems slim, to say the least.

And in the few cases where international courts stressed the importance of state cooperation post maritime delimitation, they did so for reasons of national economic interest rather than to accommodate existing private rights. To date, the dispute between Eritrea and Yemen is the only case in which states were explicitly requested to respect offshore private rights post delimitation. However, the request related solely to artisanal fishing rights, which already enjoyed protection under local custom. On the contrary, no reference was made to the protection of commercial private rights (ie concerning petroleum, industrial fishing), which also existed in that area.

The practice followed by the judges of the sea has three serious implications for international law. Firstly, it contradicts the doctrine of acquired rights, which is fundamental in public international law. Secondly, it may create a 'persuasive precedent' militating against the preservation of private rights in future maritime delimitation cases.[156] Thirdly, it may further reduce states' already limited recourse to conventional means to preserve offshore private interests post delimitation – and ultimately hinder the development of a customary rule obliging states to preserve reallocated private rights in the ocean.[157]

4.4.3 Implications for Non-State Actors

The fact that similar rights are treated differently on land and at sea post delimitation has important implications for individuals operating in areas that change states due to a subsequent delimitation treaty or ruling.

---

[156] For an analysis of this term, see Chapter 3, Section 3.4.2.
[157] On the impact of case law on custom, see Chapter 3, Section 3.4.2.

4 Uneven Preservation of Reallocated Private Rights

When preserved by conventional or judicial means (as is typically the case on land), reallocated private rights are enforceable vis-à-vis the absorbing state. But when, as more often happens at sea, this is not the case, the private rights concerned become fully exposed to the absorbing state's interference.

This means that a reallocated private right has a much greater chance of surviving on land than at sea.[158] When an offshore private right finds itself transferred from state A to state B, it will become subject to the jurisdiction and the laws of the absorbing state. If this state challenges the existence or the nature of the absorbed right,[159] or refuses to recognize it for reasons of national interest,[160] the right may eventually vanish.[161]

To protect its interests against the absorbing state, the private actor will have to turn to that state's domestic courts. However, the effectiveness of such a move is uncertain, as it is likely that these courts would favour their government over the foreign person.[162] Even if the private actor's claim is based on the international doctrine of acquired rights, the acceptance of this claim by domestic courts will be entirely dependent on the place international law

---

[158] In most maritime examples, the private actors simply abandoned the area in which they operating upon its redistribution to the other state. On some occasions, the absorbing state subsequently granted new rights to other private actors. For example, in the maritime boundary delimitation between Guyana and Suriname, the part of the CS (oil block) that was originally explored by CGX Energy Inc on behalf of Guyana was granted to Apache Corporation upon its reallocation to Suriname. On Apache's offshore assets in Suriname, see 'Apache Lines Up 5th Exploration Well in Suriname as Priority Shifts to South America' (*OilNow*, 6 November 2020) <https://oilnow.gy/featured/apache-lines-up-5th-exploration-well-in-suriname-as-priority-shifts-to-south-america/> accessed 1 April 2021. The cases discussed above in which offshore rights were reallocated did not reveal any information on whether the absorbing state compensated the evicted private actor (through expropriation or otherwise). Whether the affected private actor may claim compensation from the state that originally granted the right (eg under the doctrine of contract frustration or on the basis of damages or loss of profit or for the cover of decommissioning costs if the case involves oil rigs and other installations) is quite another question, as that is a matter of domestic, not international, law. But even if the state that originally granted the right provides compensation, this will not make the reallocated private right enforceable vis-à-vis the absorbing state. See Chapter 5.

[159] eg if the absorbing state's laws do not recognize leases or oil concessions as property rights.

[160] eg if the constitution of the absorbing state prohibits non-state actors or foreign actors from operating in its domain, or if the state asserts that recognition of the foreign contract (eg concession) is odious or detrimental to its public interests.

[161] The absorbing state's power to ignore or challenge the foreign private right stems directly from its sovereignty. See S Metzger, 'Property in International Law' (1964) 50 Virginia Law Review 594, 597.

[162] See M Dakolias and K Thachuk, 'Attacking Corruption in the Judiciary: A Critical Process in Judicial Reform' (2000) 18 Wisconsin International Law Journal 353; E Buscaglia and M Dakolias, 'An Analysis of the Cases of Corruption in the Judiciary' (1999) 30 Law and Policy in International Business 95.

occupies in the legal system of the absorbing state.[163] In some legal systems (mostly those belonging to the civil law tradition), international law is superior to domestic law.[164] In others, however, domestic laws prevail.[165] In those jurisdictions, an international doctrine may be rendered ineffective if it contradicts domestic legislation.

To avoid those challenges, the right-holder should take the route of international law to defend its interests against the absorbing state's interference.[166] The individual concerned could be well advised to refer to human rights law. There are today several instruments of international law (binding treaties, soft-law declarations) that protect human rights, including private property rights, against state interference.[167] In light of these developments and depending on the region concerned, the holder of a reallocated private right may turn to a human rights court in person or through the offices of its home state.[168]

However, the protection of reallocated private rights under human rights law is not without its difficulties. For example, all local remedies must be exhausted before the case can be brought to a human rights court.[169] A further limitation is that proceedings can be initiated only against those states that are parties to the human rights treaty invoked.[170] More importantly, even when a human rights claim is successful, this does not mean that it will be respected by the respondent state. Failing an enforcement mechanism in international

---

[163] Churchill and Lowe (n 71) 291–91; M Fitzmaurice and C Flinterman (eds), *Interaction between International Law and Municipal Law: A Comparative Case Law Study* (Asser) 1993.

[164] ibid.

[165] ibid.

[166] This discussion is part of a previous publication by the author. See M Pappa, 'Private Oil Companies Operating in Contested Waters and International Law of the Sea: A Peculiar Relationship' [2018] 1 OGEL <www.ogel.org>.

[167] Universal Declaration of Human Rights (UDHR) (signed 10 December 1948, entered into force 16 December 1948); International Covenant on Economic, Social, Cultural Human Rights (signed 16 December 1966, entered into force 3 January 1976); International Covenant on the Civil and Political Rights (signed 16 December 1966, entered into force 23 March 1976); European Convention on Human Rights (ECHR) (signed 4 November 1950, entered into force 3 September 1953); American Convention on Human Rights (ACHR) (signed 22 November 1969, entered into force 18 July 1978); African Charter on Human and Peoples' Rights (ACHPR) (signed 27 June 1981, entered into force 21 October 1986).

[168] Individuals can apply directly to the European Court of Human Rights (ECHR, art 34), but in the case of the Inter-American Court of Human Rights and the African Court of Human and Peoples' Rights, applications must be submitted to a competent commission (ACHR, art 44; ACHPR, r 33).

[169] A Cassese, *International Law* (OUP Press 2001) 82–84.

[170] ibid.

132   *4 Uneven Preservation of Reallocated Private Rights*

law, compliance with the court's judgment will ultimately depend on the good will of the state found to be at fault.[171]

If an absorbed private right qualifies as an international investment, its holder could also rely on the procedures of international investment law, which allow a private actor to appear in person before an arbitral tribunal and seek protection of its interests against unlawful state acts such as uncompensated expropriation, unfair treatment or unilateral modification of the investment's conditions.[172] Unlike human rights procedures, a claimant in an investment dispute may wish to, but is not obliged to, exhaust local remedies.[173]

However, the use of international investment law procedures presupposes that the claimant's home state and the respondent are parties to an international (bilateral or multilateral) investment treaty covering the private right in question, and that the foreign state is under an obligation to respect the absorbed investment originally created by the other state. Typically, investment protection is sought against the state that hosted the investment. Still, a claim against a third state could be successful, as it is similar to the situation where a new authoritative regime takes control and expropriates investments created by the previous regime.[174]

If none of the above options is feasible, the non-state actor's last resort is to seek diplomatic protection from its home state against the foreign

---

[171]   ibid. However, Article 46(1) ECHR provides that states are obliged to comply with the judgments of the European Court of Human Rights.

[172]   See *Saudi Arabia v Aramco* (Arbitral Award) (1963) 27 ILR 116, 205, 227; *Sapphire International Petroleums Ltd v National Iranian Oil Company* (Arbitral Award) (1967) 35 ILR 184, where it was affirmed that a petroleum concession is an acquired right and must be respected by the host state under the general principles of international law. See C Schreuer, 'Protection against Arbitrary or Discriminatory Measures' in C Rogers and R Alford (eds), *The Future of Investment Arbitration* (OUP 2009) 183; Z Douglas, 'The Hybrid Foundations of Investment Treaty Arbitration' (2004) 74 British Yearbook of International Law 152.

[173]   *Mondev International Ltd v United States of America*, ICSID (Additional Facility) Case No ARB(AF)/99/2 (11 October 2002) (2003) 42 ILM 85, para 127; *Saipem SpA v The People's Republic of Bangladesh*, ICSID Case No ARB/05/07 (Decision on Merits, 30 June 2009), where it was held that the intervention of a local court in an investment dispute can even constitute a violation of international law. The ICJ, too, has ruled that the requirement to exhaust local remedies is not mandatory. See *Case Concerning Elettronica Sicula SpA (ELSI) (United States of America v Italy)* [1989] ICJ Rep 15, paras 61–62; *Case Concerning Ahmadou Sadio Diallo (Republic of Guinea v Democratic Republic of Congo)* (Preliminary Objections) [2007] ICJ Rep 582, para 44.

[174]   The Iran-United States Claims Tribunal, for example, was established specifically to deal with investments in Iran that were affected by the Iranian revolution of 1979. See G Aldrich, *The Jurisprudence of the Iran-United States Claims Tribunal* (Clarendon 1996).

4.5 Conclusions

government.[175] But this option is not very practical either. To start with, an international claim for diplomatic protection presupposes all local remedies available in the foreign state's legal system have been exhausted.[176] Secondly, there is not guarantee that the claim will be submitted, as it at the discretion of the individual's home state.[177] Thirdly, the mechanism of diplomatic protection is designed to protect the home state's interests, rather than the individual's personal right, against injury caused by foreign state actions.[178] Hence, even if a claim for diplomatic protection is eventually successful, the remedy (eg compensation) will be awarded to the individual's home state.

It is probably because of these limitations that no international claim has so far been made for the protection of reallocated private rights post maritime delimitation. Instead, the conventional and judicial mechanisms available under international law during and after the boundary's settlement are less costly and time-consuming. But the success of these mechanisms will ultimately depend on their having equal effect in maritime and land delimitation settings.

4.5 CONCLUSIONS

The asymmetry in international law between the treatment of private rights on land and at sea continues post delimitation in the extent to which reallocated private rights are preserved. At first glance, it appears that the same conventional and judicial mechanisms are available under international law to ensure the preservation of reallocated private rights in both settings. A closer look, however, reveals that the frequency and effectiveness with which those mechanisms are used on land and at sea are far from identical.

With regard to conventional mechanisms, it is observed that reallocated private rights are better protected on land than in the ocean. The land delimitation treaties that use grandfather clauses to enforce private rights that have been reallocated to the absorbing state are far more numerous than their maritime counterparts. Also, the number of cooperation agreements entered into by states post delimitation is significantly greater on land. More importantly, the arrangements made on land post delimitation are aimed at protecting the private rights affected by the delimitation rather than promoting the signatories' national interests.

---

[175] See *Mavrommatis* (n 153); *Barcelona Traction, Light and Power Company Limited (Belgium v Spain)* [1970] ICJ Rep 4.
[176] ILC, Draft Articles on Diplomatic Protection (adopted 2006).
[177] ibid.
[178] ibid.

In the ocean, on the other hand, a larger number of cooperation agreements are made pending delimitation than post delimitation. And in the rare cases where such arrangements are concluded after delimitation, they are mainly driven by the economic and strategic interests the states have in the exploration of natural resources in the transboundary area. This demonstrates that the preservation of offshore private rights situated in the transboundary area is incidental – or even coincidental – rather than a priority for states.

With regard to judicial preservation of reallocated private rights, that too is more effective on land than at sea. Although there are only a few land disputes in which private rights have ended up being reallocated, judges have considered it important to ensure that those rights are preserved after the boundary has been settled. In addition to balancing the interests of the states involved, courts feel obliged under international law to call upon both sides to cooperate post delimitation so that the legally acquired rights of individuals in the transboundary area do not vanish.

Interestingly, the judicial stance in maritime delimitation cases has been completely different. In most cases, the issue of vested private rights was not touched on at all by the court or tribunal. It was thus left to the disputants to assume the burden of protecting the private rights affected by the delimitation. And in the few cases where judges advised states to cooperate post delimitation, they did so with a view to protecting the states' economic interests rather than preserving reallocated private rights.

The preservation of onshore rights is based on the idea that a private right and its holder constitute a legal unity which cannot be destroyed by the establishment of international boundaries. This complies perfectly with the international law doctrine of acquired rights, which preserves legally vested private rights against acts of state interference.

However, the same does not apply in the ocean. In this context, the preservation of reallocated private rights is more an act of state or judicial discretion than an obligation under international law. And when recourse is had to a protecting mechanism, it is mainly to protect the states' national interests in the transboundary area rather than private rights.

The above asymmetry has important legal and practical implications. Firstly, it prevents the formation of a state practice of preserving reallocated private rights common to land and sea. Although the systematic preservation of onshore private rights that have been displaced due to delimitation may contribute to the creation of a customary rule obliging states to accommodate such rights, the same cannot be said of offshore private rights.

Secondly, the difference between judicial attitudes to onshore and offshore private rights shows that international jurisprudence is severely fragmented.

4.5 Conclusions

The systematic preservation of reallocated private rights in land delimitation cases creates a strong precedent for their protection in future cases. It may also instil in states a greater sense of their being obliged to respect the doctrine of acquired rights when entering into delimitation agreements. On the other hand, the contrasting stance taken by judges in maritime delimitation cases prevents the development of a persuasive precedent for the preservation of reallocated private rights at sea. This in turn hinders the establishment of a general rule of international law which would apply generally after all land and maritime delimitations.

This tension in international law extends to private actors operating in contested waters. Upon being redistributed to a foreign state, an offshore private is liable to perish. To prevent this happening, the right-holder must initiate separate litigation in a special international forum (human rights court, investment tribunal) or seek diplomatic protection through its home state. However, a series of procedural and practical barriers seem to discourage non-state actors from pursuing those options.

The unbalanced treatment of onshore and offshore private rights post delimitation demonstrates that international law fails to protect all private interests equally from the consequences of potential reallocation. The question now to be addressed is whether this asymmetry is justified on legal or practical grounds.

5

Reassessing the Asymmetry

5.1 INTRODUCTION

The preceding chapters brought to light the existence of a legal problem: international law fails to afford private rights equal protection against reallocation in land and maritime delimitation situations. For one thing, private rights are less likely to be reallocated during the establishment of a land boundary.[1] And when they are reallocated, these rights are more likely to retain their original status vis-à-vis the absorbing state post delimitation.[2] Offshore private rights, on the other hand, are less effectively protected by international law from the consequences of reallocation resulting from delimitation.[3]

This chapter examines whether the above asymmetry is justified. The reasons that could potentially explain the unbalanced protection which private rights receive in land and maritime boundary-making are manifold – theoretical, practical, legal, historical, economic and political. This study concentrates on three legal grounds. The first involves the scope of the conventions of the sea: should ocean regulation be concerned with the interests of non-state actors? The second concerns the processes of boundary-making: are land delimitation and maritime delimitation too different to be harmonized? The third reason relates to the private rights themselves: are offshore private rights less worthy of international protection than land rights? These questions raise three distinct legal issues, but, treated together, they allow a holistic (re)evaluation of the identified asymmetry.

The chapter concludes that none of the above reasons can satisfactorily justify the ineffective protection afforded to private rights in the context of

[1] See Chapter 3.
[2] See Chapter 4.
[3] ibid.

136

5.2 The Restricted Scope of the Sea Conventions

maritime delimitation, highlighting the pressing need to establish an equilibrium between the treatment of private interests on land and at sea.

5.2 THE RESTRICTED SCOPE OF THE SEA CONVENTIONS

To determine whether the current treatment of private rights in maritime delimitation is justified, one must first refer to the conventions of the sea and analyse their scope and subject matter. For centuries, the international law of the sea was not an organized body of law but a cluster of scattered principles and state behaviours of a customary nature.[4] The conventions of the sea emerged in the second half of the twentieth century from the international community's attempt to crystallize pre-existing norms and codify them in a body of legislation that would be applied by as many states as possible.[5] These developments, summarized by the author in Table 2, are analysed in the subsections that follow.

5.2.1 Geneva Conventions

The first set of conventions of the sea were drafted by the International Law Commission (ILC) in Geneva in 1958.[6] These instruments divided the oceans into four zones – the TS, the contiguous zone, the CS and the high seas – providing a blueprint for which parts of the ocean could be controlled by coastal states and which were available for everyone to enjoy.

Despite their significance in the development of the law of the sea, the Geneva conventions failed to deal effectively with such important issues as the maximum breadth of the TS and the settlement of maritime boundary disputes between neighbouring coastal states.[7] And they

---

[4] H Caminos (ed), *Law of the Sea* (Ashgate 2001) 226–27; Y Tanaka, *International Law of the Sea* (CUP 2012) 20–29.

[5] International Law Commission, 'Survey of International Law in Relation to the Work of Codification of the International Law Commission: Preparatory work within the purview of article 18, paragraph 1, of the Statute of the International Law Commission (Memorandum submitted by the Secretary-General)' (10 February 1949) UN Doc A/CN.4/1/Rev.1, 8, 61.

[6] They were the Convention on the Territorial Sea and the Contiguous Zone; the Convention on the High Seas; the Convention on Fishing and Conservation of the Living Resources of the High Seas; and the Convention on the Continental Shelf. It should be noted, however, that a previous, but unsuccessful, attempt at codification had been made by the ILC at the 1930 Hague Conference. The conflicting views then expressed in on delimitation of territorial waters made the conclusion of a treaty impossible. S Rosenne, *League of Nations Conference for the Codification of International Law (1930)* (Oceana 1975) vol 4, 210.

[7] J Harrison, Making the Law of the Sea: A Study in the Development of International Law (CUP 2011) 27–36; KS Pyo, Delimitation and Interim Arrangements in North East Asia (Brill 2004) 7.

138   5 *Reassessing the Asymmetry*

TABLE 2 *Conventions relating to the sea*

Time of signing	Name of convention	Subject matter
29 April 1958	Convention on the Territorial Sea and the Contiguous Zone	The status of the TS, delimitation of the TS, the status and breadth of the contiguous zone, the rights of coastal states therein, delimitation of the contiguous zone
29 April 1958	Convention on the Continental Shelf	The status of the CS, the rights of coastal states therein, delimitation of the CS
29 April 1958	Convention on the High Seas	The status of the high seas, state freedoms therein, piracy in the high seas
29 April 1958	Convention on Fishing and Conservation of the Living Resources of the High Seas	Fishing rights of states in the high seas, obligations of states with regard to fishing in the high seas
10 December 1982	United Nations Convention on the Law of the Sea (UNCLOS)	Inter alia: the breadth of the TS, the breadth of the CS, delimitation of the CS, establishment of the EEZ, delimitation of the EEZ, the rights of landlocked states in the ocean, the status of islands, scientific research in the ocean, preservation of the marine environment, the international regime of the deep seabed, the settlement of international disputes

completely overlooked more complex legal issues like the presence of non-state actors in the ocean and the protection of their interests in contested waters.

At first blush, the Geneva conventions' silence on private interests seems justified. After all, the main purpose of those instruments was to regulate the jurisdiction of states in the ocean and to determine the states' rights and duties therein. They therefore had little to do with non-state actors and their interests.

5.2 *The Restricted Scope of the Sea Conventions* 139

Yet, this is not to say that private actors should have no place in those conventions. It bears noting that these instruments regulate utilization of the ocean through navigation, fishing and petroleum exploration. Throughout history, these activities have been largely conducted by private actors. Hence, even if the conventions of 1958 make no reference to private interests in contested waters, they should have at least generally acknowledged the presence of non-state actors in the ocean.[8] For example, they could have referred to the legal status of private actors engaging in economic activities at sea and set forth those actors' rights and duties *inter se* and towards states.

5.2.2 *UNCLOS*

An attempt was made to address the main weaknesses of the 1958 Geneva conventions when negotiating UNCLOS between 1973 and 1982.[9] Almost all states have signed this instrument, which gives it a quasi-universal character.[10] Most of its provisions are now recognized as having the force of custom, which means that they bind all states – including non-signatories.[11]

In superseding the Geneva conventions[12] and addressing many of their serious shortcomings, UNCLOS has literally transformed the law of the sea.[13] It has fixed the extent of state control at sea and determined states' rights and obligations with respect to use of the world's oceans. Among its most

---

[8] By way of exception, Article 19 of the Convention on the High Seas refers to persons engaging in piracy.

[9] Harrison (n 7) 37–40; Pyo (n 7) 8.

[10] To date, 168 states are parties to UNCLOS (including the European Union and Palestine), while only 16 (including the United States, Turkey and Israel) are not. See <www.un.org/de pts/los/reference_files/chronological_lists_of_ratifications.htm> accessed 20 March 2020.

[11] These include the provisions that establish the nature, breadth and the delimitation of the TS, CS, EEZ and the freedom of the high seas. On the other hand, the provisions regulating the exploration of the deep seabed (the Area) in part XI and the mechanisms for the settlement of interstate disputes in part XV are not customary rules. See H Caminos and M Molitor, 'Progressive Development of International Law and the Package Deal' (1985) 79 AJIL 871, 887; A Roach, 'Today's Customary International Law of the Sea' (2014) 45 Ocean Development and International Law 239; Harrison (n 7) 53–59.

[12] Article 311 UNCLOS reads: 'This Convention shall prevail, as between States Parties, over the Geneva Conventions on the Law of the Sea of 29 April 1958.'

[13] The contribution of UNCLOS to the international law of the sea is well summarized by Dupuy and Vignes. For them, UNCLOS has managed to transform the law of the sea from 'a law of movement' (which was originally concerned with maritime transport and navigation) to 'a law of emprise' (which allowed states to take physical control of the ocean), from 'a surface law' (which concerned only state activities on the ocean surface) to 'a multidimensional law' (covering the exploitation of the seabed), and from 'a functional law' (which paid little attention to the sovereignty of states) to a law where 'sovereignty has been extended to match the extension of the new uses of the sea'. RJ Dupuy and D Vignes (eds), *A Handbook*

important achievements are the creation of a legal framework regulating the delimitation of overlapping maritime zones between states with opposite or adjacent coasts, and the establishment of mechanisms allowing states to peacefully settle their boundary disputes.[14]

However, the provisions of UNCLOS on boundary disputes and delimitation mention only the rights/duties and interests of states.[15] No reference is made to non-state actors holding legal or economic interests in contested waters. These actors are literally invisible to UNCLOS, for they possess no international rights or duties in the context of a boundary dispute and no procedural standing to defend their interests against state acts before international courts or tribunals.[16]

In fact, the invisibility of non-state actors is not limited to the provisions on boundary disputes and delimitation but extends to UNCLOS as a whole. Save in connection with piracy on the high seas[17] and the exploration of the deep seabed (the Area),[18] there are no references to private natural or legal persons. And even those two exceptions relate to areas that fall *beyond* the jurisdiction of coastal states. That is surprising, to say the least, considering the significant number of private activities carried on *within* states' maritime zones.[19]

---

    on the New Law of the Sea, vol 1 (Martinus Nijhoff 1991) 248. See also Harrison (n 7) 37–40; R Beckman, 'International Law, UNCLOS and the South China Sea' in R Beckman and others (eds), *Beyond Territorial Disputes in the South China Sea: Legal Frameworks for the Joint Development of Hydrocarbon Resources* (Edward Elgar 2013) 52.

[14] Harrison (n 7) 27–61.

[15] eg arts 2–15 (referring to the TS), 33 (referring to the contiguous zone), 55–75 (referring to the EEZ), 76–85 (referring to the CS), 279–99 (referring to the settlement of disputes).

[16] See relevant provisions (eg arts 15, 74, 83, 279–96).

[17] art 105. ('On the high seas, or in any other place outside the jurisdiction of any State, every State may seize a pirate ship or aircraft, or a ship or aircraft taken by piracy and under the control of pirates, and arrest the persons and seize the property on board. The courts of the State which carried out the seizure may decide upon the penalties to be imposed, and may also determine the action to be taken with regard to the ships, aircraft or property, subject to the rights of third parties acting in good faith.')

[18] eg arts 137, 153, 168(3), 187(c), 190 referring to the right of natural and legal persons to request permission from an international body ('the Authority') in order to conduct exploratory activities in the Area, and their procedural standing to appear before the International Tribunal of the Law of the Sea (ITLOS) in order to settle any disputes they may have with the Authority in relation to those activities.

[19] For example, the exploration of the deep seabed is still very sparse. At the moment, only fifteen contractors are operating in the Area, and many of them are state-owned (eg China Minerals Corporation, German Federal Institute for Geosciences and Natural Resources). See <www .isa.org.jm/faq/who-are-countriescompanies-are-exploring-deep-seabed-minerals> accessed 20 March 2020. By contrast, a far greater number of private (seismic, drilling, scientific) operations are performed all the time on the CS. In 2015, over 1,000 oil rigs were located in the world's maritime zones. See <www.statista.com/statistics/279100/number-of-offshore-rigs-worldwide-by-region/> accessed 20 March 2020.

5.2 The Restricted Scope of the Sea Conventions

The UNCLOS stance on non-state actors is only partly justifiable. There is no doubt that UNCLOS has been successful in addressing some demanding maritime issues, and has done so in such a manner as to win over a very large number of states around the world. For those who drafted it, the Convention covered 'all matters relating to the law of the sea',[20] which, in the words of Tommy Koh (president of the Third United Nations Conference on the Law of the Sea), made it a 'constitution for the oceans'.[21] However, this claim can be now challenged. UNCLOS dealt with matters that were critical for the law of the sea at the time of its making. They were above all connected with the acts and interests of states in the ocean and therefore mainly concerned coastal states, land-locked or geographically disadvantaged states, fishing states and archipelagic states.[22]

Although crucial, those matters do not necessarily coincide with the issues that currently preoccupy the international community thirty-eight years later.[23] New questions have since arisen which UNCLOS does not address at all. They include the presence of private actors in the coastal states' maritime zones (eg migrants and refugees fleeing on boats, potential terrorists committing internationally prohibited acts at sea) and, of course, the increasing number of private operations (exploration, fishing, scientific research) conducted in contested waters.

It might be thought that UNCLOS deliberately refrained from referring to private rights in its maritime delimitation framework in order to discourage

---

[20]   UNGA Res 3067 (XXVIII) (16 November 1973) para 3, convening the third UN Conference on the Law of the Sea; UNCLOS, first para of preamble.

[21]   <www.un.org/depts/los/convention_agreements/texts/koh_english.pdf> accessed 20 March 2020.

[22]   The agenda for the UNCLOS conference included twenty-five topics: the international regime of the sea-bed and the ocean floor beyond national jurisdiction; the TS; the contiguous zone; straits for international navigation; the CS; the EEZ beyond the territorial sea; coastal state preferential rights or other non-exclusive jurisdiction over resources beyond the TS; high seas; land-locked countries; rights and interests of shelf-locked states and states with narrow shelves or short coastlines; rights and interests of states with broad shelves; preservation of the marine environment; scientific research; development and transfer of technology; regional arrangements; archipelagos; enclosed and semi-enclosed seas; artificial islands and installations; regime of islands; responsibility and liability for damage resulting from the use of the marine environment; settlement of disputes; peaceful uses of the ocean space: zones of peace and security; archaeological and historical treasures on the sea-bed and ocean floor beyond the limits of national jurisdiction; transmission from the high seas; enhancing the universal participation of states in multilateral conventions relating to the law of the sea.

[23]   See D Freestone (ed), *The 1982 Law of the Sea Convention at 30: Successes, Challenges and New Agendas* (Brill 2013); T Treves, 'UNCLOS at Thirty: Open Challenges' (2013) 27 Ocean Yearbook 49; D Freestone, R Barnes and D Ong (eds), *The Law of the Sea: Progress and Prospects* (OUP 2006); A Strati and others (eds), *Unresolved Issues and New Challenges to the Law of the Sea: Time Before and Time After* (Martinus Nijhoff 2006).

states from granting such rights in contested waters. If that were the case, then the creation of private rights in undelimited maritime spaces would have been prohibited by law. On the contrary, as explained earlier, it can be expected of states that they will create such rights, provided they act within the legal limits of their entitled maritime zones.[24] The absence of an international boundary is no reason to hinder the economic development of states or the exercise of their sovereign powers in the ocean. This is a reality that UNCLOS can ill afford to ignore.

Besides, the impact of maritime delimitation extends beyond the sphere of the states concerned. Whether on land or at sea, the establishment of international boundaries affects the international community as a whole. Its primary purpose is to ensure the peaceful coexistence of states. At the same time, however, it affects the lives and activities of any natural or legal persons situated in the transboundary area. Therefore, the rules that regulate maritime delimitation should take account of the interests of not just the states involved but also any private actors in the area under delimitation.

Moreover, by excluding non-state actors from its ambit, the law of the sea fails to conform to international law's current position on non-state actors. Prior to the twentieth century, few, if any, branches of international law conceived of non-state actors as *actors*.[25] However, their increasing role on the global stage and expanding interaction with states has made it clear that they should be recognized as having the status of subjects of international law.[26] In response to this need, most international law disciplines – such as human rights law, humanitarian law, criminal law, investment law and

---

[24] Chapter 2.

[25] See M Lachs, *The Teacher in International Law* (2nd edn, Martinus Nijhoff 1987) 5–6; L Oppenheim, 'The Science of International Law: Its Task and Method' in G Simpson (ed), *The Nature of International Law* (Ashgate 2001); A D'Amato, 'Is International Law Really "Law"?' in G Simpson (ed), *The Nature of International Law* (Ashgate 2001); W Friedmann, L Henkin and O Lissitzyn (eds), *Transnational Law in a Changing Society: Essays in Honor of Philip Jessup* (Columbia University Press 1972); P Jessup, *A Modern Law of Nations* (Macmillan 1945) esp 1–14; W Friedmann, *The Changing Structure of International Law* (Stevens & Sons 1964); A Wasilkowski, 'International Law: How Far Is It Changing?' in J Makarczyk (ed), *Essays in International Law in Honour of Judge Manfred Lachs* (Martinus Nijhoff 1984) 308; W Jenks, 'The Scope of International Law' (1954) 31 British Yearbook of International Law 1; M Shaw, *International Law* (5th edn, CUP 2003) 42–47; A Cassese, *International Law* (OUP 2001) 11–12; W Jenks, 'The Scope of International Law' (1954) 31 British Yearbook of International Law 1.

[26] The international community 'is no longer limited to States (if it ever was)' but comprises a cluster of non-state entities, including organizations (eg UN) and private persons (eg individuals, multinational corporations). J Crawford, *The International Law Commission's Articles on State Responsibility: Introduction, Text and Commentaries* (CUP 2002) 41. See also H Lauterpacht, *Private Law Sources and Analogies of International Law (With Special*

environmental law – have conferred substantive rights, duties and procedural standing on non-state actors in international forums. By contrast, international law of the sea has remained state-centric. This is all the more surprising as UNCLOS was drawn up *after* many of the treaties that have accorded a place to non-state actors in the international arena.[27]

In sum, the conventions of the sea are limited in scope, being predominantly concerned with state interests. They are clearly the result of initiatives taken exclusively *by* states *for* states. However, given the increasing presence of private actors in the ocean, and particularly in contested waters, the law of the sea's disregard of private interests is no longer justified. This stance is a relic of the era when states were the main protagonists in the ocean, but is out of tune with the world's seas as they exist today.

5.3 MARITIME DELIMITATION'S IDIOSYNCRATIC POSITION VIS-À-VIS LAND DELIMITATION

One might argue that the ineffective protection of private interests in the ocean is justified by the different characteristics of maritime delimitation compared to land boundary-making. The following subsections will explore the factors and rules that might be thought to explain the differences between the two delimitation processes.

5.3.1 Differences in Delimitation Grounds

As seen earlier, the existence of fixed land boundaries is not in itself a characteristic of statehood.[28] Notwithstanding, the presence of land boundaries is inextricably linked to state sovereignty, as the possession of a clearly-defined territory facilitates the peaceful exercise of state powers therein. This makes land delimitation a national priority for states.

Reference to International Arbitration) (Longmans, Green 1927) 73–79; H Lauterpacht, 'The Subjects of the Law of Nations' (1947) 63 International Law Quarterly Review 438; C Eagleton, 'The Individual and International Law' (1946) 40 ASIL Proceedings 22, 22–29; P Jessup, 'The Subjects of a Modern Law of Nations' (1947) Michigan Law Review 45 383; P Jessup, *Transnational Law* (Yale University Press 1956) 3; G Schwarzenberger and F Brown (eds), *A Manual of International Law* (6th edn, Professional Books 1976) 24; C Walter, 'Subjects of International Law' in R Wolfrum (ed), *Max Planck Encyclopedia of Public International Law* (OUP 2012) 640; E Brown Weiss, 'The New International Legal System' in N Jasentuliyana (ed), *Perspectives on International Law* (Kluwer Law International 1995) 65–66.

[27] eg human rights conventions, investment treaties dating from the early to mid-twentieth century.

[28] See Chapter 2.

144   *5 Reassessing the Asymmetry*

Because of its connection to sovereignty, land delimitation rests on the principle that a contested territory can belong to only one state – the state that holds the stronger or more convincing title.[29] For that reason, any factors which may prove or otherwise support the existence of such title (including private rights granted in the area) are of great importance to the states concerned.[30] This might explain the impact private rights have on land delimitation, where they are treated as factors indicative of the course the boundary should follow.[31]

Maritime boundaries, on the other hand, are associated with the exercise of states' sovereign rights.[32] Their main purpose is to enable states to take advantage of their economic and strategic interests in the ocean, which are of lesser consequence than sovereignty itself. This might explain why so many states have not yet delimited their maritime boundaries or may never do so in the future.[33]

Also, maritime delimitation rests on the principle that both states have a legitimate claim to the shared area. Hence, the purpose of maritime delimitation is to divide this space between the states – rather than to allocate it entirely to one or other of them. In order to receive as much of the shared maritime space as possible, states invoke their interests (economic, security, historical) in the region[34] and, even when referring to fishing or exploratory activities performed by private actors, will present them as national interests.

Yet, the above differences do not mean that private rights should be completely disregarded in maritime delimitation. As this study has shown, land and maritime delimitation share many common features. Above all, they are both legal processes with a common purpose. Both on land and at sea, delimitation delineates the jurisdiction of two neighbouring states. This not only enables states to coexist harmoniously, but also allows non-state actors to enjoy the legal and economic benefits associated with the presence of fixed boundaries. Hence, insofar as maritime delimitation impacts on private as well as state interests, it should take account of both – as land delimitation does.

---

[29]   See Chapter 2.

[30]   See Chapter 3.

[31]   This can be seen in land delimitation cases decided by international courts and tribunals, but also in the language and *raison d'être* of land delimitation treaties. See Chapter 3.

[32]   With the exception of the TS. See Chapter 2.

[33]   Although delimitation of the world's land boundaries is almost complete, about half of the world's maritime boundaries have yet to be established. See I Karaman *Dispute Resolution in the Law of the Sea* (Martinus Nijhoff 2012) 169.

[34]   This can be seen in maritime delimitation cases referred to international courts and tribunals, but also in the language and *raison d'être* of maritime delimitation treaties. See Chapter 3.

5.3 *Maritime Delimitation's Idiosyncratic Position*

Again as on land, the presence of private rights should be able to indicate the course the boundary should follow in contested maritime spaces. As explained earlier, long-standing and unchallenged respect (even tacit) by states of a line that accommodates private rights in the shared maritime area should turn this line into a final boundary – as it does on land.[35]

In sum, despite the seemingly different considerations at play in land and maritime boundary-making, the two delimitation processes are essentially two sides of a single coin. Therefore, both should consider private rights as factors that can indicate or otherwise determine the boundary's course.

5.3.2 *Differences in Delimitation Rules*

As seen in this study, there is no one fixed method of boundary delimitation, be it on land or at sea. But this does not mean that the establishment of boundaries knows no rules at all. As an international process, delimitation is subject to the rules and principles of international law. Many of those principles concern private rights, like *uti possidetis*, acquiescence, *effectivités* and the doctrine of acquired rights. These principles apply extensively in land delimitation, protecting private rights from the challenges of reallocation. However, that is not the case in maritime delimitation, which rests solely on the principle of equity. Does the current framework of maritime delimitation in UNCLOS explicitly or implicitly exclude the consideration of private rights? The subsections below will analyse the delimitation rules applicable in each maritime zone.

5.3.2.1 Delimitation of the Territorial Sea

With regard to the TS, Article 15 UNCLOS provides that, failing an agreement between coastal states, delimitation will follow the median line, unless a historic title or special circumstances in the area justify departing from equidistance.[36] Although the TS is part of state territory, its delimitation does not follow the rules that apply on land, such as *effectivités*. Rather, delimitation in the TS is governed by the spirit of equity. To some extent, that is justified by the fact that states possess equal legal titles in a maritime area of overlapping claims – so it would seem only fair that this area be divided between them equitably. The method that might at first sight seem best suited to securing this result is the median line, which consists of all points that are

---

[35] Chapter 3.
[36] This provision is identical to Article 12 of the 1958 Convention on the Territorial Sea.

146   5 *Reassessing the Asymmetry*

equidistant from the states' respective baselines. Yet, if this geometrical method is applied, it would appear to leave no room for private rights in the delimitation process.

Private rights can, nonetheless, have a role in the delimitation of the TS under UNCLOS if they constitute a historic title for the claimant state in the area or a special circumstance that could justify departing from the principle of equidistance laid down in Article 15. In principle, this is conceivable if the state relying on those rights can prove that their existence derives from a historic title or special circumstances.[37] Such proof could be provided by invoking the doctrine of acquiescence, meaning that the long-standing and unchallenged presence of private rights in the TS could justify a boundary line other than that fixed by equidistance.

In practice, however, a boundary other than the median line is almost never chosen for the delimitation of the TS – whether delimitation is effected through a freely negotiated treaty between the states concerned or by a judicial body.[38] The median line approach is indeed so well established that Bangladesh changed its position in its maritime arbitration with India, abandoning the angle-bisector approach for the median line approach, after its request for the angle-bisector method to be applied in its arbitration with Myanmar was rejected.[39]

In sum, UNCLOS does not expressly rule out the consideration of private rights when delimiting the TS, for they can justify departing from the median line on the grounds of a historic title or special circumstances. However, states and international judicial bodies so strongly espouse the simplified equidistance principle that in practice this leaves no room for the consideration of private rights in the delimitation of the TS. There is no doubt that the application of equidistance is associated with certain practical benefits. The median line is drawn more easily than any other line. Also, the repeated and

---

[37] As UNCLOS does not define the terms 'agreement', 'historic title' and 'special circumstances', the burden of proof falls on the state invoking them. V Prescott and C Schofield, *Maritime Political Boundaries of the World* (Martinus Nijhoff 2004) 219.

[38] eg Convention between the Government of the French Republic and the Government of the Spanish State on the Delimitation of the Territorial Sea and Contiguous Zone in the Bay of Biscay (signed 29 January 1974) art 2; *Maritime Delimitation and Territorial Questions (Qatar v Bahrain)* [2001] ICJ Rep 112 paras 175ff; *Arbitration between Guyana and Suriname (Guyana v Suriname)* (2007) 87–103; *Dispute Concerning Delimitation of the Maritime Boundary in the Bay of Bengal (Bangladesh/Myanmar)*, ITLOS Reports 2012, 4, 56–176. See also Division of Ocean Affairs and the Law of the Sea, *Handbook on the Delimitation of Maritime Boundaries* (UN 2000) 13.

[39] *Maritime Boundary Arbitration in the Bay of Bengal between the People's Republic of Bangladesh and the Republic of India (Bangladesh v India)* (2014) 5–78, Memorial of Bangladesh paras 5–48, Reply of Bangladesh paras 3.87–3.88; *Bangladesh/Myanmar* (n 38).

5.3 *Maritime Delimitation's Idiosyncratic Position*

uniform application of this method gives the delimitation process a degree of stability and predictability. However, some flexibility is needed, too, as each delimitation case has its peculiarities.[40] An excessively rigid application of equidistance could transform delimitation of the TS from a legal process into a stiff mathematical exercise.

5.3.2.2 Delimitation of the Exclusive Economic Zone and Continental Shelf

UNCLOS's twin Articles 74(1) and 83(1) provide that delimitation of the EEZ and the CS 'shall be effected by agreement on the basis of international law, as referred to in Article 38 of the Statute of the International Court of Justice, in order to achieve an equitable solution'.

It is immediately apparent that this provision resembles Article 15 in one respect and differs from it in another respect. What unites them is that the concept of equity extends to the delimitation of all maritime zones. What distinguishes them is that Articles 74(1) and 83(1) make no reference to a specific delimitation method, whereas Article 15 refers to equidistance. Instead, Articles 74(1) and 83(1) lay down three requirements: (1) there must be an agreement; (2) it must be made in compliance with the rules of international law; and (3) its purpose must be to reach an equitable solution. Delimitation of the CS and the EEZ must satisfy all three of these requirements, which are analysed in turn below.

AGREEMENT The first requirement is that there should be an agreement. This does not mean that states are legally obliged under UNCLOS to conclude a boundary treaty, as delimitation itself is not mandatory. Rather, the word 'agreement' in this context denotes that delimitation of the CS and the EEZ (like delimitation in general) is a bilateral process based on the principle of mutual consent between the states involved.[41] Even if delimitation is effected by a third body, the states involved must have the shared will to initiate proceedings[42] and comply with the decision reached. On the contrary, any unilaterally established boundaries are *ipso facto* void.

---

[40] For a comprehensive analysis on stability and flexibility in maritime delimitation, see Y Tanaka, *Predictability and Flexibility in the Law of Maritime Delimitation* (OUP 2006).

[41] Karaman (n 33) 188–89; T Cottier, *Equitable Principles of Maritime Boundary Delimitation* (CUP 2015) 219–20.

[42] Exceptionally, a state may unilaterally initiate judicial proceedings under Article 287 UNCLOS, as was the case in *Arbitration between Barbados and Trinidad and Tobago (Barbados v Trinidad and Tobago)* (2006) 45 ILM 798.

148   5 *Reassessing the Asymmetry*

Does this requirement exclude consideration of private rights during the delimitation of the CS and the EEZ? Far from it. If delimitation is reached by a treaty, states may mutually agree that their boundary will follow or otherwise respect any fishing or exploratory rights that may exist in the area. And if delimitation is effected by a third party, nothing precludes states from invoking private rights in support of their boundary claim.

INTERNATIONAL LAW The second requirement is that delimitation should comply with international law. The reference of UNCLOS to international law and to Article 38 of the ICJ Statute was added in the final draft of Articles 74(1) and 83(1) and therefore not discussed in detail by the drafters of the convention.[43] At first glance, the reference to international law seems to be unnecessary or redundant. Maritime delimitation is an international process, and as such subject to the rules of international law from start to finish.

According to the literature, the purpose of this insertion was to limit the powers of judges in delimitation cases, as the lack of reference to a particular delimitation method could leave judicial bodies with too much discretion, which might lead to inequitable results.[44] The reference to the sources of international law is intended to prevent judges from making *ex aequo et bono* decisions to the neglect of legal rules.[45] Hence, any delimitation based on international law can be assumed to be equitable.[46]

More importantly, the general reference to Article 38 of the ICJ Statute implies that all rules and principles of international law are covered, including those relating to private rights, such as acquiescence and estoppel or the

---

[43] The drafters' main concern when drawing up these provisions was to provide a delimitation method that would be acceptable to as many states as possible. See Convention on the Law of the Sea UN Doc A/CONF.62/L.78 (28 August 1981). See also *Case Concerning the Continental Shelf (Tunisia/Libyan Arab Jamahiriya)* [1982] ICJ Rep 18, Dissenting Opinion of Judge Evensen, para 4.

[44] E Manner, 'Settlement of Sea-Boundary Delimitation Disputes According to the Provisions of the 1982 Law of the Sea Convention' in J Makarczyk (ed), *Essays in Honour of Judge Manfred Lachs* (Martinus Nijhoff 1984) 639; A Oude Elferink, *The Law of Maritime Boundary Delimitation: A Case Study of the Russian Federation* (Martinus Nijhoff 1994) 33.

[45] That said, Article 38(2) of the ICJ Statute provides that the ICJ may decide *ex aequo et bono* if the disputants so agree. This has caused some scholars to suggest that Articles 74(1) and 83(1) refer only to Article 38(1) of the ICJ Statute rather than the entire article. Tanaka (n 40) 48; L Calfish, 'The Delimitation of Marine Spaces between States with Opposite and Adjacent Coasts' in R Dupuy and D Vignes (eds), *A Handbook on the New Law of the Sea* (Martinus Nijhoff 1991) 485.

[46] Cottier (n 41) 226.

doctrine of acquired rights.[47] It can thus be argued that private rights should play a role in the delimitation of the CS and EEZ.

Of course, one might insist that the only international rules applicable in maritime delimitation are those that relate to the status and interests of the states concerned, not those relating to third parties which are external to delimitation. However, such a restriction would run counter to the preamble of UNCLOS, which states that 'the matters not regulated by this Convention continue to be governed by the rules and principles of general international law'.[48] In similar vein, Article 293 provides that the settlement of UNCLOS-related disputes by international courts or tribunals (including disputes relating to the delimitation of maritime boundaries) is subject to the rules of UNCLOS 'and other rules of international law not incompatible with this Convention'.

Hence, even if private rights are not explicitly mentioned in the provisions on maritime delimitation, nothing precludes states or judges from interpreting those provisions broadly in order to bring private rights within the scope of the rules and principles of international law that will protect them against potential reallocation.[49]

Regrettably, that is not what happens in practice. Not only does maritime delimitation disregard the general rules of international law that could protect private rights in contested waters, but it not does so without legal reason. On the contrary, the persistent disregard of those rules by states and judicial authorities contradicts the spirit of UNCLOS and international law in general.

EQUITABLE SOLUTION The third requirement is that an equitable solution must be reached. The term 'equitable' is in itself vague.[50] To understand what

---

[47] Support for the use of general rules and principles of international law in maritime delimitation can also be found in the literature. See Cottier (n 41) 490; M Feldman, 'The Tunisia-Libya Continental Shelf Case: Geographic Justice or Judicial Compromise?' (1983) 77 AJIL 233–34.

[48] According to Article 31 of the Vienna Convention on the Law of Treaties, a treaty shall be interpreted in accordance with the ordinary meaning given to its terms in their context and in light of its object and purpose. For the purposes of interpretation, a treaty comprises not only its text but also its preamble and annexes.

[49] According to Article 293(1) UNCLOS, only an international rule that is incompatible with the convention would not apply. This might be the case if the protection of private rights in a particular boundary situation runs counter to the promotion of state interests or the attainment of an equitable result. But this must be proven rather than simply assumed.

[50] This subsection discusses the current meaning of the expression 'equitable result' in the context of Articles 74(1) and 83(1) UNCLOS. See Chapter 6 for a broader analysis of equity and how it should be applied in maritime delimitation.

150   5 Reassessing the Asymmetry

it means, one must turn to the *travaux préparatoires* relating to Articles 74(1) and 83(1).[51]

A look at the drafting records reveals that the equivocal nature of the term chosen was not unintended. During discussions on the wording of Articles 74 and 83, marked differences of opinion arose as to which method should be preferred for the delimitation of the CS and the EEZ. In contrast to the TS, where the long-standing use of equidistance made it acceptable to all states, delimitation of the CS and the EEZ split the participants into two camps. One advocated the method of equidistance,[52] while the other favoured the application of equitable principles.[53] The matter was referred to Negotiating Group 7 (NG7), but without success.[54]

Eventually, the president of UNCLOS, Ambassador Tommy Koh, broke the stalemate by suggesting the term 'equitable result' as a compromise between the two delimitation methods proposed.[55] His formulation, which avoided any reference to a specific delimitation method, was accepted by both groups and incorporated verbatim in the final text of Articles 74(1) and 83(1).[56]

Based on the above, it can be inferred that no fixed method exists for the delimitation of the CS and the EEZ, but the method that is ultimately chosen

---

[51] According to Article 32 of the Vienna Convention on the Law of Treaties, when the ordinary meaning of a treaty provision remains unclear, recourse may be had to the preparatory work of the treaty and the circumstances of its conclusion.

[52] This group comprised twenty-four states: Bahamas, Barbados, Canada, Cape Verde, Chile, Columbia, Cyprus, Democratic Yemen, Denmark, Gambia, Greece, Guinea-Bissau, Guyana, Italy, Japan, Kuwait, Malta, Norway, Portugal, Spain, Sweden, the United Arabic Emirates, the United Kingdom and Yugoslavia. UN Doc NG7/2 (20 April 1978).

[53] This group comprised by twenty-nine states: Algeria, Argentina, Bangladesh, Benin, Bhutan, Congo, France, Gabon, Iraq, Ireland, Ivory Coast, Kenya, Liberia, Libyan Arab Jamahiriya, Madagascar, Mali, Mauritania, Morocco, Nicaragua, Nigeria, Pakistan, Papua New Guinea, Poland, Romania, Senegal, Syrian Arab Republic, Somalia, Turkey and Venezuela. UN Doc NG7/10 (1 May 1978).

[54] Document A/Conf.62/62 (13 April 1978) Off Rec, 1973/82(X) 7–8.

[55] Document A/Conf.62/WP.11 (27 August 1981), Platzoder/Documents (IX) 474.

[56] Each group was satisfied as the other group's proposal was not expressly vindicated by the formulation. *Tunisia/Libyan Arab Jamahiriya* (n 43) Dissenting Opinion of Judge Oda, para 143. As affirmed in *Eritrea/Yemen Arbitration* (Second Stage: Maritime Delimitation) (2001) 40 ILM 983, para 116, Articles 74(1) and 83(1) were 'consciously designed to decide as little as possible' in order to secure an 'agreement on a very controversial matter'. At the same time, Ambassador Koh's solution has not gone uncriticized. See *Delimitation of the Maritime Boundary in the Gulf of Maine Area (Canada/United States)* [1984] ICJ Rep 292, Dissenting Opinion of Judge Gros, para 8, characterizing it as an 'empty formula' for failing to determine a specific delimitation method; B Oxman, 'The Third United Nations Conventions on the Law of the Sea: The Tenth Session' (1982) 76 AJIL 14–15, disapproving Articles 74(1) and 83(1) for 'introducing unnecessary language' on the one hand and 'avoiding recognized terminology' on the other.

5.3 *Maritime Delimitation's Idiosyncratic Position* 151

(eg equidistance, equitable principles) must lead to a fair result.[57] As UNCLOS does not prescribe the use of a specific method to achieve this result, states and judges are free to choose whichever method best suits the particular situation.[58] The question then is: do private rights have any role in this configuration?

As things stand today, the expression 'equitable solution' refers to the balance which must be struck between the interests of the states concerned during the delimitation of their CS and EEZ, rather than the interests of any third parties such as other states or private actors operating in the disputed area.[59]

Yet, this does not mean that private rights are not associated at all with the reaching of an equitable result. If the method of corrective equidistance is applied, as has been the case systematically during recent decades, the line as initially drawn may be adjusted in the light of relevant circumstances. As there is no exhaustive list of those circumstances, nothing prevents private rights from being recognized as a factor impacting on the boundary's final course. Likewise, if the method of equitable principles is preferred, private rights can be taken into consideration, alongside all the other factors that may affect the process of delimitation (eg unity of deposits, coastal length).

Why is it, then that states and judges disregard private rights during maritime delimitation? To a large extent, this is due to the vague language of Articles 74(1) and 83(1), which fails to pin down what exactly is meant by 'equitable result'. While it is true that ambiguity leaves room for flexible interpretations of a rule and facilitates its application to a large number of cases,[60] vagueness is not without its costs. It may cause indeterminacy, which may undermine the efficacy of the rule,[61] as in the present case. Things might have been much easier if Articles 74(1) and 83(1) had explained what is meant by an equitable result and what factors are conducive to is realization.

In sum, the UNCLOS provisions governing maritime delimitation do not expressly or otherwise exclude private rights from the process. Neither Articles 15, 74(1) and 83(1) nor the general provisions of UNCLOS prohibit the application of international rules like acquiescence or the doctrine of acquired rights (which apply in land delimitation and secure private rights

---

[57] For an analysis of which result is fair, see Chapter 6.
[58] Insofar as delimitation is based on state consent and international law.
[59] Although the interests of third states are obviously taken into account when judicial bodies decide that the boundary line should end before it overlaps with the interests of such states.
[60] T Franck, *Fairness in International Law and Institutions* (Clarendon 1995) 31–33.
[61] ibid.

152   5 *Reassessing the Asymmetry*

against reallocation) to the ocean. Disregard of those rules by states and judicial bodies goes against UNCLOS itself and international law in general.

5.4 REASONS RELATED TO THE PRIVATE RIGHTS THEMSELVES

Finally, one could argue that the lesser protection afforded to private rights in maritime delimitation is justified by the differences between onshore and offshore private rights or by the fact that offshore private rights can be protected by other legal means outside the realm of international law.

5.4.1 *Differences between Onshore and Offshore Private Rights*

Clearly, the rights which non-state actors hold on land and at sea are not identical. Based on their location, these rights possess different features. Still, does this justify the inferior treatment of offshore private rights in international law? To answer that question, one must look closely at the socio-economic and legal attributes of private rights in both settings.

5.4.1.1 Duration and Socio-Economic Value

Private rights in contested waters relate mainly to fishing, exploratory and, less frequently, scientific activities. In general, these rights are for a limited duration and associated with the economic development or social progress of the peoples concerned, rather than their domicile. The main reason for this is that the ocean is not susceptible to physical appropriation and has not yet sustained human life.[62] Land, on the other hand, is where people reside during their lifetime.[63] Consequently, the rights that individuals possess on land are long-lasting or permanent and associated more closely with the livelihood of the peoples concerned.

Still, does this justify treating onshore and offshore private rights differently in the context of boundary-making? According to the present study, the answer should be no. Save perhaps for housing rights, private rights on land are of limited duration. Some of them (eg mining, farming, grazing rights) are

---

[62] L Brilmayer and N Klein, 'Land and Sea: Two Sovereignty Regimes in Search of Common Dominator' (2001) 33 *Journal of International Law and Politics* 703, 704–708. The Bajau (known as the 'sea nomads') and other tribal groups that build their houses on boats and live in 'floating villages' are perhaps an exception, though they too rely on the shore for their survival. E Schagatay and E Abrahamsson, 'A Living Based on Breath-Hold Diving in the Bajau Laut' (2004) 29 *Human Evolution* 171.

[63] ibid.

5.4 *Reasons Related to the Private Rights Themselves*

granted to private actors for no more than ten years. Conversely, fishing has been carried on at sea since time immemorial and will continue to take place for as long as fish are available. An offshore oil permit may be awarded for twenty-five years or more. By any measure, that is a long time for a private right.

Also, in both land and maritime areas under delimitation, the rights in question can be equally important to the livelihood and economic development of their holders. The significance of farming for agricultural communities is no greater than that of fishing for coastal societies. Likewise, for energy companies and their workers the offshore exploration of hydrocarbons is as important as mining and onshore drilling.

The duration and economic value of offshore private rights situated in contested waters dictate that they should be protected in a similar manner to their counterparts on land. It is up to states and judicial bodies to respect this need. If offshore private rights (eg petroleum permits) have existed in a disputed area for several years or decades, the doctrine of acquiescence would imply that they should be considered indicative of the course the boundary should follow. Alternatively, if the rights are of a more temporary nature (eg scientific research) and not admitting of acquiescence, they can still be preserved post delimitation under the doctrine of acquired rights. But under no circumstances should offshore private rights be treated as inferior to their counterparts on land, as there is no legal justification for doing so.

5.4.1.2 Legal Value

Besides the economic importance of private rights, one must also consider their legal value when assessing the differing treatment they receive on land and at sea. It is recalled that the private rights which states grant in land and maritime areas of overlapping sovereign claims are of a proprietary nature.[64] But what are the implications of this as far as their protection under international law is concerned?

For centuries, the nature of private property has been the subject of a heated debate between two conflicting schools of thought: the conventional and the naturalist.[65] The conventional school considers private property, and property

---

[64] Chapter 2.
[65] See R Schlatter, *Private Property: the History of an Idea* (George Allen & Unwin 1951); L Becker, *Property Rights: Philosophic Foundations* (Routledge & Kegan Paul 1977).

5 *Reassessing the Asymmetry*

rights in general, as state creations, while the naturalist school considers them to inhere in each person by nature.[66]

The conventional approach prevails in domestic law, where private property is perceived as a state artefact subject to the state's regulatory and administrative acts.[67] On that basis, a property right comes into existence by virtue of the sovereign state's laws, continues to exist for as long as it conforms to the state's rules and becomes extinct when the state's law decides so.

Things are significantly different, however, in the sphere of international law. While international law seems to accept that the creation of private (property) rights is an attribute of states, it is itself a source of private property rights on many occasions. This is clearly the case in places that lie beyond the sovereignty of any state, such as the deep seabed (the Area)[68] or spaces considered as *terrae nullius*.[69] There, the law abandons the conventional approach in favour of the naturalist theory.

The existence of a perception of private property peculiar to international law becomes even more apparent when it comes to the protection of private rights from state interference. Typically, private rights are governed by the domestic rules of the jurisdiction in which they are located. However, the protection of private property against state interference is now increasingly regulated by international rules.[70] The main reason for this is that municipal laws are not always capable of adequately

---

[66] The naturalistic approach prevailed between the seventeenth and eighteenth centuries through the works of Hugo Grotius, Samuel Pufendorf, Thomas Hobbes and John Locke. The conventional approach emerged in the nineteenth century and was also supported by great philosophers like Immanuel Kant, Georg Wilhelm Friedrich Hegel and later (in the twentieth century) Charles Hyde. An analysis of naturalism and conventionalism and the other property theories to which they gave rise (eg Marxism, anarchism) would fall outside the limits of this study. Instead, one may refer to Schlatter (n 65); Becker (n 65); S Buckle, *Natural Law and the Theory of Property: Grotius to Hume* (OUP 1993); C Macpherson, *The Political Theory of Possessive Individualism: Hobbes to Locke* (OUP 1964); R Nozick, *Anarchy, State and Utopia* (Basic Books 1974); E Mensch and A Freeman (eds), *Property Law* (Dartmouth 1992).

[67] See Schlatter (n 65); Becker (n 65); Buckle (n 66); Macpherson (n 66); Nozick (n 66); Mensch and Freeman (n 66).

[68] See section XI UNCLOS, according to which the International Seabed Authority grants exploratory rights to private actors with an explicit security of tenure.

[69] As in the Jan Mayen Island, Guano Islands, and Archipelago of Spitsbergen cases. See B Ederington, 'Property as a Natural Institution: The Separation of Property from Sovereignty in International Law' (1997) 13 American University International Law Review 263, 280–92.

[70] For example, the right to private property is recognized as a fundamental human right in Article 1 of Protocol 1 to the European Convention on Human Rights (ECHR) and is also regulated by numerous international investment treaties, such as the Energy Charter Treaty (ECT) and the North American Free Trade Agreement (NAFTA).

5.4 Reasons Related to the Private Rights Themselves

protecting private property rights against state acts that cause disturbance or lead to their extinction.[71]

In such situations (eg expropriation of foreign investments, housing rights of refugees or displaced persons, cases of state succession or military occupation) international law steps in, upholding the sanctity of private property in the face of the sovereign's actions.[72] On those occasions, international law departs from the conventional position, which perceives private property as a state artefact, and adopts a natural law approach, separating property from sovereignty.[73]

Apart from the fields of human rights, humanitarian and investment law, private property rights are respected in land boundary-making, too. By allowing private rights to determine or affect the mapping of the boundary line during the process of land delimitation and by preserving any private interests that have changed states as a result of this process, the law of land delimitation follows international law's general predilection for the naturalist approach. The fact that the private rights were created by states in an undelimited space does not mean that they should perish when states decide to fix their land boundaries. International law intervenes to secure those rights against the challenges of land delimitation.

In the law of maritime delimitation, on the other hand, a different approach applies. The limited role offshore property rights play during maritime boundary-making and maritime delimitation law's failure to accommodate reallocated rights post delimitation are manifestations of the conventional approach. In contrast to the situation on land, international law does not secure offshore private rights when states decide to fix their maritime boundaries.

This divergence cannot be left uncriticized. Not only does the law of maritime delimitation conflict in this respect with international law's general tendency to protect private property rights against acts of state interference; its stance also lacks legal justification. Both on land and at sea the rights in

---

[71] Ederington (n 69) 263–331; J Sprankling, *The International Law of Property* (OUP 2014) 9; A McHarg, 'The Social Obligations of Ownership and the Regulation of Energy Utilities in the United Kingdom and the European Union' in A McHarg and others (eds), *Property and the Law in Energy and Natural Resources* (OUP 2010) 360.

[72] Ederington (n 69); Sprankling (n 71) 22–38.

[73] Apart from Grotius, who is believed to be 'the father of modern international law', the naturalist theory has been favoured by many prominent international lawyers. See J-J Burlamaqui, *The Principles of Natural and Politic Law* (1748); C Wolff, *Jus Gentium Methodo Scientifica Petractatum* (1749); F. de Vattel, *The Law of Nations* (1758). For more recent supporters of the naturalist approach in international law, see Ederington (n 69); Sprankling (n 71); McHarg (n 71).

question share the same proprietary nature. As such, they should be protected *erga omnes* (ie vis-à-vis the absorbing state as well as the state that created them). Besides, as a form of property, they are also human rights and/or investment interests, which makes them defensible under the relevant branches of international law.[74] So, on what grounds are similar rights afforded unequal protection in land and maritime delimitation? No convincing answer can be found in state or judicial practice.

In sum, the similarities between onshore and offshore private rights in disputed areas outweigh their differences. Without suggesting that private rights on land and at sea are completely identical, they are of comparable economic, legal and social value. Therefore, the unequal treatment they receive in international law is unconvincing and problematic.

5.4.2 *Protection of Offshore Rights under Private Law*

This study has demonstrated that international law does not effectively protect private rights in maritime areas under delimitation. The law of the sea is exclusively concerned with the interests of states,[75] and various procedural and substantive barriers prevent non-state actors from resorting to human rights or investment law.[76]

As a last step, it is necessary to examine whether private rights in contested waters can be effectively protected by means of private law, such as contractual mechanisms and insurance products. This could go some way to justifying or at least compensating for the lack of protection of offshore private rights under international law.

5.4.2.1 Contractual Clauses

It might be pointed out that when states grant private rights in contested waters, they include in the legal instrument drawn up for that purpose special provisions that secure private interests against potential reallocation. An example is the force majeure clause, which is widely used in exploratory permits and provides that the parties will be released from their contractual obligations upon the occurrence of an event beyond their control.[77] However, the efficacy of such a clause can be challenged for three main reasons.

---

[74] These means of protection were discussed in Chapter 4.
[75] See Sections 5.2.1 and 5.2.2.
[76] See Chapter 4, Section 4.4.3.
[77] eg Kenya's 2015 model PSA, clause 38; Tanzania's 2013 model PSA, art 26.

5.4 *Reasons Related to the Private Rights Themselves*

Firstly, the events that typically trigger a force majeure clause, such as wars, strikes, lockouts, accidents, riots and political disturbances, are unforeseeable.[78] This means that prior to their occurrence they can be neither expected nor controlled by the parties. Delimitation, on the other hand, is not always unforeseeable, especially if the private right was granted during ongoing negotiations between the states concerned[79] or if a boundary dispute already exists in the area.[80] Hence, delimitation may not qualify as a force majeure event.[81]

Secondly, delimitation is an event that has a different impact on the contract to the events that are commonly listed in a force majeure clause (eg civil war, political unrest). A closer look at the force majeure events shows that they do not actually affect the existence of the contract. What they actually do is hinder or delay the performance of the affected party's contractual obligations.[82] This effect is temporary, as it lasts only until the event in question ceases. Force majeure simply ensures 'that non-performance is no breach because no performance was due in the circumstances which have occurred'.[83] Such circumstances include physical catastrophes, strikes, civil riots and the like – which is why a force majeure clause usually accords the promisor an extension of time.[84] During that period, the contract is dormant but still existing. It is left to the parties' discretion to mutually terminate that contract if its performance remains impossible beyond a certain time.

That is not the case with delimitation, whose impact is immediate and irreversible. When the area to which the contract relates shifts from one state to another, it becomes legally unavailable, and performance of the contract is consequently impossible.[85] Hence, the impact of delimitation on a private right is more akin to frustration than force majeure.[86]

Thirdly, even if delimitation were to be considered an event of force majeure, this would not secure the affected private interests against the

---

[78] For an analysis of this term, see G Treitel, *The Law of Contract* (10th edn, Sweet & Maxwell 1999) 841.

[79] This could indicate that a delimitation treaty is on its way.

[80] This could suggest that the dispute will be referred to an international court or tribunal.

[81] Unless explicitly affirmed in the contract.

[82] W Swadling, 'The Judicial Construction of Force Majeure Clauses' in E McKendrick (ed), *Force Majeure and Frustration of Contract* (2nd edn, Lloyd's of London Press 1995) 18.

[83] ibid.

[84] ibid 9.

[85] E McKendrick, *Contract Law* (5th edn, OUP 2012) 44.

[86] Considering that the change of circumstances is unforeseeable and supervening. See M Pappa, 'The Impact of Judicial Delimitation on Private Rights Existing in Contested Waters: Implications for the Somali-Kenyan Maritime Dispute' (2017) 61 Cambridge Journal of African Law 393.

consequences of reallocation. The mechanism of force majeure is an arrangement between the parties to the contract (ie the granting state and the holder of the private right) designed to protect them from certain risks that may arise during their legal relationship. Third parties (ie including the absorbing state) are not bound by this clause. If the private right in question is reallocated post delimitation, force majeure will excuse only the granting State and the rightholder from their contractual obligations towards each other. But under no circumstances does this mean that the reallocated private right will be enforceable vis-à-vis the absorbing state.

Another risk allocation mechanism is the stabilization clause, which is widely employed in petroleum contracts between states and private actors.[87] In brief, a stabilization clause secures a private investor's interests against changes introduced unilaterally by the host state in the regulatory or fiscal conditions applicable to the contract. This can be achieved either by freezing the applicable domestic laws during the duration of the contractor by allowing the contract to be adjusted in the event of a unilateral change to the applicable legal or fiscal regime by the host state.[88]

However, it is unlikely that the stabilization mechanism would effectively protect the interests of private investors against reallocation. A freezing clause would be entirely irrelevant, as the investment area would no longer be subject to the granting state's laws post reallocation. Perhaps an economic equilibrium clause might be more suitable, as it would provide the investor with monetary compensation upon a change to the contract. But it is hard to imagine that states would readily include such a clause in investment contracts relating to undelimited or disputed areas.

The above demonstrates that contractual clauses cannot effectively protect the holders of private rights against the challenges posed by reallocation. These private law mechanisms concern the relationship between the contractor with the granting state, whereas the consequences of delimitation extend beyond this limited sphere to the realm of international law.

---

[87] See examples cited in M Mansour and C Nakhle, *Fiscal Stabilization in Oil and Gas Contracts: Evidence and Implications* (Oxford Institute for Energy Studies Paper SP 37, OIES 2016), <www.oxfordenergy.org/wpcms/wp-content/uploads/2016/02/Fiscal-Stabilization-in-Oil-and-Gas-Contracts-SP-37.pdf > accessed 20 March 2020; P Cameron, 'Stabilisation in Investment Contracts and Changes of Rules in Host Countries: Tools for Oil and Gas Investors' (2006) Association of International Petroleum Negotiators 1.

[88] See T Wälde and G Ndi, 'Stabilising International Investment Commitments: International Law versus Contract Interpretation' (1996) 31 Texas International Law Journal 215; A Jennings, *Oil and Gas Exploration Contracts* (2nd edn, Sweet & Maxwell 2008) 13; P Cameron, 'Stability of Contract in the International Energy Industry' (2009) 27 Journal of Energy and Natural Resources Law 305.

5.4.2.2 Insurance

Finally, one could imagine that an insurance product might offer private rights appropriate protection. Insurance is a common and essential risk management tool in offshore operations, especially in the oil and gas industry.[89] Insurance typically covers losses caused by accidents, blowouts, oil spills, delays in the production and supply chain, acts of terrorism or nationalization movements initiated by the host state.[90]

However, things are significantly different in the field of boundary-making. There, an insurance covering the risks to which private rights are exposed through delimitation is likely to be commercially unviable[91] – the main reason being the considerably high risk of private operations being suspended prior to completion due to interstate tension in the shared maritime space.

Perhaps some form of insurance could be offered by an international organization like the World Bank.[92] This might be possible if an existing boundary difference is unlikely to escalate into an actual dispute,[93] or where a provisional arrangement has already been reached between the states, or when the state that has created private rights in an area of overlapping claims has a much stronger case than its neighbour and the risk of reallocation is therefore low. On any other occasions (eg active boundary disputes), however, the reallocation of private rights is likely to be considered an uninsurable risk. As explained by a professional marine insurance broker,

---

[89] T Wälde, preface to DD Peng, *Insurance and Legal Issues in the Oil Industry* (Martinus Nijhoff 1993) vii.

[90] Peng (n 89); D Sharp, *Offshore Oil and Gas Insurance* (Witherby 1994); A Van de Putte, D Gates and A Holder, 'Political Risk Insurance as an Instrument to Reduce Oil and Gas Investment Risk and Manage Investment Returns' (2012) 5 Journal of World Energy Law and Business 284; T Celine, 'Risky Business: Political Risk Insurance and the Law and Governance of Natural Resources' (2015) 11 International Journal of Law in Context 174.

[91] Information gleaned from the author's exchanges with academics and professional risk analysts and brokers at the SPE Offshore Europe Conference held in Aberdeen in September 2017. According to a well-known saying among those professionals, you don't insure a house that is already on fire. Also, a look at the websites of the world's most prominent insurance companies like Lloyd's, AGCS Allianz, Meridian Risk Solutions Ltd and Axis Capital reveals that no such product is listed among the services offered (which include natural catastrophe insurance, war and terrorism insurance, pollution insurance, cyber-attack insurance). See <www.lloyds.com/>; <www.meridianrsl.com/>; <www.agcs.allianz.com/services/energy/>; <www.axiscapital.com/en-us/insurance> all accessed 20 March 2020.

[92] See Multilateral Investment Guarantee Agency (MIGA), which promotes foreign investments in developing countries <www.miga.org/> accessed 20 March 2020.

[93] As would be the case if the states involved maintain amicable relations and are likely to reach an agreement.

> [A risk caused] by a number of people sitting around a table . . . I do not think
> would ever be insurable . . . insurance is absolutely based solidly on fortuities,
> on accidents, on acts of God, on things that cannot be assessed by the normal
> person. An underwriter can make up his mind whether a risk is a high risk,
> a low risk, a bad moral risk, a good moral risk, but all of them must be bound
> up with a fortuity. . . . [H]uman argument is not insurable.[94]

More importantly, even if such an insurance product were available, it would compensate the right-holder only for losses suffered in the context of its relationship with the granting state, but would not secure the reallocated private right against interference by the absorbing state (eg eviction, direct or indirect expropriation).[95] Also, the monetary return which the affected right-holder would receive under the insurance might not be satisfactory if the disrupted operations are vital to the actor's economic development and commercial reputation. In the highly competitive energy and natural resources sector, an operator's removal from an area that has already produced important findings may open up an excellent investment opportunity for its competitors, who will seek to obtain a permit from the absorbing state.

Things will be much the same if the granting state and its licensee were to agree to create a special fund to cover any extraordinary expenses or damages that would not otherwise be covered.[96] Although this form of self-insurance would allow parties to divide the accumulated money between themselves in the event that the investment project is affected by a subsequent delimitation treaty or judgment, it would not secure the company's presence in the region nor protect its interests against the absorbing state. Again, only international law can respond to that risk.

Finally, a potential insurance for private activities in contested waters would cover only petroleum operations. Insurance for fishing or scientific research operations typically secures the right-holder against potential accidents,

---

[94] J Dawson, Managing Director, Undersea Projects Insurance Brokers Ltd – Deep Seabed Mining: Hearing before the Subcommittee on Oceanography and the House Committee on Merchant Marine and Fisheries, 95th Congress, 1st Session (1977) 379 – as cited in R Moss, 'Insuring Unilaterally Licensed Deep Seabed Mining Operations against Adverse Rulings by the International Court of Justice: An Assessment of the Risk' (1984) 14 Ocean Development and International Law 161, 181.

[95] An example is contract frustration insurance, which typically covers trade or sales contracts between private actors and foreign states that are frustrated by the action (or inaction) of the host government (eg confiscation, nationalization, expropriation). K Pasich and S Thayer, 'Political Risk Insurance' (2011) 58(5) Risk Management 27.

[96] A Perry, 'Oil and Gas Deposits at International Boundaries: New Ways for Governments and Oil and Gas Companies to Handle an Increasingly Urgent Problem' [2007] 2 OGEL <www.ogel.org>.

damage to equipment, loss of life and environmental pollution,[97] but these private activities are more likely to remain unsecured against the risk of subsequent reallocation.

In sum, no private law mechanisms, be they contractual clauses or insurance products, can satisfactorily protect private rights in contested waters. This leaves those rights fully exposed to the challenges of potential reallocation.

5.5 CONCLUSIONS

International law is one of the most diverse areas of law. It is not a unified system but a mosaic of disciplines and subdisciplines, multiple rules and manifold procedures. The same legal issue may be treated differently in different situations and in different contexts. As part of international law, boundary-making is also characterized by divergence. As demonstrated in this study, distinct processes exist for the delimitation of international boundaries on land and at sea. A degree of divergence is expectable, if not necessary: what applies in one setting does not necessarily extend to the other.

That said, divergence can be a source of problems. For land delimitation, the law operates as a unified whole. All legal issues that may arise from this process are of equal importance and are addressed responsibly and with consistent sensitivity. Although a land boundary is primarily established to secure and promote the interests of the concerned states, it will not prejudice the interests of non-state actors in the area under delimitation.

In maritime delimitation, on the other hand, the law is vehicled through a narrow prism. Whether effected by a treaty or by judicial means, maritime delimitation is exclusively concerned with interstate relations rather than with the legal issues that may arise from the relations between states and the holders of private rights in the disputed area.

This chapter has examined whether there are any legal or practical reasons for this asymmetry. A variety of potential reasons have been analysed: the scope of international law of the sea; the peculiarities of maritime delimitation compared to land delimitation; and the differences between onshore and offshore private rights. However, none of the above reasons could convincingly justify the ineffective protection of private rights by international law in the context of ocean boundary-making.

The law's failure to rationalize the unbalanced protection of private rights in land and maritime delimitation, and the significant consequences of this asymmetry, underline the need for an equilibrium. Of course, this does not

---

[97] As insurance covers the most common risks associated with the activities concerned.

mean that land and maritime delimitation should be merged or equated with each other. The sea cannot be territorialized, so the two delimitation processes must remain distinct. Yet their conflicting differences can be reconciled. The same goes for onshore and offshore private rights. Permanent housing rights on land are not identical to temporary oil concessions in the ocean. However, active private rights in both settings possess important similarities and comparable legal, economic and social value, which cannot be overlooked by international law. The equitable protection of private interests in all disputed areas is a matter of fairness. Chapter 6 will point to the direction in which a balance may be found.

6

Reaching an Equilibrium

6.1 INTRODUCTION

The final stage of this study addresses the imbalance in the protection of private rights between land and maritime boundary-making. Given that private rights have been shown to be more effectively protected on land, the book calls for the maritime delimitation framework to be reworked so that it takes account of private interests. The similarities between land and maritime delimitation processes and the need for private interests to be equally protected in both settings justify recourse to legal analogy. This will enable certain principles that apply in land delimitation to be extended to maritime delimitation.

Against this background, the chapter proposes a number of short- and long-term means which can be implemented by states and judicial bodies performing maritime delimitation, as well as by policymakers engaged in the development of international law.

6.2 SETTING THE STANDARDS TO COUNTERACT THE ASYMMETRY

In international law, developments do not occur automatically or *in abstracto*. Any course of action to address a specific legal problem requires the prior establishment of certain principles or standards. These standards set the goals that need to be achieved through subsequent legal acts.[1] They fix the

---

[1] A Wasilkowski 'International Law: How Far Is It Changing?' in J Makarczyk (ed), *Essays in International Law in Honour of Judge Manfred Lachs* (Martinus Nijhoff 1984) 308; M Shaw, *International Law* (5th edn, CUP 2003) 309. See also O Casanovas, Unity and Pluralism in Public International Law (Martinus Nijhoff 2001) 83: 'Standards are not a special category of rules or obligations, but criteria for evaluation to which rules and legal obligations are referred.'

164 6 *Reaching an Equilibrium*

framework within which the law will then act or change.[2] For the purposes of the present legal issue, this study sets the following two standards.

6.2.1 *Embracing Inclusiveness*

Following the example of land boundary-making, maritime delimitation should become a more inclusive process than it presently is. Whether on land or at sea, boundary-making should not take place in a vacuum, disconnected from the surrounding legal reality.

Instead of being a strictly technical or mathematical process, maritime delimitation should refocus on its legal purpose. Delimitation is effected by drawing a line dividing a shared maritime space between the states concerned.[3] But, as stressed in case law, there is not one correct line but rather an 'infinite number of possibilities'.[4] Which line is eventually be chosen will be determined in light of the specific facts of the case in question.[5]

The consideration of technical elements (such as coastal geography or the presence of islands) is important for the construction of a boundary line in the ocean, but so is the fact that a legally vested private right may suddenly vanish from one moment to the next. The long-standing presence of private rights in the shared maritime space should be able to determine or shift the maritime boundary's course, as does any other relevant factor. And even when this is not possible for legal or practical reasons, a reallocated private right should be preserved by international law post delimitation.

Hence, instead of concerning itself solely with state interests, maritime delimitation should consider all legal interests that may be affected, such as the interests of non-state actors that may find themselves in another state post delimitation. After all, boundary-making is a human endeavour. Whether on land or at sea, and whether effected by treaties or judicial decisions, international boundaries are established by and for human beings. The exclusion of human-related factors from this man-made process is self-contradictory.

---

[2] HC Dillard, 'Some Aspects of Law and Diplomacy' (1957) 91 Collected Courses of the Hague Academy of International Law 445, 481.

[3] *Case Concerning Maritime Delimitation in the Area between Greenland and Jan Mayen (Denmark v Norway)* [1993] ICJ Rep 38, Separate Opinion of Vice-President Oda, paras 75–89.

[4] ibid, para 91.

[5] ibid; *Delimitation of the Maritime Boundary in the Gulf of Maine Area (Canada v United States)* [1984] ICJ Rep 292, para 59; UNCLOS, arts 74(1), 83(1).

6.2.2 *Revisiting Equity*

In addition, maritime delimitation should adopt a more liberal approach to equity. The concept of equity has been an inextricable component of legal philosophy since antiquity. There is no established definition of the term, but it is generally understood as referring to justice and fairness (from the Latin *aequitas*). It should be pointed out that in international law equity does not have the same meaning as in domestic law. In common law systems, equity offers remedies in situations where case law or statute lead to an inequitable result. In international law, on the other hand, equity does not seek to override the law,[6] but rather to correct any inequalities that may arise from the application of a rule in a particular context. Here, it aims to 'reduce the harshness of law'.[7]

Despite differing understandings of the concept, it is agreed that equity must be apprehended in context rather than an abstract manner. As stressed by Aristotle in fourth century BC, what is fair and just largely depends on the circumstances of a particular situation.[8] In the words of Judge Lachs:

> [I]t is important to bear in mind that the relationship between law and equity is not one between legal system and a phenomenon exterior to it; equity is built into the legal system (...) Equity aims at proper application of law in a particular case in order to avoid decisions that are a reflection of abstract principles detached from the circumstances that a court or arbitral tribunal may face. Its function is to lead to an interpretation of a rule of law in the context of a concrete situation and to balance all the elements of the relationship between the parties concerned. Thus equity gives law vitality and makes it meet the requirements of the circumstances of each case. In sum, equity is the element to which Frederick William Maitland rightly referred when saying that it comes, 'not to destroy the law but to fulfil it'.[9]

In light of the above, two important affirmations can be made. The first is that equity tempers the 'injustice caused by a strict and literal application of law'.[10] It confers fairness on a particular legal rule by softening its sharp edges when

---

[6] This explains why, in international law, justice is not rendered *ex aequo et bono* (unless this is the will of the states involved).

[7] L Nelson, 'The Roles of Equity in the Delimitation of Maritime Boundaries' (1990) 84 AJIL 837, 839; R Jennings, 'Equity and Equitable Principles' (1986) 42 Annuaire Suisse de Droit International 27, 32.

[8] Aristotle, *Nichomachean Ethics*, bk V, cited in R Solomon and M Murphy (eds), *What Is Justice? Classic and Contemporary Readings* (OUP 1990) 38–48.

[9] M Lachs, 'Equity in Arbitration and in Judicial Settlement of Disputes' (1993) 6 Leiden Journal of International Law 323, 325.

[10] W Friedmann, 'The North Sea Continental Shelf Cases: A Critique' (1970) 64 AJIL 229, 235.

6 Reaching an Equilibrium

necessary. The second is that equity is not a one-size-fits-all concept. Its existence depends on the facts and special circumstances presented by each legal problem. What may be equitable today may not be tomorrow. Likewise, a solution that seems fit for one situation may be unsuitable for another.

Equity plays an important role in maritime delimitation.[11] International courts and tribunals pay particular attention to considerations of fairness when ruling on boundaries in disputed maritime areas.[12] This approach is indeed required by Articles 74(1) and 83(1) UNCLOS. In this context, equity relates to the parts of the shared area which the states involved will receive upon determination of the boundary.[13] Pending delimitation, the shared maritime space is legally claimed by two states. It is to be expected that each state will lose part of its legal entitlement in the disputed area as a result of the delimitation process.[14] But when is delimitation equitable?

A *stricto sensu* interpretation of equity would mean, first, that the division of the shared area should not favour one state at the expense of the other. This might suggest that the optimal solution would be to divide the area fifty-fifty between the two states. Second, it would mean that only the interests of the states concerned should be taken into account and that the consideration of any other interests (such as those of non-state actors) could lead to an inequitable result.

However, such a restrictive approach to equity should be avoided for the legal and practical reasons discussed below.

---

[11] The term itself is not used in maritime delimitation. Instead, we find expressions like 'equitable result', 'equitable principles' or 'equitable solution'. It has been observed that this is in order to distinguish equity as a principle of justice from equity as a legal norm; see L Delabie, 'The Role of Equity, Equitable Principles, and the Equitable Solution in Maritime Delimitation' in A Oude Elferink, T Henriksen and V Busch (eds), *Maritime Boundary Delimitation: The Case Law* (CUP 2018) 148.

[12] *Arbitration between Barbados and Trinidad and Tobago (Barbados v Trinidad and Tobago)* (2006) 45 ILM 798, para 229.

[13] See *Case Concerning the Continental Shelf (Tunisia/Libyan Arab Jamahiriya)* [1982] ICJ Rep 18, para 70, observing that: 'This terminology . . . is not entirely satisfactory because it employs the term equitable to characterize both the result to be achieved and the means to be applied to reach this result. It is, however, the result which is predominant; the principles are subordinate to the goal.' See also *North Sea Continental Shelf Cases (Federal Republic of Germany v Denmark, Federal Republic of Germany v Netherlands)* [1969] ICJ Rep 51, para 88; *Gulf of Maine* (n 5) para 115; P Weil, *The Law of Maritime Delimitation: Reflections* (Grotius 1989) 91; C Carleton and C Schofield, *Developments in the Technical Determination of Maritime Space: Delimitation, Dispute Resolution, Geographic Information Systems and the Role of the Technical Expert* (Maritime Briefing 3(4), IBRU 2002) 13.

[14] As 'delimitation means amputation'. Weil (n 13) 48.

6.2 Setting the Standards to Counteract the Asymmetry 167

Firstly, as international courts have explained, equity in maritime delimitation 'does not necessarily imply equality'.[15] Rather, it means that the part of the maritime space allocated to a particular state through the delimitation process should be proportional to the length of its coast, because the coast is the legal basis of its title in the ocean.[16] Hence, a state may end up with a significantly larger part of the contested area than its neighbour. This outcome will be equitable if the allocated parts are proportional to the length of the states' respective coasts.

For example, in the case concerning maritime delimitation in the Black Sea, the division of the maritime area between Romania and Ukraine was based on a ratio of approximately 1:2.1.[17] In the judges' view, this ratio was proportional to the respective lengths of the states' coasts and therefore the provisional equidistance line did not need shifting.[18] In *Croatia v Slovenia*, three quarters of the disputed area were awarded to Slovenia and the remaining quarter was left to Croatia.[19] Here too, despite an even bigger difference in the apportionment ratio, the tribunal did not make any changes to the boundary line.[20]

---

[15] *North Sea Continental Shelf Cases* (n 13) para 91; *Tunisia/Libyan Arab Jamahiriya* (n 13) para 131; *Case Concerning the Continental Shelf (Libyan Arab Jamahiriya/Malta)* [1985] ICJ Rep 13, para 46.

[16] Libyan Arab Jamahiriya/Malta (n 15) paras 46–47, 55–57; *Dispute Concerning Delimitation of the Maritime Boundary between Ghana and Côte d'Ivoire in the Atlantic Ocean (Ghana v Côte d'Ivoire)* (Judgment) (2017) ITLOS Reports 2017, 4, 146–48; A Willis, 'From Precedent to Precedent: The Triumph of Pragmatism in the Law of Maritime Boundaries' (1986) 24 Canadian Yearbook of International Law 3, 39–40; Y Tanaka, 'Reflections on the Concept of Proportionality in the Law of Maritime Delimitation' (2001) 16 International Journal of Marine and Coastal Law 433, 434.

[17] *Maritime Delimitation in the Black Sea (Romania v Ukraine)* [2009] ICJ Rep 61, para 215. See also *Ghana v Côte d'Ivoire* (n 16) para 537, dividing the area on the basis of a ratio of 1:2.02 in favour of Côte d'Ivoire, with nearly 65,881 km² allocated to Ghana and 132.842 km² to its neighbour.

[18] Although this decision was unanimous, the Court was criticized by scholars for departing from previous cases (eg *Jan Mayen*, *Libyan Arab Jamahiriya/Malta*) in which judges decided to shift the boundary's course for smaller differences in the ratio underlying the division of the maritime space. Y Tanaka, 'Reflections on Maritime Delimitation in the Romania/Ukraine Case before the International Court of Justice' (2009) 56 Netherlands International Law Review 397, 423; D Anderson, 'Maritime Delimitation in the Black Sea Case (Romania/Ukraine)' (2009) 8(3) Law and Practice of International Courts and Tribunals 305, 314.

[19] *Arbitration between the Republic of Croatia and the Republic of Slovenia (Croatia v Slovenia)* (2017) 283–364. See also A Solomou, 'A Commentary on the Maritime Delimitation Issues in the Croatia v. Slovenia Final Award' (*EJIL: Talk!*, 15 September 2017) <www.ejiltalk.org/a-commentary-on-the-maritime-delimitation-issues-in-the-croatia-v-slovenia-final-award/> accessed 20 March 2020.

[20] *Croatia v Slovenia* (n 19).

168   6 *Reaching an Equilibrium*

Equity acquires even more flexibility in the context of delimitation treaties, where the contractual freedom enjoyed by states allows them to make whatever arrangements they wish with regard to their maritime boundaries, 'even if these arrangements are not equitable'.[21] For example, it may be agreed that one of the states will be granted a significantly larger part of the shared area irrespective of the length of its coast[22] – or even the whole area in question.[23]

Secondly, taking account of private rights in maritime delimitation is not in itself contradictory to equity.[24] There is no indication (explicit or implicit) in Article 15 or Articles 74(1) and 83(1) UNCLOS that giving consideration to private rights would have an adverse effect on the attainment of an equitable result. Also, as stressed in *Tunisia/Libyan Arab Jamahiriya*, 'it is virtually impossible to achieve an equitable solution in any delimitation without taking into account the particular relevant circumstances of the area'.[25] And yet, judicial authorities take only geographical factors into account. Unless the list of relevant circumstances is closed, almost anything could affect maritime delimitation. The rejection of economic and political factors might be understandable, as delimitation is not a form of distributive justice.[26] However, this is not the case with legal factors, including active private rights in the disputed area.

Thirdly, as already mentioned, equity is strongly coloured by contextual elements.[27] 'Equity, on all accounts, is inherently wedded to the context and facts of a particular case. [It] cannot operate in a vacuum, but depends upon a particular problem which needs to be solved.'[28] This means that it should

---

[21]   L Calfish, 'The Delimitation of Marine Spaces between States with Opposite and Adjacent Coasts' in R Dupuy and D Vignes (eds), *A Handbook on the New Law of the Sea* (Martinus Nijhoff 1991) 484; K Ioannou, 'Some Preliminary Remarks on Equity in the 1982 Convention on the Law of the Sea' in C Rozakis and C Stephanou (eds), *The New Law of the Sea* (Elsevier 1983) 97–106; Y Tanaka, *International Law of the Sea* (CUP 2012) 47; I Karaman, *Dispute Resolution in the Law of the Sea* (Martinus Nijhoff 2012) 188.

[22]   eg Agreement between Iceland and Norway on Fishery and Continental Shelf Questions (signed 28 May 1980), under which Iceland received a full 200 M economic zone at the expense of Norway's Jan Mayen zone. Another example is the 1990 boundary treaty between Trinidad and Tobago and Venezuela, under which the former reportedly ceded part of its EEZ to its neighbour for political reasons. See Karaman (n 21) 188.

[23]   Although this seems less probable.

[24]   See Chapter 5, Section 5.3.

[25]   *Tunisia/Libyan Arab Jamahiriya* (n 13) para 72.

[26]   *Maritime Boundary Arbitration in the Bay of Bengal between the People's Republic of Bangladesh and the Republic of India (Bangladesh v India)* (2014) para 397. Their exclusion is contestable, however. See Delabie (n 11) 170: '[I]f we adopt a realist point of view, it is difficult to exclude, while resolving a dispute, its economic and political context.'

[27]   See nn 9, 10 and accompanying text.

[28]   T Cottier, Equitable Principles of Maritime Boundary Delimitation (CUP 2015) 29.

6.2 Setting the Standards to Counteract the Asymmetry 169

precisely consider all of the interests involved in a particular situation. If the only interests in the area under delimitation are those of the states concerned, then an equitable result should be attainable by taking account of those interests alone. But if other interests are also present in the disputed area, such as private exploratory or fishing rights, then equity requires that they, too, must be considered, as the opposite might be detrimental to their holders.

Of course, this does not mean that the interests of states should be sacrificed or otherwise undermined by a boundary line established only with the protection of private rights in mind. What is important is that the process of maritime delimitation contemplate all (whether state or private) interests involved, as happens on land.

A further feature of contextualism is flexibility. Equity is not a fixed concept but a flexible one, adapting to the current reality and changing societal and regulatory needs. In the words of Cottier:

> Moral and ethical attitudes and perceptions change as society changes. Society changes as factual conditions change due to economic or technological developments, which create new regulatory needs. . . . The function of equity therefore equally entails the advancement of the law in the light of the new regulatory needs. It offers a prime response, laying foundations for new developments which eventually find their way into the body of legal institutions.[29]

The increasing presence of private rights in contested waters underlines the need for a change in the application of equity. Ultimately, this change should be incorporated in the legal framework of maritime delimitation, including interstate agreements and judicial rulings. Hence, it is an extreme and implausible generalization to argue that if private rights are taken into account during the process of maritime delimitation, this will lead to an inequitable result for states. A fair solution can, and should, embrace all interests involved.

In sum, the above recommendations of inclusiveness and a liberal approach to equity would enable maritime delimitation to respond better to situations involving private interests. The consideration of private rights in contested waters, as well as state interests, would lead to greater social justice and fairness in the process of maritime delimitation. It would also lead to greater consistency in international law, which already protects private interests in numerous settings where state interests are also involved, such as human rights, investment law and land delimitation.

---

[29] ibid 9.

170   6 *Reaching an Equilibrium*

6.3 CHOOSING THE MEANS TO COUNTERACT THE ASYMMETRY

There are means by which the standards set out above can be implemented. They can be classified as short-term or long-term, according to their nature and the process of implementation. In general, the short-term means identified in this study are much easier to implement than the long-term means, which call for coordinated action in addition to requiring more time. That said, long-term means can ensure greater consistency in the changes made to the legal framework of maritime delimitation.

6.3.1 *Short-Term Means*

The short-term means proposed in this study relate to both delimitation treaties and rulings. Hence, they can be implemented by both states and any judicial bodies charged with maritime delimitation.

6.3.1.1 Means Pertaining to Maritime Delimitation Treaties

The principle of contractual freedom allows states to take various steps to protect private rights in the area concerned when concluding a maritime delimitation treaty. There are two particularly convenient steps they can take.

PARTICIPATION OF PRIVATE ACTORS IN THE NEGOTIATION PROCESS An initial way of protecting private interests in the shared maritime area would be to involve the private actors in the negotiation of the boundary agreement. As seen in Chapter 3, that is a common occurrence when land boundaries are fixed between two or more states. Although negotiations are heavily politicized and often conducted behind closed doors, they offer sufficient flexibility for various issues to be raised and discussed – including the interests of non-state actors likely to be severely affected by the decisions of governments or diplomatic officers.

There is in principle no reason why non-state actors should be prevented from participating in public discussions on the fixing of maritime boundaries. Participation can be either direct (ie presence of the private actors at meetings) or indirect (ie submission of their positions and proposals to the public body mediating between the two sides).

This would give the states a complete view of the precise location, extent and nature of private activities in the area from the very beginning of the delimitation process and allow them to adopt measures that will secure those interests from a potentially damaging or irreversible agreement. Further, the involvement of non-state actors in public processes could introduce greater transparency in delimitation treaties and increase the level of trust between governments and individuals. Also, as stressed by boundary experts, private actors (eg international oil companies) can enrich the delimitation process by providing capital or technical expertise.[30]

USE OF STANDARD CLAUSES Another step would be to include in all maritime delimitation treaties a standard clause protecting private interests. Such a provision would be particularly useful where a boundary's course is fixed without considering private rights. The systematic use of a standard clause in maritime delimitation treaties would elevate the protection of private rights to a level comparable to that observed in land delimitation treaties.

This model clause should be couched in general language, as this will allow it to be applied in a great many (if not all) situations where private rights are likely to be affected by impending maritime delimitation. The clause should clearly express the states' obligation to preserve those rights against the risk of their abrupt elimination following delimitation.

For example, the treaty could include a provision akin to a grandfather clause along the following lines: 'Any active private rights that may be reallocated or otherwise affected by the final boundary shall retain their status and full effect post delimitation.' Alternatively, the clause might expressly enjoin the contracting states to act jointly to similar effect: 'The Parties shall cooperate post delimitation with a view to accommodating and preserving of any private interests in the transboundary area.'

In sum, the participation of private actors in the boundary negotiation process and the use of standard clauses in maritime delimitation treaties can significantly increase the protection afforded to offshore private rights by states.

6.3.1.2 Means Pertaining to Maritime Delimitation Rulings

Short-term means can also be employed as part of judicial delimitation. Below, two recommendations are made in this connection – one procedural, the other substantive.

PARTICIPATION OF PRIVATE ACTORS IN PROCEEDINGS As in delimitation treaty negotiations, the voices of private actors whose interests are likely to be

---

[30] M Pratt and D Smith, 'How to Deal with Maritime Boundary Uncertainty in Oil and Gas Exploration and Production Areas' (Association of International Petroleum Negotiators Research Paper, AIPN 2007) 29. This should be done with caution so as to avoid potential conflicts of interest or corruption.

affected by the impending delimitation judgment or arbitral award need to be heard. Here, however, in contrast to treaty negotiations, non-state actors cannot participate directly in the proceedings, because they have no standing in the competent judicial forum. Under current procedural rules of international courts and tribunals, only states have the capacity to initiate proceedings, intervene and defend their interests directly against other states in a boundary dispute.[31] Also, the only claims states can bring during a delimitation case are those relating to their own interests in the disputed area (eg legal entitlement, historic rights, economic or socio-political interests); they cannot introduce claims related to the interests of third states or private entities.

This is keeping with the line traditionally taken in legal theory, according to which states are the sole subjects of international law, while all other entities are mere objects thereof.[32] However, most branches of international law have moved away from this position. In many contexts, non-state actors possess international rights, duties and the procedural capacity to defend their interests in international forums.[33] This suggests that the exclusion of non-state actors from delimitation cases should be reconsidered.

According individuals the right to appear before the Permanent Court of International Justice (later ICJ) was discussed by the committee of jurists appointed to draft the Court's Statute in 1920, but only two of the committee's ten members were in favour.[34] It is now high time to renew those efforts. However, the work required will be neither easy for the international community nor quickly accomplishable. Until such time as the procedural rules of international forums are radically reformed, non-state actors have no choice but to rely on existing rules when seeking to protect their interests in contested waters.

As the procedural rules of judicial bodies currently stand, non-state actors (including the holders of private rights in contested waters) can act as witnesses

---

[31] ICJ Statute, arts 34(1), 62(1); PCA Rules 2012, art 17(5); ITLOS Rules, art 31(1), although ITLOS allows non-state entities to access its proceedings under certain conditions specified in Article 20(2) of the ITLOS Statute (ie exploration of the Area as expressly mentioned in part XI UNCLOS or where all parties conclude an agreement conferring jurisdiction on ITLOS). It should be noted that international courts have been very wary of allowing interventions. For example, in *Tunisia/Libyan Arab Jamahiriya* and *Libyan Arab Jamahiriya/Malta*, Malta and Italy asked to take part in the proceedings as the final boundary would affect their interests in the area. However, their requests were rejected by the ICJ for unconvincing reasons. It was only later (eg in *El Salvador/Honduras, Cameroon v Nigeria*) that similar requests were successful.

[32] L Oppenheim, *International Law: A Treatise*, vol 1 (Longmans Green 1905) 18.

[33] eg Human rights, investment arbitration, international criminal law.

[34] See I Brownlie, 'The Individual before Tribunals Exercising International Jurisprudence' (1962) 11 ICLQ 701, 703.

6.3 Choosing the Means to Counteract the Asymmetry 173

in delimitation cases.[35] At first glance, this would seem to open the way to their participation in judicial hearings with a view to protecting their interests against the risk of reallocation.

In practice, however, things are very different. The hearing of witnesses in delimitation disputes serves the interests of the states involved, for it is used as evidence in relation to the claims they submit. Hence, the only role private rights can have in a delimitation case is to furnish support for the invoking state's assertion concerning the course the boundary should follow; they do not have a role of their own as distinct factors relating directly to the interests of the right-holders.

Yet even that supportive role is not necessarily guaranteed. As expressed in numerous delimitation cases, witness materials (such as affidavits and statements made by private individuals rather than public officials) should be treated with great caution – the main reason being that such materials may simply convey the witness's personal opinion on certain events, but not be actual evidence of the legal facts in question.[36] In that case, a private actor's statement may end up being disregarded by the judicial body.

However, there are other mechanisms in international law that non-state actors can employ to protect their interests in maritime delimitation cases. Under Article 50 of the ICJ Statute, '[t]he Court may entrust any individual, bureau, commission, or other organization that it may select, with the task of carrying out an enquiry or giving an expert opinion' on the subject matter of the case that is being heard. A similar provision is found in the procedural rules of the Permanent Court of Arbitration (PCA) and the International Tribunal for the Law of the Sea (ITLOS), in Articles 27 and 15 respectively.

Although the holders of private interests in contested waters (such as seafarers and oil companies) are not explicitly included in this enumeration of persons who can participate in proceedings, their interests can still be brought to the judges' attention through an expert opinion, provided this falls within the remit the judges have given to the person delivering the opinion (eg a renowned academic or a legal practitioner with experience in private rights in international law). Although not yet encountered in the context of maritime

---

[35] ICJ Statute, art 43(5); PCA Rules 2012, art 15(2); ITLOS Rules, art 77(2).

[36] *Case Concerning Territorial and Maritime Dispute between Nicaragua and Honduras in the Caribbean Sea (Nicaragua v Honduras)* [2007] ICJ Rep 659, para 244; *Dispute Concerning Delimitation of the Maritime Boundary in the Bay of Bengal (Bangladesh/Myanmar)* (2012) ITLOS 51 ILM 840, ITLOS Reports 2012, 4, para 112.

174   6 *Reaching an Equilibrium*

delimitation,[37] the above mechanism could be a useful tool for non-state actors when triggered by judicial bodies.

Alternatively, if the judges do not invite an expert to opine on the legal and economic impact of delimitation on existing private rights, the mechanism of *amicus curiae* (friend of the court) can be employed. Under this mechanism, which dates back to Roman times and continues to be applied in both domestic and international courts, a non-state actor (eg NGO, industry representative or individual) that is not party to the dispute but has an interest in the case may provide the court with matters of fact and law (usually in the form of a written brief) that are considered important to the forthcoming ruling and might otherwise be unknown to the judges.[38]

So far, the device of *amicus curiae* has been successfully used in trade and investment disputes, but the ICJ has displayed scepticism towards it (at least in contentious cases).[39] The ICJ's great weight and influence on international case law may explain why the device has not been employed for the protection of private interests in maritime delimitation cases heard by the PCA and ITLOS. But insofar as UNCLOS itself and the procedural rules of international forums do not explicitly prohibit *amicus curiae* interventions in maritime delimitation cases, nothing prevents right-holders from asking to be heard as *amici curiae*.[40] It remains to be seen whether judicial bodies will accept such requests and thereby expand the benefits of third-party intervention from GATT and WTO dispute settlement to maritime delimitation.[41]

---

[37]   Although expert opinions are useful in maritime delimitation cases when technical issues arise in relation to the boundary's location. See *Revision and Interpretation of the Judgment of 24 February 1982 in the Case Concerning the Continental Shelf (Tunisia/Libyan Arab Jamahiriya)* ICJ Rep (1985) 192, where the precise coordinates of Libya's oil concessions determined the boundary's course.

[38]   D Hollis, 'Private Actors in Public International Law: Amicus Curiae and the Case for the Retention of State Sovereignty' (2002) 25 Boston College International and Comparative Law Review 235, 238; D Shelton, 'The Participation of Nongovernmental Organizations in International Judicial Proceedings' (1994) 88 AJIL 611, 616.

[39]   See the WTO and NAFTA cases cited in Hollis (n 38) 238. For ICJ cases, see Y Ronen, 'Participation of Non-State Actors in ICJ Proceedings' (2012) 11 Law and Practice of International Courts and Tribunals 77, 82–86; J Razzaque, 'Changing Role of Friends of the Court in the International Courts and Tribunals' (2001) 1 Non-State Actors and International Law 169, 172–76; L Bartholomeusz, 'The Amicus Curiae before International Courts and Tribunals' (2005) 5 Non-State Actors and International Law 209, 212–25.

[40]   Under existing law, any non-state person (natural or legal) can submit an amicus curiae request. According to the literature, the applicant's interest in the case need not be judicial. Bartholomeusz (n 39) 274; Hervé Ascensio, 'L'*Amicus Curiae* devant les Jurisdictions Internationales' (2001) 105 Revue Générale de Droit International Public 897, 912.

[41]   On the benefits of third-party intervention in maritime delimitation cases, see Cottier (n 28) 504–10.

6.3 Choosing the Means to Counteract the Asymmetry 175

Given the increasing number of private rights in the ocean and particularly in contested waters, expert opinions and *amicus curiae* briefs can be expected to become important in delimitation cases. Devices allowing private rights to be protected already exist. What is now needed is for judicial authorities to become more open towards those mechanisms and to make proper use of them in reaching equitable decisions.

A NEW APPROACH BY JUDICIAL BODIES Even if private actors do not manage to participate in delimitation hearings, their interests can still be protected if judicial bodies adopt a new approach in maritime delimitation cases.

Firstly, judges need to bear in mind that from the moment they receive a request for the commencement of judicial proceedings to the handing-down of their rulings, the process of maritime delimitation is governed not only by the international law of the sea (whether conventional, customary or case law) but also by international law in general. This will permit the application of those international law doctrines (eg acquiescence, acquired rights) that can secure the status of offshore private rights against potential reallocation.

Although the application of those rules stems both from the preamble of UNCLOS and from its Articles 74(1) and 83(1), judicial bodies appear selectively to apply only those rules of international law that relate to states,[42] ignoring those relating to non-state actors.[43] There is no convincing justification for doing so, as the impact of delimitation (both on land or at sea) extends beyond the states involved to the individuals and corporations that are unfortunate enough to hold interests in the area in question. A change of stance on the part of judicial bodies would help to remove (or at least reduce) the threat of displacement of offshore rights that hangs over private actors.

International judges should also reflect on the fact that maritime boundary-making is not strictly a technical but above all a legal process. In numerous cases, judges have affirmed that 'there is not a closed list' of factors affecting maritime delimitation.[44] Yet in almost every case courts rely solely on factors of physical geography.

Without denying the practicality of relying on technical and scientific factors in maritime delimitation,[45] it is overly simplistic and highly problematical to classify relevant factors as either geographical or non-geographical. This overlooks the connection between law and real life, which is most

---

[42] eg rules which require the peaceful settlement of boundary disputes.
[43] eg the doctrine of acquired rights, acquiescence.
[44] *North Sea Continental Shelf Cases* (n 13) para 93; *Channel Continental Shelf Arbitration (UK v France)* (1978) paras 83–84.
[45] eg accuracy, quick implementation, subjectivity.

176   6 *Reaching an Equilibrium*

unfortunate given that delimitation is precisely where that connection is most apparent.[46]

The time is therefore ripe to revisit the classification of the factors that can affect the boundary's course. For example, an alternative classification of the factors that can be invoked might be: *technical* (eg presence of islands, length of coastlines) / *legal* (eg public and private legal interests present in the disputed area) / *other* (eg economic factors, ethnical or cultural links, natural resources, navigation).[47] This could significantly increase the role of private rights in maritime delimitation and their impact on judicial practice.

Arguably, private rights cannot affect maritime boundaries in all cases and at all times. In situations where the boundary will inevitably cause a (partial or total) reallocation of private rights, it is suggested that judicial bodies follow the example of land delimitation cases and request states to cooperate post delimitation with a view to preserving the private interests affected. If state cooperation after boundary settlements is systematically called for, this would contribute to the creation of a customary rule obliging states to protect private rights in contested waters.[48]

In sum, judicial bodies can secure private rights in contested waters in various ways. One approach is to consider private rights as factors relevant to the determination of the boundary's course. When this conflicts with the case facts, judges may advise states to cooperate post delimitation, so that any reallocated private rights will not vanish.

The above recommendations do not imply that delimitation rulings should be rendered *ex aequo et bono* (meaning in a juridical vacuum). This would give international judges excessive discretion to deviate from the law in favour of what they consider as fair and equitable.[49] International courts and tribunals can nonetheless protect private rights on the basis of international law

---

[46] See Dissenting Opinion of Judge Lachs in *North Sea Continental Shelf Cases* (n 13) 223.

[47] Some factors may of course belong to more than one category.

[48] As stressed in *Eritrea/Yemen Arbitration* (Second Stage: Maritime Delimitation) (2001) 40(4) ILM 983, paras 84–86, 'in the last thirty years [ie prior to 1999, when the award was rendered] there has grown up a significant body of cooperative State practice in the exploitation of resources that straddle maritime boundaries', which can give rise to an obligation for states to inform and consult each other with regard to the exploitation of shared resources. By analogy, the systematic practice of states (under the guidance of judges) to cooperate post delimitation for the preservation of reallocated private rights (whether relating to petroleum exploration, fishing or scientific research) could also give rise to a customary rule which would bind states in the future.

[49] The principle of *ex aequo et bono* is not acceptable in maritime delimitation, unless both states request the court to rule on that basis. ICJ Statute, art 38(2).

6.3.2 Long-Term Means

The long-term means this study proposes to counteract the asymmetry between maritime and land delimitation concern the regulatory framework of maritime delimitation and the decisions made by policymakers.

6.3.2.1 Future Developments in International Law of the Sea

To protect private rights during maritime delimitation the international law of the sea can develop in various ways – formal and informal, general and more specific.

AMENDMENT OF UNCLOS A first suggestion would be to amend UNCLOS so that it explicitly provides for the protection of offshore private rights in contested waters. Despite its long history spanning centuries (initially in the form of customary norms and later codified in conventions), international law of the sea has not yet attained maturity. Rather, it is law in the making, for it is constantly required to deal with new issues and to address new challenges. The dynamic nature of international law of the sea is acknowledged by both scholars and judges. As Myres McDougal emphatically stressed in 1955 (when commenting on the validity of nuclear weapons tests at sea):

> [T]he international law of the sea is not a mere static body of rules but is rather a whole decision-making process, a public order which includes a structure of authorized decision-makers as well as a body of highly flexible, inherited prescriptions. It is, in other words, a process of continuous inter-action, of continuous demand and response ... As such a process, it is a living, growing law, grounded in the practices and sanctioning expectations of nation-state officials, and changing as their demands and expectations are changed by the exigencies of new interests and technology and by other continually evolving conditions in the world arena.[50]

A similar remark was made by Sri Lanka's delegate during the making of UNCLOS:

---

[50] M McDougal, 'The Hydrogen Bomb Tests and the International Law of the Sea' (1955) 49 AJIL 356, 356–57, cited in N Klein, *Maritime Security and the Law of the Sea* (OUP 2011) 301.

178   6 Reaching an Equilibrium

[I]t is in the nature of all things that they do not remain static, that there will
be growth and there will be decay. The march of technology and changing
perceptions and aspirations will, in time, place pressures upon the regimes we
establish today.[51]

Several decades later, these words remain relevant. To a great extent, the sea
remains unknown to humanity. New ways of using and exploiting it are being
discovered all the time, and actors other than those traditionally associated
with it (ie states) are now emerging as protagonists in the ocean. It is therefore
only reasonable that the law of the sea should evolve, too. The opposite would
be irrational or even dangerous for the international community. In the words
of Judge Manfred Lachs: 'In law we must beware of petrifying the rules of
yesterday and thereby halting progress in the name of process. If one consoli-
dates the past and calls it law he may find himself outlawing the future.'[52]

Discussions on amending UNCLOS or even creating a new international
treaty on the law of the sea (UNCLOS IV) are not new in scholarly circles.[53]
Soon after its conclusion, UNCLOS was strongly criticized for poorly addressing, or even disregarding, a number of important issues in relation to ocean
governance. They included the impact of climate change on the ocean (eg
rising sea levels), the protection of the marine environment and the preservation of marine biodiversity, the exploitation of genetic resources in the deep
seabed, the policing of the high seas against internationally prohibited acts (eg
piracy, terrorism, slave trade, narcotics smuggling), the lack of a fixed delimitation method for maritime zones and the establishment of CS outer limits
beyond 200 M.[54]

---

[51] Statement of Sri Lanka, 187th meeting, Official Records of the Third United Nations
Conference on the Law of the Sea, vol 17, 48, para 161, cited in J Harrison, *Making the Law
of the Sea: A Study in the Development of International Law* (CUP 2011) 62.

[52] Commemorative address to the UN General Assembly (12 October 1973), cited in T Franck,
Fairness in International Law and Institutions (Clarendon 1995) 47.

[53] In the author's view, the establishment of a new convention on the law of the sea (UNCLOS
IV) is not foreseeable in the near future. Instead, the amendment of UNCLOS or the signing
of subsequent (implementation) agreements in relation certain aspects of the law of the sea
would be more plausible and practical.

[54] See D Freestone (ed), *The 1982 Law of the Sea Convention at 30: Successes, Challenges and
New Agendas* (Brill 2013); T Treves, 'UNCLOS at Thirty: Open Challenges' (2013) 27 Ocean
Yearbook 49–66; D Freestone, R Barnes and D Ong (eds), *The Law of the Sea: Progress and
Prospects* (OUP 2006); A Strati and others (eds), *Unresolved Issues and New Challenges to the
Law of the Sea: Time Before and Time After* (Martinus Nijhoff 2006); A Oude Elferink (ed),
Stability and Change in the Law of the Sea: The Role of the LOS Convention (Martinus
Nijhoff 2005); D Rothwell, 'Oceans Management and the Law of the Sea in the Twenty-First
Century' in A Oude Elferink and D Rothwell (eds), *Oceans Management in the Twenty-First
Century: Institutional Frameworks and Responses* (Brill 2004); M Evans, 'Maritime
Delimitation and Expanding Categories of Relevant Circumstances' (1991) 40 ICLQ 1;

6.3 Choosing the Means to Counteract the Asymmetry

This book has brought to light another issue, which is no less important that those mentioned above and likely to have an even greater bearing on the law of the sea in the future – namely, the presence of non-state actors in contested waters and, more specifically, in areas under maritime delimitation. This is part of the larger legal issue of state-centrism in the international law of the sea, which remains almost untouched in legal studies.[55] A detailed look at the rules governing the ocean (in the form of custom, conventions and judicial decisions) reveals that states are the main (if not the sole) addressees of the international law of the sea. Hence, it would be no exaggeration to say that international law of the sea is a law made by states and for states, as references to non-state entities are virtually inexistent.[56] As this study has demonstrated, the state-centrism of UNCLOS has important practical implications for persons present in the ocean, especially those with interests in maritime areas under delimitation.

An effective way of addressing this situation would be to insert special provisions in UNCLOS protecting private rights not only during but also after delimitation. This could be done by adding language to Articles 15, 74(1) and 83(1), which regulate the delimitation of maritime zones. Alternatively, a new article could be introduced worded along the following lines: 'The States shall cooperate during and post delimitation, having regard to their own interests and the interests of any non-state actors situated in the area under delimitation.'

---

[55] R Hannesson, 'From Common Fish to Rights Based Fishing: Fisheries Management and the Evolution of the Exclusive Right to Fish' (1991) 35 European Economic Review 397; S Barker, 'International Maritime Piracy: An Old Profession That Is Capable of New Tricks, but Change Is Possible' (2015) 46 Case Western Reserve Journal of International Law 387. The work of Irini Papanicolopulu is perhaps the only notable exception. In 2012, Professor Papanicolopulu referred to UNCLOS and other instruments of the law of the sea (eg Marine Labour Convention; Protocol against the Smuggling of Migrants by Land, Sea and Air; Convention for the Suppression of Unlawful Acts against the Safety of Maritime Navigation) when commenting on the uncertainty over the legal status of persons in the ocean. However, her discussion did not extend to physical or legal persons with interests in contested waters nor to the protection of those interests from the legal consequences of delimitation. Her focus was rather on the protection of human life (eg migrants fleeing with boats or fishers) under existing conventions. I Papanicolopulu, 'The Law of the Sea Convention: No Place for Persons?' (2012) 27 International Journal of Marine and Coastal Law 867. In later works, she examined whether states possess jurisdiction over persons at sea and whether there is a state duty to protect people at sea. See 'A Missing Part of the Law of the Sea Convention: Addressing Issues of State Jurisdiction over Persons at Sea' in C Schofield, M Lee and M-S Kwon (eds), Limits of Maritime Jurisdiction (Brill 2014); International Law and the Protection of People at Sea (OUP 2018).

[56] Papanicolopulu, International Law (n 55) 84.

180   6 *Reaching an Equilibrium*

The insertion of new provisions in UNCLOS requires the triggering of the amendment procedure described in part XVII of the convention. Although the drafters of UNCLOS had the wisdom to provide for an institutional mechanism to amend the convention, which to some extent confirms the view that the international law of the sea is still in the making, what they produced is somewhat convoluted. There are two amendment provisions, Articles 312 and 313, the first of which sets out a formal procedure and the second a simplified one. Both procedures can be initiated by states that are parties to UNCLOS, but they display some important differences. As Article 312 reads as follows:

1. After the expiry of a period of 10 years from the date of entry into force of this Convention, a State Party may, by written communication addressed to the Secretary-General of the United Nations, propose specific amendments to this Convention, other than those relating to activities in the Area, and request the convening of a conference to consider such proposed amendments. The Secretary-General shall circulate such communication to all States Parties. If, within 12 months from the date of the circulation of the communication, not less than one half of the States Parties reply favourably to the request, the Secretary-General shall convene the conference.
2. The decision-making procedure applicable at the amendment conference shall be the same as that applicable at the Third United Nations Conference on the Law of the Sea unless otherwise decided by the conference. The conference should make every effort to reach agreement on any amendments by way of consensus and there should be no voting on them until all efforts at consensus have been exhausted.

Article 313, on the other hand, provides as follows:

1. A State Party may, by written communication addressed to the Secretary-General of the United Nations, propose an amendment to this Convention, other than an amendment relating to activities in the Area, to be adopted by the simplified procedure set forth in this article without convening a conference. The Secretary-General shall circulate the communication to all States Parties.
2. If, within a period of 12 months from the date of the circulation of the communication, a State Party objects to the proposed amendment or to the proposal for its adoption by the simplified procedure, the amendment shall be considered rejected. The Secretary-General shall immediately notify all States Parties accordingly.
3. If, 12 months from the date of circulation of the communication, no State Party has objected to the proposed amendment or to the proposal for its

6.3 Choosing the Means to Counteract the Asymmetry 181

adoption by the simplified procedure, the proposed amendment shall be considered adopted. The Secretary-General shall notify all States Parties that the proposed amendment has been adopted.

Both procedures have their difficulties.[57] The formal procedure necessitates the organization of a conference among all state parties to UNCLOS and requires that the participants agree to the proposed amendments by consensus. Needless to say, this is a time-consuming and quite demanding process.

The simplified procedure, on the other hand, does impose an initial waiting period, but makes the entry into force of the proposed amendments conditional on the approval of all states parties to the convention. This means that the entire amendment process will be frustrated by a single objection. Also, allowing twelve months for possible objections to the proposed amendment is rather excessive for a 'simplified' procedure. Finally, under both procedures the adopted amendments need to be signed by the states parties to the convention within twelve months of their adoption, which makes the amendment process even more time-consuming.[58]

Because of the above complexities, neither of the amendment procedures has yet been triggered. Of course, this is not to say they may not be employed in the future. The changing needs of international law of the sea may eventually encourage such amendments.

CONCLUSION OF AN IMPLEMENTING AGREEMENT Even if no amendments are made to UNCLOS, there is another way of protecting offshore private rights in contested waters by conventional means – namely, through the conclusion of an implementing agreement.[59]

The signing of a separate agreement regulating the implementation of certain provisions of UNCLOS is not unknown to states.[60] Such were the 1994 agreement on the exploration of the Area[61] and the 1995 agreement on the

---

[57] See A Boyle, 'Further Development of the 1982 Convention on the Law of the Sea: Mechanisms for Change' in D Freestone, R Barnes and D Ong (eds), *The Law of the Sea: Progress and Prospects* (OUP 2006) 41–42; Harrison (n 51) 64–70.

[58] UNCLOS, art 315(1).

[59] Term used by the United Nations. See UNGA, 'Oceans and the Law of the Sea: Report of the Secretary-General' (25 November 2009) UN Doc A/64/66/Add.1, para 3, cited in Harrison (n 51) 85.

[60] By nature, an implementing agreement generally regulates issues which have not been satisfactorily covered in the convention. See the preambles to the implementing agreements cited in the following footnotes.

[61] Agreement Relating to the Implementation of Part XI of the 1982 Convention on the Law of the Sea of 10 December 1982 (signed 28 July 1994, entered into force 28 July 1996) (Area Agreement) <www.un.org/depts/los/convention_agreements/convention_overview_part_xi.htm> accessed 20 March 2020.

6 Reaching an Equilibrium

conservation and management of straddling and migratory fish stocks.[62] Both agreements now form part of international law of the sea and are applied and interpreted along with UNCLOS as a single body.[63] Recently, the UN announced the drafting of a third implementing agreement on marine biological diversity in areas beyond national jurisdiction.[64]

An agreement of a similar kind could be made to regulate the status of non-state actors in the ocean, and more particularly the rights, procedural capacity and perhaps obligations of individuals and corporations with interests in contested waters. The conclusion of an agreement referring to private actors might at first sight seem absurd. After all, international agreements typically refer to their signatories (ie states) and set forth their rights, duties and procedural capacity. But, as affirmed by the Permanent Court of Justice back in 1928, there is no principle of international law that prevents the parties to a treaty from conferring rights (or imposing duties) on individuals.[65] As later stated in the famous *LeGrand* and *Avena* cases, international treaties 'can create individual rights', too.[66] So there is no legal obstacle to including in an implementing agreement a reference to the status of private actors in contested waters or even a provision vesting them with international rights or obligations.

Although the agreement will be signed by states, it will have a direct impact on the private stakeholders. Therefore, it is important that non-state actors such as seafarers, oil companies, NGOs and other bodies involved in overseeing or regulating private activities in the ocean participate in the instrument's preparation.[67]

---

[62] Agreement for the Implementation of the Provisions of the United Nations Convention on the Law of the Sea of 10 December 1982 Relating to the Conservation and Management of Straddling Fish Stocks and Highly Migratory Fish Stocks (signed 4 August 1995, entered into force 11 December 2001) (Fish Stocks Agreement) <www.un.org/depts/los/convention_a greements/convention_overview_fish_stocks.htm> accessed 20 March 2020.

[63] Area Agreement, art 2; Fish Stocks Agreement, art 4.

[64] UNGA Res 72/249 (24 December 2017).

[65] *Jurisdiction of the Courts of Danzig (The Beamtenabkommen)* (1928) PCIJ Rep Series B No 15, 17–18.

[66] *Germany v United States* [2001] ICJ Rep 466, para 77; *Case Concerning Avena and Other Mexican Nationals (Mexico v United States)* [2004] ICJ Rep 12, para 40. See also *Société Générale de Surveillance (SGS) v Republic of Philippines* (Decision on Objections to Jurisdiction) (2004) 8 ICSID Rep 518, para 154, where it was recognized that 'under modern international law, treaties may confer rights, substantive and procedural, on individuals' (ie corporations in that particular case).

[67] It is not unknown for actors other than states to participate in proceedings leading to international conventions. Many organizations took part in various sessions during the preparation of UNCLOS, such as the International Labour Organization, the World Bank, the International Maritime Organization, the International Atomic Energy Agency, the

EVOLUTIONARY INTERPRETATION OF UNCLOS Although amending UNCLOS and concluding an implementing agreement may be effective ways of protecting private rights in contested waters, they are time-consuming and presuppose broad collaboration and consensus among state. An equally effective but more immediate step would be to interpret UNCLOS in an evolutionary way. This could be done either as a temporary measure (until such time as UNCLOS is amended or an implementing agreement signed) or as an alternative to those two options.

The evolutionary interpretation of treaties is not unknown to international law. According to the Vienna Convention on the Law of Treaties (VCLT), 'a treaty shall be interpreted in good faith in accordance with the ordinary meaning to be given to the terms of the treaty in their context and in the light of its object and purpose'.[68] On some occasions, however, it has been necessary to interpret 'a term whose meaning had evolved since the conclusion of the treaty at issue'.[69] In those cases, the term should be understood as having 'a meaning or content capable of evolving, not one fixed once and for all, so as to make allowance for, among other things, developments in international law'.[70] This does not mean that the parties' original intention will be disregarded, but rather that the term in question will be construed in a pragmatic way, reflecting its changing meaning.[71] That is particularly necessary where the treaty has been in force for a long period of time.[72]

Support for an evolutionary interpretation of UNCLOS can be found in both scholarship and case law.[73] The convention is increasingly applied in situations that raise issues not contemplated when it was drafted.[74] They

---

International Chamber of Commerce, the International Council of Women, the International Association for Religious Freedom, the International Federation for Human Rights and Pan American Federation of Engineering Societies. See UNCLOS Final Act, Appendix: Observers Invited and Participating at Sessions of the Conference.

[68] art 31(1).

[69] *Dispute Regarding Navigational and Related Rights (Costa Rica v Nicaragua)* [2009] ICJ Rep 213, para 63.

[70] ibid, para 66.

[71] See S Helmersen, 'Evolutive Treaty Interpretation: Legality, Semantics and Distinctions' (2013) 6 European Journal of Legal Studies 127.

[72] *Costa Rica v Nicaragua* (n 69) para 67.

[73] A Petrig, 'The Commission of Maritime Crimes with Unmanned Systems: An Interpretive Challenge for the United Nations Convention on the Law of the Sea' in M Evans and S Galani (eds), *Maritime Security and the Law of the Sea: Help of Hindrance* (Edward Elgar 2020) 114; Responsibilities and Obligations of States Sponsoring Persons and Entities with Respect to Activities in the Area (Advisory Opinion) (2011) ITLOS.

[74] Petrig (n 73).

184   6 *Reaching an Equilibrium*

undoubtedly include maritime security and environmental protection and should arguably include the establishment of maritime boundaries, too.

In this light, the UNCLOS provisions relating to maritime delimitation might be interpreted as requiring all interests in the disputed area to be taken into account (ie those of non-state actors as well as those of the states). This would be consistent with the modern approach to international boundaries (which seeks to secure the coexistence of states and non-state actors)[75] and equity (which seeks to achieve social fairness in a specific context).[76]

But even if the international community is resistant to an evolutionary interpretation of Articles 15, 74(1) and 83(1), UNCLOS can still be applied in a way that respects private rights situated in contested waters. According to the VCLT, 'any relevant rules of international law applicable in the relations between the parties' are to be taken into account when interpreting a treaty.[77] Such rules can be considered to include the doctrines of acquiescence and acquired rights.

In sum, the above recommendations show that the international law of the sea has the potential to protect private rights in disputed waters. All it needs is for the current UNCLOS framework to be updated by way of amendments or a separate implementing agreement or to be interpreted in an evolutionary manner.

6.3.2.2 Future Developments in General International Law

Aside from the developments in international law of the sea discussed above, the protection of private rights can be ensured through measures of general international law. Unlike the former, these measures would cover all private rights affected by boundary-making, whether on land or at sea. Such measures may be of diverse kinds.

ESTABLISHMENT OF COMMON GUIDELINES FOR LAND AND MARITIME DELIMITATION One way to counteract the asymmetry in the treatment of private rights in land and maritime boundary-making would be by drawing up a set of delimitation guidelines aimed at securing private rights equally in both settings. These guidelines could be agreed between states at an international meeting, set out by judges in future delimitation cases, or issued by UN organs as recommendations to be followed during delimitation.

---

[75] See Chapter 1; Section 6.2.1.
[76] See Section 6.2.2.
[77] VCLT, art 31(3)(c).

6.3 *Choosing the Means to Counteract the Asymmetry* 185

Such guidelines would ensure symmetry between land and maritime delimitation with regard to the factors that should be taken into account during the establishment of a boundary line. As this study has explained, there are more similarities between land and maritime delimitation than there are differences. Although land delimitation rests on the principle of a single sovereign title over the territory in question, while its maritime counterpart is based on the concept of two equal entitlements overlapping in the same ocean space, the purpose of boundary-making in both settings is to limit two contiguous jurisdiction claims. In both situations, the fixing of an international boundary is not just a technical operation but also a political and a legal exercise. In other words, delimitation is not merely about drawing a line on terrain or on paper, but a process of whereby clear boundaries destined to remain in place forever are established between neighbouring states.[78]

To achieve this purpose, international boundaries need to strike a delicate balance between the conflicting interests of states in the area in question. If a state is required to give up more than is acceptable to it, then the whole delimitation process is liable to founder. And yet, the states' interests are not the only ones that need to be taken into consideration. Whether on land or at sea, the establishment of an international boundary will affect the lives and the interests (legal, economic, social) of the natural and legal persons situated in the area under delimitation. Therefore, delimitation should have regard to the legal and socio-political reality in which it takes place.

This study has argued that, whether on land or at sea, delimitation should be governed by common principles and should treat common issues with consistency. One such issue is the presence of private interests in the area under delimitation and the bearing they have on the establishment of the boundary. As has been seen, private rights play a significant role in land delimitation. States and judicial bodies should make sure that the same happens in the ocean.

If acted on, the above suggestion would give private interests an equally active role in all situations of boundary-making. They should be recognized as important legal factors potentially affecting a boundary's course and for this reason should be taken into consideration at all stages of delimitation, from the commencement of negotiations between the states involved to the final establishment of the boundary through a treaty or a judicial decision. And if, for some reason peculiar to a particular situation, private rights are denied the possibility of influencing the process of delimitation that could lead to their reallocation, the states involved should be placed under an obligation to

---

[78] Unless states decide to amend their boundaries in the future, but only by peaceful means.

cooperate post delimitation in order to safeguard private interests by all means available under international law (eg the doctrine of acquired rights).

The establishment and application of common (and progressively fixed) practices in land and maritime delimitation can bring multiple benefits. They will facilitate the conclusion of delimitation treaties by setting a benchmark to which states can refer when deciding what factors should affect the delimitation process. They will contribute to international case law by increasing the stability and predictability of judicial practice and reducing the risk of incoherent case decisions. More importantly, states' and judicial bodies' systematic adherence to common guidelines will iron out the current discrepancies in international law between the treatment of private rights in land and maritime delimitation, ensuring that private interests are equally protected in both settings.

CODIFICATION OF COMMON PRINCIPLES OF LAND AND MARITIME DELIMITATION The importance of common guidelines for land and maritime delimitation should not be undervalued. However, as guidelines, they will fall within the sphere of so-called 'soft law'.[79] This means that their application will not be mandatory or enforceable, but instead left to the discretion of the states or judicial body responsible for establishing the boundary. Although this freedom is important, it leaves a wide margin of manoeuvre in the implementation of the guidelines.

A more effective way of protecting private rights would be to have the guidelines codified by an international body in a clear and concrete manner that allays any doubts as to their validity or binding nature and ensures that states and judicial bodies adhere to them. In international law, the body responsible for codifying legal principles as rules is the International Law Commission (ILC).[80] Since its establishment in 1947, the ILC has greatly

---

[79] Unlike hard law, soft law has no binding force. On this distinction, see M Shaw, *International Law* (7th edn, CUP 2014) 83–84.

[80] The ILC was established in 1947 by the UN General Assembly pursuant to Article 13(1)(a) of the UN Charter 'to initiate studies and make recommendations for the purpose of ... encouraging the progressive development of international law and its codification'. See <http://legal.un.org/ilc/> accessed 20 March 2020. See also ILC Statute, art 1(1). On the mission and role of the ILC in the development of international law, see H Briggs, *The International Law Commission* (Cornell University Press 1965); I Sinclair, *The International Law Commission* (CUP 1987). In the past, some scholars objected to the codification of international law on the grounds that it 'allegedly destroys or undermines the general customary law'. See K Wolfke, 'Can Codification of International Law Be Harmful?' in Jerzy Makarczyk (ed), *Essays in International Law in Honour of Judge Manfred Lachs* (Martinus Nijhoff 1984) 313.

6.3 *Choosing the Means to Counteract the Asymmetry* 187

contributed to the development and understanding of international law in various areas.[81]

One of the topics to which it has turned its attention is the place of non-state actors in international law. For example, the accountability of non-state actors for internationally recognized crimes was the catalyst that led the ILC to draw up the Draft Statute for an International Criminal Court in 1994. References to non-state actors are also found in the ILC's Draft Articles on Responsibility of States for Internationally Wrongful Acts.[82]

More interestingly, as early as 1949 the ILC proposed a codification of the law of persons that would have clarified whether non-state actors possessed international legal personality or were mere objects of international law, but its proposal was never acted on.[83] Perhaps the concept of international legal personality had not sufficiently matured at that time. Besides, codifying the status of non-state actors altogether (ie individuals, multinational corporations, NGOs and other groups of persons) and in general rather than in a specific field of international law would have been too ambitious an undertaking for a body that had been active for only two years. In the words of the late Professor Baxter, 'excessively ambitious ... schemes for the codification and progressive development of international law are almost inevitably doomed to fail' as 'in such case, codification can be law-destroying rather than a stimulus and guide to ordered conduct by nations'.[84]

However, a lot has changed in legal theory and practice since that first codification attempt. Non-state actors are of increasing interest to international law and therefore are likely to be the subject of future legal developments. Besides, codifying the place of natural and legal persons and the

---

[81] The ILC played an instrumental role in the making of the Law of the Sea Conventions of 1958. Another of its notable achievements was the adoption in 2001 of the Draft Articles on Responsibility of States for Internationally Wrongful Acts, <http://legal.un.org/ilc/texts/instruments/english/commentaries/9_6_2001.pdf> accessed 20 March 2020, which have been applied by international courts in relevant cases (eg *Guyana v Suriname*). It has also carried out important work on international criminal law, the identification of customary international law, treaty interpretation, state succession, *jus cogens*. See the reports listed on its website.

[82] eg arts 8–11 on acts of non-state actors attributable to or adopted by states; art 33 on states' obligations towards non-state actors, including reparation.

[83] Survey of International Law in Relation to the Work of Codification of the International Law Commission: Preparatory work within the purview of article, 18 paragraph 1, of the Statute of the International Law Commission (Memorandum submitted by the Secretary-General) (10 February 1949) UN Doc A/CN.4/1/Rev.1, 19–22, <http://legal.un.org/ilc/documentation/english/a_cn4_1_rev1.pdf> accessed 20 March 2020.

[84] R Baxter, 'The Effects of Ill-Conceived Codification and Development of International Law' in *Recueil d'Études de Droit International en Hommage à Paul Guggenheim* (Faculté de Droit de l'Université de Genève 1968) 146.

188   *6 Reaching an Equilibrium*

protection of their interests in the context of boundary-making is a far more plausible prospect for the ILC than general codification of the law of persons.

In sum, the similarities between land and maritime boundary-making and the need for international law to protect private interests in both settings should encourage the establishment of a common set of delimitation guidelines and the crystallization of those principles into legally binding norms.

6.4 CONCLUSIONS

This book has argued that international law should increase the protection of private rights in the context of maritime delimitation by drawing lessons from land. To achieve that, maritime delimitation should soften its hard, technical edges and become more inclusive by considering all legal issues at play within that setting. At the same time, maritime delimitation should take a more liberal view of equity than it does today, so that an equitable result can be achieved for all actors (state and non-state) with interests in the disputed area. This chapter has recommended various legal means whereby those changes may be realized. They were divided into two groups depending on the length of time they require.

The short-term means are those which can be implemented promptly by states and international jurisprudence. For conventional delimitation, the study urged that persons with private interests in the area should be actively involved in the negotiation of maritime delimitation treaties between states. It also suggested that standard clauses securing the status of offshore private interests during and post delimitation be inserted in all boundary treaties.

For judicial delimitation, the study invited international jurisprudence to be more open to allowing non-state actors to participate in delimitation proceedings through the existing mechanisms of expert opinions and *amicus curiae* interventions. It also proposed that judicial bodies revisit the restrictive geographical/non-geographical classification of delimitation factors and that they apply all components of international law, including rules like the doctrines of acquiescence and acquired rights, which can directly secure offshore private rights in transboundary areas.

The long-term means are those involving more complex procedures. They include normative changes to the international law of the sea, such as the amendment of UNCLOS or the conclusion of an implementing agreement between states on the status of non-state actors at sea, and the evolutionary interpretation of UNCLOS. Another long-term device would be to establish common guidelines on the protection of existing private rights to be applied in

6.4 Conclusions

both land and maritime delimitation, and the crystallization of those principles into a codified body of legal rules by the ILC.

Each of these means has its particularities. Some are easy to implement; some are dependent on the discretion of the bodies concerned; and some are of a binding nature, which implies an obligation to protect private rights in boundary-making. Arguably, the inclusion of a preservation clause in delimitation treaties would be a more practicable way of securing private rights in contested waters than amending UNCLOS. Likewise, it would be easier for judicial bodies to expand the list of factors to be considered during maritime delimitation (including the presence of active private rights) than for private actors to acquire standing to bring claims in delimitation cases.

Still, what is quick or easy to implement is not necessarily the most effective solution. Perhaps the best way to increase the protection of non-state rights in the ocean would be through a combination of various means. The establishment of common delimitation guidelines on land and at sea by a team of specialists (including jurists and technical experts) would prompt states and international judges to first acknowledge the importance of balanced practices in both settings, which is a prerequisite to the employment of the appropriate conventional or judicial means of protecting private rights. But above all, what is needed is a change of mindset in maritime delimitation. Without this, the protection of private rights in only some treaties or delimitation rulings would be a pyrrhic victory for non-state actors.

7

Epilogue

7.1 THE UNBALANCED PROTECTION OF NON-STATE ACTORS' RIGHTS IN LAND AND MARITIME DELIMITATION

This book has undertaken a critical assessment and proposed a reconstruction of the legal framework addressing the protection of non-state actors' rights in maritime delimitation. An increasing number of coastal states grant private exploratory, fishing and scientific research rights in marine and submarine areas to which neighbouring states with opposite or adjacent coasts also lay claim. If delimitation follows, those rights may become threatened with reallocation from the state which originally created them to the neighbouring state. The sudden displacement of private rights from one jurisdiction to another can affect the legal and economic interests of their holders.

This begs the question: do the rules of maritime delimitation protect the rights of non-state actors effectively against the disruption of potential reallocation? To address this question, the book took as a benchmark the place that private rights occupy in land boundary-making. Land delimitation was developed first and afforded extensive protection to non-state actors' interests in areas of overlapping sovereign claims. Whether private rights enjoy a similar level of protection in maritime delimitation was a question still to be examined.

It might logically be assumed that the protection which international law offers to private rights on land also extends to the ocean, confirming the traditional belief that the land dominates the sea. Land and maritime delimitation are essentially two sides of the same coin. Although not identical, they are comparable. Although not indistinguishable, they are interrelated. Both on land and at sea, delimitation seeks to set the limits of two states' contiguous jurisdictions in a peaceful manner. In both situations, the establishment of international boundaries is based on the principles of stability and finality.

7.1 Unbalanced Protection of Non-State Actors' Rights

Unless the states concerned decide otherwise, a boundary, once established, is destined to remain in place forever. But, most importantly, international boundaries affect the interests not only of the states but also of the non-state actors with legal and economic interests in the area under delimitation.[1]

However, the findings of this book were otherwise. Although land does dominate the sea prior to delimitation – in that the powers of states to control the ocean and to create private rights therein flow from their sovereignty on land – this connection dissolves during and post delimitation as different principles apply in the two settings. As observed, the treatment of private rights differs between the two. An analysis of maritime delimitation treaties and rulings revealed that the role of private rights is extremely restricted or even absent in ocean boundary-making.[2] Hence, in contrast to land, the risk of private rights being reallocated is significantly greater at sea.

The different treatment of private rights in the ocean also continues after delimitation.[3] In theory, international law offers the same mechanisms for preserving displaced private rights on land and at sea. In practice, however, those mechanisms are rarely employed by states and judicial bodies in maritime spaces. This leaves reallocated private rights exposed to the will of the absorbing state and opens the way to their possible extinction post delimitation.

The above asymmetry shows that international law fails to protect private rights in all settings. Land delimitation is profoundly anthropocentric. The protection of private interests is manifest not only during all stages of land delimitation but also after its completion. By contrast, the rules which govern maritime delimitation are state-centric. Despite its long-lived existence and evolution over time, the law of the sea remains exclusively concerned with the interests of states – even in situations like contested waters where private interests are clearly at play.

This cultivates the misconception that offshore private rights are inferior to their counterparts on land, and as such do not deserve to be protected a potential reallocation. Ultimately, this prevents the formation of a legal discipline – the international law of delimitation – which would collate and develop coordinated principles of land and maritime boundary-making.

As this book has demonstrated, there are no legal or practical reasons justifying this asymmetry.[4] Neither the general rules of international law nor

[1] Chapters 1 and 2.
[2] Chapter 3.
[3] Chapter 4.
[4] Chapter 5.

the special provisions of UNCLOS which govern maritime delimitation dictate the exclusion of private rights from the process of maritime boundary-making. Likewise, neither the concept of equity nor the characteristics of offshore private rights in contested waters can explain this legal paradox. There is clearly a conflict between the processes of land and maritime delimitation, despite the fact that both are governed by international law and as such should follow similar rules and principles, such as acquiescence and the doctrine of acquired rights.

7.2 TOWARDS GREATER COHERENCE

The greater protection that international law offers to private rights in the context of land delimitation reveals the need for changes in the rules and practices of ocean boundary-making. In light of this, the book has proposed a series of short-term and long-term responses – namely, the use of standard preservation clauses in maritime delimitation treaties, the participation of non-state actors in negotiation processes and judicial proceedings, the broadening of the factors judicial bodies consider in maritime delimitation cases, the amendment of UNCLOS, the conclusion of implementing agreements, the evolutionary interpretation of UNCLOS, the establishment of common international guidelines for land and maritime delimitation and the codification of those guidelines.[5]

The implementation of the above recommendations by states, judicial bodies and policymakers is not a foregone conclusion. Developments in international law require time, coordination and consent. Without overlooking this reality, the book urges that a dialogue be engaged in the international community over the protection of private interests in contested waters. The following lessons from land delimitation should serve as a starting point:

- Delimitation is a complex notion, comprising many elements and factors. It primarily concerns the interests of the states involved, but also affects the interests of private actors in the area in question. Hence, it should strike a balance between all these values.
- Whether on land or at sea, international law should acknowledge and protect legally valid private rights in areas under delimitation. These rights should not be treated as mere economic factors (as currently happens in maritime delimitation) but as legal factors (as in land delimitation).

---

[5] Chapter 6.

- The long-standing and unprotested presence of private rights in contested waters should be able to indicate the boundary's location on the basis of acquiescence, as it does on land.
- If the conditions for acquiescence are not met, but the maritime boundary bisects an existing private right, the latter should be considered a reason for shifting or amending the boundary's final course, as is the case on land.
- If reallocation of an offshore private right is inevitable, the affected right should be preserved by the absorbing state under the doctrine of acquired rights, as happens on land.

This work does not pretend to equate land and maritime delimitation or onshore and offshore private rights; nor does it seek to advance the interests of non-state actors at the expense of states. Its aim is rather to encourage a balanced treatment of private rights in land and maritime boundary-making with a view to creating an equilibrium justified by reasons of legal and social equity and by the increasing presence of non-state actors in contested waters.

Bibliography

BOOKS AND MONOGRAPHS

Adami V, *National Frontiers in Relation to International Law* (T Behrens tr, OUP 1927)

Adler R, *Positioning and Mapping International Land Boundaries* (Boundary and Territory Briefing 2(1), IBRU 1995)

— *Geographical Information in Delimitation, Demarcation, and Management of International Land Boundaries* (Boundary and Territory Briefing 3(4), IBRU 2000)

Aldrich G, *The Jurisprudence of the Iran-United States Claims Tribunal* (Clarendon 1996)

Anderson D, *Modern Law of the Sea: Selected Essays* (Martinus Nijhoff 2008)

Antunes N, *Estoppel, Acquiescence and Recognition in Territorial and Boundary Dispute Settlement* (Boundary and Territory Briefing 2(2), IBRU 2000)

Antunes N, *Towards the Conceptualisation of Maritime Delimitation* (Martinus Nijhoff 2003)

Anzilotti D, *Corso di Diritto Internazionale* (3rd edn, CEDAM 1928)

Becker L, *Property Rights: Philosophic Foundations* (Routledge & Kegan Paul 1977)

Becker-Weinberg V, *Joint Development of Hydrocarbon Deposits in the Law of the Sea* (Springer 2014)

Berdichevsky N, *The German-Danish Border: A Successful Resolution of an Age-Old Conflict or Its Redefinition?* (Boundary and Territory Briefing 2(7), IBRU 1999)

Blackhall C, *Planning Law and Practice* (Cavendish 2005)

Blake G and Topalovic D, 'The Maritime Boundaries of the Adriatic Sea' (Maritime Briefing 1(8), IBRU 1996)

Blum Y, *Historic Titles in International Law* (Springer 1965)

Boggs S, *International Boundaries: A Study of Boundary Functions and Problems* (Columbia University Press 1940)

Boyle A and Freestone D (eds), *International Law and Sustainable Development: Past Achievements and Future Challenges* (OUP 1999)

Briggs H, *The International Law Commission* (Cornell University Press 1965)

British Institute of International and Comparative Law, 'Obligations of States under Articles 74 (3) and 83(3) of UNCLOS in respect of Undelimited Maritime Areas' (conference report 2016)

Bibliography

Brownlie I, *African Boundaries: A Legal and Diplomatic Encyclopaedia* (University of California Press 1979)

    Principles of Public International Law (7th edn, OUP 2008)

Buckle S, *Natural Law and the Theory of Property: Grotius to Hume* (OUP 1993)

Bull H, *The Anarchical Society* (Columbia University Press 1977)

Burlamaqui JJ, *The Principles of Natural and Politic Law* (1748)

Cameron P, *Property Rights and Sovereign Rights: The Case of the North Sea Oil* (Academic Press 1983)

Carleton C and Schofield C, *Developments in the Technical Determination of Maritime Space: Delimitation, Dispute Resolution, Geographic Information Systems and the Role of the Technical Expert* (Maritime Briefing 3(4), IBRU 2002)

Casanovas O, *Unity and Pluralism in Public International Law* (Martinus Nijhoff 2001)

Cassese A, *International Law in a Divided World* (Clarendon 1986)

    International Law (OUP 2001)

Charney J and Smith R (eds), *International Maritime Boundaries* vols 1–4 (Martinus Nijhoff 1993–2002)

Chen L and van Rhee CH (eds), *Towards a Chinese Civil Code: Comparative and Historical Perspectives* (Martinus Nijhoff 2012)

Cheng B, *Studies in International Space Law* (OUP 1997)

Chevrel Y, *La Littérature Comparée* (5th edn, Presses Universitaires de France 2006)

Christy L and others (eds), *Forest Law and Sustainable Development* (World Bank 2007)

Churchill R and Lowe V, *The Law of the Sea* (3rd edn, Manchester University Press, 1999)

Clark G, *The Seventeenth Century* (2nd edn, OUP 1961)

    Early Modern Europe from About 1450 to About 1720 (OUP 1972)

Colson D and Smith R (eds), *International Maritime Boundaries*, vols 5–6 (Martinus Nijhoff 2005–2011)

Cottier T, *Equitable Principles of Maritime Boundary Delimitation* (CUP 2015)

Craven M, *The Decolonization of International Law: State Succession and the Law of Treaties* (OUP 2007)

Crawford J, *The Creation of States in International Law* (Clarendon 1979)

    International Law as an Open System: Selected Essays (Cameron May 2002)

    The International Law Commission's Articles on State Responsibility: Introduction, Text and Commentaries (CUP 2002)

    Brownlie's Principles of Public International Law (8th edn, OUP 2012)

Cukwurah A, *The Settlement of Boundary Disputes in International Law* (Manchester University Press 1967)

Curzon G, *Frontiers* (Clarendon 1908)

Daintith T, *The Legal Character of Petroleum Licences: A Comparative Study* (Dundee University Press 1981)

    Willoughby G and Hill A (eds), *United Kingdom Oil and Gas Law* (3rd edn, Sweet & Maxwell 2000)

Dam K, *Oil Resources: Who Gets What How?* (University of Chicago Press 1976)

D'Amato A, *The Concept of Custom in International Law* (Cornell University Press 1971)

Division of Ocean Affairs and the Law of the Sea, *Handbook on the Delimitation of Maritime Boundaries* (UN 2000)

Bibliography

Dugard J and others, *International Law: A South African Perspective* (4th edn, Juta 2011)

Dupuy RJ and Vignes D (eds), *A Handbook on the New Law of the Sea*, vol 1 (Martinus Nijhoff 1991)

East G, *The Geography Behind History* (Norton 1967)

Ebbin S, Hoel AF and Sydnes AK (eds), *A Sea Change: The Exclusive Economic Zone and Governance Institutions for Living Marine Resources* (Springer 2005)

Esch G (ed), *Marine Managed Areas: Best Practices for Boundary Making* (Coastal Services Center 2006)

Evans M, *Relevant Circumstances and Maritime Delimitation* (Clarendon 1989)

Evans M (ed), *International Law* (3rd edn, OUP 2010)

Fawcett C, *Frontiers: A Study in Political Geography* (OUP 1918)

Fox H and others, *Joint Development of Offshore Oil and Gas: A Model Agreement for States for Joint Development with Explanatory Commentary* (British Institute of International and Comparative Law 1989)

Franck T, *Fairness in International Law and Institutions* (Clarendon 1995)

Freestone D and others (eds), *The Law of the Sea: Progress and Prospects* (OUP 2006)

Freestone D (ed), *The 1982 Law of the Sea Convention at 30: Successes, Challenges and New Agendas* (Brill 2013)

Friedheim R, *Negotiating the New Ocean Regime* (University of South Carolina Press 1992)

Friedmann W, *The Changing Structure of International Law* (Stevens & Sons 1964) *Legal Theory* (5th edn, Stevens & Sons 1967)

Frost R, *North of Boston* (David Nutt 1914)

Frynas J, *Foreign Investment and International Boundary Disputes in Africa: Evidence from the Oil Industry* (Occasional Papers Series No 9, African Studies Centre 2000)

Fuller L, *The Morality of Law* (Yale University Press 1964)

Gavouneli M, *Functional Jurisdiction in the Law of the Sea* (Martinus Nijhoff 2007)

Grant J, *International Law Essentials* (Dundee University Press 2010)

Grbec M, *The Extension of Coastal State Jurisdiction in Enclosed or Semi-Enclosed Seas: A Mediterranean and Adriatic Perspective* (Routledge 2014)

Gretton G and Steven A, *Property, Trusts and Succession* (Bloomsbury Professional 2013)

Grotius H, *Mare Liberum, Sive, De Jure Quod Batavis Competit ad Indicana Commercia Dissertatio* (Elzevir 1609) *The Freedom of the Seas, Or, The Right which Belongs to the Dutch to Take Part in the East Indian Trade* (R Van Deman Magoffin tr, OUP 1916)

Guggenheim P, *Traité de Droit International Public* (Librairie Georg 1953)

Gutteridge H, *Comparative Law: An Introduction to the Comparative Method of Legal Study and Research* (2nd edn, CUP 1949)

Harrison J, *Making the Law of the Sea: A Study in the Development of International Law* (CUP 2011)

Harvey D, *Justice, Nature and the Geography of Difference* (Blackwell 1996)

Hershey A, *The Essentials of International Public Law and Organization* (2nd edn, Macmillan 1927)

Hey E, *The Regime for the Exploitation of Transboundary Marine Fisheries Resources* (Martinus Nijhoff 1989)

Bibliography

Higgins R, *Problems and Process: International Law and How We Use It* (Clarendon 1994)

Hill N, *Claims to Territory in International Law and Relations* (OUP 1945)

Holdich T, *Political Frontiers and Boundary Making* (Macmillan 1916)

Jennings A, *Oil and Gas Exploration Contracts* (Sweet & Maxwell 2002)

Jennings R, *The Acquisition of Territory in International Law* (Manchester University Press 1963)

Jessup P, *A Modern Law of Nations* (Macmillan 1945)
  Transnational Law (Yale University Press 1956)

Johnston D, *Theory and History of Ocean Boundary-Making* (McGill-Queen's University Press 1988)

Jones S, *Boundary-Making: A Handbook for Statesmen, Treaty Editors and Boundary Commissioners* (Carnegie Endowment for International Peace 1945)

Kaczorowska A, *Public International Law* (4th edn, Routledge 2010)

Kaikobad K, *Interpretation and Revision of International Boundary Decisions* (CUP 2007)

Karaman I, *Dispute Resolution in the Law of the Sea* (Martinus Nijhoff 2012)

Keen M, *The Penguin History of Medieval Europe* (Penguin 1991)

Kelsen H, *Principles of International Law* (Lawbook Exchange 1952)

Kemp A, *The Official History of North Sea Oil and Gas*, vol 1 *The Growing Dominance of the State* (Routledge 2012)

Kimball L, *International Ocean Governance: Using International Law and Organizations to Manage Marine Resources Sustainably* (IUCN 2001)

Kirk E, *EU Law* (Pearson Education 2012)

Klein N, *Maritime Security and the Law of the Sea* (OUP 2011)

Korman S, *The Right of Conquest: The Acquisition of Territory by Force in International Law and Practice* (Clarendon 1996)

Kraska J, *Maritime Power and the Law of the Sea* (OUP 2011)

Kratochwil F and others (eds), *Peace and Disputed Sovereignty: Reflections on Conflict over Territory in International Law and Relations* (University Press of America 1985)

Kwiatkowska B, *The 200 Mile Exclusive Economic Zone in the Law of the Sea* (Martinus Nijhoff 1989)

Lachs M, *The Teacher in International Law* (2nd edn, Martinus Nijhoff 1987)

Lagoni R and Vignes D (eds), *Maritime Delimitation* (Brill 2006)

La Pradelle P de, *La Frontière: Étude de Droit International* (Éditions Internationales 1928)

Lathrop C (ed), *International Maritime Boundaries*, vol 7 (Martinus Nijhoff 2016)

Lauterpacht H, *Private Law Sources and Analogies of International Law (With Special Reference to International Arbitration)* (Longmans Green 1927)

Lauterpacht E (ed), *International Law: Being the Collected Papers of Hersch Lauterpacht*, vol 1 (CUP 1970)

Lawson H and Rudden (eds), *The Law of Property* (3rd edn, Clarendon 2002)

Lax H, *Political Risk in the Oil and Gas Industry* (Kluwer 1983)

Lepard B, *Customary International Law: A New Theory with Practical Applications* (CUP 2010)

Lindoe PH and others (eds), *Risk Governance of Offshore Oil and Gas Operations* (CUP 2015)

Luard E, *The International Regulation of Frontier Disputes* (Thames & Hudson 1970)

Macpherson C, *The Political Theory of Possessive Individualism: Hobbes to Locke* (OUP 1964)

Mansour M and Nakhle C, *Fiscal Stabilization in Oil and Gas Contracts: Evidence and Implications* (Oxford Institute for Energy Studies Paper SP 37, OIES 2016) <www.oxfordenergy.org/wpcms/wp-content/uploads/2016/02/Fiscal-Stabilization-in-Oil-and-Gas-Contracts-SP-37.pdf > accessed 20 March 2020

Massey D, *Space, Place, and Gender* (University of Minnesota Press 1990)

McKendrick E, *Contract Law* (5th edn, OUP 2012)

McLeod I, *Legal Theory* (5th edn, Palgrave 2007)

McMahon M, *Conquest and Modern International Law: The Legal Limitations on the Acquisition of Territory by Conquest* (Kraus Reprint 1975)

Mensch E and Freeman A (eds), *Property Law* (Dartmouth 1992)

Milano E, *Unlawful Territorial Situations in International Law: Reconciling Effectiveness, Legality and Legitimacy* (Martinus Nijhoff 2005)

Miyoshi M, *The Joint Development of Offshore Oil and Gas in Relation to Maritime Boundary Delimitation* (Maritime Briefing 2(5), IBRU 1999)

Motta G, *Less than Nations: Central-Eastern European Minorities after WWI*, vol 1 (Cambridge Scholars 2013)

Nichols S, *Tidal Boundary Delimitation* (University of New Brunswick 1996)

Nozick R, *Anarchy, State and Utopia* (Basic Books 1974)

O'Connell D, *International Law* (Stevens & Sons 1965)

   State Succession in Municipal and International Law (CUP 1967)

Oduntan G, *International Law and Boundary Disputes in Africa* (Routledge 2015)

Oppenheim L, *International Law: A Treatise*, vol 1 (Longmans Green 1905)

   International Law: A Treatise, vol 1 (6th edn, Longmans 1947)

   International Law: A Treatise (8th edn, Longmans 1955)

Oude Elferink A, *The Law of Maritime Boundary Delimitation: A Case Study of the Russian Federation* (Martinus Nijhoff 1994)

   Stability and Change in the Law of the Sea: The Role of the LOS Convention (Martinus Nijhoff 2005)

   The Delimitation of the Continental Shelf between Denmark, Germany and the Netherlands: Arguing Law, Practicing Politics? (CUP 2013)

Painter J, *Politics, Geography and 'Political Geography': A Critical Perspective* (Arnold 1995)

Pan J, *Toward a New Framework for Peaceful Settlement of China's Territorial and Boundary Disputes* (Martinus Nijhoff 2009)

Papanicolopulu I, *International Law and the Protection of People at Sea* (OUP 2018)

Parlett K, *The Individual in the International Legal System: Continuity and Change in International Law* (CUP 2011)

Parry C, *The Consolidated Treaty Series* (Oceana 1969)

Peerenboom R, Petersen C and Chen A (eds), *Human Rights in Asia: A Comparative Legal Study of Twelve Asian Jurisdictions, France and the USA* (Routledge 2006)

Peng D (ed), *Insurance and Legal Issues in the Oil Industry* (Martinus Nijhoff 1993)

Pratt M and Smith D, *How to Deal with Maritime Boundary Uncertainty in Oil and Gas Exploration and Production Areas* (Association of International Petroleum Negotiators Research Paper, AIPN 2007)

Bibliography

Prescott V, *The Maritime Political Boundaries of the World* (Methuen 1985)
  Political Frontiers and Boundaries (Allen & Unwin 1987)
  and Schofield C, *Maritime Political Boundaries of the World* (Martinus Nijhoff 2004)
  and Schofield C, *The Maritime Political Boundaries of the World* (2nd edn, Martinus Nijhoff 2013)
  and Triggs G, *International Frontiers and Boundaries: Law, Politics, and Geography* (Martinus Nijhoff 2008)
Pyo KS, *Delimitation and Interim Arrangements in North East Asia* (Brill 2004)
Ragazzi M, *The Concept of International Obligations Erga Omnes* (OUP 2000)
Raic D, *Statehood and the Law of Self-Determination* (Brill Academic 2002)
Razavi A, *Continental Shelf Delimitation and Related Maritime Issues in the Persian Gulf* (Martinus Nijhoff 1997)
Reid K, *A Practitioner's Guide to the European Convention on Human Rights* (4th edn, Sweet & Maxwell 2011)
Renman D, *Markets under the Sea? A Study of the Potential Private Property Rights in the Seabed* (Institute of Economic Affairs 1984)
Rosenne S, *League of Nations Conference for the Codification of International Law (1930)* (Oceana 1975) vol 4
Rothwell D and Stephens T, *The International Law of the Sea* (Hart 2010)
Sack R, *Human Territoriality: Its Theory and History* (CUP 1986)
Sassen S, *Territory, Authority, Rights: From Medieval to Global Assemblages* (Princeton University Press 2006)
Schacht J, *An Introduction to Islamic Law* (Clarendon 1964)
Schlatter R, *Private Property: The History of an Idea* (George Allen & Unwin 1951)
Schlütter B, *Developments in Customary International Law: Theory and the Practice of the International Court of Justice and the International Ad Hoc Criminal Tribunals for Rwanda and Yugoslavia* (Brill 2010)
Schofield C, *Maritime Political Boundaries of the World* (Martinus Nijhoff 2004)
Schwarzenberger G and Brown E (eds), *A Manual of International Law* (6th edn, Professional Books 1976)
Scott A, *The Evolution of Resource Property Rights* (OUP 2008)
Sermet L, *The European Convention on Human Rights and Property Rights* (Human Rights Files No 11 rev, Council of Europe1998) <www.echr.coe.int/LibraryDocs/DG2/HRFILES/DG2-EN-HRFILES-11%281998%29.pdf> accessed 20 March 2020
Serna Martin A, *Deeper and Colder: The Impacts and Risks of Deepwater and Arctic Hydrocarbon Development* (Sustainalytics 2012)
Sharma S, *Territorial Acquisition, Disputes and International Law* (Martinus Nijhoff 1997)
Sharp D, *Offshore Oil and Gas Insurance* (Witherby 1994)
Shaw M, *Title to Territory in Africa: International Legal Issues* (Clarendon 1986)
  International Law (6th edn, CUP 2008)
  International Law (8th edn, CUP 2017)
Shotton R (ed), *Use of Property Rights in Fisheries Management* (Food and Agricultural Organization of the United Nations 2000)
Sinclair I, *The International Law Commission* (CUP 1987)
Smith N, *The Sea of Lost Opportunity: North Sea Oil and Gas, British Industry and the Offshore Supplies Office* (Elsevier 2011)

Bibliography

Smits JM (ed), *Elgar Encyclopedia of Comparative Law* (Edgar Elgar 1998)

Solomon R and Murphy M (eds), *What Is Justice? Classic and Contemporary Readings* (OUP 1990)

Spier D, *Law Essentials: Property Law* (Dundee University Press 2008

Sprankling J, *The International Law of Property* (OUP 2014)

Srebro H, *International Boundary Making* (International Federation of Surveyors 2013)

Steiner E, *French Law: Comparative Approach* (OUP 2010)

Strati A and others (eds), *Unresolved Issues and New Challenges to the Law of the Sea: Time Before and Time After* (Martinus Nijhoff 2006)

Tanaka Y, *Predictability and Flexibility in the Law of Maritime Delimitation* (OUP 2006)

Tanaka Y, *International Law of the Sea* (CUP 2012)

Tanja G, *The Legal Determination of International Maritime Boundaries: The Progressive Development of Continental Shelf, EFZ and EEZ Law* (Kluwer Law and Taxation 1990)

Taverne B, *An Introduction to the Regulation of the Petroleum Industry: Laws, Contracts and Conventions* (Martinus Nijhoff 1994)

  Petroleum, Industry and Governments: An Introduction to Petroleum Regulation, Economics and Government Policies (Kluwer 1999)

Thirlway H, *International Customary Law and Codification* (Sijhoff 1972)

  The Sources of International Law (OUP 2014)

  The Sources of International Law (2nd edn, OUP 2019)

Treitel G, *The Law of Contract* (10th edn, Sweet & Maxwell 1999)

Triepel H, *Droit International et Droit Interne* (R Brunet tr, Pedone 1920)

Tuerk H, *Reflections on the Contemporary Law of the Sea* (Martinus Nijhoff 2012)

Van Hoecke M (ed), *Epistemology and Methodology of Comparative Law* (Hart 2004)

Vattel E de, *The Law of Nations or the Principles of Natural Law, Applied to the Conduct and to the Affairs of Nations and of Sovereigns* (trans of 1758 edn by C Fenwick, Carnegie Institution of Washington 1916)

Weil P, *The Law of Maritime Delimitation: Reflections* (Grotius 1989)

Wight M, *Systems of States* (Leicester University Press 1977)

Wils J and Neilson E, *The Technical and Legal Guide to the UK Oil and Gas Industry* (Aberlour 2007)

Wolff C, *Jus Gentium Methodo Scientifica Petractatum* (1749)

Zimmermann R, Reid K and Visser D, *Mixed Legal Systems in Comparative Perspective: Property and Obligations in Scotland and South Africa* (OUP 2005)

Zweigert K and Kötz H, *Introduction to Comparative Law* (Clarendon 1998)

CHAPTERS IN EDITED BOOKS

Adams M, 'Doing What Doesn't Come Naturally: On the Distinctiveness of Comparative Law' in M Van Hoecke (ed), *Methodologies of Legal Research* (Hart 2011)

Allot A, 'Boundaries and the Law in Africa' in C Widstrand (ed), *African Boundary Problems* (Brill 1969)

Amerasinghe S, 'The Third United Nations Conference on the Law of the Sea' in M Nordquist (ed), *United Nations Convention on the Law of the Sea 1982: A Commentary*, vol 1 (Martinus Nijhoff 1985)

Bibliography

Anderson D, 'Strategies for Dispute Resolution: Negotiating Joint Agreements' in G Blake and others (eds), *Boundaries and Energy: Problems and Prospects* (Kluwer Law International 1998)

—— 'Negotiating Maritime Boundary Agreements: A Personal View' in R Lagoni and D Vignes (eds), *Maritime Delimitation* (Martinus Nijhoff 2006)

Aznar M, 'The Human Factor in Territorial Disputes' in M Kohen and M Hebie (eds), *Research Handbook on Territorial Disputes in International Law* (Edward Elgar 2018)

Baxter R, 'The Effects of Ill-Conceived Codification and Development of International Law' in *Recueil d'Études de Droit International en Hommage à Paul Guggenheim* (Faculté de Droit de l'Université de Genève 1968)

Beckman R, 'International Law, UNCLOS and the South China Sea' in R Beckman and others (ed), *Beyond Territorial Disputes in the South China Sea: Legal Frameworks for the Joint Development of Hydrocarbon Resources* (Edward Elgar 2013)

Benvenisti E, 'Customary International Law as a Judicial Tool for Promoting Efficiency' in E Benvenisti and M Hirsch (eds), *The Impact of International Law on International Cooperation: Theoretical Perspectives* (CUP 2004)

Birnie P and Mason C, 'Oil and Gas: The International Regime' in C Mason (ed), *The Effective Management of Resources: The International Politics of the North Sea* (Nichols 1979)

Bogdandy A and Venzke I, 'Beyond Dispute: International Judicial Institutions as Lawmakers' in A von Bogdandy and I Venzke (eds), *International Judicial Lawmaking: On Public Authority and Democratic Legitimation in Global Governance* (Springer 2012)

Boyle A, 'Further Development of the 1982 Convention on the Law of the Sea: Mechanisms for Change' in D Freestone, R Barnes and D Ong (eds), *The Law of the Sea: Progress and Prospects* (OUP 2006)

Brown E, 'Maritime Zones: A Survey of Claims' in R Churchill and others (eds), *New Directions in the Law of the Sea*, vol 3 (British Institute of International and Comparative Law 1973)

Brown Weiss E, 'The New International Legal System' in N Jasentuliyana (ed), *Perspectives on International Law* (Kluwer Law International 1995)

Calfish L, 'The Delimitation of Marine Spaces between States with Opposite and Adjacent Coasts' in R Dupuy and D Vignes (eds), *A Handbook on the New Law of the Sea* (Martinus Nijhoff 1991)

Crawford J and Nevill P, 'Relations between International Courts and Tribunals: The "Regime" Problem' in M Young, *Regime Interaction in International Law: Facing Fragmentation* (CUP 2012)

D'Amato A, 'Is International Law Really "Law"?' in G Simpson (ed), *The Nature of International Law* (Ashgate 2001)

Delabie L, 'The Role of Equity, Equitable Principles, and the Equitable Solution in Maritime Delimitation' in A Oude Elferink, T Henriksen and V Busch (eds), *Maritime Boundary Delimitation: The Case Law* (CUP 2018)

Dietsche E, 'Sector Legal Frameworks and Resource Property Rights' in R Dannreuther and W Ostrowski (eds), *Global Resources* (Springer 2013)

Evans M, 'Maritime Boundary Delimitation: Where Do We Go from Here?' in D Freestone, R Barnes and D Ong (eds), *The Law of the Sea: Progress and Prospects* (OUP 2006)

Bibliography

Garcia M, 'Boundary Delimitation and Hydrocarbon Resources' in G Picton-Turbervill (ed), *Oil and Gas: A Practical Handbook* (Globe Law and Business 2014)

Ghosh S, 'The Legal Regime of Innocent Passage through the Territorial Sea' in H Caminos (ed), *Law of the Sea* (Ashgate 2001)

Gordon G, 'Petroleum Licensing' in G Gordon, J Paterson and E Usenmez (eds), *Oil and Gas Law: Current Practices and Emerging Trends* (2nd edn, Dundee University Press 2011)

— 'Risk Allocation in Oil and Gas Contracts' in G Gordon, J Paterson and E Usenmez (eds), *Oil and Gas Law: Current Practice and Emerging Trends* (2nd edn, Dundee University Press 2011)

Graveson R, 'The Contribution of Private International Law and Comparative Law to International Harmony and Understanding' in J Makarczyk (ed), *Essays in International Law in Honour of Judge Manfred Lachs* (Martinus Nijhoff 1984)

Graziadei M, 'The Functionalist Heritage' in P Legrand and R Munday (eds), *Comparative Legal Studies: Traditions and Transitions* (CUP 2003)

Ioannou K, 'Some Preliminary Remarks on Equity in the 1982 Convention on the Law of the Sea' in C Rozakis and C Stephanou (eds), *The New Law of the Sea* (Elsevier 1983)

Kohen M and Tignino M, 'Do People Have Rights in Boundaries' Delimitations?' in Laurence Boisson de Chazournes, C Leb and M Tignino et al (eds), *International Law and Freshwater: The Multiple Challenges* (Edward Elgar 2013)

Kwiatkowska B, 'Economic and Environmental Considerations in Maritime Boundary Delimitations' in J Charney and L Alexander (eds), *International Maritime Boundaries*, vol 1 (Martinus Nijhoff 1993)

Lalive P, 'The Doctrine of Acquired Rights' in M Bender (ed), *Rights and Duties of Private Investors Abroad* (International and Comparative Law Centre 1965)

Lowe V and Tzanakopoulos A, 'The Development of the Law of the Sea by the International Court of Justice' in C Tams and J Sloan (eds), *The Development of International Law by the International Court of Justice* (OUP 2013)

Manner E, 'Settlement of Sea-Boundary Delimitation Disputes According to the Provisions of the 1982 Law of the Sea Convention' in J Makarczyk (ed), *Essays in Honour of Judge Manfred Lachs* (Martinus Nijhoff 1984)

McHarg A, 'The Social Obligations of Ownership and the Regulation of Energy Utilities in the United Kingdom and the European Union' in A McHarg and others (eds), *Property and the Law in Energy and Natural Resources* (OUP 2010)

Merrills J, 'The Means of Dispute Settlement' in M Evans (ed), *International Law* (OUP 2003)

Olawale E, 'Modern Sources of International Law' in W Friedmann, L Henkin and O Lissitzyn (eds), *Transnational Law in a Changing Society: Essays in Honor of Philip Jessup* (Columbia University Press 1972)

Oppenheim L, 'The Science of International Law: Its Task and Method' in G Simpson (ed), *The Nature of International Law* (Ashgate 2001)

Oxman, B 'Political Strategic and Historical Considerations' in J Charney and L Alexander (eds), *International Maritime Boundaries*, vol 1 (Martinus Nijhoff 1993)

Papanicolopulu I, 'A Missing Part of the Law of the Sea Convention: Addressing Issues of State Jurisdiction over Persons at Sea' in C Schofield, M Lee and M-S Kwon (eds), *Limits of Maritime Jurisdiction* (Brill 2014)

Bibliography

Petrig A, 'The Commission of Maritime Crimes with Unmanned Systems: An Interpretive Challenge for the United Nations Convention on the Law of the Sea' in M Evans and S Galani (eds), *Maritime Security and the Law of the Sea: Help or Hindrance?* (Edward Elgar 2020)

Redgwell C, 'Property Law Sources and Analogies in International Law' in A McHarg and others (eds), *Property and the Law in Energy and Natural Resources* (OUP 2010)

Robson C, 'Transboundary Petroleum Reservoirs: Legal Issues and Solutions' in G Blake and others (eds), *The Peaceful Management of Transboundary Resources* (Graham & Trotman 1995)

Rolston S and McDorman T, 'Maritime Boundary Making in the Arctic Region' in D Johnston and P Saunders (eds), *Ocean Boundary Making: Regional Issues and Developments* (Croom Helm 1988)

Ronne A, 'Public and Private Rights to Natural Resources and Differences in their Protection?' in A McHarg and others (eds), *Property and the Law of Natural Resources* (OUP 2010)

Rothwell D, 'Oceans Management and the Law of the Sea in the Twenty-First Century' in A Oude Elferink and D Rothwell (eds), *Oceans Management in the 21st Century: Institutional Frameworks and Responses* (Brill 2004)

Samuel G, 'Comparative Law and Its Methodology' in D Watkins and M Burton (eds), *Research Methods in Law* (Routledge 2013)

Schofield C, 'No Panacea? Challenges in the Application of Provisional Arrangements of a Practical Nature' in MH Nordquist and JN Moore (eds), *Maritime Border Diplomacy* (Martinus Nijhoff 2012)

'Defining the "Boundary" between Land and Sea: Territorial Sea Baselines in the South China Sea' in S Jayakumar, T Koh and R Beckman (eds), *The South China Sea Disputes and Law of the Sea* (Edward Elgar 2014)

and Carleton C, 'Technical Considerations in Law of the Sea Dispute Resolution' in A Oude Elferink and D Rothwell (eds), *Oceans Management in the 21st Century: Institutional Frameworks and Responses* (Brill 2004)

Schreuer C, 'Protection against Arbitrary or Discriminatory Measures' in C Rogers and R Alford (eds), *The Future of Investment Arbitration* (OUP 2009)

Shaw M, 'The International Court of Justice and the Law of Territory' in C Tams and J Sloan (eds), *The Development of International Law by the International Court of Justice* (OUP 2013)

Sinclair K, 'Legal Reasoning: In Search of an Adequate Theory of Argument' in A Aarnio and N MacCormick (eds), *Legal Reasoning* (New York University Press 1992) vol 2

Swadling W, 'The Judicial Construction of Force Majeure Clauses' in E McKendrick (ed), *Force Majeure and Frustration of Contract* (2nd edn, Lloyd's of London Press 1995)

Townsend-Gault I, 'Offshore Boundary Delimitation in the Arabian/Persian Gulf' in D Johnston and P Saunders (eds), *Ocean Boundary Making: Regional Issues and Developments* (Croom Helm 1988)

'Offshore Petroleum Joint Development Agreements: Functional Instruments? Compromise? Obligation?' in G Blake and others (eds), *The Peaceful Management of Transboundary Resources* (Graham & Trotman 1995)

'Zones of Cooperation in the Oceans: Legal Rationales and Imperatives' in MH Nordquist and JN Moore (eds), *Maritime Border Diplomacy* (Martinus Nijhoff 2012)

Walter C, 'Subjects of International Law' in R Wolfrum (ed), *Max Planck Encyclopedia of Public International Law* (OUP 2012)

Wasilkowski A, 'International Law: How Far Is It Changing?' in J Makarczyk (ed), *Essays in International Law in Honour of Judge Manfred Lachs* (Martinus Nijhoff 1984)

Wilson G, 'Comparative Legal Scholarship' in M McConville and WH Chui (eds), *Research Methods for Law* (Edinburgh University Press 2007)

Wolfke K, 'Can Codification of International Law Be Harmful?' in J Makarczyk (ed), *Essays in International Law in Honour of Judge Manfred Lachs* (Martinus Nijhoff 1984)

JOURNAL ARTICLES

'Boundary Disputes between States: The Impact on Private Rights' (1969) 69(1) Columbia Law Review 129

Aldrich G, 'What Constitutes a Taking of Property? The Decisions of the Iranian-United States Claims Tribunal' (1994) 88 AJIL 585

Alvarez-Jimenez A, 'Methods for the Identification of Customary International Law in the International Court of Justice's Jurisprudence: 2000–2009' (2011) 60 ICLQ 681

Amstutz D and Samuels W, 'Offshore Oil Spills: Analysis of Risks' (1984) 13 Marine Environmental Research 303

Andenas M and Leiss JR, 'The Systemic Relevance of "Judicial Decisions" in Article 38 of the ICJ Statute' (2017) 77 ZaöRV 907

Anderson D, 'Maritime Delimitation in the Black Sea Case (Romania/Ukraine)' (2009) 8(3) Law and Practice of International Courts and Tribunals 305

Antunes N, 'The 1999 Eritrea-Yemen Maritime Delimitation Award and the Development of International Law' (2001) 50 ICLQ 299

Ascensio H, 'L'*Amicus Curiae* devant les Juridictions Internationales' (2001) 105 Revue Générale de Droit International Public 897

Bakhashab O, 'The Legal Concept of International Boundary' (1996) 9 Economy and Administration 29

Barbara C, 'International Legal Personality: Panacea or Pandemonium? Theorizing about the Individual and the State in the Era of Globalization' (2010) 12 Austrian Review of International and European Law 17

Barker S, 'International Maritime Piracy: An Old Profession That Is Capable of New Tricks, but Change Is Possible' (2015) 46 Case Western Reserve Journal of International Law 387

Bartholomeusz L, 'The Amicus Curiae before International Courts and Tribunals' (2005) 5 Non-State Actors and International Law 209

Bastida A and others, 'Cross-Border Unitization and Joint Development Agreements: An International Law Perspective' (2007) 29 Houston Journal of International Law 355

Bibliography

Baxter R, 'Treaties and Customs' (1970) 129 Collected Courses of the Hague Academy of International Law 24

Bekker P, 'Maritime Boundary Disputes: Risk Investment in Offshore Energy Projects' (2005) 21(11) Natural Gas and Electricity 10

Benvenisti E, 'Collective Action in the Utilization of Shared Freshwater: The Challenges of International Water Resources Law' (1996) 90 AJIL 384

Blyschak P, 'Offshore Oil and Gas Projects amid Maritime Border Disputes: Applicable Law' (2013) 6 Journal of World Energy Law and Business 210

Boggs S, 'Problems of Water Boundary-Definition: Median Lines and International Boundaries through Territorial Waters' (1937) 27 Geographical Review 445

Botchway F, 'The International Adjudicatory Process and Transboundary Resource Disputes' (2001) Australian International Law Journal 146

'The Context of Trans-Boundary Energy Resource Exploitation: The Environment, the State and the Methods' [2004] 3 OGEL <www.ogel.org>

Boyle A, 'Dispute Settlement and the Law of the Sea Convention: Problems of Fragmentation and Jurisdiction' (1997) 46 ICLQ 37

Brierly J-L, 'Règles Générales du Droit de la Paix' (1936) 58 Collected Courses of the Hague Academy of International Law 5

Brilmayer L and Klein N, 'Land and Sea: Two Sovereignty Regimes in Search of a Common Dominator' (2001) 33 Journal of International Law and Politics 703

Brownlie I, 'The Individual before Tribunals Exercising International Jurisprudence' (1962) 11 ICLQ 701

'The Place of the Individual in International Law' (1964) 50 Virginia Law Review 435

Buscaglia E and Dakolias M, 'An Analysis of the Cases of Corruption in the Judiciary' (1999) 30 Law and Policy in International Business 95

Byers M, 'Power, Obligation, and Customary International Law' (2001) 11 Duke Journal of Comparative and International Law 81

Cameron P, 'The Rules of Engagement: Developing Cross-Border Petroleum Deposits in the North Sea and the Caribbean' (2006) ICLQ 559

'Stabilisation in Investment Contracts and Changes of Rules in Host Countries: Tools for Oil and Gas Investors' (2006) Association of International Petroleum Negotiators 1

'Cross-Border Unitization in the North Sea' [2007] 2 OGEL <www.ogel.org>

'Stability of Contract in the International Energy Industry' (2009) 27 Journal of Energy and Natural Resources Law 305

Caminos H and Molitor M, 'Progressive Development of International Law and the Package Deal' (1985) 79 AJIL 871

Carter D and Goemans H, 'The Making of the Territorial Order: New Borders and the Emergence of Interstate Conflict' (2011) 65 International Organization 275

Celine T, 'Risky Business: Political Risk Insurance and the Law and Governance of Natural Resources' (2015) 11 International Journal of Law in Context 174

Charney J, 'International Maritime Boundary Delimitation' (1994) 88 AJIL 227

'The "Horizontal" Growth of International Courts and Tribunals: Challenges or Opportunities?' (2002) ASIL Proceedings 369

Christie G, 'What Constitutes a Taking of Property?' [1962] British Yearbook of International Law 307

Churchill R, 'The Greenland-Jan Mayen Case and its Significance for the International Law of Maritime Boundary Delimitation' (1994) 9 International Journal of Marine and Coastal Law 1

Clapham A, 'The Role of the Individual in International Law' (2010) 21 European Journal of International Law 25

Collins E and Rogoff M, 'The Gulf of Maine Case and the Future of Ocean Boundary Delimitation' (1986) 38 Maine Law Review 1

Cree D, 'Yugoslav-Hungarian Boundary Commission' (1925) 65 Geographical Journal 89

Crommelin M, 'The Legal Character of Resource Titles' (1998) 17 Australian Mining and Petroleum Law Journal 57

Dakolias M and Thachuk K, 'Attacking Corruption in the Judiciary: A Critical Process in Judicial Reform' (2000) 18 Wisconsin International Law Journal 353

Dillard HC, 'Some Aspects of Law and Diplomacy' (1957) 91 Collected Courses of the Hague Academy of International Law 445

Douglas Z, 'The Hybrid Foundations of Investment Treaty Arbitration' (2004) 74 British Yearbook of International Law 152

Dupuis C, 'Règles Générales du Droit de la Paix' (1930) 32 Collected Courses of the Hague Academy of International Law 1

Eagleton C, 'The Individual and International Law' (1946) 40 ASIL Proceedings 22

Ederington B, 'Property as a Natural Institution: The Separation of Property from Sovereignty in International Law' (1997) 13(2) American University International Law Review 263

Ejegi J, 'What Are the Mechanisms for Resolving Disputes between Countries with Transboundary Resources? A Closer Examination' [2005] 2 OGEL <www.ogel.org>

Evans M, 'Maritime Delimitation and Expanding Categories of Relevant Circumstances' (1991) 40 ICLQ 1

Feldman M, 'The Tunisia-Libya Continental Shelf Case: Geographic Justice or Judicial Compromise?' (1983) 77 AJIL 219

Forteau M, 'Comparative International Law Within, Not Against, International Law: Lessons from the International Law Commission' (2015) 109 AJIL 498

Franckx E, 'Belgium and the Netherlands Settle Their Last Frontier Disputes on Land As Well As at Sea' [1998] Revue Belge de Droit International 338

Friedmann W, 'The North Sea Continental Shelf Cases: A Critique' (1970) 64 AJIL 229

Gao J, 'Joint Development in the East China Sea: Not an Easier Challenge than Delimitation' (2008) 23 International Journal of Marine and Coastal Law 39

Gardner R, 'Overview and Characteristics of Some Occupational Exposures and Health Risks on Offshore Oil and Gas Installations' (2003) 47 Annals of Occupational Hygiene 201

Ginsburg T, 'Bounded Discretion in International Judicial Lawmaking' (2004) 45 Virginia Journal of International Law 631

Glahn J, Schjetlein I and Haavind K, 'Modernized Risk Management in Offshore Development' (1983) 1 International Journal of Project Management 230

Gross L, 'The Peace of Westphalia 1648–1948' (1948) 42 AJIL 20

Guillaume G, 'The Use of Precedent by International Judges and Arbitrators' (2011) 2 Journal of International Dispute Settlement 5

Hafner G, 'Pros and Cons Ensuing from Fragmentation of International Law' (2004) 25 Michigan Journal of International Law 849

Hannesson R, 'From Common Fish to Rights Based Fishing: Fisheries Management and the Evolution of the Exclusive Right to Fish' (1991) 35 European Economic Review 397

Helmersen S, 'Evolutive Treaty Interpretation: Legality, Semantics and Distinctions' (2013) 6 European Journal of Legal Studies 127

Hershey A, 'The Succession of States' (1911) 5 AJIL 296

Hewitt T, 'Who Is to Blame? Allocating Liability in Upstream Project Contracts' (2008) 26 Journal of Energy and Natural Resources Law 177

Hollis D, 'Private Actors in Public International Law: Amicus Curiae and the Case for the Retention of State Sovereignty' (2002) 25 Boston College International and Comparative Law Review 235

Janis M and Brownlie I, 'Comparative Approaches to the Theory of International Law' (1986) 80 ASIL Proceedings 152

Jenks W, 'The Scope of International Law' (1954) 31 British Yearbook of International Law 1

Jennings R, 'What Is International Law and How Do We Tell It When We See It?' (1981) 37 Annuaire Suisse de Droit International 59

'Equity and Equitable Principles' (1986) 42 Annuaire Suisse de Droit International 27

Jessup P, 'The Subjects of a Modern Law of Nations' (1947) 45 Michigan Law Review 383

Jia BB, 'The Principle of the Domination of the Land over the Sea: A Historical Perspective on the Adaptability of the Law of the Sea to New Challenges' (2014) 57 German Yearbook of International Law 1

Jiuyong S, 'Maritime Delimitation in the Jurisprudence of the International Court of Justice' (2010) 9 Chinese Journal of International Law 271

Jones S, 'Boundary Concepts in the Setting of Place and Time' (1959) 49 Annals of the Association of American Geographers 241

Kaeckenbeeck G, 'The Protection of Vested Rights in International Law' (1936) 17 British Yearbook of International Law 16

Kammerhofer J, 'Uncertainty in the Formal Sources of International Law: Customary International Law and Some of Its Problems' (2004) 15 European Journal of International Law 523

Kanervisto M and Pereira E, 'National Oil Companies Operating in Upstream Petroleum Projects and Participating in Joint Operating Agreements' [2013] 4 OGEL <www.ogel.org>

Kelsen H, 'Théorie du Droit International Coutumier' (1939) 1 Revue International de la Théorie du Droit 253

Keyuan Z, 'The Sino-Vietnamese Agreement on Maritime Boundary Delimitation in the Gulf of Tonkin' (2005) 36 Ocean Development and International Law 13

Koskenniemi M, 'The Case for Comparative International Law' (2009) 20 Finnish Yearbook of International Law 1

and Leino P, 'Fragmentation of International Law? Postmodern Anxieties' (2002) 15 Leiden Journal of International Law 553

Kwiatkowska B, 'Equitable Maritime Boundary Delimitation, as Exemplified in the Work of the International Court of Justice during the Presidency of Sir Robert

Yewdall Jennings and Beyond' (1997) 28 Ocean Development and International Law 91

Lachs M, 'Equity in Arbitration and in Judicial Settlement of Disputes' (1993) 6 Leiden Journal of International Law 323

Lagoni R, 'Oil and Gas Deposits across National Frontiers' (1979) 73 AJIL 215

Lahey W and Leschine T, 'Evaluating the Risks of Offshore Oil Development' (1983) 4 Environmental Impact Assessment Review 271

Lauterpacht H, 'The Subjects of the Law of Nations' (1947) 63 International Law Quarterly Review 438

Leary D and others, 'Marine Genetic Resources: A Review of Scientific and Commercial Interest' (2009) 33 Marine Policy 183

Lee C and Liew K, 'Modelling and Risk Management in the Offshore and Marine Industry Supply Chain' (2012) 4 International Journal of Engineering Business Management 1

Llamzon A, 'Jurisdiction and Compliance in Recent Decisions of the International Court of Justice' (2008) 18 European Journal of International Law 815

Mamlyk B and Mattei U, 'Comparative International Law' (2011) 36 Brooklyn Journal of International Law 385

Mann F, 'The Doctrine of Jurisdiction in International Law' (1964) 111 Collected Courses of the Hague Academy of International Law 1

Marzuki S, 'The Dynamism of Joint Operating Agreements Involving National Oil Companies' [2013] 4 OGEL <www.ogel.org>

Maung M, 'The Burma-China Boundary Settlement' (1961) 1 Asian Survey 38

McDougal M, 'The Hydrogen Bomb Tests and the International Law of the Sea' (1955) 49 AJIL 356

and Burke W, 'Crisis in the Law of the Sea: Community Perspectives versus National Egoism' (1958) 67 Yale Law Journal 539

McGibbon I, 'Estoppel in International Law' (1958) 7 ICLQ 468

Meese R, 'The Relevance of the Granting of Oil Concessions in a Maritime Delimitation: The Jurisprudence of the International Court of Justice' [2003] 2 OGEL <www.ogel.org>

'The Arbitration between Newfoundland and Labrador and Nova Scotia Concerning Portions of the Limits of their Offshore Areas: The Relevance of the Conduct of the Parties in Maritime Delimitation' [2003] 5 OGEL <www.ogel.org>

Menon P, 'The Legal Personality of Individuals' (1994) 6 Sri Lanka Journal of International Law 127

Metzger S, 'Property in International Law' (1964) 50 Virginia Law Review 594

Milano E and Papanicolopulu I, 'State Responsibility in Disputed Areas on Land and at Sea' (2011) 71 ZaöRV 587

Miyoshi M, 'The Basic Concept of Joint Development of Hydrocarbon Resources in the Continental Shelf' (1988) 3 International Journal of Estuarine and Coastal Law 1

Monjur H and others, 'Protracted Maritime Boundary Disputes and Maritime Laws' (2019) 2 Journal of International Maritime Safety, Environmental Affairs, and Shipping 89

Morgan A, 'The New Law of the Sea: Rethinking the Implications for Foreign Jurisdiction and Freedom of Action' (1996) 27 Ocean Development and International Law 5

Bibliography

Moss R, 'Insuring Unilaterally Licensed Deep Seabed Mining Operations against Adverse Rulings by the International Court of Justice: An Assessment of the Risk' (1984) 14 Ocean Development and International Law 161

Nelson L, 'The Roles of Equity in the Delimitation of Maritime Boundaries' (1990) 84 AJIL 837

Nilsen PJ, 'The Offshore Risks of Bits and Bytes' (2010) 70(6) Offshore 84

Öberg MD, 'The Legal Effects of Resolutions of the UN Security Council and General Assembly in the Jurisprudence of the ICJ' (2006) 16 European Journal of International Law 879

Oduntan G, 'Modalities for Post Boundary Dispute, Cross Border JPZs/Unitisation Upstream Hydrocarbon Exploitation in the Gulf of Guinea?' [2009] 4 OGEL <www.ogel.org>

Ong D, 'Joint Development of Common Offshore Oil and Gas Deposits: "Mere" State Practice or Customary International Law?' (1999) 93 AJIL 771

Onorato W, 'Apportionment of an International Common Petroleum Deposit' (1968) 17 ICLQ 85

 and Shihata I, 'The Joint Development of International Petroleum Resources in Undefined and Disputed Areas' (1996) 11 ICSID Review 299

Oude Elferink A, 'International Law and Negotiated and Adjudicated Maritime Boundaries: A Complex Relationship' (2015) 48 German Yearbook of International Law 1

Oxman B, 'The Third United Nations Conventions on the Law of the Sea: The Tenth Session' (1982) 76 AJIL 14

 'The Territorial Temptation: A Siren Song at Sea' (2006) 100 AJIL 830

Papanicolopulu I, 'The Law of the Sea Convention: No Place for Persons?' (2012) 27 International Journal of Marine and Coastal Law 867

Pappa M, 'Private Oil Companies Operating in Contested Waters and International Law of the Sea: A Peculiar Relationship' [2018] 1 OGEL <www.ogel.org>

 'The Impact of Judicial Delimitation on Private Rights Existing in Contested Waters: Implications for the Somali-Kenyan Maritime Dispute' (2017) 61 Cambridge Journal of African Law 393

Pasich K and Thayer S, 'Political Risk Insurance' (2011) 58(5) Risk Management 27

Paulson C, 'Compliance with Final Judgments of the International Court of Justice since 1987' (2004) 98 AJIL 434

Penick F, 'The Legal Character of the Right to Explore and Exploit the Natural Resources of the Continental Shelf' (1985) 22 San Diego Law Review 765

Perry A, 'Oil and Gas Deposits at International Boundaries: New Ways for Governments and Oil and Gas Companies to Handle an Increasingly Urgent Problem' [2007] 2 OGEL <www.ogel.org>

Petersen N, 'The Role of Consent and Uncertainty in the Formation of Customary International Law' (2011) 4 Max Planck Institute for Research on Collective Goods 1

Politakis G, 'The 1993 Jan Mayen Judgment: The End of Illusions?' (1994) 41 Netherlands International Law Review 1

Pudden E and VanderZwaag D, 'Canada-USA Bilateral Fisheries Management in the Gulf of Maine: Under the Radar Screen' (2007) 16 RECIEL 36

Rankin K, 'The Role of the Irish Boundary Commission in the Entrenchment of the Irish Border: From Tactical Panacea to Political Liability' (2008) 34 Journal of Historical Geography 422

Razzaque J, 'Changing Role of Friends of the Court in the International Courts and Tribunals' (2001) 1 Non-State Actors and International Law 169

Rawlings A, 'The Rise of the National Oil Company: Implications for International Oil Companies' [2015] 6 OGEL <www.ogel.org>

Reeves J, 'International Boundaries' (1944) 38 AJIL 533

Rider T and Owsiak A, 'Border Settlement, Committee Problems, and the Causes of Contiguous Rivalry' (2015) 52 Journal of Peace Research 508

Roach A, 'Today's Customary International Law of the Sea' (2014) 45 Ocean Development and International Law 239

Roberts A and others, 'Comparative International Law: Framing the Field' (2015) 109 AJIL 467

Ronen Y, 'Participation of Non-State Actors in ICJ Proceedings' (2012) 11 Law and Practice of International Courts and Tribunals 77

Sanchez G and McLaughlin R, 'The 2012 Agreement on the Exploitation of Transboundary Hydrocarbon Resources in the Gulf of Mexico: Confirmation of the Rule or Emergence of a New Practice?' (2015) 37 Houston Journal of International Law 681

Schagatay E and Abrahamsson E, 'A Living Based on Breath-Hold Diving in the Bajau Laut' (2004) 29 Human Evolution 171

Schofield C, 'Parting the Waves: Claims to Maritime Jurisdiction and the Division of Ocean Space' (2012) 1 Penn State Journal of Law and International Affairs 40

Schwarzenberger G, 'Title to Territory: Response to a Challenge' (1957) 51 AJIL 308

Shaw M, 'The Heritage of States: The Principle of Uti Possidetis Juris Today' (1996) 67 British Yearbook of International Law 75

'Peoples, Territorialism and Boundaries' (1997) 8 European Journal of International Law 478

Shelton D, 'The Participation of Nongovernmental Organizations in International Judicial Proceedings' (1994) 88 AJIL 611

'The Status of the Individual in International Law' (2006) ASIL Proceedings 249

Sik KS, 'The Concept of Acquired Rights in International Law: A Survey' (1977) 24 Netherlands International Law Review 120

Singh S, 'The Potential of International Law: Fragmentation and Ethics' (2011) 24 Leiden Journal of International Law 23

Steinsson S, 'The Cod Wars: A Re-analysis' (2016) 25 European Security 256

Stirk P, 'The Westphalian Model and Sovereign Equality' (2012) 38 Review of International Studies 641

Sumner BT, 'Territorial Disputes at the International Court of Justice' (2004) 53 Duke Law Journal 1779

Tanaka Y, 'Reflections on the Concept of Proportionality in the Law of Maritime Delimitation' (2001) 16 International Journal of Marine and Coastal Law 433

'Reflections on Maritime Delimitation in the Romania/Ukraine Case before the International Court of Justice' (2009) 56 Netherlands International Law Review 397

Taylor T, 'Modern Marine Insurance: Coverages, Current Issues, and Connections' (2013) 87 Tulane Law Review 955

Thibodeau P, 'Offshore Risks are Numerous, Say Those Who Craft Contracts' (2003) 37(44) Computerworld 12

Thirlway H, 'The Law and Procedure of the International Court of Justice: Part Two' (1990) 62 British Yearbook of International Law 30

Torhaug M, 'Risk Management Updates Needed to Improve Safety Offshore' (2012) 72 (5) Offshore 156

Torstad E, 'Rethinking Risk Management for Offshore Safety' (2012) 110(6) Oil and Gas Journal 3

Touval S, 'Treaties, Borders, and the Partition of Africa' (1966) 7 Journal of African History 279

Townsend-Gault I, 'The Frigg Gas Field: Exploitation of an International Cross-Boundary Petroleum Field' (1979) 3 Marine Policy 302

Treves T, 'Fragmentation of International Law: The Judicial Perspective' (2009) 27 Agenda Internacional 213

'UNCLOS at Thirty: Open Challenges' (2013) 27 Ocean Yearbook 49

Trimble P, 'International Law, World Order, and Critical Legal Studies' (1990) 42 Stanford Law Review 811

Tsioumani E, 'Discussion of Marine Genetic Resources' (2007) 37 Environmental Policy and Law 366

Van de Putte A, Gates D and Holder A, 'Political Risk Insurance as an Instrument to Reduce Oil and Gas Investment Risk and Manage Investment Returns' (2012) 5 Journal of World Energy Law and Business 284

Van Hoecke M, 'Methodology of Comparative Legal Research' [Oct–Dec 2015] Law and Method

Vasquez J and Henehan M, 'Territorial Disputes and the Probability of War 1816–1992' (2001) 38 Journal of Peace Research 123

Vierros M and others, 'Who Owns the Ocean? Policy Issues Surrounding Marine Genetic Resources' (2016) 25 Limnology and Oceanography Bulletin 29

Wälde T and Ndi G, 'Stabilising International Investment Commitments: International Law versus Contract Interpretation' (1996) 31 Texas International Law Journal 215

Wälde T and others, 'International Unitisation of Oil and Gas Fields: The Legal Framework of International Law, National Laws, and Private Contracts' [2007] 2 OGEL <www.ogel.org>

Waldock H, 'The International Court of Justice as Seen from the Bar and Bench' (1983) 54 British Yearbook of International Law 1

Walker W, 'Territorial Waters: The Cannon Shot Rule' (1945) 22 British Yearbook of International Law 210

Willis A, 'From Precedent to Precedent: The Triumph of Pragmatism in the Law of Maritime Boundaries' (1986) 24 Canadian Yearbook of International Law 3

Woodlife J, 'International Unitization of an Offshore Gas Field' (1997) 26 ICLQ 338

Wright Q, 'The Stimson Note of January 7, 1932' (1932) 26 AJIL 342

Wright T and Diehl P, 'Unpacking Territorial Disputes: Domestic Political Influences and War' (2016) 60 Journal of Conflict Resolution 645

Zacher M, 'The Territorial Integrity Norm: International Boundaries and the Use of Force' (2001) 55 International Organization 215

212 Bibliography

ELECTRONIC SOURCES AND WEBSITES

'Border Dispute Blocks Heritage's Progress in Malta' (*Means Borders*, 23 June 2011) <http://menasborders.blogspot.co.uk/2011/06/border-dispute-blocks-heritages.html> accessed 20 March 2020

'CGX Energy Pleased with Guyana/Suriname Resolution' (*Rigzone*, 21 September 2007) <www.rigzone.com/news/oil_gas/a/50517/cgx_energy_pleased_with_guyanasurina me_resolution/> accessed 31 March 2021

'Guatemala vote to hold referendum on Belize territorial dispute' (*IBRU Boundary News*, 9 August 2017) <www.dur.ac.uk/ibru/news/boundary_news/?item no=32087&rehref=%2Fibru%2Fnews%2F&resubj=Boundary+news+Headlines> accessed 20 March 2020

African Union Border Programme (AUBP), 'Delimitation and Demarcation of Boundaries in Africa' (2013) <www.peaceau.org/uploads/au2013-en-delim-a-dem ar-of-bound-gen-iss-a-studies-elec2.pdf> accessed 20 March 2020

AGCS Allianz <www.agcs.allianz.com/services/energy/> accessed 20 March 2020

Allo A, 'Ethiopia Offers an Olive Branch to Eritrea' <www.aljazeera.com/indepth/ opinion/ethiopia-offers-olive-branch-eritrea-180607104544523.html> accessed 20 March 2020

Axis Capital, 'Explore Our Specialty Insurance Solutions' <www.axiscapital.com/en-us /insurance> accessed 20 March 2020

Cameroon-Nigeria Mixed Boundary Commission <https://unowas.unmissions.org/ca meroon-nigeria-mixed-commission> accessed 20 March 2020

Oceans and Law of the Sea, 'Submissions, through the Secretary-General of the United Nations, to the Commission on the Limits of the Continental Shelf, pursuant to Article 76, Paragraph 8, of the United Nations Convention on the Law of the Sea of 10 December 1982' <www.un.org/depts/los/clcs_new/commission_submissions .htm> accessed 20 March 2020

Council on Foreign Relations, 'Global Conflict Tracker' <www.cfr.org/interactives/gl obal-conflict-tracker#!/> accessed 20 March 2020

International Court of Justice, 'List of All Cases' <www.icj-cij.org/en/list-of-all-cases> accessed 20 March 2020

International Law Commission <http://legal.un.org/ilc/> accessed 20 March 2020

International Seabed Authority, 'Countries and Companies Exploring the Deep Seabed' <www.isa.org.jm/faq/who-are-countriescompanies-are-exploring-deep-seabed-minerals> accessed 20 March 2020

International Tribunal for the Law of the Sea, 'List of Cases' <www.itlos.org/cases/list-of-cases/> accessed 20 March 2020

Lloyd's <www.lloyds.com/> accessed 20 March 2020

Medidian Risk Solutions <www.meridianrsl.com/> accessed 20 March 2020

Muwanguzi P, 'Reconciling Uti Possidetis and Self-determination: The Concept of Interstate Boundary Disputes' (2007) <https://papers.ssrn.com/sol3/papers.cfm?a bstract_id=1023163> accessed 20 March 2020

Nova Scotia, 'Nova Scotia Says Boundary Decision Paves Way for Oil and Gas Activity' (2 April 2002) <https://novascotia.ca/news/release/?id=20020408002> accessed 20 March 2020

Bibliography

Oceans and Law of the Sea, 'Chronological Lists of Ratifications of, Accessions and Successions to the Convention and the Related Agreements' <www.un.org/depts/los/reference_files/chronological_lists_of_ratifications.htm> accessed 20 March 2020

Organization for Security and Co-operation in Europe (OSCE), 'Applied Issues in International Land Boundary Delimitation/Demarcation Practices' (2011) <www.osce.org/cpc/85263?download=true> accessed 20 March 2020

Permanent Court of Arbitration, 'Cases' <https://pca-cpa.org/en/cases/> accessed 20 March 2020

Pulkowski D, 'Narratives of Fragmentation: International Law between Unity and Multiplicity' (Inaugural Conference of the European Society of International Law, Florence 2004) <https://esil-sedi.eu/pre-2009-conference-papers/> accessed 3 April 2021

Koh TTB, 'A Constitution for the Oceans' (Remarks by the President of the Third United Nations Conference on the Law of the Sea) <www.un.org/depts/los/convention_agreements/texts/koh_english.pdf> accessed 20 March 2020

Solomou A, 'A Commentary on the Maritime Delimitation Issues in the Croatia v. Slovenia Final Award' (*EJIL: Talk!*, 15 September 2017) <www.ejiltalk.org/a-commentary-on-the-maritime-delimitation-issues-in-the-croatia-v-slovenia-final-award/> accessed 20 March 2020

Srebro H and Shoshany M, 'Towards a Comprehensive International Boundary Making Model' (2006) <www.fig.net/resources/proceedings/fig_proceedings/fig2006/papers/ts63/ts63_01_srebro_shoshani_0293.pdf> accessed 3 April 2021

Statistica, 'Number of Offshore Rigs Worldwide as of January 2018 by Region' <www.statista.com/statistics/279100/number-of-offshore-rigs-worldwide-by-region/> accessed 2 February 2021

United Nations Treaty Collection <https://treaties.un.org/pages/AdvanceSearch.aspx?tab=CN&clang=_en> accessed 20 March 2020

United Nations Treaty Collection, 'League of Nations Treaty Series' <https://treaties.un.org/pages/lononline.aspx?clang=_en> accessed 20 March 2020

University of Dundee, 'Dundee Ocean and Lake Frontiers Institute and Neutrals (DOLFIN)' <www.dundee.ac.uk/projects/dundee-ocean-and-lake-frontiers-institute-and-neutrals-dolfin> accessed 2 February 2021

Index

acquiescence, 32, 36, 68, 69, 70, 71, 78, 81, 90, 91, 145, 146, 148, 151, 153, 175, 177, 184, 188, 192, 193

acquired rights, doctrine of, 115, 119, 124, 125, 126, 128, 129

Adler, Ron, 49, 54, 194

Aegean Sea Continental Shelf Case (Greece v Turkey)
interim measures (ICJ 1976), xv, 39, 41
jurisdiction of the Court (ICJ 1978), xv, 9

African Charter on Human and Peoples' Rights (ACHPR) 1981, xxvii, 131

African Commission on Human and Peoples' Rights (ACmHPR), xxxii, 28

African Union Border Programme (AUBP), 52, 212

Alvarez-Jimenez, Alberto, 89, 91, 204

American Convention on Human Rights (ACHR) 1969, xxviii, 131

amicus curiae, 174, 175, 188

Amoco International Finance Corp v Government of the Islamic Republic of Iran, National Iranian Oil Company, National Petrochemical Company and KHARG Chemical Company Ltd (1987), xv, 28

Anderson, David, 48, 57, 61, 65, 110, 167, 194, 201, 204

Antunes, Nuno, 1, 119, 194, 204

Arbitral Award in the Matter of Delimitation of a Certain Part of the Maritime Boundary between Norway and Sweden (Grisbådarna Case) (Norway v Sweden) (1909), xv, 19, 73, 75

Arbitration between Barbados and Trinidad and Tobago (Barbados v Trinidad and Tobago) (2006), xv, 79, 81

Arbitration between Guyana and Suriname (Guyana v Suriname) (2007), xv, 40, 41, 58, 81, 122

Arbitration between India and Pakistan for the Indo-Pakistan Western Boundary (Rann of Kutch) (India v Pakistan) (1968), xv, 36, 70, 71, 72

Arbitration between Newfoundland and Labrador and Nova Scotia (Newfoundland and Labrador v Nova Scotia) (2002), xv, 79

Arbitration between Saudi Arabia and Aramco (1963), 26, 132

Arbitration between the Republic of Croatia and the Republic of Slovenia (Croatia v Slovenia) (2017), xv, 69, 79

Arbitration Concerning the Definite Fixing of the Italian-Swiss Frontier at the Place Called Alpe de Cravairola (Italy/ Switzerland) (1874), xv, 71

Arbitration in the Bay of Bengal (Bangladesh v India) (2014), xv, 79

Arbitration Regarding the Delimitation of the Abyei Area between the Government of Sudan and the Sudan People's Liberation Movement/Army (2009), xv, 68, 116

Aristotle, 165

Association of Southeast Asian Nations (ASEAN), xxviii, xxxii, 28

Asylum Case (Columbia v Peru) (ICJ 1950), xv, 85

Index

Barcelona Traction, Light and Power Company Limited (Belgium v Spain) (ICJ 1970), xvi
Becker-Weinberg, Vasco, 105, 106, 113, 153, 154, 194
best effort clause, 104, 105
Boggs, Samuel, 1, 3, 6, 10, 48, 51, 52, 194, 205
boundaries
  artificial, 3
  disputes, 7, 8, 33
  general features, 1, 2, 6, 7, 15, 191
  history and evolution, 4–6
  land, 2
  maritime, 2
  natural, 3
boundary-making, stages
  allocation, 47, 49
  delimitation, 47, 51, 59
  demarcation, 47, 54
  negotiation, 48, 57, 170
Boyle, Alan, 181, 194, 201, 205
Bramelid and Malmström v Sweden (ECtHR 1982), xix, 28
British Institute of International and Comparative Law (BIICL), xxxii, 59
Brownlie, Ian, 16, 34, 35, 46, 83, 84, 85, 172, 195, 205, 207

Cameron, Peter, 28, 108, 113, 158, 195, 205
Caminos, Hugo, 20, 137, 139, 202, 205
Case Concerning Ahmadou Sadio Diallo (Republic of Guinea v Democratic Republic of Congo) (Preliminary Objections) (ICJ 2007), xvi, 132
Case Concerning Avena and Other Mexican Nationals (Mexico v United States) (ICJ 2004), xvi, 182
Case Concerning Elettronica Sicula SpA (ELSI) (United States of America v Italy) (ICJ 1989), xvi, 132
Case Concerning Kasikili/Sedudu island (Botswana/Namibia) (ICJ 1999), xvi, 36, 71, 72, 115
Case Concerning Maritime Delimitation in the Area between Greenland and Jan Mayen (Denmark v Norway) (ICJ 1993), xvi, 79
Case Concerning Military and Paramilitary Activities in and against Nicaragua (Nicaragua v United States of America) (ICJ 1986), xvi, 85

Case Concerning Sovereignty over Certain Frontier Land (Belgium/Netherlands) (ICJ 1959), xvi, 71
Case Concerning Sovereignty over Pulau Ligitan and Pulau Sipadan (Indonesia/Malaysia) (ICJ 2002), xvi, 72
Case Concerning Territorial and Maritime Dispute between Nicaragua and Honduras in the Caribbean Sea (Nicaragua v Honduras) (ICJ 2007), xvi, 72, 79, 81
Case Concerning the Continental Shelf (Libyan Arab Jamahiriya/Malta) (ICJ 1985), xvi, 33, 77, 121, 172
Case Concerning the Continental Shelf (Tunisia/Libyan Arab Jamahiriya) (ICJ 1982), xvi, 119, 167, 172
Case Concerning the Delimitation of Maritime Boundary between Guinea-Bissau and Senegal (Guinea-Bissau v Senegal) (1989), xvi, 9
Case Concerning the Frontier Dispute (Benin/Niger) (ICJ 2005), xvi, 68
Case Concerning the Frontier Dispute (Burkina Faso/Republic of Mali) (ICJ 1986), xvi, 9, 52, 69, 71
Case Concerning the Land and Maritime Boundary Between Cameroon and Nigeria (Cameroon v Nigeria; Equatorial Guinea Intervening) (ICJ 2002), xvi, 37, 71, 73, 81, 92, 121, 172
Case Concerning the Temple of Preah Vihear (Cambodia v Thailand) (ICJ 1962), xvi, 55, 68, 70, 71
Case Concerning the Territorial Dispute (Libyan Arab Jamahiriya/Chad) (ICJ 1994), xvi, 5
Case of the Mayagna (Sumo) Awas Tingni Community v Nicaragua (IACHR 2001), xix
Cassese, Antonio, 2, 131, 142, 195
Certain Activities Carried Out by Nicaragua in the Border Area (Nicaragua v Costa Rica) (ICJ 2015), xvi, 37
Certain German Interests in Polish Upper Silesia (Germany v Poland) (PCIJ 1926), xvi
Channel Continental Shelf Arbitration (UK v France) (1978), xvii, 175
Charney, Jonathan, 1, 46, 57, 66, 90, 103, 195, 202, 205

216 Index

Churchill, Robert, 3, 18, 19, 24, 25, 41, 60, 80, 111, 131, 195, 201, 206
codification of law, 3, 137, 186, 187, 188, 192
colonialism, 3, 4, 5, 12, 18, 52, 68, 69, 116
Commonwealth, The v WMC Resources Ltd (1998), xix, 27
Cook v Sprigg (1899) AC 572, xix, 124
cooperation agreements
    land, 99–101
    maritime, 106–14
cooperation, customary duty of, 111, 112
Cottier, Thomas, 1, 77, 111, 120, 147, 148, 149, 169, 174, 195
Crawford, James, 6, 16, 34, 142, 195, 201
Cukwurah, Anthony, 1, 37, 55, 195
customary law, 17, 42, 83, 84, 90, 91, 111, 112, 123, 125, 134, 186
    elements, 84, 85, 126

D'Amato, Anthony, 86, 142, 195, 201
Decision Regarding Delimitation of the Border between Eritrea and Ethiopia (2002), xvii, 6
delimitation
    land, 9, 33, 37, 48, 68, 143, 145, 184, 186, 190, 192
    maritime, 9, 34, 38, 56, 73, 144, 145, 164, 170, 171, 175, 179, 184, 186, 190, 192
Delimitation of Maritime Areas between Canada and the French Republic (St Pierre et Miquelon) (1992), xvii, 81
Delimitation of the Continental Shelf between the United Kingdom of Great Britain and Northern Ireland and the French Republic (UK v France) Arbitral Award (1977), xvii, 74
Delimitation of the Maritime Boundary in the Gulf of Maine Area (Canada/United States) (ICJ 1984), xvii, 5, 76, 77, 92, 120, 166
delimitation rulings, 8, 11, 66–67. *See Table of Cases*
delimitation treaties, 4, 8, 11, 45–48. *See Table of Treaties*
Deutsche Continental Shelf Gas-Gesellschaft v Polish State (PCIJ 1929), xvii, 6, 16
disproportionality test, 79, 167
Dispute Concerning Delimitation of the Maritime Boundary between Ghana and Côte d'Ivoire in the Atlantic Ocean (Ghana/Côte d'Ivoire)

merits (ITLOS 2017), xvii, 40, 41, 58, 79, 82, 167
    provisional measures (ITLOS 2015), xvii, 39
Dispute Concerning Delimitation of the Maritime Boundary between Guinea and Guinea-Bissau (Guinea v Guinea-Bissau) (1985), xvii, 74, 76, 92, 119
Dispute Concerning Delimitation of the Maritime Boundary in the Bay of Bengal (Bangladesh/Myanmar) (ITLOS 2012), 58, 79, 146
Dispute Regarding Navigational and Related Rights (Costa Rica v Nicaragua), xvii, 183
distributive justice, 75, 80, 168
Dupuy, René, 2, 18, 139, 148, 168, 196, 201
duty to negotiate, 40, 41, 106, 110, 147

East Timor (Portugal v Australia) (ICJ 1995), xvii
effectivités, 68, 71, 72, 78, 90, 91, 115, 145
Energy Charter Treaty (ECT), xxxii, 154
Energy Charter Treaty (ECT) 1994, xxviii
equidistance, 10, 60, 61, 63, 64, 65, 66, 74, 76, 79, 81, 82, 83, 91, 92, 118, 145, 146, 147, 150, 151, 167. *See median line*
    corrective equidistance or three-step approach, 79
equitable principles, 60, 63, 64, 66, 74, 78, 83, 150, 151
equitable result, 60, 74, 149, 150, 151, 168, 188
equity, 9, 47, 125, 145, 147, 149, 165, 166, 167, 168, 169, 184, 188, 192, 193
Eritrea/Yemen Arbitration
    first stage (2001), xvii, 72
    second stage (2001), xvii, 79, 81, 118, 129, 150
European Convention on Human Rights (ECHR), xxviii, xxxii, 131, 132, 154
European Court of Human Rights (ECtHR), xxxii, 27, 28
Evans, Malcolm, 1, 75, 78, 178, 183, 196, 201, 202, 203, 206
ex aequo et bono, 148, 165, 176

Fisheries Case (UK v Norway) (1951), xvii, 5, 10, 19, 74, 75, 85
Fisheries Jurisdiction Case (United Kingdom v Iceland) (ICJ 1973), xvii
force majeure, 156, 157
Fredin v Sweden (ECtHR 1991), xix, 28
Freestone, David, 1, 75, 141, 178, 181, 194, 196, 201

Index

Friedmann, Wolfgang, 142, 165, 196, 202, 206
Frontier Dispute (Burkina Faso/Niger) (ICJ
2013), xvii, 68
frustration. *See* private rights: discharge of
reallocated private rights

Gao, Jianjun, 110, 206
Gavouneli, Maria, 22, 196
Geneva Conventions 1958, 74, 78, 137
    Convention on Fishing and Conservation of
    the Living Resources of the High Seas, 3
    Convention on the Continental Shelf, 3
    Convention on the High Seas, 3
    Convention on the Territorial Sea and the
    Contiguous Zone, 3
geographical factors, 79, 93, 95, 119, 168, 175
Gordon, Greg, 26, 202
grandfather clause, 97, 98, 99, 101, 102, 103, 105,
    106, 109, 118, 126
Grotius, Hugo, xiv, 1, 3, 17, 18, 33, 78, 154, 155,
    166, 195, 196, 200
Guggenheim, Paul, 86, 187, 196, 201
Guillaume, Gilbert, 89, 91, 206

Harrison, James, 137, 139, 140, 178, 181, 196
Higgins, Rosalyn, 21, 90, 197
human geography, 51, 61, 73, 117

insurance, private, 160
Inter-American Court of Human Rights
    (IACHR), xxxii, 28
International Boundaries Research Unit
    (IBRU), xxxii, 1, 63, 195
International Court of Justice (ICJ), xvii, xviii,
    xxxii, 5, 6, 9, 10, 17, 19, 33, 36, 37, 39,
    41, 52, 55, 64, 66, 67, 68, 69, 73, 74, 80,
    84, 85, 88, 89, 91, 92, 112, 119, 120, 121, 132,
    133, 148, 172, 173, 174, 176, 182, 183, 204,
    209, 210
international investment law, 28, 132, 155
International Law Commission (ILC), xxix,
    xxxii, 84, 85, 86, 124, 133, 137, 186, 187,
    188, 189
international law of human rights, 27,
    131, 155
International Seabed Authority, 21
International Tribunal for the Law of the Sea
    (ITLOS), xvii, xviii, xxxii, 40, 66, 67, 79,
    82, 91, 140, 172, 173, 174, 183
Island of Palmas Case (Netherlands/USA)
    (1928), xvii, 9, 33, 34, 36, 71, 72

Jennings, Robert, 35, 36, 69, 90, 197, 207
Johnston, Daniel, 1, 3, 4, 5, 6, 46, 57, 61, 64,
    197, 203
joint development agreement (JDA), xxxii,
    40, 109
Jones, Stephen, 1, 3, 5, 47, 49, 50, 51, 52, 55, 56,
    99, 197, 207
judicial activism, 128
judicial delimitation. *See* delimitation rulings
*Jurisdiction of the Courts of Danzig
    (Beamtenabkommen)* (PCIJ 1928),
    xvii, 182

Karaman, Igor, 8, 46, 144, 147, 168, 197
Kelsen, Hans, 35, 86, 197, 207
Klein, Natalie, 17, 152, 177, 197, 205
Kraska, James, 22, 197
Kwiatkowska, Barbara, xiv, 22, 57, 62, 63, 64,
    197, 202, 207

Lachs, Manfred, 142, 148, 163, 165, 168, 176, 178,
    186, 197, 202, 204, 208
Lagoni, Rainer, 1, 20, 48, 106, 113, 197,
    201, 208
LaGrand Case (Germany v United States) (ICJ
    2001), xvii
Lalive, Pierre, 125, 202
*Land, Island and Maritime Frontier Dispute
    (El Salvador/Honduras)* (ICJ 1992), xvii,
    69, 71, 72, 115
Lauterpacht, Elihu, 86
Lauterpacht, Hersch, 86, 124, 142
legal comparison
    between land and maritime delimitation, 11
*Legal Consequences of the Construction of
    a Wall in the Occupied Palestinian
    Territory Advisory Opinion* (ICJ 2003),
    xviii
*Legal Status of Eastern Greenland (Denmark/
    Norway)* (PCIJ 1933), xviii, 71
*Libyan American Oil Company (Liamco)
    v Government of the Libyan Arab Republic*
    (1977), xviii, 26
Loizidou v Turkey (ECtHR 1998), xix, 28
Luard, Evan, 1, 36, 70, 198

mare liberum, 17, 196
*Maritime Boundary Arbitration in the Bay of
    Bengal between the People's Republic of
    Bangladesh and the Republic of India
    (Bangladesh v India)* (2014), xviii

Index

Maritime Delimitation and Territorial Questions (Qatar v Bahrain) (ICJ 2001), xviii, 60, 79, 91
Maritime Delimitation in the Area between Greenland and Jan Mayen (Denmark v Norway) (ICJ 1993), xviii
Maritime Delimitation in the Black Sea (Romania v Ukraine) (ICJ 2009), xviii, 10, 79, 81, 167
Maritime Dispute (Peru v Chile) (ICJ 2014), xviii, 73, 80
maritime zones
  continental shelf (CS), 20
  deep seabed (the Area), 21
  exclusive economic zone (EEZ), 22
  high seas, 22
  territorial sea (TS), 17, 19, 145
Mavrommatis Palestine Concessions, The (Greece v Great Britain) (PCIJ 1924), xviii, 127
McDougal, Myres, 18, 20, 177, 208
McHarg, Aileen, 155, 202
Media Rights Agenda v Nigeria (ACmHPR 1998), xix
median line, 10, 60, 61, 64, 76, 80, 81, 145, 146. *See* equidistance
Milano, Enrico, 4, 5, 35, 37, 38, 41, 59, 198, 208
mineral clause, 104, 105
minor frontier traffic agreement, 99
Miyoshi, Masahiro, 111, 113, 120, 198, 208
Mondev International Ltd v United States of America (ICSID 2002), xviii, 132
Montevideo Convention on the Rights and Duties of States 1933, xxviii, 16

Nagoya Protocol on Access to Genetic Resources and the Fair and Equitable Sharing of Benefits Arising from their Utilization (ABS) to the Convention on Biological Diversity 2010, xxviii, 26
national oil company (NOC), xxxii, 87
natural law, 153, 155
natural resources, 3, 16, 20, 21, 22, 23, 24, 28, 29, 32, 39, 59, 61, 63, 66, 75, 76, 77, 85, 93, 107, 111, 112, 134, 160, 176
Newcrest Mining (WA) Ltd v The Commonwealth (1997), xix, 27
non-geographical factors, 61, 79, 80, 83, 95, 121, 122, 175
non-state actors, xii, xiii, 2, 7, 8, 67, 88, 93, 128, 129, 136, 164, 170, 172, 179, 182, 187, 190, 191

non-state actors' rights. *See* private rights
North American Free Trade Agreement (NAFTA) 1992, xxviii, 28, 154
North Sea Continental Shelf Cases (Germany/ Denmark, Germany/Netherlands) (ICJ 1969), xviii, 6, 10, 60, 74, 75, 78, 84, 85, 87, 92, 93, 118, 119, 175

O'Connell, Daniel, 35, 124, 125, 127, 198
Ong, David, 75, 111, 209
opinio juris. See customary law
Oppenheim, Lassa, 16, 20, 34, 71, 142, 172, 198, 202
Organization for Security and Co-operation in Europe (OSCE), xxxii, 12, 52, 53, 54, 213
Oude Elferink, Alex, 46, 58, 66, 121, 148, 178, 198, 203, 209
Oxman, Bernard, 21, 150, 202, 209

Papanicolopulu, Irini, xiv, 37, 41, 59, 179, 198, 202, 208, 209
Pappa, Marianthi, 42, 59, 92, 94, 131, 157, 209
Permanent Court of Arbitration (PCA), xxxii, 66, 67, 91, 172, 173, 174
piracy, 138, 139, 140, 178
Prescott, Victor, 1, 3, 6, 8, 10, 46, 48, 49, 50, 51, 53, 57, 59, 60, 61, 146, 199
private rights
  discharge of reallocated private rights, 129
  duration, 152
  general features, 23–29
  in areas of overlapping claims, 29–32
  in land delimitation rulings, 68–72
  in land delimitation treaties, 48–56
  in maritime delimitation rulings, 73–83
  in maritime delimitation treaties, 56–65
  legal value, 153
  protection of reallocated private rights, 133
  reallocation, 7, 83, 89, 93
  unbalanced protection on land and at sea, 136, 191
production sharing agreement (PSA), xxxii, 156
provisional arrangements, 40, 110, 159

Question of Jaworzina (Polish-Czechoslovakian Frontier) (PCIJ 1923), xviii, 36
Questions of the Monastery of Saint Naoum (Albanian Frontier) (PCIJ 1924), xviii, 6

Index

Questions Relating to Settlers of German Origin in the Territory Ceded by Germany to Poland (German Settlers) (PCIJ 1923), xviii, 127

Raibl-Societa Mineraria del Predil SpA v Italy (Raibl Claim) (1964), xviii, 28
Reeves, Jesse, 48, 210
Responsibilities and Obligations of States Sponsoring Persons and Entities with Respect to Activities in the Area (ITLOS 2011), xviii
Revision and Interpretation of the Judgment of 24 February 1982 in the Case Concerning the Continental Shelf (Tunisia/Libyan Arab Jamahiriya) (ICJ 1985), xviii, 120, 174
Rosenne, Shabtai, 137, 199
Rothwell, Donald, 10, 121, 178, 199, 203

Saipem SpA v The People's Republic of Bangladesh (ICSID 2009), xviii, 132
Sapphire International Petroleums Ltd v National Iranian Oil Company (1967) 184, xviii, 132
Saudi Arabia v Aramc, (1963), xviii
Schofield, Clive, 3, 8, 10, 20, 60, 110, 121, 146, 179, 195, 199, 202, 203, 210
Schwarzenberger, Georg, 35, 36, 70, 72, 143, 199, 210
Sharma, Surya, 4, 35, 199
Shaw, Malcolm, 5, 16, 34, 53, 90, 112, 142, 163, 186, 199, 203, 210
Societe Gééerale de Surveillance (SGS) v Republic of Philippines (2004), xviii, 182
Sporrong and Lönnroth v Sweden (ECtHR 1982), xix, 28
Sprankling, John, 24, 28, 29, 155, 200
Srebro, Haim, 48, 52, 53, 200, 213
SS Lotus Case (France v Turkey) (PCIJ 1927), xviii
stabilization clause, 158
stare decisis, 11, 89, 128
state powers
    sovereign rights, 20, 22, 39
    sovereignty, 19, 21, 37
statehood, 2, 6, 36, 66, 88, 143, 199

Tanaka, Yoshifumi, 1, 11, 19, 22, 38, 60, 78, 79, 83, 90, 137, 147, 148, 167, 168, 200, 210
Tanja, Gerard, 2, 4, 10, 34, 39, 43, 48, 200

terra nullius, 4, 34
Territorial and Maritime Dispute between Nicaragua and Colombia (Nicaragua v Colombia) (ICJ 2012), xviii, 37, 72
Texaco Overseas Petroleum Co (Topco) and California Asiatic (Calasiatic) Oil Company v Government of Libyan Arab Republic (1977), xix, 26
Thirlway, Hugh, 70, 83, 86, 88, 200, 211
title
    land, 34, 37
    maritime, 38
Townsend-Gault, Ian, 109, 110, 111, 113, 203, 211
Tre Traktörer Aktiebolag v Sweden (ECtHR 1989), xix, 28
Treves, Tullio, 141, 178, 211
Tzanakopoulos, Antonios, 90, 202

United Nations Convention on the Law of the Sea 1982 (UNCLOS), xxxiii, 18, 21, 22, 25, 66, 138, 139
    art 123, 111
    art 15, 145, 146, 147, 168
    art 293, 149
    art 312, 180
    art 313, 180
    art 74(1), 147
    art 74(3), 40, 41, 59, 104, 110, 194
    art 83(1), 147
    art 83(3), 40, 41, 59, 104, 110, 194
    evolutionary interpretation, 183–184
    implementing agreement, 181
    state-centrism, 143, 191
United States v Percheman (1833), xix, 124
unitization agreement, 106, 107, 113
uti possidetis, 52, 53, 68, 69, 91, 145

Vattel, Emmerich de, 124, 155, 200
Vienna Convention on the Law of Treaties (VCLT) 1969, xxviii, xxxiii, 183, 184
Vignes, Daniel, 1, 2, 18, 48, 139, 148, 168, 196, 197, 201

Wälde, Thomas, 106, 113, 158, 211
Wasilkowski, Andrzej, 142, 163, 204
Weil, Prosper, xiv, 1, 9, 10, 33, 34, 38, 39, 43, 78, 90, 166, 200
World Trade Organization (WTO), 66, 174

Zubani v Italy (ECtHR 1996), xix, 28

Printed in the United States
by Baker & Taylor Publisher Services